00666~2

CYBERARTS

EXPLORING ART & TECHNOLOGY

EDITED BY LINDA JACOBSON

MILLER FREEMAN INC. SAN FRANCISCO

This book is gratefully dedicated:

To neoclassical, post-industrial, world funk cybertribalists D'Cückoo, for being so d'lightful...

And to experiential revolutionaries everywhere:

"No matter how extensive the artist's means, he must use them to provoke more of the spectator's participation, not less. For without the active participation of the spectator there can be *no transfer of consciousness, no Art.*"

—Mort Heilig, "The Cinema of the Future," 1955

Miller Freeman Inc., Book Division, 600 Harrison Street, San Francisco, CA 94107 • A Member of the United Newspapers Group

Publishers of *Keyboard, AI Expert,* and *Computer Language* magazines, and sponsors of the annual CyberArts International conference

Art Direction/Design: Richard Leeds

Cover illustration: Richard Leeds

Compositor: Elizabeth Wimmer

Technical artist: Rick Eberly

Copyeditors: Gail McGrew and Dorothy Cox

Color separator: Digital Prepress International

Service bureau: Courier Connection

Printer and binder: McNaughton & Gunn

ISBN 0-87930-253-4

Library of Congress Card Number 92-60950

Printed in the United States of America

92 93 94 95   5 4 3 2 1

Photo credits: The following individuals and companies have generously supplied drawings and photographs for use in this book: p. 1, David Em, represented by Roberta Spieckerman Associates, San Francisco; p. 13, Microsoft Corp.; p. 17, Philips Consumer Electronics; p. 30, Bill Gaver, Rank Xerox EuroPARC; p.40, Loren Carpenter; p. 50, Earl Manchester/U S WEST; p. 70, ©1991 Peter Menzel; p. 74, Tod Machover; pp. 83-85, Durand R. Begualt/NASA-Ames; pp. 88, 89, Elizabeth M. Wenzel/NASA-Ames; pp. 99, 103, Curtis Chan and RolandCorp.; p. 100, RolandCorp.; pp. 105, 106, Christopher Currell/Audio Cybernetics; pp. 121, 131, Michael Masucci and Kim McKillip, Vertical Blanking/EZTV; pp. 142, 143, 145, ©1991, 1992 Stephen A. Benton; pp. 149, 151, 152, 306, back cover, Thecla Schiphorst; p. 153, © Johan Elbers; pp. 162-165, Theodor Holm Nelson; p. 171, MacroMind; p. 174, Peter Gotcher/Digidesign; pp. 181, 183, 186, Mark Lacas/Lone Wolf; pp. 192, 194, 195, Robert Edgar; pp. 196-200, Mattel Toys; p. 204, Software Toolworks; p. 216, Charlie Richmond/Richmond Sound Design; pp. 155, 221, 222, Voyager Company; pp. 243, 252, 253, back cover, Myron W. Krueger; pp. 256-262, © Kit Galloway and Sherrie Rabinowitz/Electronic Cafe International; p. 263, © Linda Jacobson; pp. 265, 268, 269, Vivid Group; pp. 273, 275, 276, © VPL Research; p. 282, Virtual Technologies; p. 283, Mr. Film and SimGraphics; p. 287, W. Industries; pp. 295, 297, Morton L. Heilig. Artworks in the CyberArts Gallery sections are used by permission of the respective artists.

The following have generously given permission to use quotations from copyrighted works: From *Human Interface Guidelines,* ©1987 Apple Computer, reprinted by permission. From the forthcoming book *The Future of Information,* ©1992 Theodor Holm Nelson, reprinted by permission. From "The Cinema of the Future," first published in *Espacios* in 1955, reprinted by permission of Morton L. Heilig.

CONTENTS

SECTION 5

OLD LAWS FOR NEW TECHNOLOGIES?

SECTION 6

CYBERSPACE AND VIRTUAL REALITIES

INSERTS

CYBERARTS GALLERY

Victor Acevedo, Elizabeth Griffiths Lawhead, Daria & Gary Barclay, Will Cloughley & Sondra Slade, Barbara Nessim, David Em, Beverly Reiser, Sandra Filippucci, Ellen Sandor, Stephan Meyers, Arthur Olson & David Goodsell, Michael Gosney & Jack Davis, Nicole Stenger, Michael Johnson, Merrill Aldighieri & Joe Tripician, Marius Johnston, Michael Ragsdale Wright, Myron Krueger

CONTENTS

PREFACE

SURREALISTIC PIXEL

cyber: Root of cybernetics *(from the Greek* kybernetes, *"helmsman"), the science of the comparative study of the operations of electronic computers and the human nervous system.*

arts: All branches of creative works and their principles; the making or doing of things that display form, beauty, and perception.

As "cyber" and "arts" come together, age-old notions of artists—and the tools they use—fall apart. Artists are shelving their splicing blocks and blades, T-squares, erasers, rubber cement, staff paper, tracing paper, graph paper, metronomes, e-charts, tuning forks, border tape, leader tape, and alignment tape . . . .

. . . and they're clearing space in their studios for digital workstations, **mice**, drawing tablets, audio and video monitors, keyboards, hard drives, floppy disks, laserdisc and CD-ROM players, sequencers, scanners, MIDI boxes, reams of documentation, and cables, cables, and more cables.

These artists, like all others, strive to create powerful, emotionally moving representations of life situations. Technology helps the artist give form to these representations. This is nothing new; any overview of the arts would lack perspective if it didn't cover art technologies—whether **analog** (clay, neon, conga, pastel) or **digital** (texture map, wire-frame, sound sample, pixel).

It is the digital, silicon-based "information technologies" that *CyberArts* explores. Although the topics range from music and sound to animated cartoons to choreography, the common thread (more like the common spool) is the personal computer—hailed not as an information-processor/number-cruncher, but as a control device. An innovation support system. A means to transcend physical limitations, both our own and those imposed by the laws of physics. Computer tools and techniques let us express and visualize complex structures and abstract ideas. Computer tools enhance the creative process by making it easy to experiment with color schemes, sound layers, scene transitions, 3D models, photo retouching, and animated char-

mouse: A data input device that supplements the keyboard; first used as a pointer in paint programs and other graphic applications. An "input device" transfers data into a form recognizable to the computer; input devices include keyboards, voice recognition systems, joysticks, and virtual reality gloves.

analog: Capable of exhibiting continuous fluctuations. Generally refers to electronic technology in which signals exist as wavelike transmissions with varying intensities of voltage or current.

digital: Refers to electronic technology in which signals (data) are represented as a series of on/off impulses (electrical states). Each impulse either corresponds to the number 1 or to the number 0. Digital data transmissions consist entirely of 1's and 0's strung together in various ways. A 1 or 0 is called a "bit." Thus, information is stored in "bits," not as a continuous wave. Digital devices use microprocessors to store and retrieve information in the form of 1's and 0's, generally dividing continuing fluctuations in value (such as sound amplitude or light intensity) into discrete steps.

art materials: Not all have undergone transition to digital existence (yet), including those used in origami, flower arranging, kitemaking, batik, tie-dying, and macrame. This may be a good thing.

behold the work: The CyberArts Gallery is divided into two sections. One displays 2-dimensional works of art that were produced with the help of computer hardware and software. The second section shows artworks that are 3-dimensional, interactive, interactive multimedia, and/or virtual reality. Gallery notes explain the artists' methods and tools. As you can see, visual art created with a PC no longer has the geometrical, hard-edged look once associated with it. Today "PC art" may look virtually indistinguishable from that created via traditional means—or totally removed from traditional art in ways that perhaps only Salvador Dali or M.C. Escher could have imagined.

hypertext: When you want to know the meaning of a word, phrase, or name, you don't have to flip to some glossary in back of the book, locate the offending term by scanning entries while awkwardly grasping the book in such a way as to not lose your place, and if you're in a horizontal position, this process causes even greater aggravation. In this book, hypertext puts the definition or explanation right where you need it, when you need it.

acters. Transferring sounds and images into digital form (which changes **art materials** into the equivalent of mathematical equations) puts the fundamental physical qualities of sound and imagery under the artist's predictable, precise control.

Equally significant is the democratizing qualities of the personal computer. More than 50 million of these boxes have been sold. Designed to work with them are hundreds of relatively affordable, high-quality video, imaging, audio, and multimedia software and hardware products that give individuals and small arts organizations the kind of power to create and produce that once was available only to Hollywood-megabuck studio facilities and the hallowed research environs of corporate entities.

Equally significant is the PC's ability to support the development of the new technologies known as interactive multimedia and virtual reality. These in turn support the development of new artforms—art that invites the viewer or listener to join in as an active participant. You can read about these technologies in *CyberArts* and **behold the work** of such interactive artists as Barbara Nessim, who says, "It's my dream come true to see everyone involved with artwork. Viewing and doing are as important as the artwork itself."

New modes of expression often require new jargon, unique terminology. Understanding the language enhances the "viewing" and "doing." Unfortunately, unfamiliar technical, philosophical, and historical references can cloud the issue and alienate people. To help prevent that, I annotated the chapters with explanatory **"hypertext."**

Our industrialized society treats art as a product. Art is compartmentalized, split asunder from the everyday life of the "average" soul. A person is either a writer *or* painter *or* musician *or* dancer *or* actor *or* designer; few people attempt to travel multiple artistic or creative avenues. The computer, however, lets us soar beyond such self-imposed boundaries.

Speaking of boundaries: Can you hand-draw a perfectly round circle or ruler-straight line? I can't. My circles look like amoebas. This problem vanished the first time I used a computer paint program. I dragged my mouse to create circle after circle, perfect 360° shapes, not one resembling any one-celled organism. No longer restricted and frustrated by lousy hand/eye coordination, my editor's mind, the critical voice, shut its mouth. My creative juices flowed. I dragged, I saved, I printed. So what if a page full of circles doesn't constitute Art? By creating, we get in touch with our inner nature, with the mystery and beauty that is life. Creating makes us feel awake and alive. It lets us get the ya-yas out. PC art tools encourage creativity, and provide a handy way to stop being a passive consumer of someone else's creativity.

Of course, being an active consumer doesn't come cheaply. You can install a full-blown 3D animation system in a corner of your bedroom, but courting the digital muse will cost you. You can buy modeling clay for a lot (a *lot*) less than you can buy modeling software. It smells better, too.

And, as the *CyberArts* authors caution, digital tools may enhance the creative process, and may perform repetitive tasks tirelessly, but they don't necessarily make it *easier* to create and produce. The interactive multimedia developer, the electronic musician, or the digital video producer spends hours, even days, just making things work rather than concentrating on creative production efforts. Too much diddling with technology leads to imagination indigestion.

CyberArts explores all these pitfalls and pleasures of integrating computer technologies into the arts. It presents the perspectives of a wide-ranging, multidisciplinary group of artists and technologists. All of them look at the computer as a creative arts medium that offers multifaceted capabilities for expression, improvisa-tion, communication, and audio/visual impact. All of them offer fascinating experiences, philosophies, guidelines, technical advice, facts, and fantasies.

We need not understand exactly how a computer works any more than we need to understand the underlying nature of internal combustion or déjà vu, but we can appreciate how they all enhance our lives.

I hope *CyberArts* enhances your creative life and artistic pursuits.

—*Linda Jacobson*
San Francisco

ACKNOWLEDGMENTS

Much of the material in this book was excerpted, adapted, and/or derived from presentations and panel discussions at CyberArts International.

CyberArts International is an annual conference and exhibition that focuses on tools, techniques, and technologies for interactive and multimedia artists. CyberArts International is produced annually by *Keyboard* magazine of Cupertino, California. For information about CyberArts International, call 408-446-1105.

Thanks to all the CyberArts International presenters and performers, for providing the material on which this book is based. The contents of this book came into being with help from the following folks:

CyberArts International conference chairman (originator of the idea) Dominic Milano; all CyberArts International conference staffers and volunteers, especially show manager Bob Gelman, Christine Pearson, Cheryl How, Hope Windle, Vicki Hartung, Louis Brill, and Ross Johnsen; Matt Kelsey and Loren Hickman of Miller Freeman Publications, for patience and support; Michael Gosney, for his Cyber-Arts International gallery curation; Jeanne Juneau at *Verbum*, for help in contacting the cyberartists whose work appears in the CyberArts Gallery; Patric Prince, for curating CyberArts International's "Art In Depth" projected stereoscopic installation and "On-Line Gallery"; Will Kreth, for salvaging the *CyberArts* text files following a frightening (but not fatal) hard-drive crash; Tina Blaine (Bean), for standing in an interminable line at the NYC Dept. of Transportation to retrieve my towed car, allowing me to sit and edit *CyberArts* galleys; and Abbe Don, for advice and inspiration.

INTRODUCTION

WELCOME TO CYBERARTS

ntegrated **interactive** *media.* Also known as *hypermedia.* Used to be known as ***multimedia.*** The dream stuff and buzzwords of million-dollar marketing campaigns in search of a market, or so you would think from the countless articles in the computer press dealing with whether the business world really needs better-looking and better-sounding bar graphs and pie charts.

Of course, the arts community needs no convincing. Better-looking and better-sounding *anything* is fine by us. Desktop tools that supposedly do it all for less? Even better. After all, "integrated interactive media" is hardly a new concept. Shakespeare, Wagner, Kovacs, Lucas, and the Grateful Dead didn't need no stinking "M" word. They called it theater, opera, ballet, television, film, rock concerts, music videos. . . .

The point being that all mega-production art forms involve lots of interdisciplinary collaboration between artists. At the core of these collaborations are technological tools and the individual creativity with which they are used. And that's what *CyberArts* is all about: bringing creative minds together in one place to discuss the latest tools available to them; assembling musicians, visual artists, movie makers, choreographers, animators, special effects creators, and other creative types to talk about *content* and how they aim to inspire, educate, and entertain through the use of emerging technologies.

—*Dominic Milano*
Editor, Keyboard *magazine*

interactive multimedia: Refers to a developing genre of computer presentations (sometimes called "titles") which integrate text, images, graphics, voice, sounds, music, animations, and video in any combination, and which present the resulting information in a way that the viewer can—via input device—genuinely and immediately affect the unfolding of the presentation. You might select which portions of the program to see, or determine how quickly the presentation moves. Another name for interactive multimedia is "hypermedia." Hypermedia offers random-access control, unlike normal video, which starts at an unchangeable beginning and runs through to an unchangeable end. Hypermedia lets you control a program's pace, explore ideas within it, and determine "beginning" and "end." Say you're watching a TV show about the history of rock'n'roll; how much time you spend watching the Elvis segment is determined by the broadcaster. (Sure, you can videotape the show and play it over and over, but eventually you'll wear out the tape. And you can't interact with it.) An interactive multimedia title about rock's history would let you explore the music and lives of different artists at the rate you choose. The title might be distributed on floppy disk or compact disc, or sent to your home over phone lines. It might run on your personal computer or home entertainment device.

SECTION ①

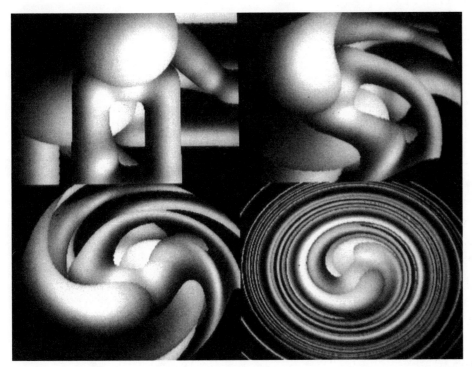

"Twist 1. 1980" **David Em**

NEW TECHNOLOGIES

AND THE ARTS

KISS YOUR TIRED AESTHETICS GOOD-BYE

ESSAYS BY BILL VIOLA, TOD MACHOVER, & PETER SELLARS

The convergence of the arts and electronic technologies raises many aesthetic questions. For instance, how might technology affect our understanding of culture? Does technology help or hinder our expression of experience? Where does "technology" stop and "art" begin? These issues and others are addressed in the following essays by three techno-artists and artistic technologists.

ON TRANSCENDING THE WATER GLASS

BY BILL VIOLA

Recognized internationally for his creations in the field of contemporary art, Bill Viola works with video and electronic media, creating videotapes and video/sound installations. In the 1970s Bill was artist-in-residence at WNET/13 TV Lab in Manhattan; in 1981, he became the first artist-in-residence of Sony's Atsugi Labs in Japan; in 1986, he worked as artist-in-residence of the San Diego Zoo. His artworks appear in collections at New York's Museum of Modern Art, L.A.'s Museum of Contemporary Art, the Art Institute of Chicago, Amsterdam's Stedilijk Museum, and Centre Georges Pompidou in Paris.

Lascaux: A cave in the Dordogne region of southwestern France, containing paleolithic (early Stone Age) drawings of people and animals.

I don't think it's possible to discuss art today *without* talking about technology. At a given time, all technologies are "advanced" technologies. A water glass represented advanced technology when people figured out that you could put liquid in a cup. In that sense, all technology is equal and all technology ultimately exists to be transcended.

I don't mean "transcendence" in terms of the evolution of newer technologies to replace older ones, but in terms of the self—the individual who is using and interacting with that technology. I've always felt that every technology I've used—from a pencil to a computer editing system—has been in the way of the creative process. The technology is simultaneously the obstacle and the path to realizing the impetus that drives one to express oneself. This impetus is as old as the human race; it's certainly older than the cave paintings in **Lascaux**, France, to which people always point as representative of the origins of what we call "art."

Creativity is a universal principle. There is profound beauty in the act of giving form to an idea and creating a thing, a material object that the rest of us can use. In all of these *things* there is a human presence. Even your favorite chair represents someone's idea and the formation of that idea.

When Australian aborigines perform their rituals and dance their creation myths, they represent cultures that have evolved continuously for over 40,000 years. Their dance today directly connects back to a time period long past. When they dance their dances that celebrate the world's creation, they describe the creation of the universe and evoke the energy of the creation of the universe. The energy of the creation of the universe is the energy that drives newborn life down the birth canal. It is the energy that inspires you when you sit at your synthesizer keyboard or your video editing system. I think we've lost a bit of that in our society, in our approach to communication with each other. Today our communication so often depends on representation or demonstration, instead of the energy of creating the universe.

One of the great illusions we've inherited from the 19th-century intellectuals is the notion that when we travel across a hill in New Guinea and discover a "primitive" tribe, we say they're living in the "Stone Age." That's nonsense. We are *all* contemporary cultures. To think that people such as the aborigines haven't changed in 40,000 years is myth and absurdity.

Another interesting notion about integrating traditional, ancient cultures with contemporary avant-garde culture is the odd alliance that forms between the two. Both represent minority art forms. Both require explanation to the uninitiated. However, jet travel has advanced to the point where we can board an airplane, and 20 hours later, walk out on a runway in New Guinea. In the coming decade, we'll see more and more convergence between old and new cultures. It's interesting that both the avant-garde and ancient, ethnic cultures are unified by a common need to explain to others what they're doing.

The thrill of technology lies in the fact that it represents real democratization of the arts. In 20 years no one will "need" Hollywood to create visual art. It doesn't take that much money to produce a feature-length video presentation. Today, most artists can afford video, which has become the medium of choice for telling the stories of alternative histories. Thanks to satellite technology, people have a previously unprecedented range of distribution and access to programming material.

As this technology gets more inexpensive, it will get into the hands of more people. Remember that infamous home video, showing the police brutally beating a black man, which was used to indict the Los Angeles Police Department in 1991. Remember what happened the year before, when the Bronx Video Collective—a group of high school students in the Bronx—decided to investigate the case of their neighbor, an 80-year-old woman who was evicted for being five months overdue with her $150-a-month rent. While trying to remove her from her apartment, five New York City riot-squad, SWAT team policemen shot and killed her. A trial was held in the Bronx and the court completely exonerated all of the police officers, because they said this 80-year-old woman had a gun. The kids in the Bronx Video Collective decided to interview her neighbors on videotape, and the butcher at the local supermarket said he always had to cut her meat into fine pieces because she couldn't hold a knife. That didn't come out in court—it came out through the Bronx Video Collective.

Yes, video is the medium of choice for both creating art and narrating alternative history, and it's now in the hands of the people, and *that's* exciting.

ON INFORMATION OVERLOAD

BY TOD MACHOVER

Tod Machover (see "Hyperinstruments" in Section 2) works at the Media Lab at the Massachusetts Institute of Technology, where he is associate professor of Music & Media, directs the Experimental Media Facility, and oversees the design and development of Hyperinstruments.

We live in a time that is more complex than any other period in human history—complex in very interesting and sometimes strange ways.

In a fundamental sense, it is our technology that creates this complexity, and it is also technology that makes us feel paradoxically more aware of the world around us yet confused as to how to interact with that world and how to assimilate it with our own.

Our art, and our aesthetic visions, serve to convey our truest knowledge of the world we live in, of our own times, and of our hopes for the future. Therefore, technology must be acknowledged as a primary shaper of our contemporary experience, and as a fundamental tool for the interpretation of our world.

Through our communications and entertainment media, we have ever more access to every culture that exists on the planet, to every historical period of human activity. We can buy compact discs containing music from any culture and any historical period. To accept the power afforded us by this easy access, the commercial mass media (and the temptation to stay at home with the CD player or the TV) propagate the notion that all this information is basically the same, and that you can passively choose or switch from culture to culture without thinking about the process. It all becomes homogenized through technological access.

Many people never leave this first level of interaction. They partake of a certain diversity without understanding its implications. I think this approach is scary, as it ignores the necessity of thinking and the great effort required to understand knowledge that comes from experience different from one's own.

People who do acknowledge the responsibility and challenge that comes with such diversity often are shocked when they realize the enormity of the task at hand. On this next level, you realize, "There's so much to know, there's so much information"; this itself is a frightening concept. Indeed, we have access to so many different ideas and so much information that it's overwhelming to consider what it means to actually know enough to function in this world.

This concept of fragmentation and bombardment with too much information takes us to another, more realistic level, in the way we face the world. Because although our technology gives us access to this complex world, and shocks us by opening the floodgate to endless experience, it is this same technology that provides us with the tools to construct a solution.

Such a solution will come, I believe, at a third level of awareness, a level where it is necessary to see below the superficial differences and discover and establish connections between worlds that at first seem incredibly different and separate. Our electronic media allow us to establish constant, non-hierarchical paths of communication, and our technological forms of expression allow us to construct new languages for such communication that can be general and specific at the same time.

Any aesthetics specific to technological forms will have this in common: They will embrace the incredible, increasing diversity of our world while simultaneously establishing connections and commonality. Both extremes will continue to develop. It is no longer sufficient to have superficial clarity and homogeneity if they deny the richness of our world. However, it is also inadequate to create forms of human expression that deal only in momentary impressions, fleeting fragments, and dismembered associations, without any attempt at coherence.

Technology is particularly well-suited to helping us express such a paradoxical aesthetic vision. As a medium, technology—especially computer-based technology—is neutral, imposing no physical constraints on materials used, or on manipulations or transformations of that material. In this sense, technology represents a sort of meta-system that can serve to relate and organize objects or categories otherwise distinct in the physical world.

In fact, one of the greatest characteristics of computational systems is that they deal primarily not with objects, but with processes. Computers force us to develop a language for describing the behavior of elements, and habituate us to imagining structures for establishing coherence. In addition, thought about process is, by definition, thought about transformation and change, which in turn encourages us to define aesthetic mutations and elaborations that give meaning to what happens "between" objects, and subsequently minimizes the importance of such objects as the building blocks for a language.

It is this mutability that gives such power to computational technology as an aesthetic tool. The machine itself has no predisposition to any particular material; any object, image, or sound is fair game for use and manipulation. In other words, any part of the real world can be integrated into such an aesthetic world. Such integration is performed by the strength of the artist's imagination, and facilitated by the conceptual power of process-oriented relationships established between these materials.

It is because of these extraordinary powers of association and integration that technology has become common to an incredibly large number of artistic approaches. A fringe activity in the mid-1980s, technologically-based art creation, has become a mainstay of commercial and "serious" domains.

Ever since I was a kid, I have felt at the apex of the kind of synthesis I describe here. I've constantly straddled a boundary between two worlds that were not "supposed" to coexist: the worlds of serious art (European classical music) and popular art (rock music), of doing (composing music) and reflecting (computer music instrument theory and design), of humanism (music, philosophy) and technology (computers), and of simultaneous interest in complexity of concept and directness of expression.

Rather than running away from these contradictions, I consistently embraced them as fundamental to my personal experience and as somehow central to our human predicament as we near the end of the 20th century. In a way, my music has been "about" this situation, expressing a search for unity and synthesis amidst great confusion and fragmentation. Sometimes this search has been represented as painful and difficult, and sometimes as smooth and almost inevitable. I've always used my technological tools to enhance both the similarities and the differences inherent in my compositional materials. It is my interpretation of this technology that has put an indelible aesthetic mark, or footprint, on my music.

We are at a crossroads in human development, and the way we choose to deal with technology will be fundamental in determining where we go next, and how we evolve.

If we are passive and complacent in enjoying the richness and diversity that technology brings us, I fear we will be reduced as human beings and we will find that we are not so much "in control" of our technology as we are prisoners of its whims, styles, and content.

If we rise to the challenge of using technology to explore, interpret, and communicate deeply reasoned thoughts about our complex world, then we will open doors to experiences that we cannot even imagine.

By acknowledging and understanding our differences, we can begin to use our technology to truly *communicate*. And facilitating such communication is—in the end—the fundamental task of any aesthetic.

ON VULNERABILITY, ABORIGINES, & WALTER CRONKITE

BY PETER SELLARS

After stage director Peter Sellars graduated from Harvard, he studied in the Far East, then joined the Boston Shakespeare Company as artistic director. By age 26 he was director of the American National Theater at Washington, D.C.'s Kennedy Center, and since then has directed over 100 productions across America and abroad. He received international acclaim for his production of "Nixon in China." As an actor, Peter was featured in Jean-Luc Godard's film of King Lear and in episodes of Miami Vice *and* The Equalizer. *On the music front, he directed a Herbie Hancock video. Peter now lives and works in Los Angeles.*

The technology at hand today is more interesting than technology has ever been. The things we can achieve with technology make the present day the most exciting time to be alive in the history of art.

I tend to treat the machines the same way I treat human beings with whom I'm working in a production, because what the machines offer is something that is inherently human. That "something" is *vulnerability*. After all, we're barely "human" when we're doing something that we're good at doing. As artists, during the act of creation, something strangely inhuman takes over us. We become more like machines. It's when we find something that we *can't* do well that we discover our vulnerability and what it means to be human.

That's why, when I work with a machine, I try to find the one thing it cannot do, and create the artwork or production around that. You do the same thing with an actor or performer: You find the vulnerability, the point at which the performer reveals something that he or she normally conceals. To achieve that requires a monstrous and heroic effort. I try to put the machine through the same process. I make demands upon the machine that it cannot meet, and the ensuing piece becomes about trying to meet those demands. Inherent in the piece is the struggle of being alive—and the absolute necessity of transcending limitations.

It's always interesting to start with technology's limitations. I find it hard to create art with a tool about which someone says, "You can do anything with this." For me, the **Synclavier** was practically useless. When it first came out, it took me awhile to figure out what it couldn't do, because what it *could* do was so obnoxiously available and obvious. It's really hard to create art out of something that obvious. "Art" is always looking for some odd, dark corner where the machine has a private nightmare.

What interests me now in working with high-tech applications in art is the process of making the invisible visible. Current video and audio tools give us the ability to see things that the human eye can't. We're basically pushing the limits of perception as far as we can. Artists spend their entire lives discussing the invisible world and trying to express the tremendous palpability, power, and presence of an invisible world. However, at this point in history, common sense no longer is adequate as a way to deal with contemporary life. We need a lot more than common sense to figure out how to clean a toxic waste site. We need a lot more than common sense to figure out how to negotiate with Iraq. It's not good enough to just go into the situation and use your noggin. What's required is *expertise*, an extreme level of expertise from people who have thought about the situation for a long time in a specialized way. In fact, we live in a period in which only the most extreme forms of specialization can move us through the complexities of our lives.

None of us, however, will live long enough to achieve specialization in anything larger than an extremely narrow band of experience. This means we are dependent on each other. We must rely on people who know things that we don't. When I create a piece of art in an electronic studio, I depend on engineers and technicians who know more about the equipment than I do. I can't take the equipment apart and put it back together, so I must engage in a collaboration with someone who can do that, someone I can trust.

When the British first arrived in Australia and encountered the aborigines, they thought that the aborigines had no culture. To the contrary, the aborigines had a

Synclavier: *Introduced by New England Digital in 1976. The first commercially distributed digital synthesizer that also functioned as recorder, transcriber, and computer-controlled composition tool. Today's Synclavier is a digital audio/music recording, production, and storage system used in studios and on stage.*

culture so highly advanced and calibrated that it was invisible to the naked eye. Aboriginal music, for example, represents the world's most elaborate system of geographic, cultural, and familial mapping: From the first two lines of an aboriginal song, you can tell where the singer is from, where they're going, who their family members are, and so on. An entire map of Australia exists in their music, because the aboriginal culture is one that has no written tradition. All of its historical and geographic life, traditions, and survival tools are embedded in its music and dance, which occupy the same place in aboriginal culture that writing has occupied in Western culture.

Music and dance are art in motion, and a basic fact in all our lives is the motion of change. We've always attempted to hold up the written word against change; we've said that some things will never change, and the written word is proof. That's one reason the aborigines avoided written words, because they figured out that the basic quality of life is constant change and continuous flux.

The only thing that holds a society together and keeps it alive is the notion that "tradition" and "innovation" are not opposing ideas. They represent the same idea. Artistic and cultural traditions constantly incorporate new material. People use the music of Mozart and Beethoven to establish a tradition that does not change, when in fact, in the lifetimes of these composers, they represented *continuing* changing response to a tradition. A tradition allows you a context in which to process new information.

Consider this: A typical aboriginal dance takes 20 to 30 seconds to perform. There-fore, 40,000 years ago the aborigines essentially invented the concept of TV commercials, the concept of transmitting a powerful message in a short period of time. For example, they will perform a dance that communicates, "Remember to take care of your sister." The dance itself contains no specific "take care of your sister" gesture; nobody puts their arms around anyone else or makes a literal visible connection with someone's sister. The message is stored in a fund of secret knowledge. All the other tribe members know that when they dance this dance, it means "remember to take care of your sister." The sense is that for those 30 seconds, a curtain opens and reveals a certain reality. Then it closes again. That 30-second period is about that moment when the boundaries of the world fall away and you can see through an opening.

Today, most of the equipment we use was created for commercial applications, and the commercial applications are inanely fascistic. They're about mass thought-control. During the past 20 years, extraterrestrials have come down in the guise of TV producers to completely sap the will of the human race in order to create a fund of brain-dead slave labor. They've taken over all the TV program distribution positions in a sort of mass takeover of the human race by a hostile planet. I know it's a plot!

This plot arose from the notion that Walter Cronkite was infallible. If he said something happened, then that must be the truth. Meanwhile, television technology was developed along the lines of 19th-century official buildings in France. It was meant to make everything look big and impenetrable. You, the viewer, were small and powerless, and the TV newscast would proceed with or without you, whether you were dead or alive. And the newscast would determine what was important in the world. The fact that 150,000 people died in Bhopal occupies 20 seconds of airtime. The next 20 seconds of airtime is occupied by a commercial for paper towels. Each subject takes the same amount of time, is presented through the same type of camera work, and carries equal implication of importance.

Our society has used most of this TV technology to flatten out differences, rather than accentuate them, and to impart the illusion that we live in a "normal" world. Certain canons of normalcy have been agreed upon by people in tall office buildings on Madison Avenue and in Hollywood, then thrust upon Americans as, "*This* is the nature of human experience." But it is *not* the nature of experience.

The objective of artists today is to take this technology—which is primarily in the hands of the oppressors and used to impart a completely false world view—and subvert it in such a way that it begins to touch elements of reality and our actual experience of time, space, and life.

● ●

STATE OF THE MEDIA

BY TRIP HAWKINS

A noted leader in the electrified, computerized field of entertainment dreams, W.M. "Trip" Hawkins is president of SMSG, Inc,. and chairman of Electronic Arts, both based in San Mateo, California. Electronic Arts is the world's largest supplier of computer entertainment software and has achieved a consistency in growth that is unrivalled in the computer game industry. Trip founded Electronic Arts in 1982 and is the driving force behind its business strategies and organization. Before launching Electronic Arts, Trip was one of the early managers at Apple Computer. He holds a degree in strategy and applied game theory from Harvard College and earned his M.B.A. from Stanford University.

VHS video: The video format found on most home and office video cassette recorders.

Does interactive multimedia represent a solution to problems inherent in our education system and on-screen entertainment? How? What hurdles do the people who make multimedia need to jump? How should they approach the creation of multimedia products that we all can enjoy?

Trip Hawkins answers these questions and others, assessing the developing industry and marketplace and the challenges facing the creative people who work with these new media technologies.

We have a job to do. We need to create what I call the "New Hollywood." In the process, we'll create a new profession, and the number of people working in this profession will increase from about 2,000 people today to about 20,000 in the year 2001. In the meantime, we need to make sure that "multimedia" doesn't become known as the hype-buzzword of the 1990s. We must make multimedia much more than that.

My dream is this: There can be a technology used in homes, schools, and businesses that is affordable and accessible to everyone, and is the interactive equivalent to **VHS video**. Remember pre-VHS video? When I was in high school, the class could watch a videotape, but we had to make a request to the school district months in advance, because the school system owned only one professional-level video player, and at that time there were dozens of incompatible video systems on the market, none of which could play the same tapes. On the appointed day, this huge, rack-mounted set of gear was brought into the classroom and we could watch the video.

Eventually, manufacturers got together to agree on the VHS standard, a good, low-cost technology. VHS took over the video world not just in homes, but in schools and businesses. It's used everywhere now. My dream is that we'll have the interactive media equivalent, and because it's interactive, it has as much potential to change the world as the invention of movable type.

The interactive medium is new. Creating interactive material, after all, is not like filming a movie or making a record—it presents all new types of design and production considerations. But we want to be able to create interactive multimedia in our lifetimes! Imagine how you would feel if you were Steven Spielberg, and you were born in the 19th century, and **Thomas Edison** was your neighbor. One day in 1890 he says to you, "Steve, come over to my place. You have to check this out!" You go over to his house, where you see the first motion picture and say, "Wow! This is incredible! I have all these great ideas about what I can create with this and what I can communicate to people with it!" But Tom says, "Gee, Steve, I'm sorry. You won't be able to do any of that for another 80 years."

This could happen to us. I've been working on "interactivity" for 15 years and we haven't made much progress. I worry about that a lot. We all need to worry about it. We need an action agenda to provide common ground on which we can all stand to help us achieve results more quickly. I'll get to that later in this chapter.

Find a Need & Fill It

In the early 1960s, **Marshall McLuhan** said television would make the classroom obsolete. I think that's proven true. Look at how television evolved to its current form, as best expressed by MTV and advertising: It's become almost video **Dada**, a completely new language for communicating. It has changed our cultural literacy and just about destroyed the classroom. Yet because television is passive, it hasn't replaced our need for learning.

Marshall McLuhan also said, "Anyone who tries to make a distinction between entertainment and education doesn't know the first thing about either." That's especially true with this medium of interactivity.

Research in the last few years has uncovered some interesting facts. In a study of several thousand homes over an extended period, results showed that watching television was one of the few activities which generally makes people feel worse after doing it. A study in 1988 focused on television habits and the school systems in six countries, including the United States, England, and South Korea. Researchers asked 12-year-olds, "How do you feel about your knowledge about science and math?" Then they tested them in science and math. The researchers also asked how much time they spent watching television and how much time they spent studying. They learned that the South Korean kids, who spent the least amount of time watching television, felt the worst about how much science and math they knew, yet scored the highest in science and math tests. The American kids, who watched the most television, felt the best about what they knew, yet scored the lowest. Imagine asking these American kids, "How much do you know?" "Not much." "How do you feel about that?" "I feel fine. I feel good." This is a real problem.

The United States has the world's worst education system. It's expensive, and it takes the longest to complete. So people sit at home, watch TV, and get depressed.

The solution is interactive multimedia. In the sense that audio is the medium of hearing and video is the medium of viewing, multimedia is the medium of "doing." It lets you do things. It's real life in a box. Studies at the University of California proved that the single best way to increase your intelligence is through interaction. In one experiment, one group of rats lived the way "normal" lab rats do, while another bunch of rats were given human infant toys to play with. Later the scientists measured the changes in the rats' brain size and complexity and found a difference. The brains in rats who played with toys were larger. I guess we better not give rats too many toys!

The fact that we learn by playing is a concept that is fundamental to all mammals. Nevertheless, when we invented the modern classroom we stamped "play" into the dust. Our institutional classroom processs is also stamping out creativity. We must get back in touch with the fact that the best way to learn is by playing and doing. Do you remember the last time you purchased an appliance or electronic device? Did you read the instructions before you tried to use it? Probably not. Most of us want to do things. We want to interact with the items in our daily lives. That's how we learn.

There was once a man who understood this principle, but pursued it before any technology existed to help him. That man was John Dewey, the education philosopher who lived about a hundred years ago. He developed a concept of teaching through experience. For example, he took a group of kids to a sheep farm. They watched the farmers shear the sheep's wool and took wool samples back to the classroom. They also collected raw cotton samples. Back at school, Dewey divided the class into two groups. One group darned the wool; it was a tedious process. The other group tried to pick the seeds from the cotton; it was almost impossible. After a period of time, the wool group had produced much more fabric material than the cotton group. Dewey did this to show why wool was society's staple fabric for thousands of years, and why cotton couldn't be used in the ancient past. Then he brought out a miniature cotton gin, dropped the cotton in it, turned the crank, and presto, produced more cotton in a minute than the wool group had produced in a couple of hours. In this way he illustrated the power of the Industrial Revolution. What a wonderful approach to education!

Today it's impractical to haul kids out to sheep farms, or the equivalent of sheep farms in other industries. Dewey's approach didn't get far in the educational system, but it represented a brilliant idea.

CD-ROM

Jumping the Hurdles

The multimedia industry is a mess today. More than 30 different hardware systems, all incompatible, including **CD-ROM**, **CDTV**, and **CD-I**, are aimed at the consumer market. That's not the case with multimedia software. People in the multimedia industry spend too much time recreating software products for the various hardware platforms (computer families) instead of creating *new* software products. This is crazy. It creates confusion for customers and retailers, most of whom get turned off by the idea of "multimedia" because of the lack of standards.

CD-ROM; CDTV; CD-I:
Compact Disc-Read Only Memory, Commodore Dynamic Total Vision, and Compact Disc-Interactive, all competing (incompatible) formats for storing different types of information digitally on a compact disc. CD-ROM is the oldest and most prevalent. A device that plays a CD-ROM disc is called a CD-ROM drive, and it connects to personal computers. CDTV, a consumer multimedia system that connects to televisions, is a product from Commodore Business Machines. CD-I is a home entertainment system based on a player that connects to any TV and stereo system; it was introduced to the retail world in October 1991 by Philips Consumer Electronics.

redrawn: A computer screen image and a TV screen image are drawn differently. A TV image is divided into 525 horizontal lines. The electron beam inside a TV set draws every other line on the screen until it reaches the bottom, then returns to the top to draw the alternating lines. This happens 30 times a second. Computers generally draw every line in the screen image from top to bottom. It's this difference in image presentation that challenges multimedia developers who want to display sharp, TV-like images on a computer monitor.

pixel: Contraction of "picture element," the smallest resolvable element in a computer-generated image. Picture resolution is measured in the number of pixels (usually in horizontal and vertical dimensions) used to create the image. The more pixels per inch, the higher the resolution. For example, Apple's high-resolution monitor supports 640 x 480 (HxV) pixels.

image compression: The translation of data (in this case, video and graphics) to a more compact form for storage or transmission, so it takes up less space in computer memory.

In 1948, CBS introduced the LP (long-playing) format for music. RCA thought, "We're not going to let the LP dominate the industry." Three months later, they introduced the 45-rpm record. These formats were positioned against each other as higher-fidelity, long-playing music media. Two formats competed—not 30, just two—and people bought fewer records in the next four years. It doesn't take much to create confusion.

The confusion in multimedia today is worse. This alone should motivate us to change the industry. When Electronic Arts started in 1982, 135 companies made entertainment software. Today, only six or seven of those companies are still in business, and many more have come and gone. Few multimedia companies turn a profit. And if we don't have profits, we can't create jobs and support creative thinking. As a result, fewer jobs exist, and fewer computer software products are sold, which means fewer people around the world are benefiting from the technology.

How do we change this? To turn "multimedia" into a mass-market reality, first we must examine animation technology. Maybe you've noticed that computers seem somewhat slow, and often when you're trying to create graphics, and you change something, the screen isn't **redrawn** instantly. As objects move around on the screen, their movements are jerky, and there aren't nearly enough colors to make it look anything like television.

Many people in the computer industry misunderstand this problem. They think, "Let's put full-motion video on the computer screen. That will make it look like real video." But this doesn't make it interactive. Turning the computer into a digital movie projector won't motivate the average, non-computerized person to buy a computer.

Instead, let's all focus on the computer's interactive capabilities. Interactivity requires real-time animation. In other words, if I'm flying a plane on-screen, and I turn the plane to the left, the screen must redraw instantly to keep up with the world I'm creating as I am making those decisions. That's "real-time animation." The computer must be able to immediately draw the scenery, other planes, and all the other objects in the environment. It must make all those objects look good, through high resolution (image sharpness and clarity) and color depth (how many colors it can display), and it must animate them smoothly.

In an animated TV picture, the **pixels** change (are redrawn) on the screen at a rate of more than six million per second. In most current personal computer and video game systems, the rate of change is about one million or less per second. TV-quality is the minimum threshold the consumer expects. All this requires huge amounts of computing horsepower, and we don't have enough of that—yet. And it isn't cheap enough—yet.

People involved in multimedia also treat **image-compression** technology as if it were some kind of Holy Grail. They say, "With compression technology, we can run full-motion video." Great. But it's no replacement for animation technology. It's like saying, "I'm going to put all my data on CD-ROM and treat the connection to the computer like a fire hose: I'll spray all this stuff on the CD as quickly as possible into the computer memory, up on the screen, and try to get it moving on there at 30 frames per second."

The problem is, it's difficult to interact with a fire hose.

If you want to interact with software, you must be able to make decisions that will literally invent—redraw—the screen. The fire hose approach won't allow this. We can't assume that compression technology will replace the need for more animation. Today, the best compression technology is **MPEG.** And it's not good enough. We need a breakthrough to improve image compression.

CD-ROM technology presents another problem we must solve. CD-ROM is a gigantic storage device, but the CD-ROM drives are too slow to transfer information **in real time**, especially when compared to a video game cartridge or computer hard disk. Using it resembles pulling an 18-wheel truck by a bicycle. We need to improve the engine. If the engine were more powerful in terms of animation and compression technology, then we could start making sensible use out of its great capacity.

Imagine that we can store the borough of Brooklyn on a CD-ROM. We need to move it over to a powerful computer in Manhattan. A one-lane bridge connects the two. Using compression technology, we can cram all the people in Brooklyn into a taxicab, zip it over the bridge, and unload them instantly. However, the bridge has only one lane. Traffic moves so slowly that we have to cram all of Brooklyn into one trip, which requires an incredibly high compression rate, and when we reach Manhattan and expand, or de-

compress, the taxi by letting out all the people, we lose much of the original production values. They don't look as good as they did when they first climbed into that taxi. This is the problem with compression and CD-ROM, and we need to find a way around that.

A CD-ROM disc may be a big, dumb, storage device, but it's cheap. Right now the actual cost of manufacturing video game cartridges is anywhere from $10 to $20 each, because we essentially build a computer into each one. It consists of a plastic case that contains an integrated circuit board and integrated circuits. It holds up to a megabyte of data, so it's fairly large and expensive. Conversely, it costs about thirty cents to make a CD. And you get over 500 million bytes of information. That's a 10,000-to-1 price/performance improvement.

Today, one megabyte of **RAM** costs about $30 in parts. When you figure there's at least a 3-to-1 relationship between what parts cost and retail price, that means for every $30 in RAM, the addition of each megabyte adds $100 to the retail price. We can't just go put eight megabytes in a machine like you can with a Macintosh in the office, because it will add $800 to the retail price, and people can't afford that. The price of the multimedia player or "appliance" must fall under $500. Only then might it interest almost any household and almost any student in any school.

What's The Prize?

Here's my take on what might happen once we overcome the obstacles. If we imagine that we're in the pre-**Gutenberg** stage of the multimedia "revolution" . . .

MPEG: Refers to multimedia standards proposed by the International Standards Organization (ISO) for digital compression and decompression of moving images/audio for use in computer systems. MPEG stands for Motion Picture Experts Group. (See chapter on image compression.)

in real time: responding instantaneously

RAM: Random Access Memory; data that can be called up from a computer's internal storage to be read, changed, or erased. When a computer has lots of RAM, it's more powerful and can support faster, more visual, and more complex software.

Johann Gutenberg: Born in 1400, this German invented movable type (c. 1450) and launched the modern craft of printing. Before that, knowledge stored in the form of written language was reproduced by hand or wood-block printing, and only rich people could afford to buy books.

what will occur when we invent the multimedia version of the printing press?

Movies. The music industry went digital with the audio CD, and now there's the same opportunity for the film industry to move toward digital by using CD-ROM as a movie storage medium. The reasons laserdiscs aren't hugely successful are that they're not digital and they're more expensive to produce than VHS videotapes. The major movie companies say, "Everybody owns a VCR. VCR tapes are cheaper to make. Why should I try to make **laserdiscs**? It would just increase my production costs." So they don't support the video laserdisc, and when they do, the discs retail for $89.95, and they're not distributed broadly, so the laserdisc market will never really develop.

By going digital with CD-ROM, however, movie companies find a manufacturing cost that is much lower than videotape's, and a medium that is much more durable than videotape. The image quality is much more consistent, the CDs don't need to be rewound, and they don't wear out. Once the quality level is high enough, then movie companies will switch to CD-ROM. The film industry, in fact, ultimately will define the compression technology standards, because they're the ones who will create the demand.

TV Programs. Once the **fiber-optic cable** networks are in place, the cable TV industry will be able to supply hundreds more channels to the home. However, you won't sit down at home in the evening and start clicking the remote control through 600 movie channels to decide what to watch. Instead you'll have some kind of front-end computer system with a menu with which you'll have an ongoing dialogue.

You might use this system to watch a network broadcast of a sporting event, for example. While the event takes place, you can retrieve data about the game, the players, and their career stats. You'll also use an on-line TV guide that automatically programs your VCR. People also will be able to shop from the convenience of their own homes. The system could contain an electronic "profile" of you in which you've stored information about who you are, what you like, and what you look like. The system will send you just the sections of the shopping network broadcast that interest you, and you can browse through the items and watch computer-animated models of yourself walking around on screen modeling the stuff. When you want to buy something, the system uses your credit card number to order it automatically.

Games. As the visual quality of computer software reaches the image quality of television, the audience will expand. Today, the video game audience is basically limited to imaginative boys who put up with the abstractions on a video game screen. The original Nintendo video game screen displayed 12 colors and animated at 50,000 pixels per second. Compare that to television, which displays 200,000 colors that are animated at six million pixels per second. You can sit down with a kid and you can say, "See that blue boxlike shape over there? That's your spaceship. That red circle over here is Planet X. You have to go to Planet X and rescue the princess." The kid will say, "Okay, let's go!" Show the same thing to adults and

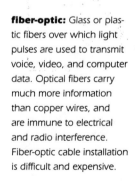

laserdisc: A.k.a. videodisc, a 12-inch plastic disc that holds thousands of video images and hours of sound.

fiber-optic: Glass or plastic fibers over which light pulses are used to transmit voice, video, and computer data. Optical fibers carry much more information than copper wires, and are immune to electrical and radio interference. Fiber-optic cable installation is difficult and expensive.

they'll say, "That doesn't look like a space-ship. Why would I want to go to Planet X?" Adults are waiting for something they can relate to. Picture, for example, a golf game for a 50-year-old guy who plays golf and loves watching it on TV. He can watch something on the screen that looks to him like his weekend TV broadcast and yet he's in there, playing in a foursome with Jack Nicklaus, who knows him by name. That adult is going to be really interested in something like that.

Simulations: interactive movies & TV shows. These give people experiences that are hard for them to have in real life, such as flying a jet or working as a foreign spy. As the medium improves, it becomes possible to make it much more vivid. When a TV show is created, the production team collects information that is edited down from a huge pool of raw material, then transformed into a single linear piece of film. The viewer starts at one end and goes to the other end, and that's the only way to experience it. An interactive TV show would somehow take all the information and let you use it and play with it in any way you desire.

For example, let's say you're watching an interactive episode of "Wild Kingdom." It starts out with normal narration, "We're here in Africa to learn about the continent's animals." You see rhinos and lions on the screen, and you think, "I'd like to find out about lions." You use something like a joystick to point at a lion, the camera instantly zooms in on the lion, and the narration starts talking about lions. Then you say, "I want to see the lion hunt." You point at a "hunt" **icon**, and now you see the lion hunting, and the narrator de-

scribes the lion's eating habits. Suddenly you think, "I want to be the lion!" You select another on-screen icon, and immediately see images of the world from the lion's perspective, and you get to make the hunting and eating decisions that a lion must make, while the narrator tells you how you're doing and gives you survival hints. I can just see kids wanting to be competent lions. Next thing you know, they're digging deeper into this information resource, learning about lions from different parts of the world, discovering which ones are endangered, and hearing about the various international organizations that are trying to save the lions.

Hobbies. Any hobby that requires reference or storage, from photography to cooking, will benefit from new media. I'd love to have Paul Newman on disc to coach me through a barbeque sauce recipe, tell me what ingredients to assemble, how to calculate all the quantities, and remind me to start simmering the carrots by a certain time. This uses the computer's

Unveiled in department stores and major electronic system retailers by Philips Consumer Electronics in October 1991, the Compact Disc Interactive system kiosk is equipped with a 27-inch color TV, CD-I player, and brochures for 60 CD-I software titles. A continuously playing demonstration disc encourages shoppers to try the system.

icon: A graphic symbol used in a computer program to represent an object or process; on the Macintosh screen, for example, you would select a "file folder" icon to access documents.

intelligence and TV-like audio/visual display to make cooking much more fun.

Education. In 1990, 15 states approved a change in the definition of "textbook" to include electronic media. The "textbook" can now be laserdisc, CD-ROM, or floppy disk. In the state of Texas, a laserdisc-based science course includes workbooks and laserdisc presentations, and 70 percent of the Texas schools switched from using a regular textbook to teaching that course via laserdisc. That's pretty amazing. It represents a huge change.

All this stuff is possible now. In the next few years, the cost of accomplishing these things will decrease. It's a matter of focusing industry effort and letting time pass for this all to happen. We must be careful what we ask for, because we might get it. The next question is: Once we have the right interactive hardware medium, how do we create the proper software?

Multimedia Design Goals

These are my suggestions to the people who are conceiving and developing interactive multimedia "titles" and products, whether they're for entertainment, education, or business:

1. Make it innovative. Most media start out with imitation. In the transition from the book to radio, the first radio program consisted of some guy reading a book. In the radio-to-television transition, the first TV program simply consisted of some radio personalities with a camera pointed at them. It takes decades for people to exploit a new medium. We must work hard to innovate, take risks, and do things that are truly new. Like pioneers, we must be willing to get out there and take a few

arrows in the back, choke on trail dust, and hack around until we discover what's new and different about the medium.

A good example is the work I've done with John Madden, the TV announcer and former football coach. Electronic Arts decided to make a football simulation computer game that gave people the feeling of playing real football. We thought, "John Madden knows football. Let's involve him in this. Let's ask him to help design the game." To meet with him, we had to fly to Denver and join him while he was on the road, traveling by train. He doesn't like to fly. We spent two days on a train talking about football and how to design this game. The design process went on for four years. Everybody in the company joked about it; they said we should kill the idea, the product would be a joke, a disaster. They said, "It's only because Trip wants to do it that we're still doing it." But I knew we could get it done. Well, this product has become the No. 1 best-seller in our company's history. Over a million copies have been sold. Most adults probably know John Madden as an announcer more than they know him as a football coach, but kids come up to him and say, "You're the guy in the computer game." Today, John enters the locker rooms of professional teams, and the football stars hassle him if they don't like the way their player is rated in the computer game. In the last couple of years, John's taken a greatly increased interest in the quality assurance aspect of the player ratings. It's become politically important for him.

2. Make it simple. One way to look at this is to ask, "What is the most complex mass-consumer skill?" People know how to use a telephone, but do they know how to operate an outdoor barbecue? I don't. Do they know how to turn off the flashing "12:00" on their VCR? The best example is the automobile. No multimedia title or program should be more complicated to use than driving a car. You might think, "Driving a car is simple!" Then you realize that our society doesn't let anybody drive until they're 16, and first they must take a training course, pass a test, and acquire a license. Meanwhile, police are out on the roads all the time, checking that people are driving the right way.

What's "simple"? First, the design should *present the user with one way of doing things.* If there's more than one way to accomplish a task, people get confused and stop trying. When I worked at Apple Computer, we had a war about how many mouse buttons there should be—one or two. Some engineers thought the mouse should have six buttons, because that's how many buttons bartenders can handle on their drink mixers. The one-button camp won, of course, and the rest is history.

Don't use "modes" in the program or title. Depending on what mode a device is in, one set of buttons may have different uses, and you have to interact with them in different ways. If I unknowingly put a computer program in "delete" mode and hit a button, the whole screen might disappear—to my utter confusion and frustration. You can't have the same key do different things depending on the modality of the software. That's one reason Macintosh users must select something and only after the process of selec-

tion can they perform an operation on it. The Mac doesn't make it easy for you to unknowingly delete something.

Eliminate clutter on the screen. To a computer-literate person, every single pixel on the screen is significant. The average human looks at a computer screen the way a cat looks at a TV screen. Software designers actually ask people to pick out four tiny pixels in a single, blinking, vertical line. To see these pixels requires an incredibly advanced skill. I still see lots of computer game software titles in which you must click the mouse button to hit a target that is incredibly tiny.

Give people audio and visual feedback when they select something or when they otherwise take action. I still see software that doesn't do that. They have you selecting menu items or clicking on buttons but there's no feedback to tell you whether you did it.

3. *Make it hot.* "**Hot**" refers to high definition in the McLuhan sense. Make the animation as good as possible—by using more colors and higher resolution—because you're competing with film and television. You must provide high resolution to attract people's attention, and move beyond the abstract in terms of creating illusions.

4. *Make it cool.* McLuhan defined a "**cool**" medium as one that has low definition, which requires your mind to fill in more aspects of the scene, thus you become more involved. By definition, multimedia is the coolest medium of all, because it requires interaction. If you don't do something, the character or action doesn't move, or at least isn't as interesting as it would be if you interacted with

Hot and Cool: McLuhan also distinguished betwen "hot" and "cool" media; a hot medium provides lots of information and requires little audience participation ("filling in" of information). Print and radio are hot. A cool medium provides little information and requires lots of audience participation. Telephone and TV are cool. TV, he argued, requires audience participation because the screen shows a fuzzy collection of tiny dots that the viewer must "connect" and fill in.

it. Coolness encourages involvement, and involvement leads to stimulation.

I'm not suggesting that every program resemble an arcade game, which requires tremendous involvement. Most people are afraid of arcade games because they're embarrassed when they fail. In multimedia titles, you can vary the amount of interaction. You have to give users the feeling that they're in control and they're responsible for making something happen.

5. *Make it deep.* Deep like the ocean. The ocean must seem inviting, so I will wade out into it. It must draw me in. Initially it must be safe and shallow, but then let me go as deep as I want. In the earlier "Wild Kingdom" example, you have a huge pool of information that people enter gradually or all the way, as quickly as they want. As they get more involved and motivated, they keep coming upon new information.

6. *Make it fun.* People don't simply want more information. They want to have a good time. The program or title must provide immediate, positive, and fun feedback. When designing the Apple Macintosh, we wanted people to do something productive with it within 20 minutes of opening the box. When people open a new game, you want them to have fun within 20 seconds. Therefore, when you design a title, always ask, "What visual treat or reward should we give people right off the bat, based on something they've done interactively?" This relates to the environment you create and the ways in which people can control it. It's what makes an interactive experience interesting. When you design the environment, give people information and enough

digitize: To transform information (such as audio or video) into a digital format that can be used by a computer.

overlay: One image placed over another.

control over that environment so it's fully engaging and not frustrating.

7. *Make it cheap.* Everyone who creates multimedia would probably like to operate on a Francis Ford Coppola budget, but have to act more like the B-movie king, Roger Corman. Don't think, "I'm going to make a movie, then turn it into software," because that's too expensive and not applicable. Take advantage of the fact that most visual images are displayed on a screen with fairly low resolution so you can get away with some tricks by creating illusions without a huge amount of effort. If you were to show the same thing on 90mm film, flaws would be more readily apparent.

When we created the computer game, "Dr. J and Larry Bird Go One on One," we needed to create realistic sound effects. We bought tickets to a professional basketball game, brought a tape recorder to the arena, recorded the sounds, then returned to the office where we used a sampling keyboard to **digitize** the sounds. It's a good example of successful production efforts that aren't expensive and complicated.

Multimedia Presentation Techniques

What will the user see on the screen? This relates to the program's graphics production. What occurs on the screen alters the effectiveness and style of the overall illusion. Here are a few techniques used in graphics production:

One technique is "simulcast," in which you watch something on the screen and simultaneously can call up a menu or **overlay** that provides additional information. This works well in such applications as sports programs, where you call up information about the players.

The second technique involves "**sprites**." Consider the on-screen scene as a theatrical set. People in the audience watch the stage from a fixed angle, and on stage they see props and actors. As long as the audience only sees these objects from one angle, you can create pretty strong illusions of movement and action with the props and actors. A sprite can be scaled to look larger or smaller, to tilt and turn, or to appear as if it's moving toward the audience. You can replace it with similar sprites set in different positions to give it depth and make it appear three-dimensional. This technique resembles the production of a traditional animated film: The animators create a beautiful, static background, and in front of it place images of animated characters drawn on clear material, so you can see the background behind them. The animator moves the camera while changing the foreground images to make it appear as if the entire scene is moving. This is the fundamental production model used for most video games today.

Another technique employs motion video for segues between scenes. If you're creating a multimedia title that contains periods of interactivity between scenes, the segue can consist of a little movie clip that sets the stage for what's going to happen next.

Another popular technique is called "video wallpaper" by some people. I call it a "tunnel." Suppose I pump a lot of information onto disk, enough to fill a **frame** as large as the screen. However, the main action on the screen at any time occupies a much smaller space. Imagine an interactive helicopter game as an example. I fly a real helicopter down Broadway in Manhattan to film all of Broadway. I return to my studio and digitize the film. In the game, the helicopter flies down Broadway, spinning upside-down and zigzagging, moving back and forth, moving according to the player's control. The "tunnel" simply runs in the linear sequence of the original film I shot. The illusion is that you're flying down Broadway. It only works as long as the helicopter stays in the tunnel. If you make a sharp left turn, you'll run into a building, because the system can't sustain the helicopter entering a different tunnel. Therefore, with video wallpaper, something constant occurs in the background, while the player's causing other actions to occur in the foreground. The stuff in the foreground consists of animated sprites.

As you can see, creating multimedia is much different than making movies and recording music.

How To Get "There" From "Here"?

I would like to propose an action agenda of issues that we, as a new industry, should address and support.

• *Standards.* Can you imagine how frustrated you would feel if you had to buy gasoline for your car at only one type of gas station? How did we find ourselves in a situation where we face 30 different incompatible multimedia systems all competing for the same audience? If the creative community develops a common voice and says, "We're not going to put

sprite: Screen image, moveable under program or manual control through an input device. Sprites may be characters (such as those in video games), cursor shapes, or specific patterns. Defined by a two-dimensional array of pixels, they normally are smaller than full-screen size, unlike cels, which are complete animation frames.

frame: A single, complete picture in a video recording, film, or animation. Standard video (as seen on TV) runs at 30 frames per second. Film runs at 24 frames per second. The type of cartoons on Saturday morning TV run at about 14 or 15 frames per second.

up with this," the hardware companies will listen.

• *Performance.* The CD alphabet soup contains all these different systems, and we need to express a common voice that none of the systems is good enough. They're adequate for practice, and that's about it. None will appeal to the consumer in a big way.

• *Lobbying & Laws.* When considering multimedia content, we must deal with issues of availability, **copyright**, and use of images, sounds, and text, and how much we pay to acquire them. We need an organization to help define these issues and change some laws.

Laws are supposed to serve society's best interests. However, laws are not forward-thinking because they're created before the invention of technologies that relate to those laws. Our industry needs to protect itself from outdated laws. Consider the issue of software rental. You legally can rent a videotaped movie; you legally can rent a Nintendo game. It's illegal, however, to rent a record or computer software. Why? In the case of recorded music, a music industry lobby was able to effect the banning of renting music recordings. The lobby was powerful and spent years working on the issue.

The CD-ROM medium is the same as the CD that contains music. We can argue that if a CD contains a movie, you legally can rent it; however, if the CD contains music or computer software, you can't legally rent it. So what happens when the CD contains a Nintendo video game? Is it legal to rent it, or not? Obviously the laws must be changed.

Another example of needed change concerns the fair use law. People in the multimedia industry are already talking about how to apply fair use to what we're doing, but we need something more far-ranging. Then there's the issue of royalties on blank media. After a long battle, the recording industry convinced the government to put a tax on blank digital audio tape. The tax goes to compensate members of the creative community for all their music that is digitally taped by people. The taping is against the law, but the government looks the other way. It would make a big difference to our creative community if we had a tax on blank media, because if someone can use a digital medium to create perfect copies that last forever, we face the serious problem of copyright violation.

• *Patience.* As in any profession, we need training, better tools, and networking methods so we can find each other to collaborate on projects. We also need to create jobs and attract financing. The scene isn't going to change overnight. Van Gogh didn't sell a single painting in his lifetime. George Seurat, the artist who pioneered pointillism, never sold a painting. We, too, will experience a struggle.

• *Motivation.* I'd like to see something in our industry, on the level of the Academy Awards ceremony, that recognizes the best efforts in each aspect of the creative process. This would be fun and motivating, and would publicize our products. We need to create public awareness, which will accelerate the process of change in people's lives, which is what this is all about. We need to organize the creative community to get our voices heard.

Things You Can Do Today

If you want to design and produce multimedia titles, prepare for where the technology's heading and perform an autopsy on what's already here. How? Buy a video game system and play the best video games. Buy a personal computer, CD-ROM drive, and the best CD titles. Go to arcades and play the games. Visit theme parks and examine the ways in which electronics are used in the newest attractions. Go to the movies to see the ways they're produced and the ways in which the stories are told. Buy a camcorder and start making movies; learn about video production.

Become a student: Study the audio/visual media that you don't understand. Read the trade magazines. Attend the professional conferences.

Don't overlook the fact that this medium is about play. Don't forget to play!

If you want to be in the multimedia business now, understand that most of the money is involved in game production. If you're not interested in games, try to produce something for these CD-ROM systems that is platform-independent. If your product is locked in on one hardware platform, it means you're not going to survive financially. You must create titles that you can move from one platform to another, covering enough platforms so the lack of a standard won't kill your business. If your title is platform-independent, it won't have fast animation, so you must focus on products that are information-oriented, rather than animation-oriented.

As for me, I'd like to try to apply all these interactive technologies to the reinvention of school. If we're any good at this, we can give all this technology and its applications to other schools and, maybe eventually, put the current public school system out of business. That's my life ambition. It's a big dream, but it means a brighter future for our children and our children's children.

SNOW'S TWO CULTURES REVISITED

PERSPECTIVES ON HUMAN-COMPUTER INTERFACE DESIGN

In this chapter, renowned cyberartist Bill Buxton explores the relationship between the traditionally divergent communities of scientists and artists, and describes the "meeting place" created for them by today's communications technologies. According to Bill, "my intent is not to present a detailed map of this 'meeting place.' Nor is it to present some reductionist treatise on the dangers to society of technology and how they can be solved. Rather, my plan is to jump (somewhat cavalierly) among anecdote, musing, and argument to identify some of the landmarks that make up this 'place.'

"My hope is that the rough sketch that emerges will provide some sense of how the roles of the two cultures can converge and complement one another. Since I am speaking primarily to the arts community, my emphasis is mainly on the role it has to play in this meeting."

BY BILL BUXTON

Bill Buxton launched his career as a musician. He became involved in electronic and computer-based instrument design, which brought him into the fields of computer graphics and user interface design. Long associated with the University of Toronto, he now serves as associate professor in its computer science department and as a scientific director of the Ontario Telepresence Project. He also enjoys a long-time relationship with Xerox's Palo Alto Research Center, where he explores new methods of input and interaction, and multimedia and media-space techniques. With Ron Baecker, Bill co-edited Readings in Human-Computer Interaction: A Multi-Disciplinary Approach, *published by Morgan Kaufmann. His newest books include* Haptic Input to Computer Systems *(about input techniques and technologies) and, with Sara Bly and Bill Gaver,* The Use of Nonspeech Audio Displays in Human Computer Interaction *(both published by Cambridge University Press).*

In 1959, Sir Charles P. Snow presented a landmark lecture on the relationship between the science community and the community of the arts and humanities, or "literary intellectuals."

Snow later wrote an essay ("The Two Cultures: And A Second Look," published in 1964 by Cambridge University Press) in which he characterized these two communities as having lost even the pretense of a common culture. He argued that they had lost the ability to communicate on any plane of serious intellectual endeavor—from the perspective of creativity, "intellectual life," and normal day-to-day living. It was in this essay that he coined the term "the two cultures" to characterize the polarization of these two communities.

My intent here is to take a renewed look at the relationship between these two cultures and discuss how the technologies of computers and telecommunications provide a potential meeting ground for these otherwise polarized worlds. Consider the **interface** where humans meet technology: My belief is that the resulting problems are so critical to society at large that they require and compel both "cultures" to work together to resolve them in a socially acceptable way.

The gulf that was articulated by Snow is amply evident today, even (especially?) in the very area where I claim that the potential meeting ground exists. We see it expressed as the old "them-and-us" attitude, as manifested in complaints such as, "Those engineers! Those programmers! *We're* the intellectuals; *this* is how we write/paint/draw. Those cybernerds have no concept of what we do, much less know how to build our tools!" This them-and-us attitude, of which this is a caricature, is destructive, unnecessary, and extremely counter-productive.

But if there are two cultures, and we believe that the gap between them must be bridged, why can't we do so by education? After all, isn't that one of the goals of a liberal arts degree—to give us the opportunity to balance our literacy in the arts with that in the sciences?

Would that it were so simple! In fact, Snow's original lecture was directed largely at the issue of education. In it he also pointed out why this was no magic bullet. Simply put, the modern world is just too complex. Even by the 18th century, when the Encyclopedists were active in France, the complexity of the world was beyond any individual to absorb. As Snow pointed out, trying to use education to create a new generation of neo-Renaissance men and women is not a viable approach to the problem.

Yet, parenthetically, that is close to one of the "lies" being sold today with multimedia, namely, that you, too, can be a Renaissance man or woman. You can be a good graphics designer, sound designer, scriptwriter, salesperson, and scientist, all at once. This is nonsense—unless you're far brighter than me or anyone else I know.

Renaissance teams? Yes. Individuals? No.

Let's look at such teams. I'll use my own initiation as an example. Back in 1969 I saw a computer for the first time, and used it to create a film soundtrack. This computer was really a music workstation: it had four voices and real-time multi-timbral digital sound, it used common music notation, it provided color encoding of the parts, and it let me use both hands to efficiently enter music (a chording keyboard for my left hand to enter note durations, and a pair of thumb-wheels for the right hand to specify pitch and entry point in time). Even the tape recorder was under computer control.

I worked on that system at Ottawa's National Research Council. The same computer also had one of the first interactive animation systems, which was capable of performing automatic **in-betweenings** from key **frame** to key frame. This was the system on which Pierre Foldez created his award-winning animation, *Hunger*. Pierre did his animation on the system during the days, while I worked on my film score at night.

interface: [noun] The interconnection or method of communication between two objects; an interface may be hardware or software. Examples include a computer keyboard (an interface between human and computer) and a doorknob (an interface between human and door). [verb] To interconnect or communicate.

in-betweening: Transitional effects between two versions of an animated character performing an action or an object in motion. The "in-betweening" function creates a series of frames in which the character or object makes incremental moves between the first "key frame" and the subsequent action in the last "key frame."

frame: A single, complete TV (or video or film) picture. In the U.S., a video frame consists of 525 horizontal lines, composed of two scanned fields of 262.5 lines each. One frame is scanned in one-thirtieth of a second; therefore, a single second of video footage consists of 30 frames. A single second of film footage consists of 24 frames.

I spent a week with this system, finished my score, and went home. I thought that was what computers were, and it impressed me. You walk in, do your score, and walk out. What could be easier? I was sold. Even though I was a musician, I decided to take a computer course. That's when I hit the wall and slid into the culture gap!

I had the dubious pleasure of studying "Burroughs Extended Algol." This had nothing to do with my experience creating the soundtrack. I couldn't figure out how to reconcile these two experiences. Nevertheless, I persevered because my initial experience was so strong and positive that I *knew* that there was another way. After all, I had experienced it.

Looking back, I see that this experience laid the basis for my subsequent life in design and research: I was just trying to get back to where I started.

I was lucky. My first experience occurred with people who were sensitive to the arts and extremely enlightened about human-computer interaction. They also realized that the creative arts offered an excellent base to find guinea pigs for studies in the design of human-computer interfaces. This was an important lesson that I learned from them: Who else does creative stuff and is foolish enough to stay up all night and work on a computer? Not your typical dentist or lawyer! An artist understands how a pencil should work and feel. Likewise, musicians make a lifetime pursuit out of expressing powerful ideas through a mechanical intermediary. They understand what an "instrument" is. In short, to design an interface that has the qualities of a good sable brush or a quality musical instrument is

something to strive for, regardless of application domain.

I use the analogy with brushes and instruments because they are the intermediaries between something that exists in the mind and the resulting realization in the external world. Like computers, these technologies also have "users"—yet it is almost an insult to describe them as such, because of the skill they bring to the task. Where these types of tools differ from most computers lies in the quality, finesse, and subtlety with which they can capture this skill. Therein lies both the core of the problem and the key to its solution.

I would wager that the first violinist of the Los Angeles Philharmonic uses a violin bow—I'm talking about the bow, not the violin—that costs more than a Sun computer workstation. Think about that in terms of the message it conveys regarding the importance accorded to quality tools (especially given the relative income of artists and their ability to afford them). Yet expensive computers that perform "serious" functions don't let you do what you can do with a pencil, such as draw a line whose thickness depends on how hard you push. Even for a so-called "graphics workstation" you must buy special hardware and software to do a dumb little thing like that.

So far we've been talking about the problems of artists as users of computers, evincing a "consumer-as-victim" type of whimpering. That's not the intent. Let's explore territory where aspects of the arts are applied to solve some problems that confront us. These solutions benefit not just artists, but the "user community" in general.

For our example, let's use the currently hot topic of scientific visualization. First, consider this: Today we're in a computational and communications revolution, which is often called the "information revolution" and which is frequently compared to the Industrial Revolution. This "information revolution" is a myth! Instead, what we really have is a *data explosion*. But data does not become "information" until it informs or can serve as the basis for decision-making.

Over the last few years, every magazine that covers computer graphics has published articles about scientific visualization. Scientific visualization involves the graphic rendering of complex data in a way that helps make pertinent aspects and relationships within the data more salient to the viewer. The idea is to tailor the visual presentation to take better advantage of the human ability to recognize patterns and see structures. From this perspective, scientific visualization represents one step forward in the move from a data to an information technology. We can see a clear role here for those in the visual arts and graphics design, since it is precisely the skill set they possess that forms the essence of the visualization technique.

Unfortunately, scientific visualization doesn't go far enough. And why is it just "scientific" visualization? We should be pushing for the application of similar techniques in domains other than science. Even if we restrict ourselves to the term "visualization," we still face problems. The visual system is not the only sensory modality we can use to extract meaning from complex data. For example, without the use of an audio channel, we would

be handicapped in performing complex tasks in the everyday world, such as driving or crossing a busy street. Likewise, we are seriously disabled in terms of our ability to function in the domain of information systems due to the current impoverished use of sound.

Therefore, let us choose a term that better captures the full sensory richness of the user. Let us pursue *perceptualization*, rather than visualization. In so doing, we open up the possibility of building upon the skills of musicians and sound designers as well those of visual artists.

However, the terms "visualization" and "perceptualization" conjure up the image of the human being as multi-sensory sponge and the concept that information is presented to be absorbed. This is not how humans learn and it is not how we develop an understanding of complex phenomena. The process of understanding more closely resembles exploration. We learn by becoming actively engaged with the material. Instead of pursuing scientific visualization, we should strive for *interactive perceptualization*.

When we think along these lines, we see less tension between art and science. We start to expose a meeting ground for the two cultures. The ability to tailor systems to reflect how we sense, think, and problem-solve requires contributions from both the arts and the sciences. Neither has a monopoly. Each needs the other.

The principal design sensibility underlying these ideas is one of designing to exploit the user's existing skills—the skills acquired through living in the everyday world. If we embrace this "skills perspective," we open the door to understanding the ubiquitous (but misdirected) objectives of "ease of use" and "user friendliness." As objectives for design, both of these are poorly formulated. Our focus on skill leads us to a much better formulation of our design objective: *to design systems that accelerate the process whereby novices begin to perform like experts.*

Expert performance isn't simply faster than novice performance. It represents not only a quantitative difference, but a qualitative difference. The way we structure our activities in the process of creating—how we think, how we formulate problems, how we structure our activities, how we move our hands and so on—differs from expert to novice. When we formulate the objective in this way, whether we're designing educational software or drawing programs or music systems, we are forced to ask, "What are the essential skills involved in what I'm trying to support or encourage?"

By examining the differences in how experts and novices work, we can better design systems that channel behavior along the desired path. We can start building strong, specific systems tailored to support specific functions.

However, people possess different types of skills and expertise. How do we use the general dogma just expressed to establish design criteria that reflect these different skill levels? My approach is best described using a metaphor of three mirrors. In this metaphor, we think of the technology as a type of skill. From this, the quality of a design is directly related to the fidelity with which that skill set is reflected.

The first "mirror" reflects the user's motor-sensory system. How well does the system reflect the user's sensory and motor skills? Generally, the image is distorted. If you held up a mirror to a typical microcomputer, you would have to assume that the user either has one eye with monochrome vision or sees only fully saturated colors, has ears with a **frequency response** of about 200 **Hz**, understands no spoken language, has no legs, and has one arm ending in about 60 uniform-length fingers that only have two joints. Given the evidence, these conclusions are as reasonable as they are wrong. Either we should change our bodies or change our machines.

Let's say we blindfold a few good flautists and hand them two flutes, a poor one and a good one. Without playing a note, the flautists know how much respect for their skills is built into the tools simply by touching them. The distortion at this level reflects a lack of respect for the skills of the user, distortions that would never be tolerated from a flute designer.

Now let's look at the second mirror. For this one we ask, "How well does the computer system reflect our cognitive structures: how we think, how we solve problems?" Unlike the motor sensory characteristics, these structures are invisible and harder to quantify. Yet there is ample evidence in the frequency of errors that distortions at this level are as great or greater than those reflected in the first mirror.

The third mirror is perhaps the most important, yet the most neglected. This one reflects our social skills. With this mirror we ask, "How well does the design reflect how I go about my day-to-day work and how I interact with people and groups?"

Virtually all computers were designed for use in the one-person/one-computer, face-to-face configuration. That's not how life is. And it doesn't reflect how we work. In our daily life, we meet people, enjoy social interactions, jump from idea to idea, from person to person, and from group to group. The degree to which computer systems support these types of interaction is impoverished, to say the least. This third mirror might as well be painted matte black, for all the information that it reflects.

It doesn't have to be this way. Again, let's go to the arts for an example. Think of a musical instrument that is designed to be played by four people and resembles a non-competitive game (because the only way you win is not by competing with the other people but by collaborating with them). Such an instrument exists. It's called a string quartet.

The string quartet doesn't simply represent four instruments. When performed properly, it represents one instrument played by four people. In other words, it represents one technology capable of capturing the collective efforts and skills of a group in order to solve a particular (musical) problem. What we need, and what is starting to emerge from the world of "**groupware**" and "computer-supported collaborative work," are technologies that can capture group efforts in solving a broader class of problems, and do so in a manner that reflects and exploits our social skills.

This discussion of group activity brings us back to Snow's observations that our hopes should not be that education can breed a new-generation Renaissance person. If we accept this notion, our only option lies in teamwork and collaboration, and in technologies that can help support, foster, and encourage such activities. We must remove the distortion from the three mirrors!

This task requires the use of expertise of the "two cultures." Therefore, we must take steps in terms of design and organization to build up the long-neglected trust relationship between the two groups.

In conclusion, I'd like to describe a situation that epitomizes the creativity and benefits which can result when we start to let this happen.

This situation occurred at Rank Xerox's Cambridge EuroPARC lab, a satellite of Xerox's famous Palo Alto Research Center (PARC). It was carried out by two colleagues, Bill Gaver and Randall Smith.

Their underlying goal was to study collaborative computer-mediated work and problem-solving carried out by two individuals in separate locations. These subjects were connected by a reciprocal audio/video link that let them see and speak to each other and the task they jointly worked on was displayed on the screens of their computers, which were connected by a local area network.

The task involved operating a simulated cola bottling plant. As the underlying system was called the "Alternative Reality Kit," or ARK, the study was called "ARKola." A key aspect of the study related to investigating the effectiveness of non-speech audio as a means to augment the subjects' ability to efficiently operate the simulation. Some subjects ran the simulation with the audio, and others without it.

According to Bill Gaver, "In this experiment, we were interested in exploring

groupware: Software designed for teams of people working together on shared information; team members might be in the same building or working together from locations miles apart.

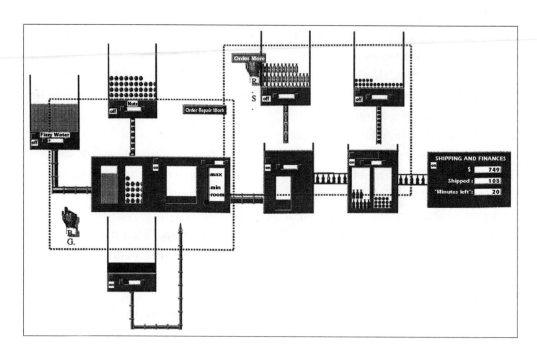

The simulated bottling plant used in the ARKola experiment. Each of the shaded rectangular objects represents one of the machines in the factory. For example, the left-most one is the source of "fizzy water," and the right-most one is the "shipping and finances department." The two larger dotted rectangles illustrate what part of the factory each of the two "operators" is viewing. Operators can move their view independently, but neither can see the whole factory at one time. At the moment, there is little overlap between the two views. The two hands seen in the figure are controlled by the operators' mice. Given that the factory was larger than the operators could monitor visually, the sounds made by the various machines played an important role in helping the operators detect, diagnose, and repair problems. (Figure courtesy of Bill Gaver, Rank Xerox EuroPARC.)

the usefulness of sound in a large-scale collaborative environment. In particular, we were interested in whether sound would be useful in helping subjects with a number of simultaneous, interdependent processes, some of which were not visible on their screens.

"We implemented the project in the shared ARK environment, a large-scale collaborative system developed by Randall Smith of Xerox PARC. The task we gave subjects in this environment was to run a simulated cola bottling plant. Their goal was to work with their partner to make money and produce as much cola as efficiently as they could."

The cola bottling plant consisted of nine machines connected by a series of pipes. Basically, water and nuts were pumped from tanks into a machine called the "cooker." The cooker heated the cola; when it reached the right temperature, nuts and water were combined to produce cola, which then was added to a holding tank. At the

same time, some of the cooked cola was pumped out of the cooker and into the bottle-filler machine. This machine filled bottles with cola and sent the full bottles down the line to the capper machine. The capper sent capped, full bottles to the end of the factory line, to a "shipping and finances unit" machine.

Bill explains, "The shipping and finances machine counted the successfully produced bottles and paid the operator a set sum for each bottle. It also took away money when new supplies were added to the holding tanks. The current balance appeared on the computer display. Half the machines make the cola, and the other half bottle and cap it. Bottling supplies run out occasionally and must be refilled by the operators. Refilling tanks cost money. The operators' goal was to produce as many bottles of cola as possible without wasting too many supplies."

A view of the bottling plant appeared on the computer screens. The entire plant wasn't visible at one time. Instead, the subjects used their hands to scroll over the virtual underlying surface of the "world," and collaborating partners saw different views of the world and could divide tasks in order to oversee different machines.

"Sounds helped the operators achieve their goals," Bill says. "Some sounds provided information about the status of on-going processing. Other sounds indicate trouble, such as empty bottles reaching the shipping and finances unit. For example, the heater made a sound that changed in pitch as the temperature rose. The bottle-filler machine emitted a dripping sound to indicate a tank overflow—which meant a waste of material and a waste of money. When the machines ran smoothly, another sound indicated successful operation."

Can non-speech audio cues actually help operators oversee work tasks and collaborate better with other people who see a different part of their working environment? I believe so. ARKola represents a "multimedia" system in which the use of our senses and interactive media combine to help accomplish fundamental tasks, instead of serving as some secondary artifact, or a "lollypop" intended to reward the worker or sweeten an unpleasant task.

The design of the ARKola system required a great amount of musical skill in creating the sounds. It's not "Art," but nonetheless it represents a meeting ground between the two cultures that can support improved design.

In 1959, Snow might have said that knowing the second law of thermodynamics was a measure of scientific literacy. However, today our "two cultures" have a technology-based common meeting ground and vocabulary.

When we consider the potential of emerging technologies to affect our society, taking advantage of this meeting ground is compelling and essential for the health of the society.

As someone from the arts who works in technology, I can easily be cast into the role of champion or advocate of technology. But given technology's ceaseless advance, one can either try to achieve a degree of literacy and help shape its evolution in humanistic directions, or bury one's head in the ground. With an equally healthy dose of skepticism and optimism, we arrive at a healthy degree of "skeptimism" in approaching the topic: an approach that is based on respect for the skills and contributions from both cultures.

· ·

COMPUTERS AS INSPIRED COLLABORATORS

BY JEFFREY RONA & CHRIS MEYER

*Jeffrey Rona is a composer, arranger, synthesist, sound designer, and author. As a musician, he's worked with such artists as Philip Glass, Basil Poledouris, Jon Hassell, Hans Zimmer, Tina Turner, and others on film scores, albums, operas, and concerts. As a product developer at RolandCorp., he designed some of the first musical software tools for personal computers. He also composes and performs with his own ensemble. From 1986 to 1992, Jeff served as president of the MIDI Manufacturer's Association, the worldwide consortium of musical equipment makers responsible for the **MIDI** specification.*

Music technologist and engineer Chris Meyer has worked as a product developer with Sequential Circuits, Digidesign, and other music technology companies. He currently heads RolandCorp.'s R&D Center in Los Angeles, where he works as chief engineer. Chris is a former technical chairperson of the MIDI Manufacturers Association, and he instigated a number of significant enhancements to the MIDI specification.

The computer provides artists with a new collaborator and a new type of collaborative process. Recent advancements in the capabilities of computer systems raise several technical and philosophical issues for artists to consider.

In this chapter, Jeff Rona and Chris Meyer discuss the implications of the computer's contribution to the creative process, and they explore the reasons for choosing to collaborate with machines over people and vice versa. Although they focus on music here, the issues apply to all arts that incorporate computer-based tools. As Chris points out, "Some people work with software and machines for reasons of efficiency and inspiration. Some work with machines because they are not as judgmental as humans." Chris and Jeff ask, "What is the point of collaboration? What do people intend to achieve from collaboration?" and other questions—some of which they answer.

What if there were a computer program that could take over large elements of the compositional or creative process? Would you consider it a "collaborator"? Several music software programs today are capable of producing infinite variations of your input—but "collaboration" involves more than theme and variation. Variation is an important part of collaboration, but it's not the only desirable contribution to the collaborative process.

In many successful collaborations, the goal is not so much to elicit variation, but inspiration—to provide new raw material along the way. In a successful collaboration, two entities inspire each other in an ascending spiral to reach a final artistic destination.

MIDI: Acronym for Musical Instrument Digital Interface, an industry-standard protocol that lets electronic instruments communicate with each other and with computers. Introduced in 1983, MIDI revolutionized the music industry, and today can be found in various signal production and control devices on stage and in the studio. With a personal computer, some software, and a few MIDI-controlled instruments, one musician can write, perform, and record an entire orchestral composition.

Why do creative people collaborate? They disagree with the people who think that if one person creates the work entirely by himself or herself, that work is the purest and most perfect, because it's undiluted by outside inspiration or interference. This attitude is similar to that of a synthesizer teacher in Cincinnati who was asked, "What music do you like to listen to?" He replied, "I try not to listen to anything, because I don't want to be influenced."

People also say (and sometimes rightfully), "Too many cooks spoil the broth." Problems arise when you have six people in the recording studio arguing, "Make the bass louder"; "No, lower the bass."

Some of us want to collaborate because we want more musical ideas. Some of us collaborate because we enjoy working with someone else. We think the reason most people want to collaborate with others is so that something other than their own experience can be brought to the work.

In our case, nothing has had a stronger impact on the refinement of our music and creative process than the people with whom we've collaborated. Over the past decade, for example, Jeff has collaborated with choreographers. Choreographers listen to music differently than musicians. Right off the bat he found that he liked the way they listened better than the way his classical music teachers taught him to listen. He was taught to have critical ears. Choreographers, on the other hand, have critical feet. He found that their way of listening to music involved listening to the *energy* of the music. They didn't listen to the resolution of a particular chord pro-gression. They listened in a refreshing way that was revealing to Jeff. As he started to compose music for dancers, it forced him to critically reevaluate his writing. It's changed who he is as a musician.

The point of hypermedia is to involve all the senses, and that should extend to involving many different kinds of creative people. The production of modern media—movies, TV, new forms of video—requires various technical areas of expertise. The success of the end result doesn't lie in how each element succeeds in and of itself. There are bad movies with good music, good videos with bad art, and bad TV shows with good acting. What matters is how individual collaborative personalities mesh to produce the successful synergy—because the point of collaboration is *synergy*.

The point of working with another person or entity is to see or hear things you never would have imagined. Whether both collaborators are musicians, or one is a graphic artist and the other is a sound designer, collaboration involves each person's personal vision and aesthetic influencing the other to bring something new out of them.

The idea of diluting personal vision is important. Certainly some people choose not to or should not work in groups, because their best work is done by themselves. Outside of that, a look toward the future—and where the new media technology is taking us—reveals the idea that collaborations will become more important over time.

Let's say that, for whatever reasons—personal, stylistic, or forced by management—you decide to collaborate on an artistic work. Do you collaborate with another person, or do you collaborate with a machine? What are the similarities and differences between collaborating with a human and collaborating with a machine? Why pick one over the other?

The environment we create when we work with people is radically different from the environment we create when we work with machines. It's so different that it affects process and product.

Collaborating with a machine offers many advantages. There's the old joke about drummers always showing up late to rehearsal, while drum machines show up on time. Machines don't get into screaming matches with their spouses during a practice session. (They do sometimes argue with their peripheral devices.) Computers are clean and convenient. You go in, switch on the system, and typically it powers up, ready to go. You can collaborate with it at any hour.

Sometimes you get better feedback from a computer, in terms of **algorithmic** composition or **fractal** generation. Some people feel the computer is a tool that offers input they can't get from other people. Or the computer is a tool that provides the most convenient way to finish a job. Some people feel very, very comfortable working with their computer or a particular computer program. Sometimes the program is almost impossible to use, but so powerful that it's worth putting up with; people regularly use programs they find fickle, but feel these systems supply tools and help achieve results not otherwise possible.

We've met people working toward computer science degrees mainly because they didn't like to deal with humans. Humans are judgmental. Machines are not. However, we've tried to explore how we can make machines judge what we do and see how many people that ticks off.

People talk about programming computers to analyze our creations. It's not a difficult task to instruct a computer to go through a composition, parse out aspects of the performance, and use that as a model to make judgments. Still, it can't say, "Gee, I don't know about that phrase. I think we can do better."

That augmentation is another aspect of collaboration. Is it not good to sometimes hear someone other than yourself say, "Maybe you could come up with something better," or "I think it stinks"? It's difficult to create and criticize simultaneously. You can't be a composer, creator, and editor at the same time. One activity switches off the other; when you start criticizing yourself, you start shutting down your creative process. However, when two collaborators work together in a synergistic way, there's always somebody who'll say, "I think we could do better than that." A computer can't provide that viewpoint.

People often collaborate with others because they want another critical judgment processor. They don't want to work alone. Sometimes you work with another person because you get along well; the two of you are "in tune" and can create a relaxed, happy environment. Sometimes you work with someone you don't like, yet he or she is so brilliant that they bring you further along or add something to the process. Despite their lack of personal charm, you seek them out because you think the results will be better.

algorithm: A mathematical term indicating any series of instructions, decisions, and steps used to solve a problem or perform a task.

fractal: Fractal art generation is a computer process that creates complex, repetitive, mathematically defined geometric shapes and patterns that resemble those found in nature.

In his book *Shared Minds: The New Technologies of Collaboration*, Michael Schrage explores successful collaborations and seeks common elements in them. He talks about such people as James Watson and Frances Crick, the discoverers of the DNA model, and posits that all successful collaborators have a common shared space for working. He writes: "The shared space is actually a medium. And what you find out is that if you alter the properties of the medium, you alter the quality of the collaboration. Watson and Crick's shared space was the metal DNA models that they crafted based on their experiments, which let them work outside the mental and physical isolation of their usual mode of work. Now, we can build those models on our Sun [computer] workstations. The problem, however, is that despite the sophistication of the technology, most computer systems are still designed for working in isolation."

When Jeff was studying computer music, his university received the very first instrument from a small, new company called New England Digital. You typed on a keyboard and entered code into this system, and eventually it compiled everything, and out of a speaker would come a crude **FM** sound. It was an algorithm-based system; that is, it could improvise if you taught it rules, and it dealt both in timbre and in composition. He worked with that system for untold days and nights. One day, he made a mistake. He accidently sent a series of negative numbers into the **oscillator**. Suddenly, the most incredible sounds he ever heard from the machine started coming out of its speaker. And he fell in love.

It also made him realize that software systems are not very forgiving of mistakes. Today we bemoan the fact that most software is almost too well-written. It doesn't provide for totally unexpected results.

We are told to hate television because it's passive, because all the decisions are made for us as to what appears on it, and all we do is take it in. We're also told that anything we interact with—including a computer program—liberates our imagination, because we get to make choices. However, it represents a level of passivity that is removed and hidden; the choices we get to make are the choices given to us by a program. We're still doing what someone else allows us to do. Is it possible to remove the computer programmer from the composition?

When you write music for the piano, the piano maker's involvement is minor except, perhaps, for the quality of the piano's tone. This is not the case in **intelligent music-composition systems** or interactive music performance technology, available these days in various commercial instruments and software. In the typical intelligent-music system, a musician plays an instrument while a computer monitors the performance and reacts to it with musical information of its own. It might generate music or it might modify the music being played. Can you ever completely remove the programmer from this type of collaboration, even if you're working alone with the computer? Would you want to?

Humans don't necessarily work in defined ways. You know that when you strike a note on the piano, you'll hear a sound. If you play a musical phrase for a human,

FM synthesis: A digital sound synthesis technique in which **f**requency **m**odulation is used to create complex audio waveforms. "FM" is a change in the frequency or pitch of an audio signal, and is perceived as a change in tone quality.

oscillator: One of the basic elements in a synthesizer, this electrical device creates a repeating electrical waveform. The shape (form) of the wave determines its harmonic content, which in turn is a vital part of its timbre (tone color). Basically, the oscillator is the part of the synthesizer that makes the sound.

intelligent music composition & interactive music performance technologies: Computer-based systems that generate music in response to human input, or somehow change the music being played by humans. The idea of programming a computer so it can complete a compositional process is not a new one; the first composer to use computers this way was Lejaren Hiller at the University of Illinois in 1957, producing "Illiac Suite" for string quartet. The computer produced the score using numbers that represented pitch, duration, and instrumentation.

you don't know what that person will play in response. Is that, then, the primary difference between collaborating with machines as opposed to humans? Machines tend to do the same thing over and over again, while humans are unpredictable?

Let's differentiate between tools, then, and collaborative systems that are intelligent systems which go beyond being "simply" musical tools. They become part of the compositional process. They invite us to acquiesce in our own creative input and allow the computer to do more.

When you are inspired to compose music, one of the first things you do is choose the instruments that will best express your feelings. If you are inspired to paint, one of the first things you do is select a brush. And one of the most critical points in the creative process is this choice; your choice of tools relates directly to the final result. Likewise, our decision to collaborate with people or with machines.

Michael Schrage (we quoted him earlier) also writes for the *Los Angeles Times*. In a 1990 article, "Quill or Computer Makes No Difference," he stated, "Using an Apple Macintosh can lead to sloppier writing and fluffier topics, according to research by a University of Delaware writing instructor."

The article emphasized how the tools we use influence not only how we express ourselves, but what we express. He related how he had reviewed a word-processing program for the IBM PC, giving it a very negative review. He said that it was much too difficult to use, it was an impediment to writing, and it wasn't worth buying. Many people—users of

the program—wrote to him to say, "How dare you put this program down? It's an incredible program!" Every one of those letters was handwritten. In his article, Schrage pointed out that the people who wrote those letters probably didn't give their method a second thought. They had to get something passionate out, which is not possible with a program that makes expression difficult.

The point is: Choosing the programs we use is as important as choosing the humans with whom we collaborate.

Another issue to consider is this: When you work with a machine, where does it cross the line from being a tool to being a collaborator? The breakthrough occurs when you get the program to do unpredictable things. Then you start learning how to master the unpredictability. Theoretically, you could drive a person insane so they start doing unpredictable things, and after a while you start learning how to deal with that and can use that.

In fact, it works that way whether you work with a person or a machine. At one point the "collaboration" is 100 percent you and 0 percent the other. Then you start giving a bit of creative power to the machine or person. You might command the computer, "Play the bass line with these notes," or, in the case of some algorithmic composition programs, you'll tell the system the percentage of variation they're allowed to introduce, or how often to introduce a fill in some programs. You might tell the human, "Go ahead and swing the time if you want." You might reach a critical point where you depend on the other for at least half the final result. Many users of music and graphics software say, "I'll let the computer do more than half this job because I'm not up to it." Same thing working with people. We know some professional musicians who are very good at surrounding themselves with talented players, making a record, then putting just their own names on it.

This brings up another grey area. If we work with another person, we tend to give that person credit. If we work with another machine, we tend *not* to give the machine credit. Why? Isn't it right to credit the computer or the person if you used something they contributed that you didn't think of yourself? That's when someone or something crosses over the line from being a tool to being a collaborator.

The amount of instant gratification and simulated virtuosity that comes from collaborating with computers tends to *supplant* as opposed to *enhance* the inspirational process. The computer-person interaction offers a possibility of inspirational atrophy.

Intelligent instruments, however, are different. When we start handing over a large part of the process to a machine, we put less of our souls on the line. Plenty of music, some of it good and a lot of it bad, has resulted from interactions between humans and "intelligent machines." Certainly much more music will be written, and as the quantity grows, so will the quality. Given the ability to generate musical events at a near-infinite scale with newly found ease is like Bach saying, "Forget about the finale, just keep copying, more and more." *Something* good is bound to come up. Same thing if you gave a roomful of monkeys a synthesizer each, instead of the proverbial typewriter.

When we use machines, can we express thoughts or feelings about the human condition any more succinctly than we have in the past? Do we need 20th-century tools to express 20th-century feelings? Is there such a thing as "20th-century feelings"? Is there a big difference between the way you feel when you get dumped for another person, and the way an ancient Egyptian felt when dumped for another ancient Egyptian?

Probably not. The same feelings keep coming up over and over throughout history. The definitions of "music" and "art" have changed over the course of the centuries, but our desire for feeling, passion, story, resolution, beauty, lightness, and darkness hasn't changed. Art is an inspiration for the people we're trying to reach with it, and the inspiration comes not from the musical notes, not from the clay or pigments, not from the pixels, not from the tools, but from an artist's ability to express feelings and tell stories. The tools we use to express feeling and tell a story must fit the creative desire and the circumstances of the art's creation.

We have yet to find emotions that can be expressed with a synthesizer that can't be expressed as well or better with "low technology." In other words, what are we adding to the vocabulary of artistic expression when we use high-technology tools? Those of us who consider ourselves artists should remember that at the outset of each new work, we are faced with an infinite array of choices with which to express ourselves. From those, usually only one choice is the "right" one, and that's what the piece becomes.

When we choose to develop new compositional systems, let's not fool ourselves into thinking we're creating the future. We're augmenting the present. We can do this as individuals or we can explore the synergy of working as collaborators. Maybe your best collaborator is a person. Maybe it's a machine. Maybe it's a person you'll never actually meet, someone who lives across the ocean or the world. Maybe you'll find the best combination of purpose, medium, environment, people, systems, and/or algorithms that allows a perfect way to reach out and communicate with another person. Does it matter in the end to the person who listens to your music or admires your art that the experience was generated by human or machine? Does it really matter to us as artists and creators?

• •

IS IT TECHNOLOGY OR IS IT ART?

COMMENTARIES BY CARL MACHOVER, DAVID EM, BO GEHRING, & ELLEN SANDOR

In August of 1991, a New York Times *critic complained about an example of art created with the help of technology. He said, "The 18th and 19th centuries were the ages of inventions, but 20th-century art has taken them over. The beauty of Christo is not, I suspect, in the miles of umbrellas or streamers across the landscape, in the ultimate seeing of them whole. The art is in the doing, in the assembling of materials, the logistics of installation, the raising of money, and the dickering with farmers over the use of their corn fields. The finished product completes an equation, but it is less a climax than a denouement. Solving the problem, in other words, is more fun than looking at the answer."*

In the following commentaries, former National Computer Graphics Association president Carl Machover and three contemporary artists respond to this and similar criticism.

BY CARL MACHOVER

Carl Machover heads the New York-based firm Machover & Associates, a computer graphics consulting firm serving users, suppliers, and investors. He is a founder and former president of the National Computer Graphics Association and has been involved in computer graphics since 1958.

animation: A series of pictures displayed in rapid sequence that present the illusion of motion. Creating computer-generated animations requires the coordination of pictures (and, usually, sounds) in a time-based sequence, often with sophisticated transitions and visual effects. Current animation software programs automate some of these processes.

vector display: A device that stores and displays data as line segments. A "vector graphic" is a representation of an object based on a complex mathematical description.

THE NEW TOOLS

Some of you may know that 1988 was the first year in which an Academy Award went to a computer **animation**. That animation was *Tin Toy*, which was produced by northern California's Pixar. You may not be aware that ten years before that, a computer animation called *Le Faim ("Hunger")*, created by Pierre Foldez of Canada, received a nomination for an Academy Award. *Le Faim* employed a relatively simple process of animation using a **vector display**, which means that all the images appeared as simple outlines, but nonetheless it was extremely powerful.

People criticize computer art by saying that it really is a depiction of **algorithms**; in other words, I make pictures of certain physical phenomena, and thus I create "artistic" images. This type of criticism often is directed toward the use of **fractals**. One of the first people to use fractals was Loren Carpenter in his pioneering film, *Vol Libre* (1980). This film illustrates the principal issues involved in the art-versus-technology debate. Is a piece considered "art" because it consists of artistic images? Or is it considered "technology" because the artist has "only" superimposed a mathematical principle on a graphic image? That question lies at the heart of our discussions about art, creativity, craftsmanship, and the degree to which we can use computer technology to create what you might describe as "automatic art."

I recently heard someone complain about the "extraordinarily high" cost of some of the new computer graphics equipment. The system they mentioned cost about $4,000. The hardware used to create *Le Faim* cost almost $300,000, and you certainly couldn't drive down to your local discount computer store to buy soft-

A frame from Loren Carpenter's fractal-based, 1980 film, Vol Libre

ware for it. Today, most of us can afford entry-level computer systems and we all have access to a broad range of standard software, both conditions that contribute to the current widespread use of this kind of technology.

Now we also have access to digital paint programs that let us use a personal computer to make extremely realistic images—whether we're creating a building for use in an animation, or designing a building that will be constructed in "real life." Technology has reached the point where artists can create computer-generated images that are much softer than the "hard edge" that computer art often has been accused of having. But when automobile manufacturers use beautiful, computer-generated images to design cars, instead of using physical models, do we call that "art"? Or is it technology? The distinction is not clear.

We must also consider the fact that we have access to output devices that eliminate the traditional craftsmanship of production. Thermal dye transfer, for example, is a process which produces hard copy of images that look as if they were created by hand, by painting. Digital photographic techniques allow us to produce highly artistic photographs. New video technologies, such as **HDTV**, are reaching computer artists, including Yoichiro Kawaguchi, who has used it to create such artworks as "Flora."

When we try to define the contribution of the artist and the contribution of the technologist, we can only say that the blend of technology and art grows increasingly interdependent and increasingly complex.

THE NEW ATTITUDE

BY DAVID EM

David Em gained international prominence in the early 1980s for his pioneering works of computer art. His digital paintings, prints, and films have been exhibited around the world, including the Pompidou Museum in Paris, Madrid's Spanish Museum of Contemporary Art, and Tokyo's Seibu Museum. His work has been profiled in many TV programs, magazines, and books, including Gardner's Art Through The Ages, *the widely used art textbook. His own book,* The Art of David Em *(Harry N. Abrams) is the first collection of computer art published by a major art publisher.*

Computer art has hit some interesting territory ever since artists began working with the medium in the 1960s, or whenever we say the clock started running. The computer provides a medium through which one can express one's sensibilities. The question, "Can you make art with computers?" is a ludicrous one. You can make art with mud! Anyone who looks at a computer and says, "Gee, do you think you could actually make art with that?" should have their eyes examined. It's a non-issue. So why do people treat it as an issue?

Whether a particular image is "art" is another issue entirely. Within the art world, people have always been asking, "Is this *art*?" They asked that when **Duchamp** exhibited a urinal over 50 years ago. Today that urinal is one of the most written-about works of art of the 20th century.

The current "technology versus art" debate is reminiscent of the 15-year lag experienced by the Impressionists when they first presented their work as art in the late 19th century. It's not an issue related to technology; it's a perceptual issue. That is what is happening now with computer art. Many people think the art world is avant-garde and forward-looking, but it's not. The most conservative people I know work in the art world, and they're not necessarily the artists. Indeed, "artists" and "the art world" represent two different things.

Let's use photography as an example. It took 100 years before museums said, "Yes, photography is art," and started exhibiting photographic art and setting up photography curatorial departments. It won't take 100 years before they accept computers; the evolution of computer art is happening quickly. To the artists who use computers, it may seem slow. The computer medium has been in existence for some 20 years. But, come the year 2000, the art world's attitudes will change, particularly among the people who grew up with this stuff and never knew a time when computers did not exist.

I presented a lecture a few years ago in New York City for a group of graphic art designers who were totally enamored of the concept of computer art. They realized that their future depended on getting involved in this technology. The trade magazines in the commercial art world *assume* that their readers are computer-literate; they write about computer hardware, software, graphic file formats, and so on. But it's very rare for magazines in the fine art world to even mention computers. Computer art is not "real" to them. But when I talked to those commercial art designers and explained, "This is what computer graphics is. This is a **pixel**; this is a

Marcel Duchamp: (1887-1968) Born in France, this painter worked in Europe and the U.S., and is often credited as "the father of concept art."

pixel: Contraction for "picture element," the smallest controllable spot on a computer display screen. The more pixels per square inch, the sharper and clearer the image.

raster: A type of video display technology used for personal computers. Televisions also use raster monitors.

resolution: The measurement of image sharpness and clarity on a video display, usually measured by the number of pixels per square inch. The higher the resolution, the better the image quality.

raster," and so on, they were extremely receptive and interested.

That night I visited my sister in Connecticut. She has four kids. At the time, they were between 4 and 11 years old, and they asked me questions such as, "What's your computer's **resolution**? What kind of software do you use?" I thought, "Where are they getting this stuff? Are they learning it in school? Are they reading about it in kid's magazines, are they hearing about it on Sesame Street?" However they get the information, such osmosis is part of the way kids experience life. When these kids grow up and become art curators (many curators, in fact, are people in their twenties), they'll move into the art system, replacing the older generation, and "computer art" will be considered art.

THE NEW ME

BY BO GEHRING

Bo Gehring has created award-winning film segments, TV commercials, and broadcast graphics. He first worked in compu-ter graphics in 1972 at Synthavision, the entertainment offshoot of MAGI (Mathematical Applications Group, Inc.), a company involved in mathematical simulations. MAGI coined "Synthavision" to suggest that realistic images could be synthesized mathematically, a new concept at the time. Bo later moved to California created computer graphics, feature film segments, and advertisements for such clients as ABC-TV, Universal Studios, and General Motors. In the early 1980s, while working to improve aircraft cockpit displays under U.S. Air Force and Defense Department sponsorship, he independently invented a means of using binaural audio as a cockpit display. Today Bo's Focal Point 3-D audio technology is used in virtual reality and entertainment applications, including music recording and live performance.

The Kitchen recently celebrated its 20th anniversary with a successful benefit featuring Laurie Anderson performing at Town Hall.

I n my Synthavision days, my focus was primarily technical, although I had attended art school (night classes at the School of Visual Arts and the New School for Social Research). At that time—it was 1972—there was a place in New York City called **The Kitchen**, which produced video shows. A typical Kitchen show featured a wall of video monitors with a group of people sitting there, watching the monitors. I felt like I was observing the communication of an alien species, because as an analytical type of person, I couldn't see any information content in the material. By the time you saw 1,000 frames of this video, you saw all it had to offer. It was like the world's biggest lava lamp, and I quickly grew tired of it. Not that the technology wasn't fascinating—it's just that it didn't have much creative depth or range of expression. It was hard to tell whether the different artists possessed unique visions. The technology itself seemed to be in the creative driver's seat.

In New York, around this same time, Milton Glaser was having a powerful effect on the world of graphic design. After spending years establishing a successful commercial art studio, he was able to get his work shown at the Museum of Modern Art. Of course, it didn't appear in the gallery space itself; that area was reserved for "high art." They installed Glaser's work in a room where they showed the design things. The *New York Times* did review it, however; it said something like, "Milton Glaser, the commercial artist, has a show of drawings at the Museum of Modern Art." That was the entire review. And yet the importance of his work could hardly be overstated—he's one of the few artists who influenced our entire cultural iconography. So isn't his work "Art"? I would have thought so, but evidently the definition depends on context.

This brings us to the question, "What is this stuff we create with computers? Is it art?" Let's cast our minds back to the early days of painting when people used egg tempura and tiny brushes. They had to mix this egg stuff by hand. It dried and hardened very quickly, but if you painted with it at the right moment, the colors were pure and the lines were extremely crisp. Then along came this messy, dirty, dreadful thing called "oil painting." It changed the nature of painting. It represented a change in painting technology and technique, because the oils stayed wet for a long time. Oil painting was messy; you had to use big, wide, sloppy brushes. The acceptance of oil painting represented an attitude change, because if you looked closely at oil paintings, everything looked smudgy, unlike the appearance of egg tempura paintings. I bet those egg tempura folks said, "This isn't art, this is *oil*!" Today, with computer art, we're in the same position.

Fifteen years or 50 years from now, most people won't even know that. My kids will be adults. They're so computer-literature now that it frightens me. They won't care about the "art versus technology" issue because to them, it is not an issue.

When I worked with Synthavision, I was an analytical technologist. My work there made me start thinking about the "other side," where the artists lived and worked. Those days in the mid-1970s were a time of great creative freedom. It was the heyday of innovative ad campaigns such as Volkswagen's, and the agencies' creative staffs were trying to outdo each other in wild dress and hairstyles. Coming from MAGI, which basically was a group of distinguished mathematicians, I'd visit ad agencies and tell their art directors, "We can use mathematical models to make a better picture of your aspirin box than your regular photographer can. Moreover, once we have the model in our computer, we can spin it around, animate it, and do all these wonderful things that your photographer can't do." I was excited and enthusiastic, but I realized after I left the meetings that the agency people had looked at me as if I came from the moon.

Years later, I moved over to their side. I owned a studio and enjoyed working with some of the top commercial directors. Frankly, that new me would not have talked to the old me. The new me realized that the old me was just hyping some technology which was trying to find its way into the ad market, technology that wasn't fully ready for professional use.

Nevertheless, creative projects (then and now) that use technology fascinate me, because for the technology to work on a creative level, somebody must control it—there must be human spirit present in the process.

When you produce television commercials, you don't have the luxury, as you do with "high art," of taking time to complete something that can go through creative changes in the process. You start with a definitive storyboard (a detailed, illustrated, scene-by-scene representation of the script), and the finished commercial must resemble that storyboard. To deal with this approach you need a team of workers led by an art director and a technical director, who are always at each other's throats. The technical director tries to use all the new technology in the commercial so they can win a prize from the computer graphics industry; the art director wants to keep it pure and win Clio awards from the advertising industry. This creates a healthy tension.

Typically, these projects go one way or the other: They are dominated either by the art or by the technology. No matter which way they go, underlying the project is the fact that people remember only its *human value*. This has nothing to do with technology. The technology is a medium, and the most successful creative works represent great human vision. For all the technology I've worked with, I'm really a **Luddite**. If the finished piece doesn't sing in human terms, then it ain't worth seeing.

Many art critics duck the issue of computer art by saying that they just don't understand this type of art, thus it's not "Art." The world's oldest screen for incompetence is the claim, "I don't understand it."

Luddite: Opponent of the introduction of labor-saving machinery. The original Luddites, followers of legendary Ned Lud, were a group of workers in England (1811-1816) who smashed new labor-saving textile machinery that threatened their jobs. Modern opponents of technological change are sometimes called Luddites or "neo-Luddites."

THE NEW ROCK STARS

BY ELLEN SANDOR

Mixing art and science is nothing new to Ellen Sandor. After earning her M.F.A. in the mid-1970s from School of the Art Institute of Chicago, she focused on neon sculpture—artworks that required electrical power for illumination. In 1983 Ellen masterminded (Art)^n Laboratory as a collaborative group dedicated to the fusion of art and science. Today she is (Art)^n's director and producer. Based at Chicago's Illinois Institute of Technology, (Art)^n is renowned for its 3-D images, "PHSColograms" (skol-o-gram). PHSColograms represent a visualization of mathematical and scientific data, brought together in an art form that influences scientists, mathematicians, physicians, and the art world. PHSColograms show molecules, viruses, trees, geometric patterns, aircraft, human torsos

We call our work "virtual-photography," and it is extremely process-oriented; it's three-dimensional photography created digitally from start to finish. Our work wasn't always digital. In the early days we built movable, sculptural dioramas and photographed them with huge bellows cameras. Each exposure took 45 minutes and each complete 3D image took almost seven hours to photograph.

Today, all our tools are highly advanced and sophisticated, but we remain true to the juxtaposition of garage art and high tech, operating from our headquarters at Illinois Institute of Technology and with the Electronic Visualization Laboratory of Chicago's University of Illinois. We still take an old-fashioned approach to creating art; we just happen to work with amazing scientists in the process.

Inspired by **Man Ray's** Rayographs and **Moholy-Nagy's** photograms, we devised the term "PHSColograms" by combining elements of the words "photography," "holography," "sculpture," and "computer graphics." The PHSCologram viewer sees a three-dimensional image suspended inside an electrically illuminated metal and plastic box. To create a PHSCologram, we start with a sophisticated computer graphics program that lets us sculpt an image that isn't flat and two-dimensional like a painting, but resembles an imaginary sculpture (a "virtual sculpture"). We sculpt real or imaginary objects that exist only as information in a computer program.

After we created a virtual sculpture of the AIDS virus [*shown in the CyberArt Gallery*], for instance, Stephan Meyers of (Art)^n recorded 13 different perspectives of the image onto computer disk. It's like taking 13 photographs from different angles. We then divided all the images into thousands of extremely thin, vertical strips. By "interleaving" these strips, we turned the 13 pictures into one picture. The picture was printed in negative form, and we used the resulting large negative to produce color slides of the sculpted image.

We laminated the film and a barrier screen on the back of a piece of Plexiglas, and placed the whole assembly inside a light box. We achieve the 3D effect by deceiving the eyes with venetian blind kind of effect. Tiny slits in the barrier screen let you see only one image at a time from any angle. Because of the way your eyes are placed in your head, you see a different image with each eye, which the brain interprets as 3-D information. In its final form, the PHSCologram looks as if you could reach out and touch it. The creation of the PHSCologram involves precise control over all the elements in the process.

Unlike a hologram, a PHSCologram is full color, and its creation doesn't require laser photography. The materials we use may suggest a certain distance from the realm of "pure art," but the PHSCologram image balances a reticent precision with the age-old attraction of shifting, glowing forms. In fact, our early PHSColograms, such as *Man Ray 1983*, were loaded with references to specific figures in art history. Like Man Ray's experimental works, PHSColograms blur the line between form and content. Unlike Man Ray's works, PHSColograms—particularly the purely computer-generated ones—are based on concrete scientific and mathematical data and thus serve as "information vehicles," yet they satisfy one's desire to view aesthetically pleasing images.

We create art that makes political statements and has emotional content, and it is not those statements and content that create controversy. What *does* create controversy is the fact that we perform scientific imaging that transcends into art. Some critics have a problem dealing with images that *they* consider to be pure science and that we claim are art. In 1990 Feature Gallery in New York City showed a PHSCologram exhibit containing only science-based images. *Art in America* was furious and published a negative review. Their article, however, inspired some wonderful, positive articles in other publications!

The people we work with to create PHSColograms are scientists, physicians, and mathematicians, and they are the rock stars of the future. They're ahead of their time. In the 1990s they'll help us show the world that art and science really do blend well.

Man Ray; László Moholy-Nagy: Photographers active in the 1920s and 1930s. Man Ray was an American dadaist and Surrealist best known for his experimental photography and sculpture. (He said, "I photograph what I do not wish to paint and I paint what I cannot photograph.") Moholy-Nagy, another Surrealist, belonged to the Bauhaus design movement (which promoted the adaptation of science and technology to architecture). He described his work in his books **The New Vision** (1928) and **Painting, Photography, Film** (1925), in which he wrote, "In the photographic camera we have the most reliable aid to a beginning of objective vision. . . . This will abolish that pictorial and imaginative association pattern which has remained unsuperseded for centuries and which has been stamped upon our vision by great individual painters."

CONTENT DISTRIBUTION: WHAT'S THE MEDIUM?

ESSAYS BY JOHN ATCHESON, PATRICK FORD, & EARL MANCHESTER

With developments in multimedia technology occurring rapidly and regularly, so too are new strategies for distributing multimedia titles (also known as "content," or "programming") themselves. These essays point out key issues involved in distributing the new media titles on a widespread basis. Whether these distribution methods serve to provide a large portion of the general population with easy, affordable access to multimedia, video, and musical artworks remains to be seen.

DISTRIBUTION PATHS: DISC VS. NETWORK

Today we can split interactive multimedia distribution technologies into two categories. The first is local storage, or disc, technology, which includes CD-ROM and the two competing consumer CD-ROM standards, CD-interactive (CD-I), promoted by Philips, and CDTV, promoted by Commodore. The other category of distribution is *network* technology.

Disc technology puts the multimedia content directly into users' hands. They can use the discs repeatedly and at any time, just as they do with music CDs or computer software. Network technology involves the distribution of the multimedia content from one central location into multiple homes.

Our current, primary network technology is fairly low-bandwidth: the standard telephone technology. With standard telephone technology, **modems** provide the data transfer. Modem technology is advancing rapidly; not too long ago, 9600 **baud** seemed very fast. Now it's practically a standard. Newer modems can transfer 54 kilobits of data per second, and some run even

BY JOHN ATCHESON

John Atcheson is founder and president of San Francisco's MusicNet, a leading developer of interactive music programming. John also served as vice president of sales and marketing for Digidesign, a developer of high-end audio products for the Apple Macintosh, and as multimedia marketing consultant to Macromedia and Apple Computer.

modem: Short for **mo**dulator-**dem**odulator, this device converts computer signals (data) into communication signals that can be sent over standard telephone lines.

baud: A unit of measure of data transmission approximately equal to bits per second.

faster than that. So it's not unreasonable to imagine limited multimedia content distribution over standard phone lines.

Another current **network** technology is ISDN (Integrated Services Digital Network), which essentially is two channels of data moving at a rate of 64 kilobits per second, delivered in conjunction with a standard telephone line going into the home. Now that the Public Utilities Commission has approved the service, regional phone companies can deliver ISDN today. ISDN is not widespread, however, primarily because most central switching offices are not equipped to deliver it. Moreover, ISDN could be called "intermediate-**bandwidth**," not a high-bandwidth service.

Let's turn to true, high-bandwidth network technology. The most extensive high-bandwidth "pipeline" today is **coaxial** cable, which now carries cable television into about 60 percent of the homes in America. Coaxial cable potentially can transmit multimedia programming in two different ways. The first is a "continuous loop," which circulates information on an ongoing basis. By circulating the information, people can pull specific content off the network at any moment. For example, if you're playing a video game and you press a button to cause a certain action, the reaction to that button-push gets pulled off the loop and appears on your screen. The beauty of continuous loop technology is that it does not require two-way communications to be effective. This is important, because two-way cable is generally not available.

The next step up the ladder is the use of "hybrid" technology, which combines the high bandwidth of coaxial cable with the two-way communication capabilities of the telephone. For example, a hybrid system would allow us to blast information over the cable into the home, view it on the computer screen or some future TV-like device, then send messages back through the phone line. For example, we could send a message such as, "I want to see the next screen now," or "I want to open the door to the cave that's displayed on my system," and so on.

Ideally we'd use coaxial cable for bi-directional data transmission. Unfortunately, very few cables currently installed in homes provide for two-way communications. That's largely because the cable companies, when they first laid the cable, saw no applications for two-way communications. But there's no reason we can't use two-way communication over coaxial cable. Unfortunately, to go back and retrofit systems for two-way use is extremely expensive.

We're also starting to move into some experimental, forward-looking technologies, such as ADSL—a new telephone technology that breaks telephone tradition by sending extremely high bandwidth out to the home with the ability to carry low-bandwidth signals back to the central office. *[ADSL is described in Earl Manchester's part of this chapter.]*

The Holy Grail of interactive multimedia distribution is the network ideal: fiber-optic cable going into every home in the country. Unfortunately, widespread installation of fiber-optic cable will cost between $100-200 billion. We can safely assume that's going to take a while.

Let's consider the advantages of each distribution technology. On the disc side,

network: An interconnected system of hardware and software in which individual users share resources. A network can span great geographical distances.

bandwidth: The range of signal frequencies that a piece of audio, video, or computer equipment can encode or decode; data transmission rate.

coaxial cable: Data transmission medium with a single-wire conductor insulated from electromagnetic and radio frequency interference. It's what carries cable TV into the home.

the first advantage to mention is portability. You can take a disc anywhere. You can't take a network anywhere; you have to be tapped into it somehow. Next, discs are a "hard good." People like to be able to hold or touch or see the things they buy. They like to see that these purchases are "real" items, ones they can keep for a long time. Perhaps the most significant advantage of disc, however, is that the technology is available today. We don't have to wait while the technology's development undergoes further iterations.

Turning to network technology, perhaps the key advantage concerns the "universal library" concept. A CD-ROM consists of a single disc carrying a finite amount of information. In contrast, if you're using network technology, you have access to all kinds of information all the time. Naturally, this requires the use of huge disk drives, especially when you want interactive video on call; but nonetheless you essentially can call up anything at any time. Next, a network provides up-to-date information. We can go into that central **server** and update the data on a daily or even hourly basis, so anyone who taps into it will receive the latest information. Another advantage of network technology is that your network access can be personalized. When all data is maintained on a central server that can be updated regularly, we also can store a brief file containing information about each person's tastes and preferences. For instance, we can keep track of the fact that you always play a certain adventure game at the expert level and always follow a certain path in the game. Then we can always present the game to you at the expert level; maybe

server: A computer that provides shared resources, such as files and printers, to the computer network.

even occasionally suggest an alternative path that you might enjoy.

One other great advantage of network technology is that it is linkable: We can communicate with other people as we interact with the technology. I can play a game with a neighbor who lives down the street—or a friend in another city. Likewise, network technology gives me the ability to order products and services. I could use the network to order concert tickets, for instance. You can't do that with a disc.

The technology we choose for multimedia distribution has a direct impact on the way multimedia content is produced and marketed, and on the types of multimedia devices, or "players," that people need to buy for accessing the multimedia.

If you're dealing with disc technology, you simply take your source material to a standard disc mastering house for disc duplication, encourage people to buy the right disc player with the appropriate operating system, video and audio decompression, video and audio output, and CD-ROM drive, and sell the disc through retail outlets and/or the mail.

If you're dealing with network technology, you have to go out into the field and install an entire network base. This brings up a classic chicken-and-egg problem. You can't sell the players until the network's in place; you can't get the network in place until there are players in the home. And you can't do either until there are four or five compelling applications that will drive the market. To top it off, the delivery of multimedia content over a network requires a sophisticated host computer with large disk drives—extremely large, hundreds of gigabytes of storage, or even terabytes.

The players that serve as the front-end to a multimedia network are similar in many ways to the players necessary to play discs. However, the CD-ROM drive is replaced by communication technologies. Communication technologies have an advantage over CD-ROM drives in that they are solid-state, so we need not worry about mechanical problems or high manufacturing costs.

A final point: These two distribution approaches are not mutually exclusive. The distinction between these two technologies is less like VHS vs. Beta than audio cassettes vs. CDs. It is extremely likely that sometime in the following decade, most people will enjoy multimedia through both disc *and* network technology. The only thing we know for sure at this point is that the success of both these technologies rests on the strength of the multimedia content that is and will continue to be developed.

DISTRIBUTION, BABY-BELL STYLE

BY EARL MANCHESTER

Earl Manchester, transport architect at U S WEST Technologies, is an expert in advanced communication technologies. He has worked with Pacific Telephone, Pacific Northwest Bell, and U S WEST. These days Earl is developing the Asymmetric Digital Subscriber Line (ADSL) concept.

This segment describes the concept, development, and capabilites of a technology championed by a "Baby Bell" telephone company for the distribution of multimedia programming.

U S WEST is a regional telephone company, one of the seven RBOCs (Regional Bell Operating Companies, or "Baby Bells") left over from the divestiture of Bell Telephone. We've been working on a concept called Asymmetric Digital Subscriber Line (ADSL), a very high-speed, high-bandwidth "pipe" that will go out to residential homes. Installation is planned to begin in the mid- to late-90s.

ADSL's data transmission scheme, "T-Carrier," features the same bandwidth as compact discs, which works out well for us. ADSL would support the transmission of video, stereo audio, text, and graphics.

Today the phone companies have an extremely large embedded base of copper wiring: A pair of copper wires (actually, 1.2 pair, on the average) goes into every home in the U S WEST region. We'll run T-Carrier over this wire pair, the same wiring that supports telephone conversations and provides the dial tone. The ADSL service would work in conjunction with the proposed ISDN (Integrated Services Digital Network) and with regular telephone service. Although they ride on the same copper pair of wire, these services are independent. None interferes with the other two.

On the customer premises, we would install a box that takes the ADSL signal off the copper wire, recovers the T-Carrier signal, and decodes it, using a special

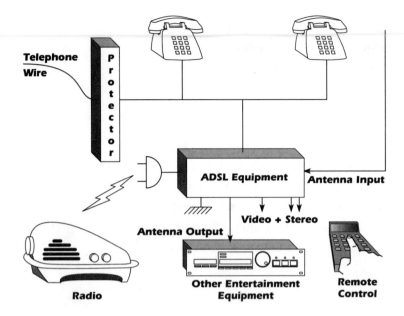

The ADSL System set-up in the home

algorithm to decompress the video signal. You would take your existing RF input, whether it's coming through an antenna or cable TV cable, and run it through the box. The box would insert the channel of information coming from our network, causing it to flow "downstream" into the rest of your viewing equipment. A remote control device would control this box and facilitate menu selection. Your telephones would be unaffected and remain plugged into the wall where they always were.

Our central office would handle the switching via a "multicast" switching system. Let's say you're watching a football game, and so are a large group of other people in other houses. The broadcasting company with the contract to cover the football game would send the video feed to us. We would feed just one digital stream containing the game broadcast to our central office, but would want to be able to copy that stream to as many ports (people's homes) as needed at any time. That's why we call it "multicast-

ing"; it involves repeating the same signal to multiple ports at once. The multicast switch also helps us track who's getting what program, so we know who to charge for what amount of time. It also provides testing and analysis functions by providing performance data and automatic message accounting.

Let's look at some services we might provide via ADSL. Live broadcast is an interesting concept. You might have heard about the tests taking place with "ACTV," interactive television, where the viewer can control the viewing angle. If you're watching that football game, for instance, you can choose to watch it from behind the end zone or from a bird's eye view. You make that choice and watch the action in real time. ADSL would be able to provide the same capabilities.

Current cable TV services provide "pay-per-view video," a system in which you pay for a certain movie to be run to your home. The movie runs continously, however; you can't stop and start it at any point. If someone knocks on your front door while you're watching the movie, you can't pause the film while you go greet your visitor, because the movie's running into thousands of other homes at the same time. Since ADSL equips each home with its own "data pipeline," you could simply push a button on your remote control to pause the movie, cancel it, or spool it out into a data storage space in your home so you could watch it later.

Home education represents another potential application area. A great deal of retraining is occuring in corporate America these days, because technology is changing so rapidly. It would be possible to use ADSL to transmit a class specific to your field into your home, so you can learn about a subject in your living room. If your children attend public school in the daytime but need additional help with a subject in the evening, they can call up the subject via the ADSL service and receive tutoring from a remote location.

We also imagine the possibilities for electronic game-playing through ADSL. A person can play a video game in their home with another player who lives across the city, across the state, or even in a different country.

Targeted advertising has strong potential for revenues, and we're interested in that because this entire process will be expensive. If you know exactly who's watching a program sponsored by your company, you could target your commercials to reach only those viewers. The phone company could assist vendors in directing the commercials to the right people at the right time.

Home shopping is another application that could use live video. You could flip the "pages" of a "catalog" on your TV screen and watch someone model the clothing or item that interests you. You could interact with the video, and even order the item in the process.

We think that the supply of video content is best handled by other companies. There might be a video vendor in New York, for instance, that would feed its video via MCI or Sprint to Denver, where

U S WEST is headquartered, and we then would feed the video to the multicast switch for distribution into people's homes. The video vendor could send its live, compressed video feeds to satellite or something we call a "disk pack." If a vendor feeds a video signal to us, and we send it out to a customer, the vendor would want to know if the video feed actually arrived at its destination. Using the multicast switch, they could request that the video signal be looped back to them on a different channel. Even if the vendor is located across the country, the loop would enable them to know that the video actually reached a particular customer. We also expect to go into a partnership with cable television companies to help them serve regions that they don't normally cover.

If we do achieve high levels of data compression with the new technologies, cable TV companies theoretically could send 500 channels instead of 50 or 100 channels down the cable. Direct broadcast satellite is starting to come out from its headquarters in Bellevue, Washington. In fact, direct satellite broadcast is another potential method of distributing video and multimedia information to the home.

One reason we're developing ADSL is because it's extremely important for us to find ways to support the people working in the new arena of interactive multimedia. One of those ways is to provide broad distribution channels for their products.

THE MULTIMEDIA PC, TODAY & TOMORROW

BY PATRICK FORD

Patrick Ford is product manager for the multimedia computing group at Microsoft Corporation. Involved in interactive video production since 1983, he has produced multimedia for Sony, Ford, and other large organizations, and he cofounded the International Interactive Communications Society.

MIDI: Musical Instrument Digital Interface, a standard protocol that allows digital music instruments (such as synthesizers) to communicate with each other and with computers.

I n 1983 I was a doctoral student at Stanford University at the Institute for Communications Research; I studied human communication and sociological effects of communication technology, and took a minor in computer science. That's when I became interested in the merging of communication technologies, such as video, and computer technologies, such as computer graphics.

At that time the interactive video industry, while interesting in terms of technological development, exhibited many problems. One problem involved the quality of the content; another problem concerned the need for a standard hardware platform for using this new mix of data. I decided to form a company to develop interactive video programs. We wrote a business plan, stating that we wanted to produce **CD-ROM**-based information titles, and we included some financial projections that said CD-ROM **peripherals** would be standard equipment on all PCs by the year 1987. Well, that's only just beginning to happen now.

Today, one of Microsoft's goals is to encourage hardware manufacturers and software developers to support the standard platform, the Multimedia Personal Computer (MPC). We launched the MPC

CD-ROM: Compact Disc–Read-Only Memory, a laser-encoded format for storing information digitally on a compact disc. A device that can read a CD-ROM disc is called a CD-ROM drive. A CD-ROM drive that meets the MPC standard can deliver data at a rate of 153 kilobytes per second.

peripheral: A piece of hardware connected by cable to a computer, such as a disk drive or printer, that gives the computer various external capabilities.

in October 1991. One goal in defining the MPC platform was to use existing technology such as CD-ROM drives and video-based, 256-color graphics, with fully integrated, digital audio and **MIDI** files, all in a package that a person can buy for about $2,000 retail. We see great opportunities in the business market for this type of technology, and as the business market adopts it, it helps bring the price down. Then the technology can migrate to the home market.

The MPC consists of a PC, model 386SX or above, and two additional components. One is an audio subsystem that supports at least 8-bit, 22kHz **waveform audio**, sound synthesis, MIDI input and output, CD-quality audio, and accepts three audio sources plus an auxiliary source, such as an external video tape or a videodisc. An internal mixer blends all these sources and sends them to a stereo output.

The other component is a CD-ROM drive that must maintain a 150-kilobyte data transfer rate while using no more than 40 percent of its bandwidth. We specified this high-performance requirement because it supports software-based digital video, in small, on-screen windows, without requiring additional **compression** hardware. Therefore, it provides a low-cost method for distributing video on CD-ROM. We're working with many CD-ROM manufacturers to help them improve the performance of their systems.

Over 20 different computer manufacturers are developing multimedia PCs and MPC upgrade kits, which consist of a CD-ROM drive and audio circuit card. By mid-

1992, Microsoft had shipped over 2,500 MPC developer's kits to software vendors. Several dozen multimedia titles were put into distribution by the end of 1991, including *The Guinness Disc of World Records, Compton's Multimedia Encyclopedia,* many games, and educational titles, such as discs that teach foreign languages.

All the MPC machines and MPC software titles sport the MPC trademark for the same reason that video tape products share the VHS trademark: When you buy any VHS tape and any VHS deck, you know they'll work together—"plug-and-play compatibility." That's critical when you're considering the distribution of this type of technology to markets that aren't necessarily technically sophisticated.

Microsoft is working with CD-ROM technology because it's something we can use today to deliver vast amounts of information to a very broad audience. We're also looking beyond that to CD-ROM "write-once" technology (so people can create their own programs and throw them onto a disc), magneto-optical storage, and **local area networks** for delivering video information. In the not-too-distant future, most computers will be able to receive video information via a network; later, they'll support two-way video communication in real time.

IBM's research showed that 99 percent of current multimedia users are what they call "browsers," or consumers of the technology, as opposed to the producers. By the mid- to late-90s that will change to 50 percent, and eventually, all of us will produce as well as consume multimedia.

Video cameras, attached to our computer terminals, will be standard equipment. Combining multimedia technology and live video will be a common occurrence. One constraint preventing that from happening today is the vast amount of storage space required for multimedia data. It will be some time before we all have disk drives that hold gigabytes of data—but not too far in the future, local network servers will provide that amount of data capacity. The industry now must develop the high-capacity networks and high-capacity data storage devices, along with user interfaces that let people deal easily with all the data.

Microsoft hopes that the Multimedia PC will provide a successful first step toward reaching this point. We're also studying television-based CD players, and systems such as Philips' CD-I (compact disc-interactive) and Commodore's CDTV, with an eye toward developing systems that will blend in with other home devices: "smart" televisions, "smart" telephones, and hand-held digital information devices.

Throughout the decade, we'll see a blurring between the computer and the television. Today we mostly use our televisions as a sort of "video terminal"; it's a video workstation that we use to plug in our VCR, cable TV box, and camcorders. Soon we'll be plugging in our CD-based information devices, and eventually all of these systems will merge into one basic digital information device. Once that happens, the sky's the limit on the amount and type of information that people will be able to access in their homes.

waveform audio: A technique for recording voice and sound effects using digital audio samples.

Local Area Network: A system of software and hardware connected by a common data transmission medium and limited to a geographical area less than about 10 kilometers. It's the most common means of connecting several personal computers into a larger system that allows users to share information and resources.

compression: A process that squeezes data into smaller files that take up less space.

EXPLORING CREATIVITY

QUESTIONS BY S. JOY MOUNTFORD
ANSWERS BY FRANK THOMAS & DAVID EM

Joy contacted two important artists—whose artistic tools lie at opposite ends of the technology spectrum—and asked:

How do great things get created, and how do people work together on the process of design? How do people initiate the process of creative discovery to generate ideas in animation, graphics, and visual arts? Do people under creative pressure experience "blocks" similar to those experienced by writers? Do they have special ways to free their imaginations to be more productive and more creative more often? What tools do artists use to communicate ideas to their co-workers?

No technology tools exist today to support brainstorming or idea-sketching—unless you count text-outliner software programs. Devising a means to support creative, expressive skills seems to allude the existing technology medium. One problem lies in how to closely match the thought process of discovery to the available limited "tools" of expression.

In the following essays that address some of these questions, the artists point out that people go through a process of designing, in which iteration is a key element. This process occurs whether the artist uses traditional tools or computer systems.

I've often heard people say that computer companies don't truly care about working with "real" artists. To the contrary, much of our work at Apple Computer is motivated by our work with visual communicators such as David Em and Frank Thomas. Our aim is not to change the types of tools that various artists use to create in their medium, but rather to enhance the development and design of new software tools for them to use. We're trying to design the interface to meet the needs of a range of users. We're most interested in providing a rich environment in which people can visualize ideas before actually producing them. We're trying to bridge the gap between traditional visual art skills and the range of new uses that a computer can enable.

BY S. JOY MOUNTFORD

*S. Joy Mountford manages the Human **Interface** Group in Apple Computer's Advanced Technology Group. She also serves on the conference committee of the Association for Computing Machinery's Special Interest Group in Computer-Human Interaction, which convenes annually to address the issues of computer hardware and software interface design and implementation.*

interface: [noun] The interconnection or method of communication between two objects; an interface may be hardware or software. Examples: a software program's screen design (interface between the human and the functions enabled by the program); a doorknob (interface between the human and the door). [verb] To interconnect or communicate.

Don Norman, a professor at the University of California at San Diego, discussed these issues in his book, *The Psychology of Everyday Things* (Addison Wesley). He lectures around the world on the design of real-world interfaces, such as VCRs, doorknobs, and signage. He has great impact on interface design. He points out that our use of everyday things is fraught with problems. We rent cars, but can't figure out how to work the dashboard controls. We stay in hotel rooms, but can't find the light switches and can't turn on the shower without scalding or freezing ourselves. By the way, the softcover version of Professor Norman's book is renamed *The Design of Everyday Things*, because people bought the initial hardback volume thinking that the book was about psychotherapy. This indicates the need for user testing!

ON "EUPHORIA AT FOUR" & OTHER TRICKS OF THE TRADE

BY FRANK THOMAS

Frank Thomas worked at the Walt Disney Studio from 1934 to 1978 as a supervising animator on films ranging from Snow White *to* Jungle Book *to* The Rescuers. *His best-remembered scenes include the Dwarfs crying around Snow White's bier, Bambi and Thumper on ice, and Lady and The Tramp eating spaghetti. This award-winning animator has co-written several books about his work at Disney and is currently writing a fourth book about famous villains in Disney films. Since retiring, he has lectured on animation throughout the world.*

As I watch what artists are doing with all the new, wonderful technologies, I feel like an old dinosaur. I try to keep up with it all, but I fail miserably. (I've failed many times in the past, so I'm used to it.) I have more trouble with the computer than I ever did with a pencil. I sit there punching little keys on the computer keyboard, and nothing that's anything good comes up on the screen. I think, "I could walk over to my desk and animate this in ten minutes. I've been working on this stupid animation on the computer for two weeks already and I don't have anything done." People tell me, "Don't worry. The Wright brothers had the same trouble. You're about at the same stage that they were when they started building planes."

In the movie industry today, there is a great shift from the use of traditional tools to the use of computer-generated graphics. The work being done with computers boggles my mind. To discuss what we did 50 years ago doesn't seem pertinent to today's problems, yet the problems of creativity and the issues of approaching and recognizing creativity are pertinent. Some of the things we did a half-century ago probably are valid today.

Let's go back 50 years to the days when we were with the Disney studio, alive with creative opportunities. There were many different jobs at the studio. Not everybody did animation or designed characters. There was story work, there were gags to work out, there was business to handle. There was drawing to do, from designing characters to creating the movement of those characters to getting life into the drawings of those characters. That was crucial—how do you put life in a drawing of an animated character? There was acting, too—the acting of the characters—which was very important, and there was filmmaking. No one person was good at all those things. I know, because I tried.

Freddy Moore was the best animator at Disney when I went to the studio. I was fortunate to study under him. Freddy's forte was drawing. Freddy had no interest in the story. That was somebody else's job. Gags? He could put over a gag that someone else thought of, but he couldn't think of it himself. He didn't seem to understand filmmaking at all. But this allowed him to focus. One of the big factors in supporting creativity is to focus all your energies on the one thing you're trying to do. Freddy was trying to establish personalities and show how those characters felt, in drawings that you would like to look at, drawings that were clear and that made a strong statement. He had a confidence that showed up in his pencil line.

There's a part in *Snow White* where Sneezy's beard is being tied around his nose. That's a challenge to an artist—to draw a character with a beard tied around his nose. Freddy had a way of solving problems like this. All of us in the department would do our work first in rough form, where we didn't have to tie ourselves down to the exact details or precision of the character—we could could get the overall feeling of it first, then clean it up afterwards. None of Fred's drawings of Doc and Sneezy and Happy and Grumpy had a rigid, geometric form—unlike the

way people create characters in computer graphics. With the computer, you draw half of a character, then you draw a mirror image to duplicate it, thereby making the other half, creating a solid object. That forces you into the difficult position of trying to stretch or manipulate a shape that's constructed as a completely symmetrical one. In our drawings, however, we tried to break away from symmetry—we tried to make something look the way you felt it ought to be, rather than concentrate on great precision.

Another element of creativity is *superstition*. Whenever Fred felt that he wasn't drawing things right, he'd switch to a different colored pencil. Word went around the studio like wildfire: "Freddy's drawing with *blue* pencil! Hey, Freddy's drawing with a blue pencil!" Then everybody would switch to blue pencils. Sometimes that made things go better and sometimes it didn't do anything for you. Then the word would come through, "He's using orange now!" So we all would switch to orange pencils. Freddy worked with one pencil for maybe two weeks, or maybe two months. A fellow in the story department, the son of a famous baseball player, said, "You animators are just like those baseball players. Someone tells them they're in a slump, and they think, 'Hmm, I'll hold the bat higher. Hold it like this. Move it back. Turn my toe in toward the plate before I swing.'" You might notice this on TV: The batter takes a strange stance, but as soon as the ball's thrown, he immediately drops back into the standard position to take a swipe at the ball. Well, we animators *were* the same way—we'd use anything to help us. We'd say, "This paper's too rough. No, this paper's too smooth. No, that's not it—it's the chair, the chair's too low. No, it's too high." We'd keep changing things, changing things. So, if you made a good drawing with a blue pencil, that's it, you stuck with the blue pencil: "From now on, that's what I'm going to do, for the rest of my life"—or until Fred changed it.

What do you do when you start running dry, when you're sitting there looking at a blank piece of paper? How are you going to do anything that's worth doing? You'll find that you can get a lot of stimulation from news photos. Pictures—provocative pictures in particular—offer an awful lot to help keep you going. Doing something out of the ordinary also helps some people. Before I went to the studio I studied with Pruitt Carter, a very good magazine illustrator. This was back in the days when magazine illustration was akin to fine art. Pruitt Carter would look at my drawings and say, "You're in a rut. You're doing the same thing over and over and making the same mistakes. Why don't you go to Santa Monica and take a ride on the roller coaster?" This was back when they had a roller coaster in Santa Monica, and it was a good idea, but I didn't do that because I don't like roller coasters. They scare me. But I'm an emotional guy. I'm probably more susceptible than other people.

Pruitt studied with Walter Biggs, who was even more of a fine artist. Walter's studio was on the second floor, overlooking a courtyard. When he would find that he couldn't paint any more, he'd throw all his paints and brushes out the window, pick up a broom, beat himself over the head until he was bloody, and then he'd stagger downstairs and go to a bar two doors down the street. He'd stay there for three days. Now *that's* getting a new outlook on your problems! His building had a custodian who was used to Walter's ways, and he'd go into the courtyard, pick up all the paints and brushes, and bring them back up, so when Walter came back, going "Mm . . . well!" he could pick up his paintbrush and everything was ready to go again. I thought that was kind of a violent way to handle the problem.

One other interesting scientific fact concerns the euphoria that we all felt at the studio at 4:00 p.m. We always called it "Euphoria at Four," because you'd work all day, trying hard to come up with something creative, and you couldn't get it, and suddenly, right around 4:00, it would all begin to come together, and you'd feel elated. You'd say, "*Now* I've got it, finally!" And then they'd say, "Time to stop." And you'd say, "No! I can't stop, I can't stop!" "You'll miss your ride home. It's 5:00, come on, get out of here." So off you'd go. The next morning, you'd come in, all anxious to pick up where you'd left off, and you'd see the worst-looking drawing you'd done all day! Then you'd think, "I left it on the desk all night! What will the janitors think of me?"

If you keep working too long on a project, not only do you become blind to it, you lose perspective on it. Yet something inside you says, "It's OK. You're doing fine, fella, you're doing fine. Keep going." That's *wrong*. You have to do something to break that rut. For instance, I get some of my best ideas when shaving. I use an electric razor, so I think that has something to do with brain waves and electric current.

Another source of stimulation depends a bit on why you're being creative in the first place. Some people are driven by curiosity. That's how I am with the computer. "What can I do with this thing? It's wonderful! It's just magic!" I can't get it out of my system, even though nothing good ever happens. Others are driven by a "go-get-it" attitude. They want to be the first. They want to be the best. They don't want to be on the winning team, they want to be the *winner*. Of course, when the juices stop flowing, you have to go at it in a different way. Others work from fear—they fear that they're not the best, or they fear that someone's going to find out they're not the best. If they're commercially oriented, they might have fears about their job, and worry, "Gee, I was hired—I'm supposed to be good. Come on, kiddo, let's be good! Come on, let's do something about this." There may even be some guilt in there—remember those people who sacrificed so much to save the money to send you to art school? You're letting them down because you're not doing anything good, and your poor old grandmother ruined her eyes sewing by candlelight night after night.

What else keeps you going? We all need support, certainly. If you drew a horse and your third grade teacher said, "That doesn't look like a horse," that killed your artistic drive for the rest of your life. To keep that drive, you need some successes and you need support. When we were working for Freddy at the studio, there were three of us in the room. He'd say, "Fellows, I've got to do a scene this afternoon. Tell me how good I am."

So we'd say, "Boy, Fred, you're the best artist, the *best* there is. God, you're good!" And he'd say, "Well, it isn't *that* big of a scene, you know, it's just a little one." But he'd stand there and nod, "Yeah, yeah. That's good. I'm ready to go!" Then he'd work very quickly, sitting on his stool. His legs weren't long enough to reach clear to the floor, so he'd rest them on the edge of the runners on the chair, and he'd sit there, humming, "La de da de da," and he'd pull out a piece of paper, "La de da," and in about two hours he'd do as much work as other people would do in two weeks. Confidence!

Confidence is awfully important in anything you do. But you can't just say, "Now I'm going to be creative," and do it. You have to focus your energy on the project at hand, bring together everything you know that's related to the project, and hope that something's going to pop into your head at about the time you say, "Well, I'm not getting anywhere here so I'll—Oops, wait, I have an idea!" Sometimes that doesn't work. It didn't help me.

Watching films is great to get inspired. When we were starting on *The Rescuers*, we wanted to have some way for the little mice in the film to travel from New York City to the bayou country down south. We thought they ought to ride on some kind of bird. Someone suggested we put them on a 200-pound robin that has to be catapulted off the ground because he weighs too much. Once he's up there, he can glide, but he has trouble landing. We tried a few gags with that approach and they were pretty good, but they didn't do enough for us.

Well, we happened to see a film of the true-life adventures of the albatross on some Pacific island. The albatross is the size of a goose. It's a big, heavy bird, with both eyes facing forward, not on the sides of its head like a chicken. We could see in the film that the albatross has great difficulties taking off and landing, which are considered the main parts of flying an airplane. When an albatross takes off and flies, it stays up in the air for days at a time. If you saw one land, you'd know why! The film showed the albatross landing, bumping into another albatross, and they both just sort of spit the sand out of their mouths and went about their business as if they were saying, "Pretty good landing, huh?" Watching those nature films gave us the character we were looking for. We said, "Why don't the mice fly down on the back of an albatross, and we'll draw him like a World War I flyer wearing a scarf and goggles, and he'll think that he's the best flyer there is!" If you see the film *The Rescuers*, you can see the results.

Let's think about the restrictions and challenges behind creativity. Too many restrictions will shut off your creativity; if you can't do the things you want to do on the computer, for instance, because it doesn't have enough memory to run the program you want, or something breaks down, or your software limits what you want to do. It's the same problem if you're trying to animate a scene and you have problems with story or layout or footage or music or sound effects, and you can't get them all to work together. With so many restrictions, you'd think you would not be able to do *anything*. And that's often true.

On the other hand, challenges often force you into producing something far more creative than you would have ever done by yourself. You find that you're doing things that are rather dull—you've

been doing them often, the same way, all the time. You don't want to do that; you need something to jar you out of the rut. Once I was told to animate a snake for *Jungle Book*. I felt restricted by the fact that a snake has no shoulders, no arms. How can a character scratch his head and shrug? We did an awful lot of studying to figure out how to make that snake. We gave one snake a prehensile tail; he would lift it to take his glasses off, or to hold a pen and write. With another snake, who didn't need a pen or wear glasses, probably the biggest challenge was figuring out what to do when he was tickled. How do you do that with a snake? Challenges force you into doing something far more creative.

I was talking about this problem with a musician who writes music for TV shows. He said there were two main ways to focus your energy on what you want to create. You can wait until the last possible minute you can get it written, then you *have* to do it, and it doesn't matter whether it's good or not; the point is, you've done it! Or you can assess all the restrictions in the project—how long it has to be, how many instruments you'll use, what it's supposed to say, what you can't do, what you can do. This gradually forces you into one little area in which you can write. This musician also pointed out something you could do if you use a computer to create. The software often lets you do many different things that aren't necessarily what you need, but you can at least put something up on the screen. The theory is that it's easier to correct something than it is to come up with something brand new. So this musician would punch keys wildly, get something up on the screen, and say, "Well, *that's* no good." Then he'd change this and he'd change that, and finally, he had his work all done, and he felt that he hadn't been creative at all but simply used his experience and wisdom to salvage something from the junk the computer put up on the screen for him.

At film studios today they use all kinds of electronic devices. They do lots of computer and video work, and they put together a scene in one afternoon that it would have taken us three weeks to do. If you were going to animate 20 scenes in a sequence, you'd start on the project by thinking about it and thinking about it and thinking about it until those characters were alive to you and you'd put them to bed with you every night and brush their teeth while you brushed yours. You really *knew* these characters. If you didn't know everything about them, you were in trouble when you tried to animate. They had to be someone that you enjoyed being with. You'd spend all this time thinking about your idea until it matured.

This reminds me of the great comedy routines of the vaudeville days, when routines were worked out by the performers over a period of weeks and months. They did three shows a day, and if you did three shows a day, you'd get tired of something that didn't get laughs, so you'd keep trying to build the act. The performers perfected acts that were surefire with an audience. When you saw one in a theater, you knew you were seeing top quality, top grade. You don't see that anymore, because everything today happens too quickly. People don't have the chance to really think about what they're creating, because they're just being creative, thinking, "This is good, this is good, turn this knob, I'm going to do this, press this button. *There*, it's done." You haven't lived with your idea; it hasn't had the chance to mature in your mind. I'm afraid that we're going to have a flood of movies, films, TV, and commercials, all based on output generated by computers that is shallow and empty. That would be a big shame, and I think it's the biggest loss confronting us today. How's that for a somber note to end on?

FOLLOWING PATHS

BY DAVID EM

David Em landed in San Francisco in the early 1970s after leaving the Pennsylvania Academy of the Fine Arts, where he had fashioned sculptures from polyvinyl chloride (PVC) and polyethylene. In 1975 David was invited to Xerox Corp.'s prestigious Palo Alto Research Center to work with their Superpaint computer system, the predecessor of many current computer paint programs. Later that year he moved to Southern California to work on the supercomputers at Jet Propulsion Laboratory (JPL, home of computer imagery pioneer Jim Blinn). Contributing to the advancement of space exploration, JPL supports NASA with computer enhancement of photographs from outer space. In 1985 David set up his own art studio. From 1978 to 1984, David worked on a Digital Equipment Corp. (DEC) PDP 11/55 minicomputer with an Evans & Sutherland 8-bit frame buffer, Picture System 2 display system, and Conrac RGB monitors. After 1984, he worked on an upgraded system based on a DEC VAX 780 and a Gould/DiAnza 24-bit frame buffer. He primarily used computer paint programs written by Jim Blinn. Today he works on Apple Computer's Quadra workstation, using a range of computer imaging, paint, and 3-D modeling programs.

n thinking about the creative process, I realized that I never exactly had a creative "block," but had often experienced times when it just wasn't happening. I started to examine why and I realized that a couple of things occur in the creative process. One of them is a path: When you're creating, you're on a path, you're going somewhere. It's a mysterious path. You don't know where each step will lead. Paths often lead to other paths, and sometimes paths come to an end. The other aspect of creativity is the cycle. Art, after all, is life. In fact I don't really believe in art. "Art" is a corrupt notion. Creativity, however, is an exciting aspect of the human experience, and the minute it's defined as "art," all kinds of problems start to develop, such as attitudes like, "You are an artist and I'm not," or, "You are a dancer and I'm not," or, "You are a poet and I'm not." People feel separated from the experience of art, but we all have creativity. We may not all be geniuses, but everyone should draw, paint, and dance— everyone should do all these "art" things. Much of this involves being in tune with what's inside of you, and also connecting it with an outside experience.

I had a traditional training in art. When I became interested in technology, I was told that technology was not art. That's why I left art school. Around that time I was building sculptures with plastic and became interested in how light fell on the sculptures. I wanted to put that onto film. Someone asked, "Why don't you do it in video?" and handed me a video camera. I recognized something powerful in it, even though I had never seen it before. Right around then, in the early 1970s, I was

living in San Francisco, where many people were doing new things with electronics and images. One day I visited a friend's studio. He was throwing out an ancient color television, the kind with the round tube. The TV couldn't receive signal transmissions, but when you turned it on there was motion on the screen, a kind of fascinating animation. The colors were distorted on the screen in an interesting way that created strange, beautiful images. I took it home to my studio. I became fascinated by electronic light. I looked at that light on the screen and started building mirrors around it. Eventually I built an entire room around it. After a while, it occurred to me that there had to be a better way to control what was going on in the room, and that's when I starting looking for a computer, without consciously realizing that the computer would deliver that control for me.

When I first started working with computers, it was the light coming from them that provided a source of inspiration. Many of my early images grew out of that light. Today, we look at the concept of computer art backwards; we say, "Isn't a lot of early computer artwork very geometric?" It was, but only because that's what the machine did. It also was exciting back then to say, "Look at what this medium does that nothing else can do!"

When I started using the computer to make images, many people connected those images with science fiction, even though the images had nothing to do with science fiction. I was creating them in a NASA facility, JPL, and my inspiration came from the computer and from deep-space imagery. At that time the Voyager

8-bit: Refers to a computer monitor's ability to display colors. An 8-bit monitor can show 256 colors at once.

frame buffer: A buffer is a temporary storage device; it accumulates data from one device functioning at a particular speed for release to another device functioning at another speed. In computer graphics, a frame buffer is used to store all data required to make up a complete frame of images. From the buffer, data is fed to the image-generation part of the system for display on the screen; data cannot be fed directly from computer to screen.

3-D modeling: Geometrically defining the shape of a 3-D object; the first step in creating 3-D animation, involving creation of complex objects using basic shapes (blocks, circles, cones, etc.).

spacecraft was constantly transmitting pictures of Jupiter and Saturn to JPL, where they were decoded and displayed. While the scientists around me used computers to take snapshots of outer space, I used them to design and document worlds of my own. So the inspiration was very much science fact, and not at all "futuristic." It was exciting when the images came in, watching them come back from a robot in space. Being a part of that, the feeling of living on those planets, served as a major source of ideas.

The computer opened doors for me. I made space-inspired images for a few years, but at one point I reached the end of that path. I found that I was repeating myself, the colors were starting to drain away, and I was getting bored with what I was doing. I asked myself, "If I'm bored, what's the rest of the world going to make of these things?" Yet I would work around the clock.

As part of the creative process, at least in my case, before an intense period of creative work I don't do anything for two weeks. I'll get a couple of big, fat books and do nothing but read and sleep. Then I start working—non-stop activity. It goes on around the clock. Five hours of sleep per night.

I was working like this but not getting the "juice" anymore. I remember one evening while I was working at JPL. Actually, it was about six in the morning by then, and the sun was rising. Nobody was around. I walked outside where some flower beds had been planted. It was springtime and flowers had just come up, and I remember looking at them, fascinated by the amount of color and light and life pouring out of them, and how lacking these traits were in what I was doing.

At the time I had been creating pictures with 8 bits of color, and I constantly thought about how I could make the colors look good with 8 bits—8 hues and 32 intensities. That alone caused stress that I didn't realize I had. Soon afterwards, I visited the Prado museum in Madrid, Spain, where I saw a painting by Velázquez which had been painted four centuries ago. It blew my mind.

Velázquez is one of the great heros of art and I had never understood why. I always thought his paintings were interesting, but you have to actually stand in front of them before you can realize that they cannot be reproduced. No matter how good the reproduction, it just doesn't get the feeling in the painting. The painting I saw was about ten feet tall and 14 feet wide. I spent a long time looking at it, thinking, "With computer images, there's something that's not being delivered, something I want. There's also something *I'm* not delivering." Velázquez was a master of light. He spent his life looking at light and it was stunning to see the resulting relationships in his paintings. I thought, "How coarse these things are that I'm doing, dealing with the light of outer space, which is sort of the sun, a single-point light source that creates real easy shadows—*boom*, there it is."

I realized I'd reached the end of something and I decided to get out of computers. I went to New Mexico and spent a while not doing much—just looking at clouds and light and morning and evening; looking at the stuff I had completely lost track of while in the lab.

A couple of years later I taught a seminar for computer programmers at the California Institute of Technology. I spent a day talking about light to them. It turned out that nobody in the group understood that light in the morning is different from light in the afternoon, which is different from light in the evening. That blew my mind. These were the people who were going to write lighting algorithms for computer programs! So we all trooped outside and started looking at light. Everybody had known about the differences in light from a *theoretical* basis, and in a sense I had worked the same way, using the computer to show light. That realization led me to start painting again and looking at natural light. At a certain point, I felt, "I'm ready to go back to computers," and I did.

That's when I started making a new series of images, using the computer medium. I felt an incredible renewal that came from *not* doing it for a while before that. I had reached the end of a path. I had reached the end of part of a cycle, but the cycle itself never ends. It's part of a greater thing, and when you reach the end of certain paths, you must accept that.

Meanwhile, as I dealt with my internal problem, avoiding the computer, an entire technical community was dealing with external problems. By the time I got back into the computer, the technology was 24-bit color, which meant I could create full-color images. My inability to do so a couple of years earlier had bothered me. Now the computer system could handle whole new levels of subtlety; my perception had grown, and so had the computer's capability to express.

Funnily enough, after two or three years, I returned to monochromatic spaces, and got about as far as I felt I could. Then I thought, "Well, I'll take some more time off."

I was 14 years old when I started seriously studying art. I read everything about art that I could find. I knew about every artist and every art movement; at least, I *thought* I knew about all kinds of art. Most of us are taught about art from an ethnocentric viewpoint, however, and there were things I never learned in my studies. After I decided to take another break in my work, I wandered around southeastern Utah and found things that my art training never touched. Part of this discovery included rock art and pictoglyphs: things that are carved, or pecked, into rocks. It represented a new, mysterious world— mysterious because we don't know who made most of these pictoglyphs and we don't know what they represent. Their context was fascinating: They were always situated near water and you could **echo-locate** them, because they almost always were located in an area where you could make echoes. You could shout and listen and follow your echoes to find those visions. I looked at a lot of them. They started to seep into my consciousness, and in 1991, when I did an artist-in-residency at Apple Computer, all this stuff— without my expecting it—came pouring out into my art. Thus a new series of artworks that I never could have predicted came out of an experience.

As I considered the topic of "exploring creativity," I realized that the sources of creativity are somewhat mysterious. What got me on the path of making my most recent pictures involved a set of steps in-

echo-location: The determination of the position of an object by the emission of sound waves which are reflected back to the sender as echoes. It's how bats get around.

timately connected with the time almost two decades earlier when I looked at the light coming from a distorted, electronic screen. My fascination with electronic light ultimately led me to wandering around canyons and mesas, looking for ancient pictures scrawled on walls. This has led me to create a new series of artworks which, in turn, will lead somewhere else—somewhere I can't even dimly imagine today.

SECTION ⬤2

MUSIC AND SOUND

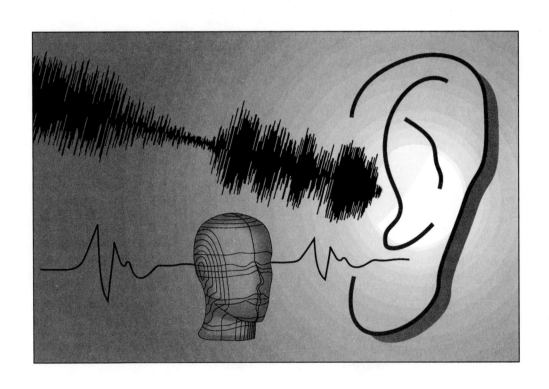

HYPERINSTRUMENTS

A COMPOSER'S APPROACH TO THE EVOLUTION OF INTELLIGENT MUSICAL INSTRUMENTS

BY TOD MACHOVER

Composer Tod Machover is active in many forms of new music. After studying at the Juilliard School in Manhattan, he worked in Paris from 1978 to 1985 at IRCAM (Institut pour Recherche et Coordination Acoustique/Musique). Since 1985 he's worked at MIT's Media Lab, where he is associate professor of Music & Media, directs the Experimental Media Facility, and oversees development of Hyperinstruments. Tod's music has been performed worldwide. The American Institute of Arts & Letters, the Kennedy Center, and other organizations have honored him. Tod's sci-fi opera VALIS *was commissioned for the tenth anniversary of Paris' Pomipidou Center and produced again in Japan in 1990; the New York Times called the* VALIS *compact disc (Bridge Records) a "best recording of the year." Tod's release* Flora *(1990, Bridge) contains four Hyperinstrument pieces. The title track is a collaboration with legendary computer graphic artist, Yoichiro Kawaguchi. Tod's more recent work includes a series of pieces for "hyperstring" instruments for cellist Yo-Yo Ma, the St. Paul Chamber Orchestra, and the Los Angeles Philharmonic. He also is working on new opera projects, including one with director Peter Sellars.*

"Hyperinstruments" come from the fertile minds and venerable realm of the Media Lab at the Massachusetts Institute of Technology. Developed under the direction of Tod Machover, with technical coordination by Joseph Chung, Hyperinstruments are designed to augment and expand performance virtuosity in real time, using "intelligent," interactive, musical instruments and computers. The current generation of Hyperinstruments uses MIDI controllers and synths, samplers, custom signal processors, special input controllers and instrument sensors, and Apple Macintosh computers. This chapter provides an introduction to the background, philosophy, and use of Hyperinstruments.

I grew up studying classical music and playing the cello. My mother is a pianist who also taught musical creativity, and my father has been involved with computer graphics since the dawning of that field. Ever since I was a kid, the idea of combining music and technology was close to my heart. I also grew up performing and listening to rock music, and the general idea of bringing together (or at least confronting) seemingly divergent worlds has always been an obsession of mine.

After a year at the University of California at Santa Cruz and another year studying and performing in Florence, Italy, I attended the Juilliard School to major in composition. At that time, in the mid-1970s, it was difficult to work with electronics at Juilliard, although I managed to learn something about computer music through private tutoring. I initially was drawn to computers because of my interest in writing extremely complex music that juxtaposed many layers of contrasting music. It was pretty hard to play, and I wanted to learn to program it, to hear myself, and to show other musicians what it sounded like. My experience as a performer soon convinced me of the importance of developing computers as a live performance medium. Since then I've been developing performance

real time: The speed of the computer coinciding with the speed of the user; no delay in computer response time, giving the impression of instantaneous response.

MIDI: Musical Instrument Digital Interface, a "language" created in collaboration by competing synthesizer companies who first offered the MIDI specification to the musical instrument industry in 1982. MIDI represents an agreement on a software format for representing musical events and a hardware design for communicating those events. MIDI's initial goal was to enable musicians to hook up keyboards, guitar synthesizers, and drum machines made by competing companies. Essentially, MIDI is a simple computer language optimized for musical applications which allows electronic instruments to transmit and receive musical information (such as pitch and time value of notes, dynamics, modulations, etc.) and operating information (such as program changes in a synth's memory). MIDI cables don't carry audio signals (electrical sound waves); they transmit commands in the form of computer data. These data streams travel single-file through the cabling between instruments, MIDI-equipped computers, and MIDI devices such as special effects units. MIDI does not change an instrument's sound; it lets you use a keyboard "controller" to play many "slave" instruments, layering their sounds.

systems that involve **real-time** computers combined with instruments—sometimes existing instruments, and sometimes ones built from scratch.

Our work on Hyperinstruments started in 1986. It grew out of my experiences composing my opera, *VALIS*, for the Georges Pompidou Center in Paris. The Center had asked me to conceive an elaborate project that combined image and sound in a new way. I treated it as an opportunity to redefine "opera." As it's almost virtually impossible to rehearse a complicated computer setup within a traditional opera structure (insufficient rehearsal time, anti-technology attitude problems, and so on), I decided to start from square one by building my own theater, designing purely electronic scenery, inventing a new opera orchestra, and—in some sense—attracting a new audience to opera. I based *VALIS* on Philip K. Dick's science fiction novel of the same name, which provided an opportunity to explore the implications of the kinds of technology I wanted to build.

The Pompidou Center's entrance hall is the size of an airplane hangar, and I decided to build the theater in that hall because thousands of people walk through there every day (thus exposing to this project people who normally would not attend an opera or a contemporary music concert), and because I could set up the visual and sound installations the way I wanted. We built enough seating for 700 people, with standing room around the edges. The stage was constructed of real marble, built in the form of a labyrinth. A large computer-controlled video wall provided all the scenery, with additional

scenery provided by several columns of computer images. We also included an extremely sophisticated laser installation to convey the "pink light," the strange mystical bombardment experienced by the opera's main character (the explanation of which forms the central argument of the opera).

Just as we built the theater from scratch, my idea for the instruments was to depart from the traditional opera orchestra and use real-time, live computer instrumentation. I essentially wanted the fewest number of musicians controlling the most amount of music: the most layers of music and the most amount of subtle control over the music, necessitating the most sophisticated musical setup I could devise.

The technology we developed for this opera project came to be called "Hyperinstruments." By focusing on allowing a few instrumentalists to create complex sounds, we continually improved the technology and reduced the number of actual musical instruments. The resulting opera orchestra consisted of two performers: one keyboard player and one percussionist. They controlled all the music for the opera, almost all of it live.

The Hyperinstrument system is based on musical instruments that provide various ways for musicians to play music into our computers. The simplest method is via an instrument similar to an existing traditional instrument, such as a **MIDI** keyboard or percussion controller. More and more, however, we're using extremely sophisticated controllers that monitor hand gestures.

The output of those instruments goes to an Apple Macintosh II computer, the "brain" of the Hyperinstrument. There, a special **artificial intelligence** software environment analyzes and interprets real-time performance data. This environment, "Hyperlisp," is based on the programming **languages** Allegro, common LISP, and Language, and was developed by Media Lab graduate student and software engineer, Joe Chung (my principal collaborator in Hyperinstrument design). All musical data coming from the live instruments are analyzed and interpreted in real time in the Mac's lisp environment, then turned into MIDI or musical data that is output to a bank of sound-producing devices, MIDI **synthesizers**, **samplers**, or more complicated signal-processing devices.

One theory behind the Hyperinstrument development concerns the potential for live performance. Music is a performance art. You can achieve magical results in a recording studio, where you have the chance to redo and overlay parts, but you should be able to accomplish things on stage that are just as wonderful and retain the dimension of direct human expressivity, communication, and spontaneity. To achieve that while performing live, onstage in a concert setting, we need the power of "smart" computers following the gestures and intentions of fine performers.

Working with fine performers is a key aspect of our approach to the Hyperinstruments. In the past, we haven't built systems for novices (although we're working on our first such system). In fact, the systems reward skill. Hyperinstruments are extremely sensitive to the special nuances of the finest performers, and employ those

skills to expand and enhance performance, all under the performer's control. The better you play, the better the computer reacts.

How simple or how hard should it be to learn and understand such sophisticated instruments? We usually work with virtuosic performers who don't have much experience with electronics. We want this type of terrific performer to be able to come into our studio and understand the concept of the instrument or implementation in 15 or 20 minutes. We want them to understand, "Okay, I see that if I move my hands a certain way, or breathe a certain way, I can produce a certain effect." The musician must be able to understand the concept quickly—but if the musician can learn the entire instrument in 20 minutes, then we've produced not an instrument, but a toy. So the instrument must be easy to understand *conceptually*, but worthwhile and rewarding to practice so the musician can improve on it over time. It must have depth while being easy to learn. Such systems are not easy to design.

We also strongly believe in designing performance systems that let the performer control the system, and in some ways afford the performer even greater musical power than he or she normally would have. I'm not interested in systems in which the computer acts as an accompanist, playing a role of its own, or in systems that prevent the performer from knowing what to expect from the computer. The performer must remain in control at all times.

Another important aspect of live-performance computers of the future involves the performer's ability to take on

artificial intelligence: The development of programs to enable computers to mimic certain aspects of human intelligence, such as as the ability to reason, learn, solve problems, and make decisions. Artificial intelligence programs enable computers to play chess, prove theorums, and so on.

language: A system of commands and statements used to create software for computer use.

synthesizer: An electronic device that contains in one unit, or several linked units, all the resources necessary to generate and modify sound electronically. A synthesizer sound is called a "patch" (the term originates from the fact that early modular synthesizers required "patch cords" to connect the output of one component to the input of another). Creating new sounds on a synthesizer is called "synthesizer programming."

sampler: An electronic device that makes and plays back a digital recording ("sample") of any type of sound. The original sound can be acoustic (such as the sound of a clarinet or a dog bark) or electronic (such as the output of a synthesizer). Feeding a sound into a sampler and recording it is called "sampling."

varied music-making roles. We build our systems mainly for performers, but they work with powerful computers, so they also can be used as improvisation systems and composition systems, and also let the performer control the music's overall shape. Instead of simply playing one note at a time, the performer can react like a conductor. We believe the musician of the future should be a combination of performer, improvisor, composer, and conductor, and be able to switch easily between those roles, or to combine them in new ways.

This approach is illustrated in the piece "Towards the Center," which I composed in 1988/89 for six musicians and conductor. It is scored for six instruments, four of which (violin, cello, flute, clarinet) are amplified and slightly transformed electronically. The keyboard and percussion parts are performed on MIDI con-

Tod Machover enters hand-movement data into the computer by playing a cello Hyperinstrument. Photo © 1991 Peter Menzel.

trollers (Kurzweil Midiboard and KAT four-octave mallet percussion system) connected to the real-time Hyperinstrument system. The computer system was designed to follow, complement, and emphasize the work's musical development, which differs functionally in virtually every one of its sections (including such concepts as rhythmic enhancement and "complexification"—which we call time warping, timbre tremolos, and automated arpeggios). In "Towards the Center," the relationship of control versus independence (of the two electronic soloists) is mediated by machine. At moments the players are free of each others' influence, while at other times they group together to form a single "double instrument," where each controls only part of the musical result.

One aspect of musical enhancement that greatly interests me concerns rhythm. In a live performance, it can mean making musicians more precise than they normally are. It also can mean making the rhythm "crazier," or more complex, or creating delicate combinations or relationships of synchronization that are difficult to play without the help of a computer.

In certain kinds of music that's not an easy thing to do. Such procedures work well in an improvisatory context where it may not be crucial for a certain note to fall precisely on a certain beat. But when you're dealing with a precise score in which you know that in a certain measure you want a particular musician to play a particular note on a downbeat, and the computer to adjust the rhythm to precise sixteenth notes, the only way to do that is to have the computer there, running in real time, and when a performer plays the note, the computer holds that note and waits until the next sixteenth note, and plays it where it considers a proper sixteenth note should go. It won't let the note fall between the cracks.

In one section of "Towards the Center," every time the keyboard player plays an individual note, that note triggers a repeated note passage. The repeated notes play in the tempo of what everybody else is playing. As you press on the key—creating **afterpressure** on the controller—that rhythm is deformed, and it becomes more and more complex. It actually becomes faster as you press harder on the key. As you lift your finger, the rhythm snaps back into synchrony with the rest of the performers. By pressing the keys and triggering various events, you bring synchrony in and out of an ensemble setting in a complex way. The rhythm is adjusted to be more precise than normal, going into a section where the rhythm keeps going in and out of synchrony, by the performer pressing the keys and the computer adjusting the result.

Another Hyperinstrument used in "Towards the Center" and other pieces is called an "automated arpeggiator," and usually is played by a keyboardist. The keyboardist controls the general shape, texture, and articulation of extremely fast notes that are rhythmically precise. The notes come out so quickly and the rhythm is so delicate that you could never play it by hand. But we don't want it all controlled by computer; we want some combination of human and computer. To accomplish that, we store chord progressions and complex rhythm patterns in the computer. Every time the keyboard

player plays a note, the computer decides whether the note belongs there or not. If the computer decides it's a correct note, it decides which chord it belongs to, looks in a library, and selects a rhythm pattern that corresponds to that chord, assigning each note of the chord in time to the appropriate note in that rhythm pattern.

This keyboard uses various other methods to control the final result; for example, depending on how loud you play each individual note, the notes in the rhythm pattern coming from the computer grow louder or softer. This lets you shape the pattern in the computer. If the computer expects five notes, and I don't play note number one, the computer reorders the notes in the pattern so that note number two becomes note number one. Thus, the notes injected into the pattern will be different and the rhythm shifts accordingly.

Additionally, when I press on this keyboard, the afterpressure of each individual finger brings up an extra bank of **timbres** that articulate each individual note. This allows the performer to introduce different chord notes in an irregular way rather than just playing them as block chords, thus bouncing the notes around and playing against what the computer expects you to play. What emerges is an extremely delicate effect. Most keyboard players get the idea in ten minutes, but usually practice many hours to achieve beautiful, controlled effects.

While the keyboardist performs these automated arpeggios, the percussionist does something else. I started with the idea that one thing computers can do that live instruments can't is make gradual transitions of sound color. Just as a

afterpressure: Refers to an electronic keyboard's ability to sense how hard the player is pressing a key.

timbre: A musical sound's distinguishing sound qualities, other than pitch and loudness; for example, an oboe has a "reedy" timbre that distinguishes it from a trumpet that's being played at the same pitch and volume.

computer graphic image of a person's face might transform into a lion's face, computer sound can start with one sound image, such as an oboe, and transform over time to sound like a human voice or anything else.

Current synthesis gear technically allows us to achieve such effects, but no current musical instruments let us perform and control such transitions—at least not in the sophisticated way that a musician could practice and perfect. We try to use existing instruments to interpret techniques that performers know how to master, and extend them to control such effects.

For instance, percussionists are good at selecting different physical objects, controlling rhythm and how hard they hit, but no existing percussion instruments give percussionists the opportunity to control and change the overall shape of a percussive sound in time.

Therefore, we adopted the concept of a percussion **tremolo**, a technique that percussionists easily master, and translate it into timbre. We take a series of discrete sounds and measure the speed of live tremolo, separating the tremolo speed from its loudness: The faster the percussionist tremolos, the more complex and "unnatural" the sound becomes. We continue measuring the tremolo speed, and the Hyperinstrument contains an entire bank—a "map" of timbres—that start with pure sounds and progress to complex ones. The faster the tremolo, the more complex the sound made by the computer. Percussionists typically slow down and speed up in a somewhat jerky motion, however, and we don't want the sound to transform that way. We want it to be con-

tinuous, so we include a filter in the Hyperinstrument software that slows down and smoothes the timbral transition.

One thing that interests me is combining electronics with traditional instruments and sounds to increase the sound palette of the traditional orchestra, sounding distinct and contrasting, but also capable of mixing so well that you can't tell what's what. Also, computers provide the potential to link various performers through the system; instead of connecting one individual to an instrument connected to a computer, two or more people play one instrument.

As we consider these possibilities, we realize there are many parameters of musical performance to control, aspects that are difficult to control with one pair of hands or feet. In many situations you might want a percussionist to concentrate on the rhythm of a section, the keyboardist to concentrate on the notes or harmonic content, and the string player to concentrate on the inflection or the phrasing. Instead of thinking of that as three separate lines as we would with a string quartet, we can think of it as one instrument played by three people. That led us to build "double instruments" and "triple instruments."

One such double instrument is based on our desire for two players—percussionist and keyboardist—to work together to control a sort of giant color organ, an instrument that controls complicated timbres. I wanted the keyboard player to control the overall content of the sound spectrum—the **partials**, **harmonic** series, and sound quality—and the percussionist to control the behavior of each individual

tremolo: A regular pulsation in loudness. For the singing voice, it's sometimes known as "vibrato."

partial: Any of the pure, or harmonic, tones forming a complex tone.

harmonic: A sound whose frequency is mathematically related to the fundamental (the note sounded). The simplest harmonic is one octave above the fundamental. The fewer harmonics present, the purer the note sounds, approximating the timbre of a flute or soprano voice.

partial. Think of it in terms of a microscope, where you want the keyboard player to control a less-magnified portion—the overall sound structure—while the percussionist looks at individual parts of the sound under the microscope.

We approached this in "Towards the Center" by combining percussion and keyboard instruments. When the keyboard player plays any note with the left hand below middle C, this plays the note (actually a pedal or fundamental tone for these complex spectrums) and also redefines the timbres and pitches for the keyboard above middle C. At the same time it sends an enormous collection of notes to the percussion controller. When a note is played on the keyboard above middle C, all the pitches and timbres are redefined, and a collection of inharmonic or harmonic partials are sent to the percussion controller. A percussion player is great at choosing rhythms and playing delicate nuances, but it's difficult to do that while playing a four-octave mallet instrument. If you have seven notes from which to choose, it's even more difficult when you're trying to play that subtly over four octaves. So we send the notes automatically from the keyboard instrument to the seven white keys in one octave of the percussion instrument. This provides the percussionist with the equivalent of a seven-note chord automatically determined by the note played by the keyboardist.

As the keyboardist presses more on a left-hand note within a seven-note octave, a "filter" opens up on the percussion controller, spitting out more and more notes to each pad on the percussion controller. Using eye contact, the two players indicate when the percussionist wants the equivalent of a denser spectrum, or wants the keyboardist to eject more notes. The percussionist then can concentrate on picking the part of the spectrum into which the notes are sent. The general spectrum is determined by the keyboardist, and the way those notes are articulated is determined by the percussion controller.

For performing the music of the future, MIDI controllers don't provide adequately sophisticated **performance data**, and are somewhat limited in capabilities. For this reason we're interested in connecting complex acoustic instruments, such as string intruments, to Hyperinstrument systems, and inventing completely new performance controllers.

Toward this end, we have experimented with systems that can capture complex gestures and turn them into musical controls. Our first such experiment, conducted in 1989 and 1990, concentrated on marshalling the expertise used by a conductor, concentrating on left-hand rather than right-hand technique. To do this, we tried various glove-type **gesture controllers**, and chose a device designed by Exos, a company in the Boston area. Their Dexterous Hand Master was developed by Dr. Beth Marcus and adapted for musical use by the Hyperinstrument group. It is an aluminum "skeleton" that fits onto the fingers with Velcro. It uses sensors and magnets to measure the movements at each finger joint. When you move your finger, the angle of the magnet is measured and translated into the angle of the finger joint. This system works fast enough to monitor the most subtle movements of a finger as well as

performance data:
One of two types of data transmitted by MIDI, performance data refers to the physical action taking place on the keyboard, drum machine, synthesizer, etc. When a note is played or a button pressed, MIDI instantly sends out a message about which button was pressed and how quickly, which note was played and how hard it was struck, which slider was moved and how far, and so on. (MIDI also communicates voice data, which consists of the specific parameters that make up a sound on a particular instrument.)

gesture controller:
Input device that translates hand movements into computer data.

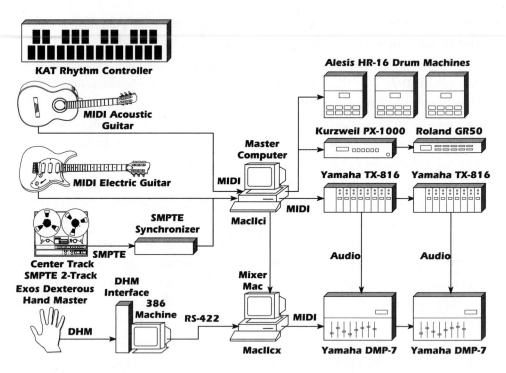

Hyperinstrument set-up for Tod Machover's composition, "Bug-Mudra"

KAT Rhythm Controller

MIDI Acoustic Guitar

MIDI Electric Guitar

SMPTE Synchronizer

Center Track SMPTE 2-Track

Exos Dexterous Hand Master

DHM Interface

386 Machine

DHM

SMPTE

RS-422

Master Computer

MacIIci

MIDI

MIDI

Mixer Mac

MacIIcx

MIDI

Alesis HR-16 Drum Machines

Kurzweil PX-1000   Roland GR50

Yamaha TX-816   Yamaha TX-816

Audio   Audio

Yamaha DMP-7   Yamaha DMP-7

the largest hand gestures, with great precision, accuracy, and speed.

I composed the piece "Bug-Mudra" for use with this glove controller. The piece premiered at Tokyo's Bunkamura Theater in January of 1990. Commissioned by the Fromm Music Foundation of Harvard University, "Bug-Mudra" is scored for two guitars (one acoustic and one electric), percussion (KAT electronic mallet controller plus three acoustic suspended cymbals), and conductor. The three instrumentalists are connected to the Hyperinstrument system, as is the conductor, through the Dexterous Hand Master worn on the left hand. The glove measures the nuances of the conductor's left-hand gestures, translating them to influence the piece's overall sonic result. By the way, the title "Bug-Mudra" comes from *mudra*, the word for hand gestures in classical Indian dance, and *bug*, referring to computer "bugs," a pun on the difficulty of get-

ting such a complex interactive system to work in a live concert situation.

In this piece, the guitar and percussion signals are sent into the first Hyperinstrument system, while the glove is analyzed by an IBM PC (now we use a Mac II), which monitors and classifies the finger gestures. That information is sent to a second Macintosh. This Mac contains a series of programs that interpret the finger movements and gestures, and turn those into controls which then influence the music in various ways. In different sections of the piece, the glove movements influence loudness mix, spatial placement, and the overall timbre of the whole piece.

In "Bug-Mudra," my right hand conducts tempo and speed, while I use my left hand for balance between instruments and for changes of color and articulation—much as traditional conductors use their hands to indicate that a cello section, for instance, should play louder, while the violins should play softer or with more attack, and so on. The glove interprets all my gestures, every little motion. The hand has various degrees of freedom: I can curl the tip of my index finger or the middle portion, or just bend the lower portion of my finger. The glove also measures the induction angle, so I can move my finger back and forth. I can change the effect by a small amount or by the full amount. The piece's entire timbral content—all the sound color of these instruments—is determined by movements of the hand.

An even more elaborate Hyperinstrument piece is "Begin Again Again...," which I composed in 1991 for cellist Yo-Yo Ma. The work is scored for solo cello and live computer electronics, using the Hyperinstrument concept. About 28 minutes long, the piece consists of ten sections, all distinct in character, which are grouped into two large-scale movements. As in much of my recent music, "Begin Again Again . . ." combines many forms of musical expression, from rock music-like drive and intensity to melodious singing to the timbral exploration of cello sounds—all to create a diverse but coherent artistic statement.

The Hyperinstrument system developed for "Begin Again Again . . ." allows the cellist to control an extensive array of sounds through the nuance of his or her performance. We developed many new techniques so the computer can measure, evaluate, and respond to as many aspects of the performance as possible. The most prominent sensors include: a special sensor worn on the right hand to measure wrist movement while bowing;

finger-pressure sensors built into the bow; a radio transmitter that indicates where the bow is making contact with the string; four thin strips placed on the fingerboard under each string that measure left-hand position; and special **pickups** placed on the bridge that facilitate the computer's task of analyzing the cello's actual sound.

Information from all these sensors is sent to a Macintosh IIfx computer, which analyzes the data and provides an ongoing interpretation of the performance. This information is used in different ways at different movements in the piece. At times the cellist's playing controls electronic transformations of his or her own sound; at other times, playing nuance shapes many aspects of the computer-generated accompaniment, changing orchestration, adding emphasis, and simplifying or densifying the musical texture. Sometimes the cello's influence on the computerized accompaniment is clear and direct; sometimes it is indirect and mysterious. My goal has been to create many levels of relationship between soloist and computer, much as the classical concerto dramatizes such relationships between soloist—not as a dichotomy, but as a new kind of instrument.

The members of the Hyperinstrument team who worked with me for over a year to make "Begin Again Again . . ." possible are Joe Chung (technology coordinator and chief software designer), Andy Hong (digital signal processing and software design), Neil Gerschenfeld (sensor design and construction), Jim Davis (software design), Casimir Wierzincski (digital signal processing), and Betty Dexter (administration).

pickup: Electromagnet designed to "pick up" acoustic vibrations and convert them into electrical impulses.

The piece's title refers to its musical form and its expressive content. "Begin Again Again . . ." is a set of variations in which the same melodies and harmonies are returned to over the course of the work, each time expanded and elaborated in new and unexpected ways. This serves as a metaphor for change in our lives: of breaking with the past while retaining what is dearest to us; of opening doors to unknown possibilities; and, finally, of renewed hope and affirmation.

Our Hyperinstrument concepts have been further developed in my composition "Song of Penance," which combines a "Hyperviola" with a large orchestral ensemble and enables the soloist to control and manipulate a vast array of sung and spoken vocal sounds, and in our project to enable amateur and non-expert musicians to expand their skill and stretch their musical imaginations through such a system. We also will continue to apply Hyperinstrument techniques to large-scale opera and to interactive public installations.

It seems that each time we solve a particular problem, new technological challenges and musical visions pop up. We're happy about that, but it sure keeps us busy!

SOUND ENTERS THE THIRD DIMENSION

This chapter delves into the concepts behind spatially enhanced sound, also known as "superstereo," "stereo-surround," and "3-D audio." Here you'll find an introduction to the concept, an overview of some commercially available 3-D sound systems, and some hard-core technical explanations.

PSYCHOACOUSTIC SATISFACTION— OR PSYCHOBABBLE?

BY LINDA JACOBSON

Linda Jacobson is a journalist and editor who focuses on emerging entertainment and communication technologies and the people who use them. In 1980, with a background as a musician and a B.S. in journalism from Boston University, she started her career as a technical writer for audio and video equipment makers. After moving to the West Coast, she served as an editor for Mix, *a recording industry publication, and helped develop* HyperMedia *magazine (now* NewMedia) *and* EQ: The Creative Recording Magazine. *Linda's work appears in* Keyboard, A.I. Expert, MacWEEK, Grammy, *and many other high-tech magazines. She assembled and edited this book, and is glad that you're reading it.*

digital audio tape (DAT): A relatively new stereo tape format in which sound is recorded as a digital code. DAT cassettes are smaller than the familiar audio cassette.

Does this 3-D sound stuff really work? I'm one "earwitness" who can testify that it does. One afternoon late in 1991, a technology explorer named Christopher Currell visited my house. He was carrying a **digital audio tape** player and a bag full of cassettes. He hooked the tape deck to my 15-year-old stereo system, popped in one of his tapes, and punched the "play" button. Then he told me to sit on my couch, close my eyes, and point to the location of the sounds and music as they came out of the system. I listened. I pointed up, and I pointed down, and I pointed sideways, and I pointed toward some imagined horizon in the distance. Not once did I point at the stereo speakers.

That's what 3-D sound's all about.

"Three-dimensional sound" generally refers to a new type of audio technology that lets recording artists enlarge their musical canvas, and gives listeners the opportunity to enjoy the results without buying extra speakers, expensive headphones, or special decoders.

With a 3-D sound canvas, the artist can paint a realistic sound "picture" that can be gleaned through garden-variety, two-channel stereo speakers or headphones. With 3-D sound tools, the artist can place sounds in three-dimensional space

mixing: The process of blending and routing audio signals while controlling their relative levels. In the "mixdown," signals on several recorded tracks are combined to create the final mono or stereo version of the recording.

signal processing: A technique used to change the characteristics of an audio signal (other than overall level). Signal processors include such devices as equalizers, delay lines, compressors, and reverberators.

psychoacoustics: The branch of science that is concerned with human perception and interpretation of sound.

binaural: Involving the use of both ears. Binaural recording is a stereo recording process that employs two microphones which are positioned to emulate the sensitivity and spacing of two ears on the average human head. The microphones are (preferably) placed in an artificial or dummy head, but often merely spaced the same distance apart as human ears, or placed on or in the recordist's own ears. Two completely independent recording channels are used, and the two signals are fed to the reproduction system (headphones, historically).

Vocalist Lou Reed was the first rock musician to release a commercial recording made with a binaural dummy head; the album is **Lou Reed: The Bells** (Arista Records), recorded in 1979 in West Germany.

and control their direction, distance, and depth; the perceived motion of the sound source; and the image's size and stability, consistency and positioning.

New, commercially available 3-D systems that work in the recording or **mixing** process are said to do everything from expand the stereo imagery to make sounds seem to jump from speakers and swirl about the room. All these systems enhance the "presence" of music coming from ordinary hi-fi systems, the clarity of mixes, and, according to some musical experts, the accuracy of acoustic instrument recordings.

That's why artists such as Sting, Madonna, Michael Jackson, Suzanne Ciani, Robbie Robertson, Paula Abdul, Janet Jackson, and many others have used some kind of spatial sound processing in the production of their newer releases.

Traditionally, when recording studio engineers mix for stereo, they spread the music along an imagined flat line that has a speaker at each end. The new 3-D sound technology blurs that line, spreading it above, below, and beyond the speakers' edges. Some systems can place, or *localize*, a sound not only at the line's left end, right end, and center point, but in the "up," "down," "front," and "back" positions. Other systems accurately recreate the original recording environment, providing an "acoustic photograph" of music and sounds filling a room. ("Omnidirectional," then, is a more appropriate title than "three-dimensional," but somehow "O-D" just doesn't ring the same chimes.)

All the systems work in different ways but share a goal: to trick the brain. They fool us into *perceiving* that the sound is coming from somewhere other than the speakers (or headphones). That the trick works is due to recent advances in computer technology, **signal processing**, and **psychoacoustic** research.

People have been trying to create 3-D sound via **binaural** recordings since the 1880s, but music lovers never cared for the results because they had to wear headphones to enjoy the effect. This approach reproduces the ambience of the original sound environment, but it can't recreate the time-of-arrival and "shadowing" cues provided by a flesh-covered skull sporting ears and filled with grey matter. When listening to a binaural recording through two speakers, you experience *interaural crosstalk:* Sounds from the left speaker reach your right ear while sounds from the right speaker reach your left ear, which further smears the imagery.

Today, however, computer scientists bring us new 3-D systems that can mimic our auditory system (ear plus brain) by supplementing binaural recording with *transaural* processing, in which **phase** information is manipulated to effectively eliminate interaural crosstalk so that we can hear "3-D" sound in horizontal and vertical sound fields via two speakers. They also duplicate the localization cues provided by our bodies, emulate the interaural time delays and filtering effects that occur when we hear music and sound, and electronically recreate those effects in real time.

Whether 3-D sound truly transcends stereo or simply serves as a studio production tool to enhance the listening experience, it heralds the beginning of a new phase in sound recording and puts a new twist on arranging music for recording. As new age music composer Suzanne Ciani says, "Motion is rhythm." (And, as the saying goes, "riddim is life.")

This new sound technology doesn't affect only music lovers. It's used to complement and enhance visual imagery, impart information, and facilitate "situational awareness," in aerospace and aviation centers, movie theaters, theme park attractions, video game arcades, and virtual realities. As the overall goal of using 3-D sound is to impart a sonic sense of depth and presence, and increase intelligibility and accuracy, by improving audio quality and finding new ways to manipulate and move sounds we enhance the overall listening experience *and* affect the listener's perception of reality.

"Perception" is the key word, because 3-D sound is about what we *perceive* we hear. I like to think that this *CyberArts*

chapter pays homage to the likes of Edgar Bergen and Charlie McCarthy, Jerry Mahoney and Knucklehead Jones, Waylon Flowers and Madame, the stars of ventriloquism. After all, when we consider the definition of ventriloquism—"the art or practice of speaking so that the voice seems to come from some source other than the speaker"—we realize that 3-D sound is electronic ventriloquism.

In fact, some 3-D systems even use a *dummy*, an almost anatomically-correct, artificial head that is equipped with tiny microphones in its ears. The dummy's design objective is to faithfully record the original recording soundfield. I'll leave it up to this chapter's brains to describe the use of dummies and 3-D sound technology. They all have their own recipes for extracting multidimensional sound from two channels of audio . . . they're all electronic ventriloquists.

phase: Describes the relative position of two soundwaves with respect to one another, usually measured in degrees. (When an instrument plays a note, its pitch is determined by the frequency of regular vibrations of air that are created; these vibrations are soundwaves. Soundwaves are cycles of alterations in air pressure: compression followed by rarefaction.)

THE VIRTUAL REALITY OF 3-D SOUND

This technically oriented section delves into 3-D audio techniques, 3-D reverb, and describes psychoacoustic research into 3-D sound and what's being done to improve the technology.

BY DURAND R. BEGAULT, PH.D.

Durand Begault is a researcher in psychoacoustics at the Aerospace Human Factors Research division of NASA-Ames Research Center in Moffett Field, California. He received his Ph.D. at the Computer Audio Research laboratory at UC San Diego in 1987 and his M.F.A. in electronic music and recording media from Mills College in 1981. He also remains active as a musician and recording engineer. His recent projects include directing a hardware development project for 3-D sound communications at Kennedy Space Center, and a 3-D sound Traffic Collision Avoidance System for commercial air carriers.

"Three-dimensional audio technology" is a generic term for a group of new systems that relatively recently made the transition from laboratory to commercial marketplace. Such terms as "dummy-head **synthesis**" and "spatial sound processing" promise many things, but all are related in that they create a "psychoacoustically enhanced audio display." Just as stereo and quadrophonic sound were introduced as improvements over their predecessors, 3-D audio technology is hailed as the latest innovation for both **mixing consoles** and **reverberation** devices.

synthesis: The process of producing sound electronically; sound is assembled (synthesized) out of simple waveforms that are manipulated and combined in various ways. A waveform is the characteristic shape of a soundwave when represented graphically; the content (form) of the wave determines its harmonic content.

mixing console: A device that blends and balances audio signals.

reverberation; reverb: A form of continuing echo, produced electronically or acoustically, that gives sound a livelier presence. Reverb is caused by the sum of acoustic reflections from environmental surfaces, and is a normal, expected part of sound. Sound recordings that lack reverb seem unnatural.

The idealistic goal of 3-D audio technology is to control every act of spatial hearing, using nonspecialized playback systems. This control should be possible over standard loudspeakers and headphones. "Control of spatial hearing" refers to the ability of the producer or the listener to:

• interactively replicate an existing, spatial auditory condition, such as a violinist playing while moving back and forth across the stage in Carnegie Hall;

• create new spatial auditory conditions, such as hearing that violinist play while moving rapidly around your head like an angry insect in a tiled bathroom the size of an aircraft hangar; and

• **transmute** freely and easily between these varying conditions, such as hearing that violinist play in a closet and suddenly the closet turns into Carnegie Hall.

To control this experience, however, we need to break it down conceptually into manageable categories. These categories are somewhat arbitrary, primarily because they overlap—one thing influences another. For instance, if I twist a knob to change one aspect of the sound, I change another aspect along with it.

In 3-D audio processing, we call our sound source the "virtual source." This virtual sound source can have distance, elevation, and a position in **azimuth**, and it usually exists within an "environmental context." The environmental context doesn't mean you literally hear the room's sound; instead, you hear how it affects the sounding source. For example, you can tell something about the quality of a room, whether it's large or small, carpeted or tiled, just by hearing

the sound of a person speaking inside the room.

With 3-D audio technology, we would like to place any number of sound sources at a given azimuth, elevation, and distance from the perspective to the listener. We'd also like to freely change the environmental context, as in the example of the violinist in the closet and Carnegie Hall.

Finally, the ideal 3-D audio technology would allow the movement of sound sources, with a smooth transmutation between conditions. If you're listening on headphones, we might place a sound to your right, and when you turn your head to the right, the sound source seems to move toward the left, instead of moving with you, as with normal sound over headphones. We've achieved this at NASA by using a device with a head position-tracker attached to it; we update the audio spatial processing based on the listener's head position, as is done for visual displays in virtual reality systems.

Current professional recording technology, such as mixing consoles and reverberators, let us control the distance and azimuthal perspective within a two-dimensional plane, and the environmental context in a limited fashion—but not in three dimensions. When you're working on a mix and you set the auditory perspective for stereo through the mixing console's **pan pots**, and you use the console's **effects return** to bring in more reverb, it changes the perspective of the sound somewhat. You don't have direct control over the localizing the entire mix, where you can make the guitar, for example, appear to come from the upper right and the bass appear to come from

transmute: To change from one form, condition, nature, or substance into another.

azimuth: Refers to left/right tilt.

pan pot: Short for "panoramic potentiometer." A pot is a device, typically attached to a knob or slider, used to adjust an aspect of the signal passing through it. A pan pot adjusts spatial positioning: In a mixing console, two volume controls for the left and right channels of a stereo mix are wired in such a way that as the left channel's level increases, the right channel's level decreases, and vice versa. This affects the amount of signal going to the left and right speakers (or headphones).

effects return: A mixing console input that receives the signal from an effects device for blending with the main audio signal.

the lower left. Instead, you approach the instruments in isolated ways, and they end up creating different perceptual effects.

Current 3-D audio technology provides greater control over azimuth and elevation over environmental context than what we had with traditional stereo, but is nowhere close to the aforementioned ideals.

Traditional stereo recording captures two of the basic cues for hearing in three-dimensional space: *interaural-amplitude differences* and *interaural-time differences* that result from the fact that we listen with two ears. Over the last 60 years psychoacoustic research has progressively stressed the importance of the spectral modification caused by the outer ear, head, shoulders, and torso. The cause of this sound modification is referred to as the "head-related transfer function" (HRTF). The HRTF causes the interaural phase and spectral differences for a given sound-source position.

The head-related transfer function seems especially important when we need to distinguish between sounds coming from the front and from the back. It also can cause sounds over headphones to seem more externalized, as if they're coming from beyond the headphones.

Our three principal clues to sound location are interaural level differences, interaural time differences, and HRTF-induced spectral differences. If we send a monaural signal through a mixing board, and use a pan pot to change its placement in the stereo image, we're using interaural level differences. If we're listening to two speakers in a room, we're hearing time-delay differences introduced by the fact that the sounds from the closer speaker reach your ear before the sounds from the one farther away. If we're listening over headphones, we're hearing level differences.

When audio engineers record a string quartet or brass ensemble, they use the standard **"X-Y" miking** technique traditionally used for stereo recording. This captures amplitude differences and time differences. In Germany, however, around the early-1970s, we saw the introduction of what was called ***Kuntskopf*** or "dummy-head" stereo recording. Engineers there took a mannequin head, put a realistic **pinna** on each side where the ears would be, and placed microphones inside the head. This way they could capture the head-related transfer function through the outer ear. More recently, in 1979, Neumann Acoustics introduced the KU-80 artificial head (later the KU-81), and in 1989, Head Acoustics GmbH of Germany introduced their own fiberglass dummy head. This sophisticated product included "modeled" pinnae and shoulders, since these body parts are thought, by some researchers, to contribute to the HRTF's modification.

Using these dummy heads, you can record a live concert and capture spatial sound in a much more dramatic way than you can with a normal stereo miking technique. But wouldn't it be great to capture any sound, any time, *then* spatialize it? Record something with a single, standard microphone and later arbitrarily place the sound's position in space, instead of being restricted to the way it was placed when you originally recorded it?

If you don't have access to a dummy head, it's possible to do this by using a "spatial processing filter." Such a filter

amplitude: Level or volume of an electrical or acoustical signal. Acoustically, amplitude is the pressure level of sound and it determines the sound's intensity and strength.

"X-Y" miking: A technique in which a pair of microphones are aimed at crossed directions with the mike elements almost touching, feeding two channels for stereo pickup.

Kuntskopf: German— **Kunst** is "artifice," **kopf** is "head."

pinna: That soft, shell-like fold of skin on the side of your head, also known as your "outer ear." It helps you determine which directions that sounds are coming from.

was created in a project with our fellow researchers at the University of Wisconsin at Madison. We placed extremely tiny microphones in someone's ears; custom ear molds kept the microphones in place. Then they blindfolded and seated that person in a soundproof chamber in which a series of loudspeakers was mounted at the position they wanted to synthesize. Next, over those speakers they fired something called an "impulse." We can learn the difference between the impulses' original spectra and what happens to it when it reaches the ear. The impulse response was measured to obtain the HRTF for each of the positions that we wanted to simulate.

In these tests, we removed the transfer function of the headphones by doing an "inverse convolution"; that is, we took the **frequency response** of the headphones, then compensated for it, so what people were hearing was "flat" except for the HRTF. (Maybe in the future we'll be able to buy chips that plug into our stereo systems to eliminate the spectral characteristics of lousy speakers or headphones.)

Once we measure the impulse response for the left and right ears, we put the mathematically modeled HRTF spectrum into a pair of filters that let us filter the left and right channels.

This measurement technique results in extremely long impulse responses, which translate into many digital *multiplies*. The more multiplies you have, the more expensive the system costs. You have to use more chips, or more advanced chips, to accomplish the processing. That's why we'd like to reduce the number of multiplies used in these head-related transfer

functions. I've been working with filter design programs so I can reduce a filter's 1,024 multiplies, or coefficients, down to 65. It doesn't capture all the nuances in the spectrum, but what interests me is learning if the reduction makes any *perceptual* difference. In other words, if I reduce the number of coefficients, does it make any difference in the ability to localize the sound? If not, then it means I can achieve the same results for a tenth of the cost, and I can use a common Motorola 56000 chip, which is the heart of most personal computer-based, digital sound systems.

Although we use state-of-the-art equipment, the HRTF measurements have a poor low-frequency response. The little microphones we put in the ear tend to **roll off** at low frequencies; this means that if you were to play a piano scale from low notes to high notes, through one of these spatial filters, you'd hear the scale grow louder as the pianist moved closer to middle C. As a matter of fact, there was a related problem with the initial dummy-head recordings; people didn't like the resulting spectral balance. Therefore, in addition to building simpler filters, I'm working on correcting for this low-end frequency response.

Once we achieve all these goals, we'd like to implement movement. This brings up the Convolvotron, the real-time sound spatialization device developed by Dr. Elizabeth Wenzel of NASA and Scott Foster of Crystal River Engineering. We use the Convolvotron system at NASA-Ames.

The diagram of the Convolvotron illustrates several measured positions at one, two, three, and four, for which we've measured the impulse responses. It also

roll-off: A gradually increasing loss or attenuation beyond a given frequency point.

frequency response: Frequency is the rate of vibration of a soundwave or audio signal; low-pitched sounds have low frequencies, while high-pitched sounds have high frequencies. Frequency is expressed in Hertz (Hz) and kilohertz (kHz), equivalent to cycles per second. The range of normal human hearing is 20 Hz to 20kHz. Frequency response refers to the range of frequencies that an audio device can reproduce.

shows the desired position for the sound. Let's say the sound source position moves back and forth. We have our measured positions, and we use an **algorithm** to calculate the "in-between" positions. As we use the head-tracking device to measure the location of the head, we can create new position data that follows the head's movement. The basic idea is that from a sampling of auditory space, we can figure out what unmeasured positions might look like.

Some of you may know about "spatial reverb." Before we explore that concept, let's define "reverb."

We can think of "reverb" as a series of time-delayed, filtered copies of sound that reach you indirectly, as a result of bouncing off walls and surfaces around you. You can figure out what the reverb might look like by using a visualization technique such as *ray-tracing*, where you pretend that sound reflections resemble light reflections. You could describe the sound of a reverberant environment by showing a direct sound and its "early reflections" (the first bounces of the sound off the walls) coming toward you. Then you calculate the early reflections' angle of incidence to a listener and you apply head-related transfer functions to the delayed sound as well as to the direct sound. Then we simulate dense reverberation, which basically is many, many reflections, by using exponentially decaying **white noise** with different distributions, and the result is spatial reverberation.

Instead of having single-channel reverb, the idea with spatial reverb is to impart a sense of greater spaciousness. The idea is not a new one, but in the mid-

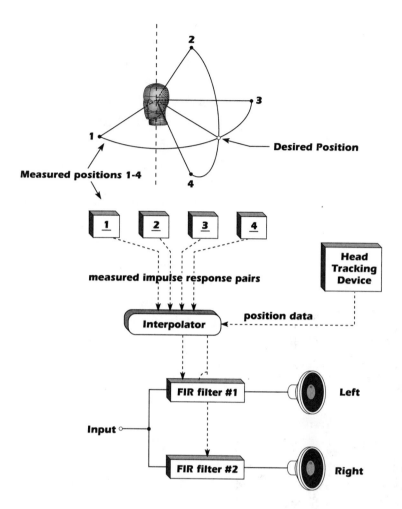

The Convolvotron

1980s at Northwestern University, Gary Kendall and Bill Martens started working on it in earnest. Essentially, in creating spatial reverb, you figure out the direction that the reverberation is coming from, and you "directionalize" it with head-related transfer function filters. The goal of using spatial reverb is to try to recreate the entire sound field.

Ray-tracing is complex. Proper ray-tracing must be done in three dimensions. In any physical modeling of acoustic spaces, such as in concert hall acoustics, acousticians have tried to predict things like reverberation time, and after spending millions of dollars, they end up having

algorithm: A mathematical term indicating any series of instructions, decisions, and steps used to solve a problem or perform a task.

white noise: Noise which contains all frequencies at the same intensity; it sounds like a hiss.

to tear down buildings or otherwise disappointing the fund-raisers, because their physical models of the concert hall didn't account for things such as light bulbs. A few years ago, Carnegie Hall was replastered and repainted, and some people say the acoustics changed, in spite of the best efforts of the acoustic modelers.

In ray-tracing, you estimate how the reverberant energy might hit the listener, then calculate its angle of incidence. In terms of signal processing, I split the input into three paths: I perform a direct sound filtering by the HRTF, then calculate the source-to-wall distance for a reflection, then filter by the wall—you basically put into the computer different kinds of walls (different materials and widths) and estimate the transfer function for that particular wall. This is valid only for higher frequencies on the walls, for lower frequencies tend to be **diffuse** in the way they reflect off the wall.

Finally, I measure an angle of incidence—a calculation for the wall-to-listener distance—filtering by the angle of incidence for the reflections. Then the directed early reflections of sound are passed to left-right headphone outputs. Future reverberation devices also will attempt to capture features of a reverberant environment in more ways than the simple left-right stereo techniques.

At this point, people are trying to determine which early reflections are critical from a psychoacoustic perspective. Although we can create all kinds of physical modeling of auditory space, it's more relevant to figure out what is most perceptually important.

The second diagram illustrates the possible sources of "localization error" that can occur when you're using a 3-D audio system. This relates to headphones, not loudspeakers. The evaluation of 3-D audio system performance depends on three significant types of input. First, and perhaps the most important, is the particular set of head-related transfer functions in use. We can measure one person's ears, but everyone's outer ears are different. The third diagram shows a graph of the HRTF of two people measured at the same position in the anechoic chamber with the loudspeakers. You can

diffuse: Spread out or dispersed.

Possible sources of localization error: why does X ≠ Y?

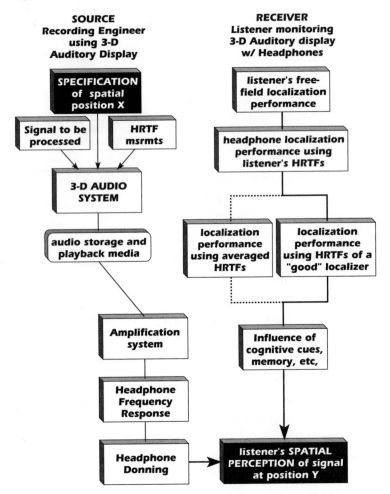

tell that there are quite a few spectral differences between them.

When trying to compensate for this difference, we ask ourselves, "Should we average the difference?" If we take the averaging approach, however, we remove many distinct features, because if we average between two values, we end up with something in the middle that eliminates individual, and important, characteristics.

Another solution is to measure the ears and HRTFs of many people, see how well they localize sound, then say, "We'll use the ears of the best localizer." In the future, in fact, I think we'll see musicians and recording engineers carrying around special sets of data for ears, the same way keyboard players carry around synthesizer **patches** now and say, "This is my Hammond organ sound, and I don't let anyone use it!" People with 3-D audio systems will say, "These are Brian Eno's ears, and I don't let anybody see them," and on the backs of CD packages you'll see credits like, "This CD was recorded with Michael Jackson's ears."

Let's briefly examine the sources of error that influence the basic capabilities of 3-D audio systems: the head-related transfer function measurements and the signal to be processed. Different kinds of sounds are easier or more difficult to localize. If you play a note on a piano with a sharp attack, the sound is much easier to localize than something with a very smooth, even volume. A number of errors can come in, either through the way you store the sound, or the way you amplify it, or even due to the frequency response of your headphones, which also will af-

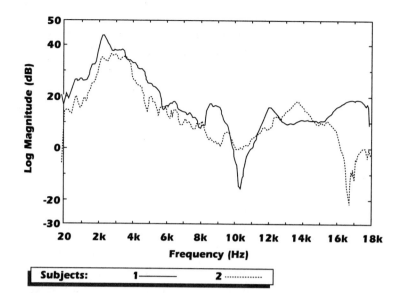

Subjects: 1———— 2 ············

HRTFs, two people measured at the same position in the anechoic chamber

patch: A synthesizer sound.

fect the sound, and even the way you're wearing the headphones on your head.

The problems increase when you try to reproduce 3-D sound over loudspeakers. Different rooms will add different reflective characteristics to a sound, and thus affect the listener's localization accuracy. Consider how a physical space affects our ability to localize sounds. For instance, sometimes I hear a telephone ringing in my office and I'll think it's my phone, but it turns out that it's my officemate's phone. Sometimes I'll be driving in my car and I'll hear a sound—*boom*—and I'll think, "Oh no, something's wrong with my car!"—because lots of things go wrong with my car. Then I look to my left and see that it's another car that's lost its muffler. So many conditions come into play when we hear sounds, and it's important to realize that our localization ability varies widely from day to day and situation to situation.

When we consider, then, how a person localizes with their own ears, we wonder how well they'll be able to localize while listening through synthesized

cognition: The process of "knowing" in the broadest sense, including perception, memory, judgment, and so on.

HRTFs. Add to that the influence of past experience and **cognitive** cues.

In considering the effectiveness of 3-D audio, we also must consider the problem of "front-back confusions." For example, front-back confusion occurs when you're supposed to hear something as if it's coming from the front, but instead you hear it to the rear. One 3-D demo tape included the sound of somebody drinking a glass of water. You listen and say, "Wow, that sure sounds like it's in front of me!" When was the last time you tried to drink a glass of water from behind your head? The point is, cognitive cues influence your perception. Many 3-D demos include the sounds of race cars zipping by, which instantly impart the impression of sound movement. The race car demo *always* "works"—even with mono systems!

Three-dimensional sound has great potential, but one must be aware of what we demand from it. A while back, I saw an advertisement in the newspaper for a television set. The ad showed a small picture of an ear with the caption, "psychoacoustics." It said that the TV's sound system "enables viewers to sit virtually anywhere in the room while still retaining a sense of direction of all the instruments in the orchestra." Great, so it gives me a sense of direction—but *what* direction?

Perhaps accurate localization isn't so important. How many of us who listen to classical music want to be aware of the exact fugal technique used by Bach or the **timbral** changes of **Varese**? When you hear their music, you know something's being manipulated, but you don't necessarily even need to discriminate the

timbral: Referring to a sound's distinguishing qualities, other than pitch and loudness.

Edgard Varese: (1883-1965) French composer who is considered a founding member of the avant-garde. In the 1920s he started exploring the possibilities of composing for electronic instruments.

violins from the violas to enjoy the listening experience.

Similarly, we can use a 3-D audio system to distribute sound sources so that there's a spatial quality present that couldn't be achieved with stereo. There's great potential for that. For example, my work today involves a commercial airline's flight simulator. We're working on a traffic collision avoidance system found on most commercial airplanes. Basically, a warning system goes off when you fly your Boeing 737 into the airport when there's another plane too close for comfort. Currently the airline uses visual warning systems, but I'm researching the use of a 3-D sound system to localize the sound to the position of the traffic outside the cockpit window. Although there's a certain amount of error in terms of where the traffic is located, so far I've found that the pilot and co-pilot know how to tell who should be looking out the window, just by whether the sound appears to come more from the left or more from the right. This essentially lowers their workload and makes for a safer flying experience and less chance of an airport accident.

The more you listen to 3-D sound, the more you learn to discriminate between different sound positions. Through an interdisciplinary approach to the design and evaluation of 3-D audio systems, it may be possible in the near future to successfully confront the challenges involved. The need for additional work in the psychoacoustic domain is apparent—development of products always outpaces research. Already it is possible to perform creative audio processing with HRTF filtering techniques that is not possible with other traditional stereo technologies. But ultimately, it will be the specific demands of recording engineers and music listeners that will determine the quality of 3-D audio systems.

LAUNCHING SOUNDS INTO SPACE

BY ELIZABETH M. WENZEL, PH.D.

Among the first people to help develop a commercially available 3-D sound system is Dr. Elizabeth Wenzel. Beth received her Ph.D. in cognitive psychology (with an emphasis in psychoacoustics) from the University of California at Berkeley. She then conducted research at the NASA-Ames Research Center, working on the auditory display of information for aviation systems. Since 1986 Beth has directed the NASA-Ames Spatial Auditory Displays Lab in the Aerospace Human Factors Research division, where she heads development of real-time display technology and conducts research in auditory perception and localization in "virtual acoustic displays."

Our project started as an outgrowth of the "**VIEW**" (Virtual Interface Environment Workstation) project at NASA-Ames in 1986. The VIEW goal was to develop a multimedia virtual display based on **stereoscopic optics**, updated in real time using computer graphics techniques.

Most information-display research emphasizes the visual aspects of display. Many researchers, however, point to the importance of the auditory system as an alternative or supplementary information channel. That's why our Spatial Auditory Displays Lab set out to develop the auditory equivalent of a virtual visual display, one that is completely interactive: People wearing the head-mounted visual display in the VIEW environment would be able to turn their heads and hear the audio adjust accordingly. For example, if a sound came from the left, and they turned their head to the left, the sound would seem to come from in front of them. To achieve this, we developed a signal-processing device capable of generating **externalized**, three-dimensional sound cues for real-time presentation over headphones. This device is called the "Convolvotron."

Basically a digital signal processor attached to a head-position tracker and installed inside an IBM PC computer, the Convolvotron accepts four sound sources and processes them according to the way you move your head. [*The next section by Scott Foster provides detail about the system's development.*] The applications of a spatial auditory display such as the Convolvotron involve any situation in which the user's spatial awareness is important, particularly when visual cues are limited or absent. Examples include air traffic control displays, advanced **teleconferencing** environments, the monitoring of **telerobotic** activities in hazardous situations, and scientific **visualization** of multi-dimensional data.

From my viewpoint as a perceptual psychologist, I define 3-D sound in terms of the "cues" we try to synthesize or represent. Ours is a simple scenario: The listener remains in a fixed position in space and is asked to tell us where the sounds,

VIEW: Virtual Interface Environment Workstation project launched in 1985 by NASA-Ames researchers, the first to combine head-mounted visual-display output devices, gesture-recognition (data glove) input devices, speech recognition, 3-D audio, computer graphics, and video imaging technology. VIEW was developed to plan space missions and research data display and manipulation concepts.

stereoscopic optics: Technology involving optical devices and pairs of images to create three-dimensional illusions.

externalized: Refers to the fact that the sounds are intended to appear to come from outside your head at a particular location in space, rather than inside your head, as is usually the case when you're listening over standard stereo headphones.

teleconferencing: The use of electronic methods and equipment to facilitate real-time communications among groups of people at two or more locations.

telerobotics: The remote operation systems that translate human movements into the control of machinery.

visualization: Graphical representation of abstract data that normally appears in the form of text and numbers.

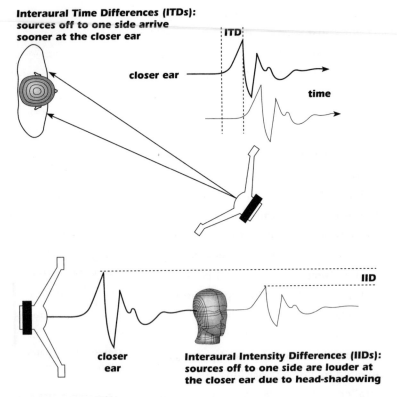

Interaural Time Differences (ITDs): sources off to one side arrive sooner at the closer ear

ITD

closer ear

time

IID

closer ear

Interaural Intensity Differences (IIDs): sources off to one side are louder at the closer ear due to head-shadowing

Primary localization cues: time and intensity differences

interaural: Relating to the combined effects of listening with two ears.

delay line: A device that delays an entire audio signal by a certain length of time, usually from 0 to 500 milliseconds. Commonly used in recording for echo and other special effects.

gain: The amount an amplifier increases the power of an audio signal, usually expressed in decibels. An "audio signal" is a varying voltage that carries information representing sound. Audio signals can be recorded, transmitted, processed, and so on.

which may come from any direction around him or her, are located. The first diagram illustrates the listener's two primary **interaural** cues, time and intensity. As you can see, a sound source coming from the right arrives first at the closest ear, the right ear. It also seems louder at that ear, due to an effect called "head shadowing": Your head gets in the way of the sound waveforms. Many simple stereo-recording techniques take advantage of this head shadowing. It's relatively easy to introduce these time and intensity cues into a sound signal, using digital or analog techniques. Analog techniques include a simple volume or balance adjustment between the left and right channel, or the insertion of an analog **delay line** between the channels. Similar effects are achieved digitally by using mathematical **gain** changes or delay lines.

At NASA-Ames, we're interested in helmet-mounted displays that present sound over headphones, not speakers. When you listen to cues that have been manipulated over headphones using standard stereo techniques, you tend to hear something "inside" your head; in other words, it isn't externalized. If you change the interaural time and intensity cues, the apparent left/right location of the sound simply bounces back and forth between the ears, moving along your interaural axis. It doesn't sound natural.

Another problem that arises when you present only time and intensity cues is known as "perceptual reversal" or "front-back confusion." When you try to manipulate a sound's position by manipulating only interaural time and intensity, you essentially create an ambiguous situation that psychoacousticians refer to as "the cones of confusion." When you manipulate only interaural time and intensity, it is as if you are assuming that the listener's head is a stationary sphere with two symmetrical holes for ears. The geometry of this situation predicts that a particular value of interaural time (or intensity) corresponds to any location along a conical surface, as shown in the second diagram. If you increase the value of the interaural time or intensity, the corresponding lateral (two-dimensional) position of the sound may tend to move farther out, but its true three-dimensional position is still ambiguous. When the interaural time or intensity cue is your only clue to location, any point on the entire conical surface could serve as the location of the sound source. For example, a sound located in the front would sound just the same as (or produce the same interaural cue as) its mirror image in the rear. Perceptually, this could result in a front-back confusion.

This is why we need yet another set of cues: the pinna cues that result when the sound interacts with your pinnae or outer ears. When you hear a sound coming from a particular direction, the sound is spectrally "colored" because it reflects and **refracts** off the folds and curves of your outer ears. It also bounces off your shoulders and torso and **diffracts** around your face. We can think of the resulting coloration as having a pair of **graphic equalizers**, one for each ear, which change the sound's timbre before it reaches the inner ear and brain. Depending on the sound source's position, the shape or "coloration" of the two graphic equalizers will change, and usually is different in the two ears. Thus, a source position in front will produce a different pair of "graphic equalizer shapes" or spectral colorations than a position in the rear. Over the course of your life, your auditory system has learned to pick up on these spectral differences to distinguish front from back (or up from

down); it has learned to disambiguate the cones of confusion.

In the development of our 3-D sound techniques, we've measured the interaural time and intensity cues as well as the pinna cues, and graphically shown the resulting spatially-dependent coloration effects.

If we graphed head-related transfer functions for a sound source directly in front of the listener, it would show a bumpy pattern for the spectra as a result of the sound's interaction with the listener's ears and other body structures—but the

Conical loci of source positions having constant Interaural Time Differences (ITDs) or Interaural Intensity Differences (IIDs)

+z

+y

+x

Larger ITD or IID

Smaller ITD or IID

Cones of confusion

refraction; diffraction: Respectively, the bending and the breaking up of soundwaves as they pass by some physical object.

graphic equalizer: An electronic device that adjusts certain portions of the frequency spectrum to alter the tone of an audio signal. A graphic equalizer operates simultaneously at several pre-set frequencies, any of which can be amplified or attenuated independently of the others. Many high-quality home and car stereo systems include graphic equalizers.

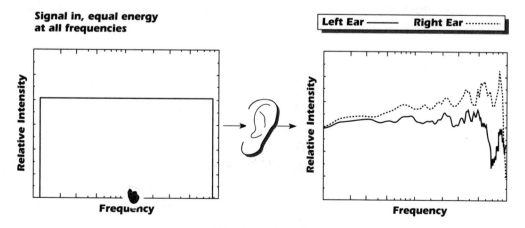

Signal in, equal energy at all frequencies

Relative Intensity

Frequency

Left Ear ——— Right Ear ···········

Relative Intensity

Frequency

Spectral shaping by the pinnal (outer ears)

source at +90 deg azimuth, 0 deg elevation (directly to the right)

pattern of the bumps would be about the same size and shape for both ears. If we graphed a sound source coming directly from the right, it would show large "bumps" in the responses of the two ears that would be more intense overall in the right ear and also have different shapes in the two ears. This results in large intensity (magnitude) differences between the two ears with a distinctive pattern that corresponds to that location.

The way in which these effects vary is extremely complicated. It's difficult to develop a single equation that could be used to simulate the cues—to vary a sound's elevation versus its azimuth, for example. Instead of attempting to write equations, we took another approach, one of brute force. In collaboration with Fred Wightman at the University of Wisconsin in Madison, we seated people inside in an anechoic chamber—a "dry" or free-field environment, one which completely absorbs all reflected sound—and we inserted tiny probe microphones down into their ear canals, as close to their eardrums as possible. Then we presented a **broadband** sound over a loudspeaker and measured what happened to the sound as it entered the ear canals. We stored the resulting measurements as a pair of digital filters—one filter for each ear. This method, usually called an "impulse response" technique, allows you to measure the spectral coloration effects, or pinna cues, for that particular location, as well as the interaural cues—the time and intensity differences—for both ears at once.

We repeated the measurements with a movable arc of 6 speakers that was rotat-

broadband sound: A complex sound.

ed so we could measure 144 equidistant locations in a spherical array around the listener. The objective was to use a "map" made from the resulting listener-specific digital filters (which are also called spatial filters, location filters, or head-related transfer functions) to digitally process localized sounds, building a synthesized, spatialized recreation of the original. We loaded the map of filters from an IBM PC/AT personal computer into the memory of the Convolvotron, the real-time, digital signal processor designed by Scott Foster. The Convolvotron filters any input, non-localized sound with the digital spatial filters in real time and presents the resulting synthesized sounds over headphones. When we do our job right, the listener perceives the input sound as if it were coming from the location in which we originally measured the sound.

We worked with real people, not artificial ("dummy") binaural recording heads, because outer ears vary from person to person, and the importance of that in sound perception was not yet clear to us. We assumed that we would achieve the best effect if we used real ears to record the sounds. We wanted to examine what happens when people listen through their own ears, as opposed to someone else's.

Since we made these measurements for use in information displays, we didn't simply worry whether the sound was "good" or "spacious," but also whether it was spatially *accurate*—are we hearing the sound come from the place we intended it to come from?

The basic working assumption of our synthesis technique is that if one can produce, using headphones, actual ear-canal waveforms that are identical to those produced by the anechoic or free-field sound, then we should be able to duplicate the free-field experience. To judge the accuracy of our assumption, we performed a series of perceptual studies that compared localization of real sound sources versus localization of synthesized sound sources.

In general, we've found that people make a variety of errors in sound localization, for which we eventually hope to compensate using digital synthesis techniques. The errors occur when you present a sound source and ask people to identify where the sound comes from; they tend to give various answers. However, most of the errors are relatively small; people err by only a few degrees in the azimuth direction and in elevation. That's not too surprising. The interesting error concerns "reversals," which probably result from the cones of confusion. People frequently experience these reversals when they listen to recordings made with binaural techniques and sometimes even when they listen to real-world sounds: A sound source in the front can sound as if it's coming from the rear, and vice versa, or a sound source from above can sound as if it's coming from below. Therefore, although the pinna cues are present in our digital spatial filters, sometimes these cues are not strong enough to help disambiguate the correct location along the cone of confusion that corresponds to the simple interaural cues.

As I mentioned before, we measured our digital filters for particular people's ears with the idea that the sound synthesis process should work the best for a given individual when the synthesis is based on measurements made for his or her own ears. However, it's probably not practical to expect to measure "personalized" spatial filters for each person who wants to use our system. Thus, an important practical issue concerns what happens when you "listen through another person's ears." What happens to your ability to localize a sound source when it has been synthesized from digital filters measured for someone else's ear structures, not your own?

In general, we've found that the ability to localize a sound's azimuth or left-right direction is not greatly affected by various manipulations, whether you listen through your own ears or somebody else's. This dimension is robust, from person to person. Sound azimuth was synthesized nearly perfectly for all listeners.

Localizing the sound's elevation, however, proved less robust and more subject to individual differences in listeners' spatial hearing. It seems that people vary in their ability to discern the up-down direction of sounds. You might expect this because the sound's interaction with (or spectral colorations caused by) the pinna provide the primary cue to elevation, and this cue's quality is likely to vary significantly from person to person, depending on the shape of their ear structures. When you listen to the synthesized sound through your own ears, elevation accuracy is fairly good. When you listen through the ears of someone we consider a "good localizer"—someone who localizes sounds well in the real world—you get a slight increase in variability, but generally, elevation perception remains intact.

Occasionally we come across someone who can't localize sounds well; we say that he or she has "bad pinna." Basically, this person has no elevation cues, whether listening to a real or synthesized sound sound source. They can't tell "up" from "down." If you listen through this person's ears, you too will lose elevation perception.

This observation argues for some data-sifting in terms of which spatial filters to use as the digital filters in your own real-time system. You must perform some kind of basic perceptual test, such as comparing your ability to localize real sounds versus sounds synthesized from filters made from your ears. If your localization is good for both real and virtual sources, consider yourself a good localizer. You then can use your spatial filters to synthesize sounds for other listeners, and you can feel confident that the localization cues produced by your filters will work fairly well for most people.

Similarly, if you want to make your own spatialized audio recordings using an artificial binaural head, make sure the head can deliver the required interaural and pinna cues, or verify that the manufacturer has measured the head's ability to deliver the appropriate cues for good localization. In some sense, using an artificial head is really no different than using a real person's head, even if the artificial head is based on some sort of "average" person's ear structure. Who knows whether this average structure results in good cues for localization—unless those cues have been tested in perceptual studies?

We've also learned that, as a function of the individual differences from ear to ear, reversals tend to increase under syn-

thesized conditions. For most people, reversals with real sound sources occur about five percent of the time. The incidence of reversals increases to about ten percent when you listen to sounds synthesized from filters based on your own ears, and further increases to 30 percent or more when you listen "through" someone else's ears. Therefore, our objective now is to find ways to generalize our systems for a wide variety of people—because we don't want to put people in an anechoic chamber and shove mikes down their ears every time we want them to go into in a virtual environment!

There are several methods that can compensate for some of the difference effects. We've already alleviated some ear-difference problems by our development of the Convolvotron, which transcends the use of fixed sound sources by letting people move around so they can pick up on how sounds change dynamically as they interact with a virtual acoustic environment. For example, when listeners turn their heads, the virtual sound sources don't move with them; they stay in their proper position. People gain lots of location information by tracking the changes in localization cues over time and in response to their own head movements, so it's important that the virtual sounds behave as they would if you were walking through an actual environment.

We also need more complex simulations, not just dry, anechoic ones; we have to be able to model actual **room reflections** in real time. That's one reason the Convolvotron was developed. It lets us synthesize a single source plus six reflections, so we've taken the first step

room reflections: *Refers to soundwaves that have bounced off surfaces in a room.*

toward the real-time simulation of complex environments.

Thanks to my colleagues at the University of Wisconsin, psychoacousticians Frederic Wightman and Doris Kistler, for their critical contributions to the research and development of the Spatial Auditory Displays Project.

THE CONVOLVOTRON CONCEPT

This section covers the issues involved with presenting a 3-D audio "world" (a simulated environment) over headphones via the digital signal processing system, the Convolvotron. The Convolvotron is an extremely high-speed processing system that delivers three-dimensional sound over headphones. It consists of a two circuit boards designed for installation in and control by an IBM personal computer. The system outputs audio signals and compensates for the head motion of the listener and/or the motion of audio sources. As the listener changes the position of his or her head, the perceived location of the sound source remains constant. For example, sound perceived to come from behind the listener will "move" smoothly to the right side of the listener when she or he turns to the right.

BY SCOTT FOSTER

*Scott Foster founded Crystal River Engineering in 1987 to develop digital signal processing equipment for spatial audio and navigation systems. One of his first clients was NASA-Ames, for which he developed the Convolvotron 3-D sound system. Scott retained commercial rights and launched production of the Convolvotron in 1989. Today it's used in various applications, primarily for **virtual reality** systems. Before establishing Crystal River, Scott worked at Hewlett-Packard on digital signal processing and at Atari as a research scientist, focusing on audio synthesis. He holds a degree from Massachusetts Institute of Technology.*

In audio systems such as the Convolvotron, the idea is to calculate a synthetic, head-related transfer function in real time for each sound source in a virtual environment. The resulting simulation is a dynamic model; the sound sources can move around in real time. When you wear the headphones and peer into the **stereoscopic** display in a Convolvotron set-up, the system's **head-position tracker** lets you look around and move through a simulated environment, with the sounds adjusting accordingly. We can adjust the sounds' reflections and even the positions of the simulated walls at any time through the computer system, based on an IBM PC/AT.

The head-related transfer function [*described in the previous sections by Durand Begault and Beth Wenzel*] essentially represents a measurement of the transfer characteristics of sounds from points in space to the eardrums of a listener. This measurement takes into account the effects on the sound of the head, pinna, shoulders, nose, paunch, and other body parts. It doesn't include environmental information, because the signals we're manipulating are meant to be presented over headphones, not loudspeakers.

If you carefully measure these transfer characteristics and implement them

stereoscopic: Giving the illusion of three-dimensional imagery.

position tracker: A system that tracks the movements of parts of the body and sends information about position and orientation to the computer for processing.

virtual reality: Generally refers to technology that provides the ability to interact with data in a way that enables "entering" and navigating through a computer-generated, 3-D "world" or environment and change your viewpoint and interact with objects within that world. Virtual reality is characterized by "immersion" (it feels as if you are "inside" the environment).

directly into a system such as the Convolvotron, you can achieve the right effects. Our colleagues Fred Wightman and Doris Kistler at the University of Wisconsin performed studies that show that sound signals which arrive in the listener's ear canals via headphones are nearly identical to signals which arrive in the listener's ear canals via a loudspeaker in an anechoic chamber. They've also shown that people give approximately the same localization performance when they hear a simulated **anechoic** chamber as when they hear sounds produced by an actual loudspeaker in an anechoic chamber.

That's good for those of us who want to spatialize sound. The problem, however, is that we still only have an anechoic simulation. If you've ever spent time in an anechoic chamber, or any other extremely dry space, you know it's an awful place to try to localize sounds, especially when you try to distinguish sounds coming from the front from sounds coming from the back.

Other psychoacousticians have shown that you can't provide distance cues in an anechoic chamber. Unless you can move around, or the sound source can move around, no information in a single sound waveform can pass through the space and arrive at your head in a way that lets you judge its distance from you—unless the sound source is really close to your head. People in actual rooms can determine distance, even when they're not familiar with the room. If you give them time to familiarize themselves with the room's acoustics, they can easily determine how far from them various sound sources are located.

Another challenge of spatial audio via headphones concerns "externalization." Occasionally you present sound signals over headphones, and they're heading down the listener's ear canals, yet the listener reports that the sound seems to be coming from inside their head. This tends to happen more often when the listener listens with someone's ears other than their own [*see previous section for explanation*]. The sound does seem to move around, but always inside or near the head. It's difficult to create a sound image that's well outside the head when you're dealing with an anechoic simulation.

When you're producing a simulation of this type, if you don't provide distance cues, you can't create true "3-D" audio. To treat spatial audio as a 3-D process, you must include distance. That's why a simulated world must include a "reflection model" or "reverberation model": When you send sound over loudspeakers, you hear sound reflections; sometimes the reflections are part of the recorded track, but they're also always part of your listening environment—the sounds from the speakers reflect off walls, furniture, and other objects. That's why it's vastly simpler to deal with headphone presentation when you're working with 3-D sound.

The way we provide distance cues with the Convolvotron is by computing and presenting reverberation models. Our reverb models consist of three parts: the direct path from a sound source, the sound's early reflections (the first reflections from nearby surfaces), and the sound's late reflections, what we call the "tail," in which soundwaves rattle around and are largely diffuse.

anechoic: Without echo; an anechoic environment is one where little or no sound is reflected. An anechoic chamber or room is designed to absorb all sound within it, thus preventing sound reflections or reverberation.

In the computer that hosts the Convolvotron, we created an image model in which we dealt with each reflector or "scatterer" in the simulation—each wall of a computer-generated, virtual room, for example. We reflect a sound source in the room to the other side of that wall and let it radiate into the room, resulting in a "propagation delay" for the new path length, a spreading loss of energy, and an appropriate "directional transfer function" for that image as well as the direct path. We do the same for other walls, the floor, and the ceiling. We know that the floor reflection is extremely important, as are the first few lateral reflections. We've been refining these image models in an attempt to create a more realistic 3-D effect and to help us investigate these issues in a systematic way, using a computer program so we don't have to work in anechoic chambers.

If we can understand the ways in which the human head affects our ability to determine the locations of sounds, then we can implement those characteristics to simulate a series of direct sound paths and reflections, including reflection characteristic models for walls, with the goal of creating a complete virtual environment. Unfortunately, doing that properly requires lots of signal processing power. You just can't cut corners on a head-related transfer function simulation. It's takes 30 to 50 **MIPS** for each sound source image. To simulate many walls and sources, you need heavy-duty signal processing power; for example, the computation of an environment model containing six walls and four sound sources requires about a billion computer operations per second.

Nevertheless, we continue to build monstrous signal processing systems, and use them to study the 3-D sound situation. Perhaps in a few years we'll study how to cut corners without destroying the efficiency and quality of the auditory display.

MIPS: Acronym for "millions of instructions per second," a common measurement of data-processing capability; the more MIPS, the more computer horsepower.

SOUND LOCALIZATION & SPATIAL ENHANCEMENT WITH THE ROLAND SOUND SPACE SYSTEM

Here Curtis Chan outlines the basics of sound localization theory and transaural processing, relating them to the development of the Roland Sound Space (RSS) processing system, the first commercially available sound localization and enhancement system to let recording engineers move sounds in space. He describes uses for sound localization systems and presents some observations from RSS field tests. The RSS System, which was developed specifically for professional, high-end audio applications, retails for about $22,000.

BY CURTIS CHAN

When Michael Jackson's album, Dangerous, came out in late 1991, it featured 3-D effects conjured up by Michael and engineer/co-producer Bruce Swedien on the Roland Sound Space (RSS) system. This unique sound localization system was introduced by the Japan-based music technology company, RolandCorp., in 1991. At the time of the RSS introduction, Curtis Chan was general manager of RolandCorp. U.S.'s Pro Audio/Video Group, where he oversaw new product planning, sales, and marketing. Before joining Roland, Curtis worked for Ampex and Sony, where he managed product development and the marketing of digital audio and digital video technologies. He recently formed his own company to offer consulting services for the audio, video, multimedia, and data storage industries.

SOUND ENTERS THE THIRD DIMENSION **95** **CYBERARTS**

Within the last half-century, stereo reproduction has been concerned primarily with re-creating an approximation of the sound pressures and timing differences of different sound sources with respect to their original or manipulated positions when they reach the listener's ears. In standard two-speaker systems, stereo reproduction techniques offer good frontal horizontal plane-imaging. However, they don't attempt to re-create impressions of "sound localization," impressions that sounds move from front to back or up and down, which spatially enhances the audio information.

Over the last three decades, researchers have extensively studied the psychological and psychoacoustic models of directional and spatial perception. These studies, in part, culminated in the development of sound localization and enhancement processing systems. As a result, it was possible to create a sound localization encoding system capable of localizing sound and expanding the aural soundfield reproduced by a pair of equidistant loudspeakers. The advent and integration of digital signal processing and **VLSI** technology allowed RolandCorp. to develop and manufacture the Roland Sound Space processor, which reproduces sounds in a way that paints an infinitely adjustable, sonic "**hologram**." It lets you create a "soundscape" consisting of image width, depth, and height, well beyond the boundaries of the speakers. The recording artist or engineer can control all these parameters in real time, and reproduce the results on two speakers on a normal stereo system. The RSS doesn't require special decoding equipment and is compatible with any stereo playback equipment or medium as well as stereo or mono program transmission sources, such as FM and AM radio broadcast.

Auditory Fundamentals

Psychoacoustic research has determined that the localization of sound is based upon four primary phenomena:

1. Interaural time difference: the difference in a sound's arrival time between the listener's two ears;

2. Interaural intensity difference: the difference in the sound's volume between the ears;

3. Pinna effects, which result from **phase** shifts and **timbral** changes caused by soundwave reflections in the outer ear; and

4. Head shadowing, a phenomenon dependent upon where a sound emanates from around the listener and the different paths it must follow, moving around the head and shoulders, to reach the listener's two ears, resulting in perceived volume and arrival time differences. In addition, the listener's outer ears and head will cause different soundwave reflections, refraction, and absorption effects to occur in relation to the sound's spectral content and angle of incidence.

The soundwaves reaching the listener's ears are affected by sound source propagations within the listening environment and the propagation system created by the reflection, diffraction, and resonance effects generated by the listener's head, ears, and shoulders—

phase: Relative position of two soundwaves with respect to one another, usually measured in degrees.

timbre: Distinguishing sound quality; pronounced "tam-bur."

VLSI: Very Large-Scale Integration, a manufacturing and design process that allows great quantities of electronic components to fit on a single, quarter-inch square chip.

hologram: A three-dimensional image, created via photographic techniques, that can be seen without any special viewing device.

this overall effect is the head-related transfer function.

Stereo Recording & Reproduction

For many years, engineers have been working to improve recording techniques and playback hardware to achieve more realistic sound reproduction. "Surround sound" and "Quadrophonic" represent two attempts. However, despite best efforts, two-channel (stereo) recording (and two-channel playback) are still the standard. Sound engineers use two basic types of recording techniques to reproduce two-channel sound: the *multi-microphone* and *one-point stereo* recording techniques.

In the multi-microphone technique, each instrument or sound source is recorded with its own microphone (or with two or more microphones). The outputs of the microphones are fed to a mixing console, where the relative volume of each instrument is controlled by the recording engineer—primarily by manipulating each channel's **panning** and "left speaker" and "right speaker" level controls to determine the positioning of sound sources in the mix. Coincident microphones produce only level differences. In some "concert hall" type of applications, spaced microphone techniques often are used to produce time and level differences between the left and right channels (in other words, a microphone feeding the left channel might be placed closer to an instrument than the microphone that's feeding the right channel). Psychoacoustically, we identify those signals as offering a sense of acoustic spaciousness.

Research also has shown that spaced microphones can result in summed (left+right channel) signals reaching the ears that are completely contradictory in the directional clue given by the *precedence effect* (perceived sound direction is dependent upon the signal which is advanced in time, relative to the other signal) and by the summed sound pressure upon the ears. Thus, listeners mistake the resulting "phasiness" as "spaciousness." Unfortunately, crosstalk artifacts (cross transmissions of left-channel sound reaching the right ear, and right-channel sound reaching the left ear) result in an increase in interaural correlation on top of that already perceived from the speakers. The net result is that the spacious effect is perceived to be confined to an acoustic soundscape existing only between the two speakers.

The *one-point stereo* technique uses two similar microphones placed closely together, several meters from the sound source. The outputs of the two microphones are then combined in a matrix system to form the left-and right-channel signals. One-point stereo recording is used mainly for recording orchestras, chamber groups, and vocal ensembles (usually in a naturally reverberant space). Sounds recorded in this way have a great sense of "presence." This recording method is used rarely on its own these days, but is often used in conjunction with the multi-microphone technique.

Subjective tests performed by psychoacoustic researchers found that many listeners preferred sounds reproduced by near-coincident pairs. These slightly spaced or near-coincident microphone techniques offer a pleasing compromise to the other techniques. The microphones

panning: The placement of a sound signal within a stereo perspective (left, right, center, and anywhere in between).

are close enough together to give moderately good imaging due to the level differences and do not have excessive **low-frequency** phase differences. They also exhibit an element of precedence effect and introduce a degree of decorrelation between the channels that supports the listener's perception of spaciousness in the reproduced sound.

Binaural Recording & Reproduction

A logical extension of the one-point stereo recording technique is the binaural recording technique, using an artificial head fitted with microphones in the dummy's ears. Typical dummy heads simulate the "shadowing effect" of the head on high-frequency signals, as well as the timing differences between the ears. Many newer dummy heads also simulate the effects of the outer ears, which are important for accurate front-back and up-down perception. It is critical that the playback systems do not double these effects by introducing them both in the recording process through the dummy's outer ears and on playback through the listener's outer ears. This is dependent upon the microphone placement inside the dummy head, the type of headphones used by the listener, and how much those headphones obstruct the listener's pinnae.

Although binaural recording does a good job of reproducing the ambience associated with the original soundfield, one common malady as a result of the outer ears being obstructed by headphones is the listener's inability to perceive forward sound localization. This problem is caused by the disturbance to the *conch* resonances of the outer ear. The "conch" is the principal cavity in the pinna, and its resonance affects the way sounds are heard. Headphones disturb this resonance so some form of sound processing is needed to restore natural hearing. Research also shows that a significant part of the resonance effect varies with the sound direction, necessitating a direction-assignment to the sound signal processing. This processing must be an integral part of the headphone design, and cannot be accomplished by the recording engineer in the studio with a mixing console or special effects device.

Although most binaural recordings played over headphones work well, they are less convincing when played over loudspeakers. However, by processing the binaural signals through a filter that can flatten the transfer function of the front direction, satisfactory playback through loudspeakers can be attained with results similar to that obtained through the one-point stereo recording technique.

This digital filter implementation is part of Roland Sound Space system. The RSS system allows binaural signals to be processed and played back through loudspeakers by the cancellation of crosstalk (left signals reaching right ear, and vice versa). Multi-microphone signals also can be processed and localized in real time through the RSS to create a sonic hologram that differs from conventional mixing techniques. This process is called transaural processing and it results in "transaural stereo" played back through a pair of loudspeakers.

Transaural Stereo & The RSS System

Conventional stereo assumes that the end point of the recording and reproduction chain are the sound source drivers (the instruments that make the sounds). Transaural stereo, similar in concept to binaural stereo, takes the end point of the recording and reproduction chain to be the actual sounds at the listener's ears. It differs from binaural stereo in that structured composite signals are output to loudspeakers, rather than direct signals supplied via headphones to the ears. The composite signal structure consists of the left and right audio components minus the left-to-right and right-to-left crosstalk components, which have been filtered via the RSS transaural processor.

The RSS system processes the sound recorded with the multi-microphone technique and allows the recording engineer to create a full "sound space." By processing signals recorded via the binaural technique with the transaural processor, the sound is heard as if it were recorded with the one-point stereo method.

Basically, the RSS system works by processing the input signal through a binaural and transaural digital filter system that represents the head-related transfer function, which is determined by the direction from the listener relative to the sound source and the direction from the listener relative to each of the two speakers. To accomplish this, during our prototyping stage we constructed a head-related transfer function measuring system. In this system we measured a human listener's aural responses to sounds played from a compact disc. We collected these responses by locating two small microphones by the listener's

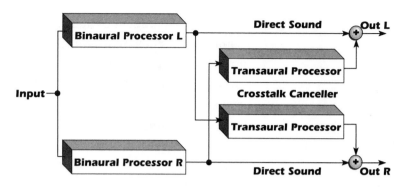

RSS system diagram

ears, each microphone placed about 5mm from each external ear canal. We recorded and analyzed the output from the speakers, the time difference for a signal to reach the left and right ears, and the distance gap of the measuring moment.

The RSS System consists of two processors, one binaural and one transaural. The binaural processor places input signals to a desired direction, similar to what can be obtained through binaural recording. The transaural processor works at playback with two speakers to cancel the crosstalk signal from the left speaker to the right ear and from the right speaker to the left ear.

The prototype hardware consisted of several digital signal processors ("DSPs") and an NEC PC-9801 personal computer that controlled the DSPs and the **A/D-D/A** unit. The **sampling** frequency was set to 44.1kHz (compact disc-quality), and there are four **channels** for processing. The floppy disk in the computer contained the data regarding the head-related transfer function, which was transferred, along with data relating to the sounds' direction, to the DSP. Direction input was accomplished via computer mouse control: A graphic representation of the soundfield was displayed on the

A/D-D/A: Analog-to-Digital & Digital-to-Analog convertors, electronic devices. The A/D portion converts analog electrical signals to digital values whose numbers represent the level and frequency information contained in the original analog signal. The digital signal then can be manipulated by the computer-based processing system. The D/A portion converts the digital numbers representing level and frequency information back to a continuously varying analog electrical signal. The analog signal then can be output as sound from a loudspeaker or headphones.

sampling: The process of digitally recording any type of sound.

channel: A single audio signal path. Generally, each channel carries a different signal. Not to be confused with "track," which refers to a path on magnetic tape that contains a single channel of audio information.

44.1 kHz and **48kHz:**
Refers to a primary factor
that affects the quality of
sampled sound: the sam-
pling rate, or how often
a measurement of level is
made. "48kHz" equals
48,000 samples per second.

24-bit: Refers to a primary
factor that affects the quality of sampled sound: the
resolution with which the
signal levels are measured,
expressed as the number of
"bits" in the digital word
that is stored. The greater
the number of bits, the
higher the sound quality.
The sampling rate of most
computer sound systems is
8-bit or 16-bit.

AES/EBU: Refers to the
Audio Engineering Society
and European Broadcasting
Union, international stan-
dards-setting organizations.

MIDI: Musical Instrument
Digital Interface.

**Roland Sound Space
Processor**

computer screen, and the engineer used the mouse to click on a point for the desired sound position.

Our objective was to develop a sound localization system that met profession-al audio standards and yet was capable of being moved without undue hardship. This meant extensive use of DSP and VLSI integration. The packaging and design objectives were to design a system that would be intuitively and ergonomically functional, able to withstand shock from shipping, reliable, flexible in operation, and offering high sound quality. The system al-so had to be designed so we could man-ufacture it easily.

Our efforts culminated in the de-velopment of the RSS system. It con-sists of the Sound Space Processor, two A-D/D-A units, and the Sound Space Controller. It incorporates **24-bit** inter-nal processing circuits, and the processor can handle four channels simultaneous-ly. Input to the Processor is accomplished via digital connection that conforms to the **AES/EBU** data format. When connected to the A-D/D-A units, the system also can accommodate analog inputs and outputs.

All input/output connections are made via standard 3-pin connectors. Each A/D-to-D/A unit accommodates two input chan-nels and four output channels, so, for every input, you get two (left and right) signals coming out.

To ensure high sound quality, the two-channel A/D converter achieves 18-bit processing, while the four-channel D/A converter uses 20-bit processing. In order for the unit to work in both the professional and CD standard, the A/D converter is selectable between **44.1kHz** and **48kHz**.

The Sound Space Controller provides four sets of rotary dial controls for azimuth (left, right, front, back) and elevation (left, right, top, bottom) for controlling sound placement for four separate chan-nels—it allows the simultaneous con-trol of up to 64 individual sound sources. By rotating the dials on the Controller, the engineer can place sounds within a 360-degree horizontal radius and give the user control over the vertical elevation. The combined settings of these dials de-termine the placement of the associat-ed sound. The Controller also allows linking of channels, so you can use one dial to move a stereo image. The system operates in real time, so the engineer can hear the results immediately. As **MIDI**-based equipment is so prevalent in varied professional audio applications, the RSS system can output and receive MIDI information, so the system can be controlled via MIDI.

Since we envisioned that film sound engineers and high-end music produc-tions would use the RSS to localize sounds in more than four channels, the system allows up to 15 additional units to be connected and controlled by one Controller.

Sound Creation Using the RSS System

Before and after we introduced the RSS, we conducted field tests to determine its strengths and limits. We brought it into professional music recording, film, and video facilities to be used on actual working projects. This helped us better evaluate the system under real-life situations.

We found that there are no problems when mixing RSS-processed signals with "normal" signals. In fact, depending on the application, mixing both RSS-processed signals with unprocessed signals allows for greater creativity and flexibility in the arrangement of the composite sounds. It also was found that processing RSS signals through signal processing equipment such as equalizers and reverbs did not affect the perception of sound localization. However, we determined that engineers must process the individual channels in a consistent manner.

We also learned that the RSS system holds up well during data **compression**, and used a "blind" listening test to determine that the listener could not discern any sonic differences concerning the localization effects between compressed and uncompressed signals. We also successfully aired TV and radio program material processed through RSS. In our initial investigations, there were no discernable artifacts noticed when listening to the off-air results. The same program also was duplicated on video cassette and replayed back on a stereo S-VHS deck with no degradation to the localization ef-

fects. However, mixing engineers are cautioned to use the sound localization controls judiciously, as extreme settings might result in compatibility with AM mono broadcasting systems (that is, the 3-D processing might result in loss of some portions of the sound when listened to through a mono system). As a precaution, studio engineers should routinely test for mono compatibility while mixing. One such test on the recording of a pop song involved the localizing of multiple sounds in which the chorus and background vocals were made to "wrap" around the main singer, with the stereo image spread beyond the speaker boundaries. In this case, careful use of the RSS, combined with monitoring of the mono mix, avoided the possibility of lower-level sounds being "lost" in the background when the stereo mix was collapsed to mono.

The stability and valid range for placement of sound in the 360-degree soundfield vary, depending on the spectral density of the sound. We found that the impression of placement of sounds is more believable with sounds that cover a wide frequency spectrum. In this event, most natural and electronic instrument sounds could be placed easily.

In film and video soundtrack production, we found that sounds can be layered together in a similar manner to video **compositing**, in which one builds multiple layers of sound. Each layer (track) has its own unique composition and placement of sounds. These individual layers are mixed on the console and output through the speakers. Reverbs can be used to help process the RSS sounds to add a sense of depth. An engineer also can

compression: The translation of data to a more compact form for storage or transmission.

compositing: The mixing of multiple layers of images into one image.

add realistic ambience to the soundfield beyond the speaker boundaries, and can use a reverb to dynamically control a realistic, expanded stereo image. This is accomplished by inputting the reverbed ambience background signals from the mixing console to the inputs of the RSS system, while also leaving the unprocessed signals in the normal stereo mix. In one RSS application, the azimuth dials on the RSS Controller were set to the 4 o'clock and 8 o'clock positions. This resulted in having the normal reverb signals in the main mix, and the RSS-processed signals outside in the normal mix. Then a dynamic impression of "acoustic depth" can be attained by adding sound delay (15-50 milliseconds) to the reverb signal, adjusting the azimuth dials and mixing the relative levels of the two signal returns via their respective channel faders on the mixing console.

After many experiments, we found that vertical motion of sounds is difficult to discern. Some sounds were placed easily using the elevation control, and seem more "believable" because of the type of sound. It also is plausible that we can relate psychologically to sound impressions that we associate with vertical movement; for example, it is more believable to hear the sound of a bird chirping and relate that to a vertical movement rather than to try to imagine a piano flying overhead.

Another limitation concerns the ability to control distance or depth of the soundfield without having to use additional peripheral devices such as delay lines and reverbs. Good natural results can be obtained when using the RSS-processed

signals in conjunction with reverb and delay devices.

Another area requiring improvement is the listening position. The optional listening position is set on a bisector that connects the two speakers each at a 60-degree angle from the listener. We also tested the RSS-processed signals with various stereo reproduction devices. We were surprised to learn that we attained good results from systems ranging from expensive recording studio monitors to portable stereo tape players. The sound localization is very good along the bisector that is equidistant from the speakers moving in a forward or backward position. As you move away from the bisector, however, the sound localization effect diminishes. Nonetheless, when compared to normal recordings, a greater sense of spaciousness is achieved with the RSS-processed sounds, even though the localization effect is lost. These results are best achieved in a somewhat reverberant listening environment, such as a listening room, studio, or typical household where there are both reflective and absorptive surfaces. We found listeners cannot easily hear the RSS-processed signals in a very echoic ("live") room.

Where To Use The RSS System

The RSS system lends itself to any application that can benefit from sound localization and spatial enhancement. Some possible applications include:

• music recording, to give the artist, producer, and engineer another layer of creativity in which to create a sonic hologram in which to envelop the listener;

• audio for video and film soundtracks,

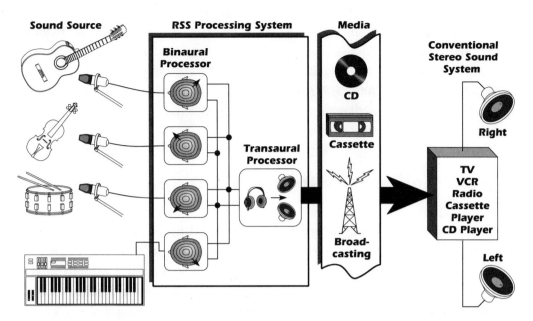

Sound Source

RSS Processing System

Binaural Processor

Transaural Processor

Media

CD

Cassette

Broadcasting

Conventional Stereo Sound System

Right

TV VCR Radio Cassette Player CD Player

Left

to integrate an extra level of sound effects generation into the production to distinguish and dramatically enhance it (dramas might use sound localization for background effects, while educational programs might use RSS to help focus on specific subject matters or points of interest), and to add acoustic depth and width to the musical score;

• AM/FM stereo and TV broadcasts;

• live sound events (concerts, recitals, multimedia presentations, etc.);

• theme-park rides and entertainment, in which localized sound effects can be coordinated with special video effects to add realism to the scene;

• flight cockpit simulation, to help pilots learn to fly complex systems using localized sound cues;

• in-flight headphone entertainment for airlines, in which localization impressions are maximized since the sound reproduction is via headset; and

• video and interactive games.

The study of sound localization through binaural and transaural processing and the field of psychoacoustics will continue to develop. Every year, new theories and practices lead to further refinements and progress in our understanding of sound localization and spatial enhancement technologies.

The development of the RSS System greatly owes to the recent progress in VLSI and DSP technology. The continued improvement of these signal processing technologies means that it will become possible in the near future for the RSS process to be an integral part of other products, such as mixing consoles. We hope this type of system provides incentive for people to be more creative in their audio mixing. We also hope that the benefits derived from transaural recording techniques and sound localization will dramatically change the way that people listen to "stereo."

The creative options and enhanced realism provided by this sound localization controller and other similar devices make their introduction as historically important as the development of stereo itself.

If you'd like to see the originally published technical paper with Roland's HRTF derivations and mathematical equations, contact the Audio Engineering Society in New York City and request the report, "Sound Localization & Spatial Enhancement, Realization of the Roland Sound Space Processor," presented at the 1991 AES Conference.

Virtual Audio: New Uses for 3-D Sound

"Virtual": being something in effect, although not so in name; for all practical purposes; actual; real

"Audio": of hearing; of sound

"Virtual Audio": a recorded sound experience that contains significant psychoacoustic information to alter human perception into believing that the recorded sound experience is actually occurring in reality.

By Christopher Currell

Christopher Currell is a composer, musician, and producer who spent nearly three years recording and performing with Michael Jackson on the "Bad" album and tour. Chris now explores high-end interactive technology via his Los Angeles-based company, Audio Cybernetics, developers of the Virtual Audio 3-D sound system. Working in conjunction with Germany's Head Acoustics, Chris has developed several system prototypes. The music recording industry serves as breeding ground for Virtual Audio; the first commercial U.S. releases to implement Virtual Audio were Connie Champagne's La Strada *(Heyday Records, 1991), D'Cückoo's release,* D'CüCKOO, *(D'Kayla, 1992), and Slamming Gladys (Private Rocks, 1992). Chris plans to bring Virtual Audio to the areas of virtual reality and communications and to put Virtual Audio on a $500 chip for use in video games and digital musical instruments. In the meantime, he continues to record and produce music.*

Educating people on the subject of 3-D sound is vital. Although this technology is not new, until recently the 3-D sound process was presented as a mysterious "black box." It's time for a change—for the benefit of people who want to use it for creative purposes. After all, we wouldn't hear much recorded music if studio tape recorders were mysterious "black boxes" that engineers didn't know how to operate. Today, most recording artists want 3-D sound but they can't imagine how that might translate to their own projects. That's why we need to spread the word about what "3-D sound" can—and cannot—do.

"Virtual Audio" is a new, advanced technology. The Virtual Audio Processing System is a digital signal processing computer that reproduces 3-D sound over headphones and loudspeakers. It also creates "Virtual Audio environments" in real time. The system also includes an advanced, artificial, binaural recording head. I've found that both the binaural recording-head approach and the computer-processing approach suit specific applications, so we need to combine the two types of technologies, depending on the desired results.

We use the artificial head primarily in situations where you'd use a regular microphone, such as in the studio to record guitar, piano, voice, and so on. The resulting clarity and direction of the sound sources are excellent; when you build a mix recorded with the artificial head, different sounds don't get "lost" in the mix because the tracks are in phase and correctly articulated for human hearing.

Many people would like to be able to give their already recorded, multitrack or two-track mixes some spatial qualities, or "move" things around in the mix. The Virtual Audio Processing System allows this, so they don't have to re-record their tracks with the artificial head. In fact, most of the practical applications of Virtual Audio will incorporate the computer technology. Additionally, the computer system is necessary to create room simulations with proximity effects ("proximity" refers to a sound's distance from the ear).

We're currently researching different levels of 3-D sound processing, in terms of real-world applications. On one level we have the artificial recording head. You can take it anywhere or use it in the recording studio, similar to the way you use a microphone. To find out where to place the artificial head to capture the best Virtual Audio effect, you simply walk around the recording environment and *listen carefully*; wherever it sounds best, that's where you place the head, and that's how the resulting recording will sound through headphones. Speaker playback is also greatly improved with this method. However, with two speakers the sound will not "wrap" around your head, although with four speakers (each pair carrying

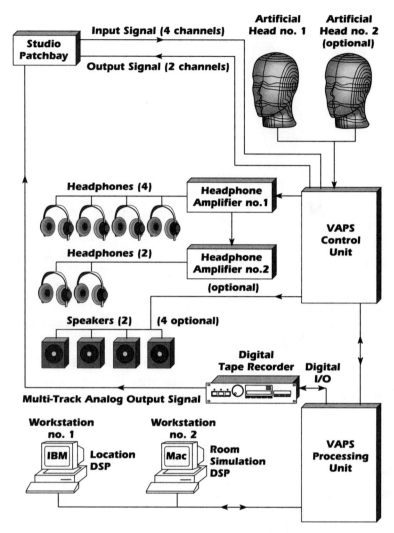

the same left and right signal information), a headphone-type surround-sound experience can be achieved.

On the next level we have the computer system. In the most basic type of Virtual Audio processing, we can run a two-track mix through our hardware and software, which lets us process the sounds of the pre-recorded tracks with spatial imaging. We generally use four channels of processing for a two-channel mix. We have found through many tests that good results are achieved if we locate the stereo channels at approximately 306 degrees

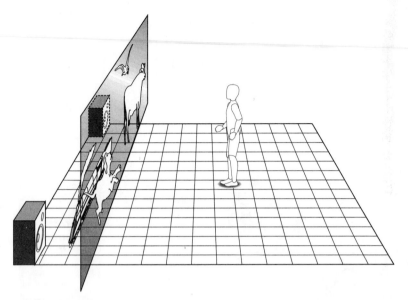

Conventional audio creates a flat, "two-dimensional" sound field.

Virtual audio creates a "three-dimensional" environment.

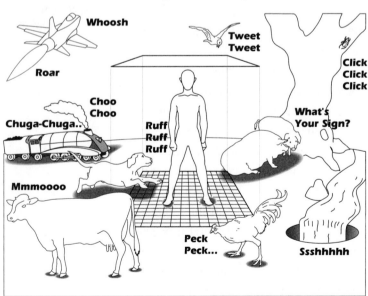

for the left channel and 54 degrees for the right channel on the horizontal axis. We can position the channels in any direction, depending on how "wide" we want the image to be. For the "rear," we can position the same stereo channels to approximately 106 degrees for the right rear channel and 254 degrees for the left rear channel. We then apply delays on the rear channels and raise or lower their levels. On headphones, this procedure simulates simple but realistic room reflections "behind" us and makes the music sound as if it exists in three-dimensional "space."

On headphones we can achieve a complete 360-degree soundfield, because the left and right channels are discrete. With two loudspeakers, we achieve a natural, expanded soundfield that is positioned far past the confines of the speakers. The two-track Virtual Audio process can widen the image to the left and to the right, extending it past the speakers. If, for example, your recording includes the sound effect of a car driving by, the sound starts way beyond one speaker and travels way beyond the other speaker. If the recording has airplane or helicopter sound effects, they seem to come from above the speakers. From a head-on position in front of the speakers, you sense a definite increase in the depth of the music space: Things appear to jump out, depending on the acoustics of your speakers and the room.

One thing we must understand, however, is that to achieve any kind of 3-D effect on two loudspeakers, we must deal with room acoustics and the physical characteristics of the speakers themselves. If we're waiting for a magic box that creates amazing 360-degree sound through two speakers, we'll wait forever because of the laws of physics—unless we want to build and provide a custom recording studio along with every record or CD. Thus, what we're trying to achieve with the Virtual Audio process is *optimization* of speaker playback.

In addition, the success of a Virtual Audio-processed, two-track mix depends on the quality of the original production.

If the effects in a film soundtrack, for example, are clean and they pan well (move from left to right), and something called "taste" is used in the production, the Virtual Audio mix process places those sounds in a logical space and the result is quite good. On headphones, the process removes that annoying sound-in-the-middle-of-my-head phenomenon.

The next step in Virtual Audio processing involves multitrack mixing, in which we process each individual track and give it room simulation. In other words, we create "walls," and we control each wall: We can place that wall anywhere in the simulated room. The sound source then can move around within the simulated, 360-degree space. This Virtual Audio environment and the reaction of the sound reflections within it provide for realistic effects. The multitrack method, in fact, gives the most impressive results.

In most contemporary recording projects, people tend to use effects and reverbs in a surreal manner, in the sense that they don't necessarily relate to "reality." With Virtual Audio processing of a recording, we can achieve some unusual effects when all those reverberant fields occur within 360 degrees.

Mixing music in this way requires a new way of thinking, because the creative potential is limitless. When we think about the possibilities for advanced Virtual Audio recording, we must consider what kind of spaces we want, and what kind of effects or impression we want to create on the listener. For instance, we can make a studio recording of a band sound as if we recorded it live, in concert. We can "build," or simulate, a huge hall, then

play back the recorded music in that room and it will sound as if the music was originally recorded live in a room that size. We also can combine artificial head recording and computer processing. We can use the artificial head to record an outdoor environment. Then, back in the studio, we mix in prerecorded sound effects, directionalize them, and create a similar space around them. The room simulation achieves interactive reflections. We then put the directionalized and room-simulated sound effects inside the prerecorded artificial-head space, and mix the whole thing down to two-track for stereo.

Virtual Audio Systems is now working on the computer-human interface, to help the recording engineer easily and quickly manipulate all these parameters. We're building a 48-channel Virtual Audio processing machine that will allow mixing automation and mixing of Virtual Audio in real time, easily and quickly.

When you mix the sound for a scene in a film or television show, you could give each scene a different ambience by creating a different three-dimensional space, or environment, for every scene. This causes the atmosphere to change throughout the film, even if only on a subtle level, which is emotionally effective for people watching the finished film.

In the future, we also need to easily change points of view in the Virtual Audio environment. When you use a computer program for 3-D graphics modeling, you can render the object (give it realistic attributes such as texture, shading, and lighting) for every different position; you can view an object, for example, from behind, then from below. We need to achieve the same effect with audio. If we switch the camera work in a scene to a shot from above, all the sound imaging must move accordingly, including the change in sound reflections. It has to be easy and quick to do, so the recording engineers and producers can stay in creative mode, not in techno-mode.

Thanks to all the current research, in the near future everyone will be able to use this new technology. Today, at the high-quality level, it's very expensive to use, because of the amount of number-crunching necessary to render the head model and room simulations. At Virtual Audio Systems, we believe the first cost-effective step for artists and producers to use Virtual Audio will be through leasing time on the system for their projects. For example, the 48-channel processor is a supercomputer that will cost over a million dollars. This isn't a practical investment for home media enthusiasts who want to give their audio material some spatial qualities. At first, only professionals in the recording industry will be able to afford to use the 48-channel processor. In the meantime, our company is working on cost-effective methods to get Virtual Audio into the hands of everyone interested in recording with it.

Eventually, when digital signal processing power goes up and its cost comes down, the Virtual Audio Processing System can reside on a single chip that will let us use joysticks or piano-like keyboards so we can fly sounds around in a 360-degree field.

May audio never be the same!

SOUND DESIGN FOR COMPUTER SOFTWARE

BY TOM RETTIG

Tom Rettig is the sound design manager for Broderbund Software, Inc., a publisher of personal-computer software for entertainment, education, and productivity. He has created music and sound effects for many of their award-winning products, including the famous "Carmen Sandiego" series. He also directs Broderbund's technical development of audio and works closely with manufacturers of sound hardware for personal computers.

square waves: A "wave" (waveform) is a visual representation of a synthesized (electronically created) sound; a computer's square wave is associated with a buzzing sound.

DAC (digital-to-analog converter): Converts digital data to analog electrical signals that can be output over loudspeakers or headphones.

CD-ROM: Compact Disc-Read-Only Memory. Introduced in 1985, CD-ROM stores vast amounts of data (up to around 600 megabytes of words, sounds, and images) in digital format on a compact disc, like the ones used for music. A CD-ROM is "read" by a CD-ROM drive, which is a peripheral device attached to a desktop computer.

Windows: Windows 3.0 is a graphical user interface for the DOS operating system produced by Microsoft. Developed in 1981 by Microsoft Corp., DOS (Disk Operating System, sometimes called "MS-DOS") is the standard operating system for IBM PCs. The operating system is the software that controls the computer's hardware, manages program operation, and handles data flow to and from peripherals and storage devices.

The first PC, introduced by IBM in 1981, emitted one sound: a cold little "beep" that let you know you completed an operation or made a mistake. Today's PCs emanate the sounds of a Baroque orchestra or a Florida swamp, and audio has become an integral component of the computing environment. This chapter discusses the use of sound in personal computer software, considerations for sound design for current computer hardware, and the balance of technical and aesthetic considerations.

When the first IBM PCs came out, the only sounds they could generate consisted of **square waves**. They didn't even provide volume control. PC users are familiar with the beep tone that's used to alert you, usually to some error condition. Early computer game developers pushed the capabilities of these machines, using the beep tones to play simple tunes.

When the Apple Macintosh debuted in 1984, it was the first personal computer that came standard with a **DAC**, a digital-to-analog converter, for playing digitized sound, thus creating a relatively sophisticated sound environment on a personal computer. With its built-in sound capabilities and growing **CD-ROM** support, the Macintosh is no stranger to sound-laden software.

In late 1990, Microsoft Corporation announced the Multimedia PC (MPC) standard in conjunction with ten other computer companies, including Tandy, AT&T, Fujitsu, NEC Technologies, Olivetti, and Zenith Data Systems. The MPC's main components are a CD-ROM drive, sound card (or "sound board," an expansion board placed inside the PC to improve the quality of the PC's sound output), and the **Windows** 3.0 operating system with multimedia extensions. MPC computers and upgrade kits started shipping a year later, providing PC fans with a means

sample: A brief recording of sound. A sampler is a device that records sounds directly, stores them as digital data, and plays the sounds when triggered. The term "sampling rate" refers to how often the analog-to-digital converter analyzes (samples) the incoming analog signal and assigns a number to it. The faster the rate, the better the system can represent the sounds. Standard CD-quality sampling rate is 44.1kHz, which means 44,100 samples per second.

11K: "K" refers to "kilobyte," the standard measure of data used with computer memory. It equals 1,024 bytes. It's easy to confuse this "K" with the lower-case "k" in "kHz," which usually stands for "kilohertz," the standard measure used to indicate how many times an audio signal vibrates per second. One kilohertz is equal to 1,000 vibrations, or "cycles," of sound per second.

to hear lush music and sounds coming from their computers. The software product must support the PC's sound board, however, before it can benefit from the board's improved sound quality.

Today, scores of companies market hardware and software systems for composing, arranging, producing, and recording studio-quality sounds and music on every kind of desktop computer. Software developers are taking full advantage of these systems to enhance and support the visual content of their products.

Types of Sound Data

For a computer to handle sound, the sound must be *digitized*, or transformed into a digital recording. "Digital recording" refers to the process of converting sound into numerical data. The sound first travels through an analog-to-digital converter, which analyzes the audio signal and converts it into the binary format (consisting of a series of 1's and 0's) that the computer understands. This data typically is stored on the computer's hard drive. Upon playback, the numbers travel through a digital-to-analog converter for transformation into an analog electrical signal, which is the format "understood" by audio amplifiers and speakers.

The data format for sound in computer software is typically "8-bit." This refers to the system's ability to provide 256 levels of amplitude resolution, or how many different numbers are available to represent the original analog signal. Eight-bit sound systems are the most popular for digitizing sound on computers.

The quality of the digitized sound can range from monophonic, AM-radio quality (8-bit audio **sampled** directly into the system at 7, 11, or 22kHz) to stereo, compact disc quality (16-bit audio at 44.1kHz). Digitizing sound results in the most realistic audio, which is important for voice and sound effects. However, this method is data-intensive: Each *second* of sound takes from **11K** to 22K bytes of disk space. The higher the quality, the more computer memory and processing speed are required.

Sound synthesis—creating the sound electronically, as opposed to recording "real" sounds—offers a means for providing sound at lower data rates, but you can't replicate certain sounds, particularly speech. Synthesis is, however, ideal for music.

The most common format for synthesizing music involves MIDI files, which people sometimes confuse with MIDI, the musical instrument digital interface that allows computers and digital musical instruments to communicate. Software developers use "standard MIDI files" to trigger musical sequences to play from a MIDI-equipped synthesizer or sound module.

The MIDI file contains not an actual sound recording, but instructions that are sent to the MIDI instrument, so the MIDI file doesn't take up much space. In DOS/Windows machines, the "instrument" is provided by the synthesizer hardware contained on the sound cards. The data in the MIDI file tell these instruments what sounds to play, at what speed, and when to play them.

One complicated data-management issue relates to "instrument definition" data, because you have to create unique instrument-definition data for each individual synthesizer supported by various personal computers. Let's say we use a certain kind of synthesizer to create bass, piano, and guitar sounds for the musical score. We ultimately must "map" those instruments to other synth environments: I play the score back on different sound cards, and create the instrument definition data for each particular type of sound card. This means that the score will sound pretty much the same from sound card to sound card.

A part of the MIDI specification known as "General MIDI" simplifies this process. General MIDI provides a means by which all kinds of synthesizers can use a common instrument "palette." In theory, no matter what type of General MIDI instrument you use, the guitar, or bass, or piano should sound the same.

In the DOS/Windows world, sound cards support digitized sounds and MIDI data, similar to the way a computer's video card lets the system display text and images. In the Macintosh world, however, there is no built-in synthesis hardware. All sound in a Macintosh comes from its main **CPU**, which supports playback of standard, 8-bit digitized sounds. If we want to include higher-quality sounds, then our Mac software products must include a way to emulate sound synthesis. The MIDI files still contain the same notes and instructions, but we essentially build a sampling synthesizer right into the software product. This method is extremely processor-intensive, which means that running the software requires extra attention from the Mac's CPU. If we're using the CPU to handle animation, and al-

so want it to emulate a sound synthesizer, it must split its attention between graphics and music. This slows down overall performance.

Finally, when people create music for a software product that's going to be delivered on CD, they can use "Red Book audio." That's the industry jargon for the official Compact Disc Digital Audio Standard ("CD-DA"), introduced by Philips and Sony. The Red Book describes the technical specifications for creating audio CDs. It is the foundation on which all the other CD standards are built. As all audio CDs are manufactured according to Red Book specifications, all audio CDs play on any audio CD player.

This CD audio track standard is used for both music CDs and CD-ROM. Red Book audio offers excellent sound quality, but represents the most data-intensive approach to creating sound. Digitized sounds take up between 5K to 22K of disk-space per second; Red Book audio takes up 177K bytes per second. That's not reasonable for floppy disks, but on a CD Red Book audio can be useful. Unfortunately, current Red Book audio doesn't provide a means for synchronizing with graphics.

Current Hardware Platforms

When we design PC soundtracks and create musical arrangements for them, we design for the best possible hardware, then pare the soundtrack of its most elegant features to make it work—and sound good—in all other environments. This typically involves variations on the arrangement. When we "port" a product over to the Macintosh, we have to rearrange the music to work with its hardware. Our goal in creating

CPU: Central Processing Unit, the computer's fundamental chip, or "processor," which is used to process instructions.

operator: A term made popular by Yamaha's DX series of digital synthesizers to refer to a set of software operations essentially equivalent to the oscillators (sound-generators) in early analog synthesizers. The more operators, the more (and richer) sounds you can create.

FM synthesis: A technique in which frequency modulation (FM)—changes in a signal's frequency, or pitch—is used to create complex audio waveforms.

voice: The output of a single audio signal path. An instrument capable of playing several voices at once is called "polyphonic."

polyphonic: Capable of producing a number of independently moving notes (or "voices," or "pitch lines") at once. On a few polyphonic synths, all the keys can be sounded at once, but on most instruments only a limited number of voices (typically 4, 8, or 12) are available.

multi-timbral: Able to play several completely different instrument sounds—such as bass, piano, and guitar—at one time.

soundtracks is to exploit the advantages of all the environments we support.

In 1987, a company called Ad Lib introduced the Ad Lib sound card. This provided the DOS-based PC with basic music capability, which excited people, because it sounded so much better than that beep tone. The Ad Lib card is a two-**operator**, **FM synthesizer** developed by Yamaha. It offers 9-**voice polyphony**, and it's **multi-timbral**. We started out using the Ad Lib card to create music and effects for our software products.

In 1989, the Sound Blaster sound card was released by Creative Labs (now marketed by Brown Wagh Publishing). Sound Blaster resembles the Ad Lib card (both produce monophonic sound, and both use the same sound-synthesis hardware). However, the Sound Blaster adds an 8-bit analog-to-digital converter for digitizing sounds and an 8-bit digital-to-analog converter for sound output. Today it is the sound-development standard on the PC, providing the environment for which we design almost all our soundtracks. We use it to provide a musical score or synthetic sounds, and add digitized sounds on top of that. This is the kind of integrated sound environment that will be an important part of multimedia computing for the next decade.

The audio requirements for an MPC (Multimedia PC) machine include an 8-bit DAC and ADC (analog-to-digital converter), so you can use it to record as well as play sounds. It has input connectors for microphones, so you can plug in a microphone to record voice or sound. It also has software-controlled audio mixing capability, so you can blend the output of

the DAC, synthesizer, and even CD audio, and adjust their relative volume levels. This gives you the advantages of the realism of digitized sound for speech and other sounds you can't create synthetically. You also can support a more consistent and "present" sound environment by producing continuous music or other synthetic ambience through synthesis. This is the kind of environment that multimedia applications will require throughout the 1990s.

Creating Sound for Software

When we set out to develop sound for a new software product, we evaluate it from an aesthetic design perspective. We divide the product's sound requirements into three categories that parallel the components of film sound: music, sound effects, and dialog. This provides us with a means to quantify the scope of the project. For example, we might decide that we want the opening title screen accompanied by fully orchestrated music with a few sound effects.

Our audio production approach mixes synthetic sounds with digital sounds to provide the best of both worlds. The type of audio data we use for each component is determined largely by the role of each sound. For music, we typically use synthesis, which helps set a mood and lets us include longer sounds. For effects, we typically use digitized sounds, which help create dramatic "punch." When supporting computers that have synthesis-only devices such as the Ad Lib sound card, we also provide synthesized sound effects. There's no way to synthesize dialog, so including it in a product requires that the customer's computer include hardware capable of playing digitized sounds. The use of dialog is not common in current computer games, although people are starting to experiment with it.

An entertainment software product typically includes music and sound effects, but the use of continuous music is not appropriate in "productivity" software such as a graphics program. Such a product might include a brief musical segment when you first launch the program, but we don't want music playing on and on while you're using the tools.

We use effects in two ways: to enhance an animation and to serve as "interface sound," which means that the computer emits some kind of sound when you press a button or perform some action. For example, our paint program for children, Kid Pix, has wacky sound effects for each tool; using the "firecracker" eraser, for instance, generates a *ka-boom!* Sound effects are an integral component of Kid Pix; they make the program more fun to use. When we plan the sound effects we want for a program, we review the need for these types of interface sounds.

Kid Pix also includes "dialog" of sorts. When the child uses the text tool to type, each letter of the alphabet is accompanied by the sound of a person pronouncing the letter. All the audio components in Kid Pix are based on digitized sound.

When we produce sounds for a product, we also must consider data size limitations. When I started working for Broderbund, we developed products that were shipped on one, two, or three **floppy disks**. This seriously restricts the amount of data we're able to provide. For example, Broderbund's "Prince of Persia" (an animated, Arabian Nights fantasy game) fit on one 720K disk; 100K of that was sound, and that represents less than ten seconds of digitized sounds. It meant that all my digitized sounds and MIDI files had to fit in 100K of disk space! Typically, 20-25 percent of the data on floppy-based products is dedicated to audio.

Soon after that, we started creating products that shipped on five, ten, and even 15 floppy disks that you would copy onto your hard disk drive before you use the product. The deluxe edition of the educational game, "Where in the World is Carmen Diego," released in 1990, comprises almost six **megabytes** of data, of which over a megabyte is sound.

On our new CD-ROM products, such as "Living Books" (stories with animations, sound effects, narration, and original music), about 50 percent of the data is dedicated audio. We expect that trend to continue.

Another important consideration concerns **RAM** requirements. The typical DOS product works with 640K of RAM, which severely limits sound capabilities. We need to decide the product's functionality and size limitations, then determine how to accomplish what we want within those restrictions imposed by RAM and the type of hardware on the customer's computer. When we make a PC program, we know every PC includes an internal speaker. Every Broderbund product that uses sound supports that speaker as well as a Sound Blaster/MPC-compatible soundtrack containing a blend of synthesized and digitized sounds.

megabyte: *A measure of computer memory equal to 1,048,576 bytes. A byte is a measure of computer data equal to eight bits. A bit is the smallest unit of data in a digital system, symbolized as a "1" or a "0."*

RAM: *Random Access Memory, an area of computer data storage that can be accessed immediately.*

floppy disks: *Also known as "diskettes," these portable, pocket-size disks are used to store relatively small amounts of data.*

There are hardware/software packages available that transform a personal computer into a professional-quality, disk-based, audio production and recording system for precise and complex manipulation of sound. This is the kind of system we use at Broderbund to create sound for our software products. We start by recording or digitizing sounds on the computer, where the sound is then stored on hard disk. We use sound-editing software to process and edit the files and convert them to the proper format for each version of the final product.

We also rely heavily on commercially available sound-effects libraries sold on audio compact discs. They provide sounds that we normally can't access. If we need a car crash sound, for example, we can't trot outside and record an automobile accident. Sound effects libraries open up a universe of possibilities, but they're also limited—it is not uncommon to find that a library does not have just the right sound. That's why professional-quality sound recording capability is essential for successful software sound design.

When we create music for our software products, we compose it by using the highest-quality synthesizer that will be supported by our final product. We use **sequencers** to edit the music data and **editor/librarians** to edit the synthesizer instrument sounds. When the compositions are complete, we create instrument definitions for all other synthesizers we will be supporting.

The Macintosh offers the best integration of these sound-editing tools, which is why all our development work occurs on the Macintosh. Also, these tools combine well with some of the Macintosh graphics programs that we use in development. Some similar tools are available for the PC, but they don't offer the kind of integration found on the Mac. Most notably, the music technology company Opcode Systems offers profound integration between their editor/librarians and their sequencers with digitized sound support. At this time, such an environment doesn't exist for the PC. The PC, or MPC, may catch up, but the Mac is at least two years ahead in terms of audio support capabilities.

We use several techniques to help successfully implement the sound within the final product. The most important one involves keeping data files as small as possible to optimize performance, whether the software product is destined for floppy disk or CD-ROM. CD-ROM provides what seems like endless data-storage capabilities, but it resembles a water tower with a straw attached: huge amounts of data come out of it a little bit at a time. When producing sound files for CD-ROM or floppy, it's to our advantage to streamline the process of transferring the data, and we do that by limiting the size of the data files.

We typically aim to create sounds that are as compelling as possible, then find ways to cut back on the sound data without losing the compelling quality. "Looping" (the act of repeating short sound samples to create a longer sound) is an effective means of conserving data. We might loop a small, 5K sound file several times to generate a longer sound.

Sound fragments also allow for mixing and matching. We can piece togeth-

sequencer: A device or computer program for recording, editing, and playing back MIDI data, the musical equivalent of a word processor. You can fix wrong notes, or make notes longer or shorter.

editor/librarian: A type of computer software that lets you alter, store, and retrieve synthesizer instrument data.

er many different little sounds and use them in different ways. Also, altering the sound's playback rate provides variety— at one point in the program it can play back at 11kHz, and at another time it can play back at the faster (higher-pitched) 22kHz rate. Thus, we get more mileage out of a single digitized sound through the use of looping, changing playback rates, and assembling several short sounds together in various ways.

Aesthetic Considerations

When the Macintosh was introduced, Apple Computer distributed a book of guidelines for software developers, *Human Interface Guidelines: The Apple Desktop Interface*, published by Addison-Wesley (copyright 1987 Apple Computer). This book includes a section on sound that lists important considerations (although some are not always applicable to entertainment software).

Here's a brief selection from Apple's *Human Interface Guidelines* on the aesthetics of incorporating sound:

Restraint: Be thoughtful about where and how you use sound in an application. If you overuse sound, it won't add any meaning to the interface, and it will probably just be annoying. *Redundancy:* Sound should never be the only indication that something has happened; there should always be a visible indication on the screen, too, especially when the user needs to know what has occurred. [This doesn't necessarily apply to entertainment software—T.R.] The user may have all sound turned off, may have been out of hearing range of the computer, or may be hard of hearing. *Unobtrusiveness:* Most sounds can be quite subtle and still get their meaning across. Loud, harsh sounds can be offensive or intimidating. You should always use the sound on yourself and test it on users for a significant period of time.

The book recommends a testing period of a week or two before you decide to include sound in your application. It also says, "You should avoid using tunes or jingles—more than two or three notes of a tune may become annoying or sound silly if heard very often."

This last point is critical. You might want really "big" sounds for some things, but you don't want the sound pounding your users in the head all the time!

Human Interface Guidelines continues, "*Significant differences:* Users can learn to recognize and discriminate between sounds, but different sounds should be significantly different. Nonmusicians often can't tell the difference between two similar notes or chords, especially when they're separated by a space of time." The guidelines also suggest that the user should have some control over the sound environment—changing the volume of sounds or being able to turn sound off altogether.

It's important to add that *repetition* poses a hazard. For example, there's a golf game program that provides voice commentary for every action you make—and it repeats the same piece of commentary every time you repeat the action. For example, when you smack the golf ball into a tree, the narration exclaims, "Oh, no. You just hit the tree!" You hear that exact same line each time you hit the tree, and after you've heard, "Oh, no. You just hit the tree!" five or six times, you're more than ready to turn off the sound.

From a general aesthetic perspective, the axiom "variety is the spice of life" holds true for software sound development. From a general technical perspective, integrated synthesis of digitized sound environments in computing is the key to successful multimedia and entertainment software.

DANCES WITH TECHNOLOGY

WILL YOU SWEEP ME OFF MY FEET OR STEP ON MY FOOT?

BY CRAIG ANDERTON

Craig Anderton is an internationally recognized authority in the field of musical electronics. He is the author of 11 books (including MIDI For Musicians *and* The Electronic Musician's Dictionary*) and a recording artist who has performed on, produced, and/or mixed ten releases. Craig was the founding editor of* Electronic Musician *magazine and now serves as editor-at-large for* Guitar Player *magazine. He contributes regularly to* Keyboard, Sound on Sound, *and other publications that cater to the music and recording communities. Craig's most recent musical release,* Forward Motion, *is on the Sona Gaia label distributed by MCA Records.*

In theory, technology exists to solve problems. But it's all too easy to be seduced by the technology itself rather than concentrate on using it to solve the problem for which the technology was invented.

I'd like to restore some perspective about technology. It's so easy to be dazzled by all the technology that we can lose our objectivity, and end up serving the technology instead of being *liberated* by it. The questions we need to keep in mind are:

• Does the technology solve more problems than it creates?

• Is the level of technology we're using appropriate for the job we need to do?

• Does the technology allow us to express our humanity and feelings more easily or does it place limitations on our expressiveness?

• Does the technology bring people together or does it encourage divisiveness?

My own interactions with technology provide some answers to those questions. Perhaps a few parables will illustrate the point. . . .

Sometime in the early 1980s I bought a Radio Shack Model 100 notebook computer so I could write while on the road. At that time, the notebook computer was such a new technology that I couldn't work on it in an airport for more than five minutes without someone coming up to me, fascinated by what I was doing. They would marvel at the computer's small size and convenience, I would nod, and after spending an appropriate amount of time talking about the technology and its price, I'd gently encourage the person to move on so I could get some work done.

Time passed. Soon lots of people had "laptop" computers. The typical laptop was no puny Model 100—no, it was an IBM-clone machine with a hard disk drive, "supertwist" display, which is a bright, backlit type of liquid-crystal display, and a battery life of an hour or two. No one came up to me at airports any more. I witnessed the zenith of laptop pervasiveness on a flight to Los Angeles. In the six seats in the row where I sat, there were six people pounding away on laptops. The laptop had arrived.

Last year, though, the funniest thing happened. People started marvelling at my little notebook computer again. "Why, it's so small and light!" some would say. Others would comment, "The letters on the display are so big and readable!" Inevitably, someone would ask what kind of hard drive it had. "None!" I would reply. "It uses battery-backed **RAM**—no saving, no loading, I just turn it on and the stuff is in there." They'd ask about battery life, astonished to hear that I typically got over 20 hours from four AA batteries, the kind you can buy at any discount store or airport shop. (Yes, there *is* a portable computer that doesn't quit on transatlantic flights.)

Folks would shake their heads in amazement when confronted with this little wonder computer with its built-in **modem**. They would ask how they could buy one. "You can't," I'd reply, to which they would assume I was privy to some hot **beta-test** prototype—only to be told that this wasn't the latest and greatest notebook computer, but the oldest one. Radio Shack stopped manufacturing it years ago.

No, I can't run **HyperCard** on it (or for that matter, any other hip, new, yuppie programs). But I'm a writer. I need something light, portable, inexpensive, and reliable so I can enter text into computer memory. I don't need a status symbol or the Next Thing. I need a tool.

One danger of being seduced by technology is that we end up buying a Ferrari to drive to the corner store to buy groceries, or that we forget about what works because we are lured by something that does far more than what we really need.

Years ago I played a trick on someone at an audio industry convention. Digital audio recording was coming into vogue and this person was going on and on about the wonders of digital. I asked whether he'd seen the latest "H-DAS" ("High-Density Analog Storage") technology. When he answered, "No," I told him the basic specifications: This system provided the equivalent of **12-bit** audio resolution out of the box, but when equipped with accessories, H-DAS machines could be upgraded to the equivalent of true 16-bit technology. A clever **oversampling** technique eliminated the need for those pesky **anti-aliasing** filters. And H-DAS was cheap: a basic H-DAS cartridge holding the equivalent of 1.2 gigabytes of data cost about $30, and cartridges with even more storage were available, albeit at slightly higher cost.

My friend could hardly wait to get his hands on H-DAS. But I told him this was just part of the story, and that everything was in place to make H-DAS a true worldwide standard. Dozens of manufacturers had committed to it, as had hundreds, if not thousands, of professional recording studios. And, I added with the *coup de grace*, no complicated editing procedures were required—you just needed a **razor blade and splicing tape**.

That's when he realized I was talking about analog multitrack tape hooked up to **Dolby SR**. Once he realized the joke, he jumped back on the digital bandwagon. Meanwhile, the smart-money folks stuck with familiar, classic, analog 24-track tape-recording because—well, it works and it's a standard. And a lot of people think it sounds better than digital, too.

(Am I down on digital? No. I use my digital audio tape deck for recording my final 2-track mixes, and I'm on the waiting list to receive the new Alesis ADAT, the 8-track, digital audio recorder that costs under $4,000 and uses S-VHS videotape as its storage medium. Most of my synths are digital. Digidesign's software for the Macintosh is great for digital audio editing on a budget. But if I needed a 24-track machine, I'd get an analog one.)

Keyboard magazine columnist Chris Meyer pulled a similar trick in one of his columns, gleefully describing a version of the MIDI specification that seemed to solve a lot of problems with the current version. Was this the fabled update, MIDI version 2.0? At the end of the column, you found out that he was describing the "Universal Synthesizer Interface"—a *precursor* to what eventually became MIDI.

And how's this for an obsolete instrument: six monophonic **oscillators** subject to **drift** and tuning problems, approximately 3.5 octave range, no **aftertouch**, no **modulation wheel**, no MIDI, and only five non-editable programs. Well, it may *sound* like obsolete technology, but Jimi Hendrix sure played it well.

Another problem: Technology can entrap you when you least expect it. Here's one example. I recently received a software update for Digidesign Sound Tools, a Macintosh-based digital audio editing program. I went about installing it in my computer, assuming it would take about five minutes. I saw that it was a "stuffed" (compressed) Macintosh file; the data was compressed so it could fit on floppy disk for shipping, with the intention that the user would "unstuff" it and copy it onto the computer's hard drive. So I clicked on its screen icon to unstuff it. Oops—disk error! I tried unstuffing it by using a standard file-decompression program; again, no luck.

Well, I had bought the decompression program's latest upgrade but I hadn't installed it, so I thought maybe *that* would do the job. I installed the program, which enabled me to unstuff the Sound Tools update and copy it over to my hard drive—but the decompression program's update put so many weird files in my system that for some reason, it became impossible to access the Mac's **Control Panel**. Time to reinstall a fresh system, right? I got out my four system disks and started . . . except the machine wouldn't read the fourth disk. Where *was* that backup? Never mind, I was running System 6.0.5 (based on what you've read so far, you've probably figured out I will be one of the last people to "upgrade" to System 7), so I figured I'd install System 6.0.7. So I got out my Nautilus CD-ROM (a monthly computer magazine on CD-ROM that includes utilities, games, industry news, etc.), went through the requisite CD-ROM set-up incantation, and found System 6.0.7. I then got out four more disks, ran the copy program, and installed System 6.0.7. Hmmm . . . now a warning message told me that HyperCard 1.2.5 would not work with the new system. Fortunately, I had Ear Level Engineering's HyperMIDI stack (a HyperCard tool for

Control Panel: Part of the Macintosh operating system software; lets you set preferences for such functions as speaker volume, repeating key rate, time clock, and so on.

oscillator, drift: The basic building block of electronic sound, an oscillator is a device that creates a repeating electrical waveform. It is subject to "drift," or the tendency to vary slightly in frequency over long periods of time.

aftertouch, modulation wheel: The former is a "touch-sensitive" feature in which the instrument senses how hard you're pressing on a key or string after it reaches its bottom-most position; the latter device is used to modify the character of the audio signal.

razor blade, splicing tape: Basic tools for editing analog audio tape.

Dolby SR: Currently, the highest-quality system used for noise reduction during analog tape recording in professional audio studios.

coming up with your own MIDI applications) which came with HyperCard 2.0, so I installed it. And then all the HyperCard stacks I use had to convert themselves to the new format. . . .

An hour and a half later, I was able to use the updated Sound Tools software in "the computer for the rest of us."

Now, don't get me wrong. I can't imagine going back to life before computers, but I don't think they're religious objects. Macintosh owners are the only people I know who think it's worthwhile to spend $50 for a program that puts pretty designs on their monitor screen when the computer's turned on but not in use. If you're not using the computer, who cares what's on the screen? I don't get excited when I find that I can use a special program to customize the cosmetic appearance of a menu (which might destroy my files in the process). I don't want to spend my future as a computer co-dependent.

From a cosmic perspective, I suppose that the point is always the journey, not the destination . . . but just try telling that to a magazine editor who's expecting your article to show up on time. I don't want to coddle my computer; I want to exploit it.

Another thought: My friends who own Macintosh computers love to show me how they have everything set up for keyboard equivalents and function keys, so they don't have to use the mouse, while my IBM PC-based friends are all excited that they can use a mouse to "point and click." I'm not making this up!

So even though I have a Macintosh IIci, I'm not getting rid of my Radio Shack Model 100. And even though I own some great synths and samplers, my tunes don't sound "real" until there's a guitar or vocal in them.

When someone tells you about the latest, greatest technology, be cynical. Ask yourself whether it's going to be a more effective tool in solving a particular problem. Public Enemy said it best: Don't believe the hype. To which I'll add, even if it is in 16-bit, oversampled stereo audio.

"Colorstorm 2 1991"

David Em

represented by Roberta Spieckerman

Associates, San Francisco, California

Tools: Apple Quadra workstation;

StrataVision 3D; Adobe PhotoShop;

Fractal Design Painter

CYBERARTS GALLERY

Michael Johnson

Orange, California

Tools: 35mm photographs
scanned and manipulated;
IBM-PC with DOS 5.0
and SVGA card; ULEAD
PhotoStyler; Iris inkjet printer

"**Love Withheld**" (from study6.tga) 1991

"**Untitled**" (from study2.tga) 1991

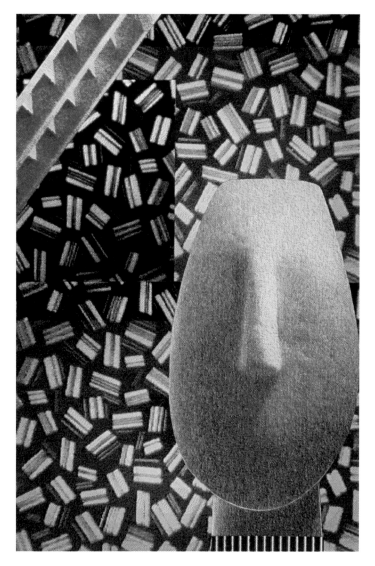

Stone Age Series: **"Rites of Passage"** 1991

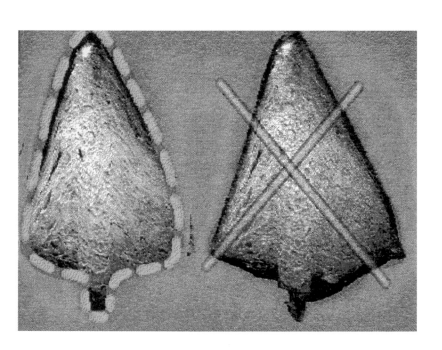

Sandra Filippucci
Sherman, Connecticut

Tools: Commodore Amiga
2500/30; NewTek
Digi-View and Digi-Paint;
textures created from
scanned images of moon
surface; inkjet printer.

Stone Age Series: **"The Interpretation of Remains"** 1991

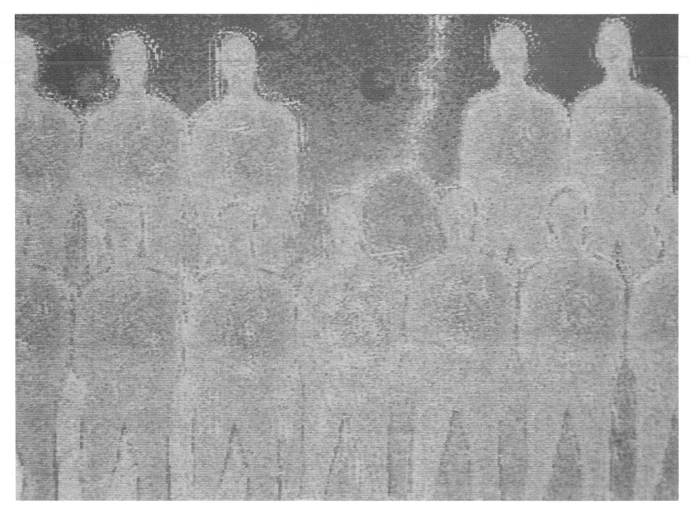

"Figure 5" 1989

Daria & Gary Barclay
Hillsboro, Oregon

Tools: Original airbrush art
scanned and manipulated;
Commodore Amiga 1000
computer, NewTek Digi-View
Gold and DigiPaint software

CYBERARTS GALLERY

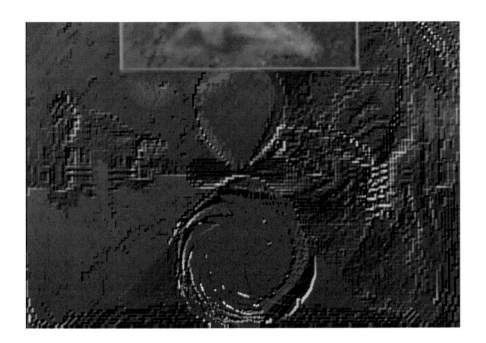

"Reel Wheels" 1990

Elizabeth Griffiths Lawhead
Portland, Oregon

Tools: Apple Macintosh IIci;
SuperMac Technology
PixelPaint Professional

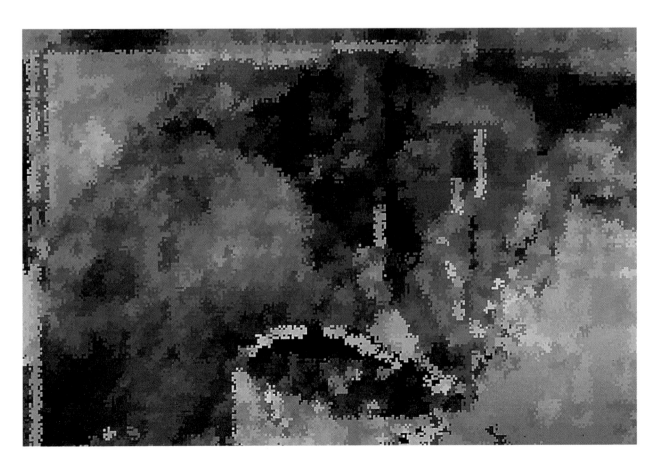

"Tapestry" 1990

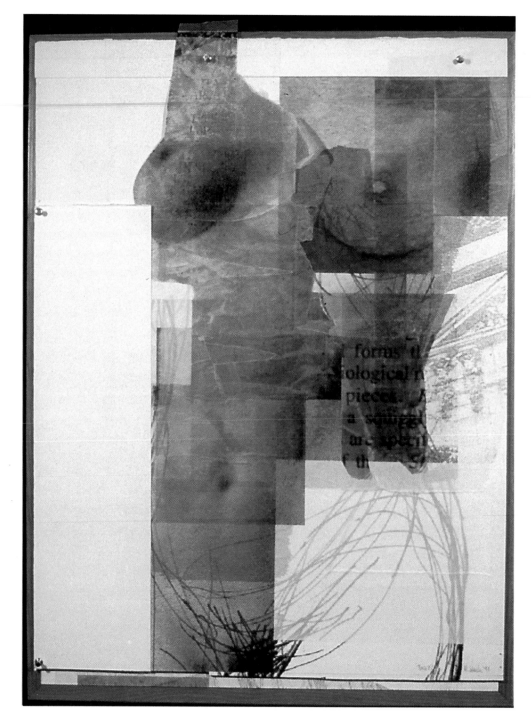

"Torso 27" 1991

Marius Johnston
Berkeley, California

Tools: Photos, drawings, and other images
are scanned and manipulated; Apple
Macintosh IIcx; ThunderWare ThunderScan;
custom photo separation software; final art
output via Apple ImageWriter II with
multicolor ribbon onto paper and vellum,
attached to masonite, framed with wood.

"Tell Me The Truth" 1990

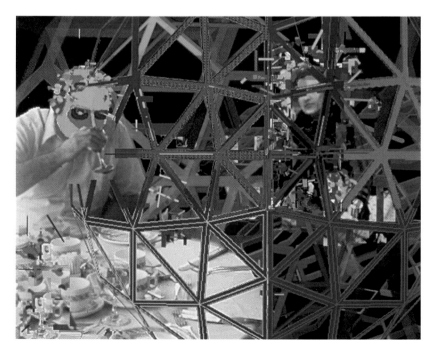

Victor Acevedo

Los Angeles, California

Tools: IBM PC/AT 386 with
frame buffer; Macintosh II;
Cubicomp 3D Modeler;
Targa Paint System; Adobe
PhotoShop; Iris inkjet printer;
watercolor paper; dyes
sealed with special UV
inhibitor emulsion

"6-26-27-'86 Version 3B" 1991

"Portrait of Patric Prince" 1991

Michael Ragsdale Wright

Los Angeles, California

Tools: Commodore Amiga 2500;
video camera; NewTek Video Toaster
for video digitizing; ASDG Inc.
Art Department Professional;
Electronic Arts Deluxe Paint 3.0;
inkjet printer

SECTION 3

"Deep Thought" videostill **Michael Masucci and Kim McKillip**
Vertical Blanking/EZTV

VISUAL IMAGERY
ANIMATION
AND GRAPHICS

GUERRILLA VIDEO

LOW-BUDGET PRODUCTION TECHNIQUES

"Musicians, artists, and writers are using the skills they mastered in the 1980s to enter the world of videomaking in the '90s," writes independent videomaker Michael Masucci. "They're making PC-based workstations part of a production chain that begins with word processors, camcorders, and MIDI gear to produce low-budget (and no-budget!) projects that can compete with traditional film productions and their large crews, heavy equipment, and extensive financial resources."

With little money, you, too, can create video art, using recycled materials for sets and props, and industrial or "pro-sumer" video and audio equipment. This chapter offers some tactics and maneuvers for video production on a shoestring budget.

BY MICHAEL MASUCCI WITH LINDA JACOBSON

Michael Masucci is based at EZTV (West Hollywood, California), an independent production facility and gallery established in 1983 to focus on live performance, video production, and desktop video and multimedia technology. His "guerrilla" videotapes have been hailed by publications ranging from L.A. Weekly *and the* Los Angeles Times *to the trade papers* Hollywood Reporter *and* Variety. *An arts activist and musician, Michael divides his time between producing original works, judging tapes for contests and grants, and curating the EZTV gallery.*

Whether you're planning to exhibit your artwork at major museums or in storefront art galleries, you're forced to deal with the ever-shrinking resources available through the federal and state grant system. In the late 1980s, the largest states drastically cut their arts funding: Massachusetts by 60 percent, New York by 60 percent, California by about 40 percent. How do artists go about producing and distributing their work when the government is offering less and less funding for the arts? They certainly don't stop creating their art; they just start looking for alternate funding and capital resources. The key word is "resources," and the first rule of guerrilla video is:

Rule #1: Be resourceful. One great way to be resourceful is to exchange information resources with others in your art community. Help each other locate talent, acquire props, and make friends with sympathetic studios and technologists (those willing to negotiate lower rates for independent producers). Arts organizations around the country are forming nonprofit charters and creating venues to stage low-budget live performances, video installations, and "intermedia," or interdisciplinary media—the term I prefer over "multimedia." (Where I come from, multimedia means a live performance event incorporating video projection, laser, or holography, not something you see on a computer!)

In 1979, environmentalist and Greenpeace co-founder Patrick Wall, a Canadian, was arrested off the coast of Japan for slashing tuna nets and releasing dolphins to save them from drowning in the nets. Patrick spent six months in a Japanese prison. After he was released (thanks to international political pressure) and deported, he landed in the United States and started an organization called Earth Alert. Among Earth Alert's members were video-makers. In 1988 they won an Emmy for their documentary about the toxic water in Marina Del Rey (a large commercial marina in Los Angeles), a film they produced with low-end, industrial-grade equipment and *no* external financial resources.

In 1989, Earth Alert asked me to help them set up a production-recycling group to save construction lumber, set props, building supplies, ladders, and all manner of production items from winding up in landfill sites, where the film and TV studios usually send their used production materials after completing a project. Hollywood spends lots of money on sets. Some sets contain actual buildings, which are strong and well-designed and last all of three months before a crew destroys them. That's ridiculous. Why not distribute these materials to independent theater producers and film-makers?

Within a year or two, this concept grew in popularity and two recycling groups were established in the Hollywood community. In early 1992, the Los Angeles city government set up "Materials for the Arts" as a branch of the city's Department of Cultural Affairs to arrange for independent filmmakers to receive used materials from big Hollywood productions.

The production teams on major film lots now recycle their props, and it's become chic for Hollywood producers to have Materials for the Arts dismantle their sets. Millions of dollars' worth of material that ultimately takes space in dumps goes to anyone who asks for it, and is distributed on a first-come, first-serve basis, usually for the cost of shipping.

You can start a prop-recycling organization of your own. Perhaps you live in a town where you belong to a band that wants to make a music video. Approach the theater department at your local college and ask if they'd like to recycle their production materials.

Where else might you find resources? Visit the media center nearest you. A well-developed media center rents low-cost video editing suites and may even give out production grants. A media center serves as an information network, providing a gathering place for film and video aficionados, artists, and producers from whom you can find out who has what you need or who knows how to get what you need. EZTV, for example, offers low-cost access to editing equipment, conducts workshops, offers production package services, and supports a network of people seeking work as computer graphic artists, actors, dancers, camera operators, and video editors. There are places like this all over the country.

If you live in a city, explore the resources available to you through your local public-access cable TV station. Public-access is one way to get your hands on equipment, assuming the station's program manager is sympathetic to local video artists. The best station I've encountered is in Tucson, Arizona. You can do just about anything in Tucson's public-access facility, even shoot a movie. Few public-access studios are so well-endowed, but at most of them, for little or no money you can have access to (typically) ¾" **video** gear to create a broadcast-quality production. The station will even air it for you. If you can afford tape duplication costs, you can hustle your tape to other local stations.

If you live in a town that doesn't have a media center, visit the area's largest university and make friends in the film or television department. Everybody needs help, especially students. If you're an actor, one great way to acquire experience and footage is to act in student film and video projects. At a good film school, the students' work is often excellent. The country's best filmmakers attended film school; some of their first films were released commercially. This leads to our second rule of independent guerrilla video . . .

Rule #2: Network. Collaboration is great, on both creative and practical levels. Find out who has the skills, talent, and/or resources you need, and figure a way to strike a deal with them to get what you need. One great approach to striking a deal when you're working on a low budget is to barter. Maybe you own a video camera and you know someone who wrote

a script that they want produced on video. Exchange your resources and skills—without exchanging cash.

You also can form an equipment co-op and arrange a group of video-makers who can chip in some funds to buy a production system. That's the way we started EZTV.

Rule #3: Use Anything You Have Access To. Not long ago, a Los Angeles-based rap group came to me and said, "We want to make a video, but we have no money, and more importantly, we have no time. Today is Wednesday. By Friday morning at 9:00 we have to ship a music video to Tokyo to be considered for a possible gig. What can we do?"

I asked, "What do you have at your disposal?"

"Nothing," they said.

But I picked their brains and it turned out they *did* have something at their disposal. They had friends. Friends = extras. Friends = cast. They could get a lot of people in one place.

Next question: Where to shoot the video? "Do you have a big place to shoot it in?"

"No."

After some discussion, we realized they *did* have a place; they just didn't know they had it. The place is called Venice Beach. There's a small stage on Venice Beach. You need a city permit to use it, but we played the guerrilla video production game of "What If?" and asked ourselves, "What if we showed up and nobody came to arrest us or kick us out? What might happen? We just might make a video!"

We decided to try it. The worst thing that could happen was someone would kick us

¾" video: Primary video cassette tape format in professional broadcasting and industrial video production.

off the beach and we'd have to find another large space.

We didn't want the entire video to consist of a bunch of people watching a rap group, so we asked the group, "What else do you guys have at your disposal?" They said, "Nothing." But it turned out they had one hour of recording studio time left over from a previous project. This meant that we had a second shooting location.

We kept asking, "What else do you have that we can use?" Two of the rappers owned matching black Corvettes, which definitely would come in handy in a music video. They also had a friend who owned a P.A. system, which would help make the beach scene appear like a real concert, even if we didn't actually use the system.

I added one more location, the space upstairs at EZTV, where we had recently demolished a set.

When I shot the video, I used a camcorder—not **Hi-8**, but regular Video 8. I used some of the cheesy video effects you get in these camcorders, such as "posterization," which makes the picture appear very high-contrast and brightly colored, a kind of psychedelic look that's now a standard effect on low-end industrial and home video equipment. (Photographers call this effect "solarization.")

This was our production schedule:

• 1:00 p.m. Shoot some footage of the rap group at a recording studio in Crenshaw district of Los Angeles.

• 2:00 to 3:00. Drive from Crenshaw District to Venice Beach. On the way, I rode in a car driving in front of the guys in their black Corvettes and occasion-

ally pointed the camera out the window at them.

• 3:00. Arrive at Venice Beach. The rap group's friends were all there and we set up the P.A. system. When 20 people gather in a public place, 20 more want to know what the first 20 are doing, so before we knew it, we had a crowd of people, all happy to appear in an amateur video.

• 6:30. As the sun set, we finished taping.

• 6:45-8:00. Dinner.

• 8:00 p.m. Back to EZTV, where I started editing the tape, completely **off-line**.

• 9:00 a.m. The next morning, the group sent their tape to Tokyo.

For the soundtrack on the video, we used a perfectly suitable lip-synching technique in the form of good old-fashioned audio cassette. It's the same technique used to create videos for MTV, only with different hardware. We didn't synchronize the sound to the picture; we simply played the group's audio tape while lining up the shots and practicing the shoot a couple of times. When you're working like this, keep in mind that different audio cassette decks don't run at the exact same speed. If you shoot your performers lip-synching to the audio on one tape deck, and edit the video while playing back the audio on another tape deck, you'll probably experience problems with lip-synching accuracy. Use the same audio cassette deck for lip-synching and video editing.

No, the rap group's video wasn't "high art," but it got the job done and it got them to Japan. It's the kind of video you can produce with some basic equipment.

Rule #4: Rules Are Rules! What's true for a cinematographer working in glorious

off-line: The first step in video editing, a process of using less-expensive equipment to make decisions about all edits in a production (source of each shot, start and end points, types of transitions, etc.). Work copies of raw footage are edited together to approximate the finished product. The next process usually is "on-line," the final editing stage, in which all shots are transferred in proper sequence from source tapes to create a master tape.

Hi-8: Video cassette tape format (8mm) for consumer and industry video. Provides a clearer, truer image than standard 8mm (Video 8) and VHS video tape.

Panavision film is true for a cinematographer working in inexpensive Hi-8 video. People in major production companies spread misconceptions about what you need to make something look "professional" or "slick." The key to imaging in photography has always been and always will be the lighting—as long as the images are created using actual objects and not just computers—and the composition (how you frame your image). The more you learn about *lighting* and the *composition* of the image, the better your finished product will be.

Rule #5: Know Your Medium. "Archival quality" and "video" are never used in the same sentence. Video's shelf life is about seven years. That will change as more and more video ends up on **laserdisc**, but for now we must live with the technical limitations of the videotape medium. Lots of people spend lots of money having their child's christening videotaped; by the time the kid graduates from college, those tapes will be blank.

I'm an advocate of Hi-8, but I'm also afraid of Hi-8, not only because of its lack of archive ability, but because it's fragile. It's like audio tape: You can get quality sound on a cassette, but it is susceptible to audio signal loss. This problem exists with video. When using the small, thin tape in Hi-8 videocassettes, the slightest amount of dust in a camcorder or playback system can render the video equivalent of a scratch, and once it's there, you can't remove it.

My approach is to sacrifice some image quality by losing generations: I shoot on Hi-8 and before I even watch it, I dump the footage onto ¾" video, then edit on two ¾" machines. This may be heresy to some people in the professional video community, but I'm not extremely concerned about the maintenance of initial image quality. Some of the best film cinematographers sacrifice resolution to achieve a painterly image quality. I often purposely degrade my images to smear them and make them less pristine. I like to "dirty" the mix. My Hi-8 camera, which Sony calls a "pro-sumer" model (whatever that means) represents, for $2,000, one of the best investments in the independent video marketplace.

Part of the reason people denigrate video work is due to the amazing cleanliness of the image. Video has fewer lines of resolution than film, but it runs faster, at 29.97 frames a second as opposed to film's 24. Thus it looks more like "real life," which is why TV news compels and "grabs" viewers. I try to kill that look. I don't want my video to look like the "Tonight Show."

Major production studios shoot their footage on Hi-8 and edit on **BetaCam SP**. When they can, they edit it on one-inch video tape, or one of the expensive digital-video tape formats. The result is good, solid image quality and fewer signal **dropouts**. But there's no rule saying you have to do it that way.

It's also important to know that ¾" video tape still works. To many video professionals, ¾" video is a dinosaur, but it's a medium that has been thoroughly refined after almost 20 years of use. The machines last a long time and the tape is durable. You can get a **cuts-only** ¾" editing system for about $10,000. That's the cost of a new system. There are many great bargains in the used equipment market.

laserdisc: Common term for optical videodisc, a 12" disc that stores video, audio, and data for playback on a videodisc player and video monitor.

BetaCam SP: A professional, high-quality, video tape format (an upgrade of standard ¾" video) developed for field production and computer animation.

dropout: A loss of picture signal during playback. Appears on screen as lines, streaks, flashing spots, or garbled images.

cuts-only: Refers to video editing with basic "cut" transitions between shots (no dissolves, wipes, fades, etc.).

½" VHS: Primary consumer video cassette tape format. "VHS" stands for "Video Home System."

S-VHS: Super-VHS, a high-quality extension of the home VHS tape format that provides sharper images and high-fidelity stereo audio. VHS tapes work in S-VHS machines, but S-VHS tapes won't work in VHS machines.

switcher: A video switching and mixing device.

frame synchronizer: A device which synchronizes two (or more) source tape machines to move in desired relationship to one another.

Dolby C: A type of audio noise-reduction system.

For an individual, $10,000 is a lot of money, so it's important to know that **½" VHS** video works, too. You can get a cuts-only VHS camcorder system for around $3,000, which you can use with a camcorder that performs basic editing effects. With another $2,000 you can buy a VHS editing system. The video you produce with such a system may not be shown on MTV, but it definitely can show your creative work.

Much equipment used in public-access TV location work is **S-VHS**, because it's highly portable. Tucson boasts one of the most advanced public-access stations in the country, and they do all their field location shoots and editing on Super-VHS. In some ways, S-VHS is more stable than Hi-8. It's larger, so you get fewer dropouts, and it's less fragile.

At EZTV, we transfer footage from Hi-8 to ¾". I layer images, going through a low-end **switcher**. We master on ¾" SP. Our choice of editing medium depends on the gig. If it's a paying job, we use whatever the budget allows. For paying jobs we shoot on ¾" Betacam SP equipment and edit to one-inch or digital video, which we rent. For our own (unfunded) stuff, we use ¾" Betacam SP, which is sharper than ¾" and has **Dolby C** sound. Stunning audio fidelity is not vital. ¾" is accessible, cheap to use, and you can rent an editing studio and a ¾" system for $20 an hour.

If you do your homework—take good production notes that identify where each shot is located on your footage—when you go into the editing room, you don't have to pay to sit there while you search through your material for each shot. You should be able to walk in and out of an ed-

it session without having to hock your house to pay for it.

Rule #6: Do It Yourself. Another way to prevent the need to pawn possessions is to use a one-person crew. When you do commercial work, the production will involve people with all different kinds of skills, but one person and one camera is all you need to create a video. When you work that way, always remember:

Rule #7: Experiment With Equipment & Techniques. When I moved from New York to Los Angeles in 1982, I had no access to technology, but I did have a relatively inexpensive video camera and editing deck. I created "video feedback" tapes for use in dance clubs by pointing the camera at the monitor to record prerecorded images; the result is, basically, a video lava lamp.

Equipment manufacturers such as Panasonic and JVC market small, one-piece video switchers and **frame synchronizers**. (It's important to remember, however, that using low-cost switchers can result in image degradation; the edits won't be transparent.) You can loop your images through one of these switchers so it feeds back—the updated version of pointing a camera at a monitor. I connect the output of the video switcher to its input, so the image loops. There are several ways to achieve different kinds of results. Try looping together the outputs of two or three decks. Experiment to discover your favorite style of video feedback.

When Video 8 was the only thing I could afford, I used Video 8. When Hi-8 came out, I traded in my Video 8 for Hi-8. As new technologies emerge, I continue trading up, just like musicians do with instruments and recording equipment. Many independent musicians own small studios that started out with one piece of equipment and, four years later, contain thousands of dollars worth of gear—acquired bit by bit, as they could afford it. Independent video makers can build their studios in a similar fashion, and create high-quality work on the way up.

In an intermedia art piece produced by EZTV in 1992, two dance companies, a group of actors, and several musicians performed a live and video-based, sci-fi piece about UFO abduction based on the testimony of psychiatrists, hypnotherapists, and physicists. We shot and edited it primarily with Hi-8 video tape, using some ¾" video footage. For audio we used the most inexpensive synthesizer keyboard and a Tascam PortaStudio 4-track audiocassette system. We edited it all off-line, using absolutely no high-end technology. We created the opening title sequence with an affordable Commodore Amiga 2000 and a **Video Toaster** system, which is not inexpensive. For every major brand of personal computer, you can buy a hardware/software package for $700-$1,000 that will turn that PC into a perfectly suitable **character generator**.

The finished art piece does not have stunning digital sound and is not on dazzling 70mm film, but it boasts high production values and expresses many interesting concepts—all for the price of gasoline, blank videotape, and some lumber and nails to bang together our props. The total cost of producing the video was about $300. Most of that went to pay for transportation for two performers who didn't live in the area.

You can learn basic video editing skills in an hour. Today's low-cost edit controllers are nothing more than the remote control you use on your VCR at home, except they control two (or more) VCRs. All you're doing in video editing, essentially, is telling two machines to start and stop. Video professionals often describe their editing systems in terms of their ability to perform "frame-accurate edits." The kinds of edits that low-budget (amateur) video equipment support are accurate to within three to seven frames. That's as much as a third of a second—not surgical precision, but precise enough for many purposes. Speaking of precision. . . .

Rule #8: You Can Live Without Time-Base Correction. You need time-base correction to produce a broadcast-quality video, but not having time-base correction (TBC) doesn't mean you can't make videos. For demonstration or non-broadcast applications, you can get by without time-base correction.

"TBC" refers to a device that replaces the initial unstable signal of video with a rock-solid signal for broadcast use. You can't perform any complicated effects on your video unless the signal is stable, because you're combining it with other signals (which also must be stable). A signal's stability has nothing to do with its picture quality, but with its strength, and stability is vital if you want to add fancy effects. A TBC is a fundamental piece of professional gear now finding its way into the hands of independent video-makers and serious "home enthusiasts."

Video Toaster: A hardware/software system (developed and manufactured by NewTek, Inc.) that turns a personal computer into a broadcast-quality video production and editing system, complete with switcher, effects generator, character generator, and many more functions.

character generator: A device that creates and superimposes text over a video image (such as baseball scores over the picture of a sports stadium in a TV news show, or the credits at the end of a program).

JVC and Panasonic both sell complete, medium- to high-end, S-VHS video production and editing systems, with built-in TBC, for about $14,000. It's not cheap, but without TBC, you can't **genlock** or create special effects. The cheapest TBCs cost about $1,000, and they can't do very much. If you want to perform interesting transitional effects (where one image replaces or superimposes another, or somehow interacts with it), you need two tape sources that are genlocked.

When you genlock video tape sources, you forget about the internal synchronization on each source, and provide a common "sync" signal to both machines. Time-base correction does that and a few other desirable things. Usually TBCs come equipped with "processing amps," or "proc amps," which let you manipulate chroma, hue, setup, and level—fancy words for lightness, brightness, color, and color saturation. Time-base correction also helps in the realm of "painterly" video. If you don't have a time-base corrector, you can achieve painterly effects by using filters and gels with the camera. You won't be able to achieve fancy transitions such as dissolves, but you'll be able to do fades.

Traditional filmmakers use various terms to describe how to switch from one shot to the next. The most common and effective way to make a transition is with the *cut*. You simply go from here to there. You don't add any "grammar." A *dissolve* usually indicates a passage of time, as does a *fade to black*. In the early 1980s, "digital video effects" became popular. Those are the things that make pictures fly into the scene, rotate, tumble, spin, split in

half, or break into pieces, the kinds of effects you can achieve with the Video Toaster, a desktop computer, a single video source, and a single edit source.

However, if you want the scene to fly out and reveal another picture underneath, you need an "**A/B roll** system." The cheapest A/B controller costs about $6,000, and it doesn't work that well. An A/B system requires three video decks: an edit deck and two sources, or an edit deck, a source deck, and a live camera. The latter setup is used in television. For instance, when a talk show host says, "Now we're going to see a clip from this actor's new movie," the station switches from live camera to a synched video source deck.

For no-budget work, I don't use an A/B system; I just push buttons and pay attention to timing. I can do that much faster than a computer can learn how to do it. EZTV does have an A/B controller, but I usually choose to manually control the "B" decks, because the response is immediate. In the time it takes me to set up a computer to do all that, I could finish three or four shots.

Nonetheless, the video revolution is taking place on the desktop. IBM PCs, Macintoshes, and Commodore Amiga computers are being used as all-in-one, stand-alone, video edit controllers. They can log and time your footage, read and write **time code**. A computer theoretically can access as many video sources as you want.

Little by little we'll replace our standard video gear with more computer-based equipment, but it's still much easier to design a shot, and build, light, and shoot a set than it is to render a completely computer-generated scene. You don't need a computer to do video; you can dive into video production today for relatively little money.

Rule #9: Anything Can Be Broadcast. It's true that any video program can be broadcast, but the **Federal Communications Commission** has put engineering barriers in place, "arbitrary standards" that attempt to define the technical excellence of the broadcast signal. A long time ago, a bunch of engineers decided what television should look like, considering aesthetics more than engineering. Today, several organizations lobby public television to broadcast more "video art." The most common reason for refusal is found on a piece of paper titled "Engineering and Technical Standards." These standards state that a public TV station cannot air video that was edited on ¾"!

The lobbying efforts of "Freewaves," a coalition in Southern California consisting of over a hundred art space organizations, succeeded in our local PBS station presenting an annual, hour-long special on video art. Most of the work in it was produced with low-end systems, primarily ¾", and it looked just fine on TV.

The problem with dealing with TV stations is that you're dealing with people who are "experts." Experts often don't have open minds. They know what they know, and they don't want to know that they don't know something. Therefore, the only way to deal with them is through the political process of lobbying. After all, shows such as "America's Funniest Home Videos" prove that the networks will show anything they want. It's just that the networks have to *want* to show it.

Rule #10: Get Your Work Seen. What do you do after completing your video tape? It depends on your goals. You can take several routes: the academic route, the struggling independent route, or the Hollywood route.

EZTV shows independent work of all kinds, including films and video from Third World communities. We import documentaries from such places as Pakistan, and we've helped establish an international curatorial organization. In doing so, we inadvertently built a distribution link. With some postage and the help of the U.S. mail, we ship tapes around the globe for viewing in all kinds of communities and venues. VHS may not be the medium of choice for the video perfectionist, but it is cheap and transportable. Before the Iron Curtain fell, people in Hungary and Czechoslovakia used low-cost camcorders to produce tapes so they could disseminate information to the world about their political activism and their country's military strategies. Via

Federal Communications Commission: In 1934 Congress passed the Communications Act, establishing the seven-person FCC to oversee the electronic media (TV, radio, telephone, and telegraph). It is responsible for handing out broadcast licenses. It also administers and interprets communications laws passed by Congress. In 1972 the FCC adopted rules requiring every cable TV station in the hundred largest markets (regions) to provide a "public-access channel." Local citizens could bring in videotapes for broadcast and sometimes produce programs using the cable company's studio. Everything that isn't commercial or libelous is carried free, on a first-come, first-serve basis, over the public-access channel.

mail and smuggling, these video documents traveled across borders.

In the States we don't have to deal with such high levels of information suppression, but we do have to scale the walls of network television and major cable suppliers to get our work shown. The essence of independent video production is that it provides an alternative to network TV. For 30 years, artists have been working in independent video, and their body of work thus far is only starting to be seen in the mainstream.

Public-access cable TV is one way to get your work seen. Now that they've been awarded the right to serve as "information providers," telephone companies can go into competition with public-access TV. That's wonderful in many ways, but probably will mean the death of public access. The FCC says that a phone company isn't "local," so it doesn't have to run local programming. You *know* that when somebody doesn't have to do something, they don't do it. In the meantime, we're applying lobbying pressure so public television will address the independents.

Want to go Hollywood with your video? Good luck. Well, independents *have* succeeded that way. A few years ago an independent film-maker shot and edited a feature on ¾" videotape. The film's production values and quality were high. It was a good-looking movie. Then he shopped for a video distribution deal. He visited a dozen distributors' offices and everywhere he went, he was asked the same question: "How did you originate?" When he answered, "¾-inch SP," they handed him the tape and said, "Thank you. We're looking for serious work." He

went that route for a year. Then he decided to lie. He returned to many of the same distributors' offices and this time he said, "I shot and edited on 35mm film." He sold his film. Now it's being distributed nationally. His "35mm film" is probably not the only one in your neighborhood video store that was shot on video tape.

You can break through the Hollywood door, but you'll probably hit the festival circuit first. Several film and video festivals enjoy high visibility, which means they're shopped by the major studios. In 1989 I showed a video at a video festival, and soon after I received a telegram from director Tim Burton (*Beetlejuice, Edward Scissorhands*) that said, "The best thing I've ever seen in independent video. Keep up the good work." In 1992, Sony Pictures Corp. saw that same video at a festival and, as a result, offered us the use of some high-end video equipment. Good things *can* happen!

The American Film Institute, based in Los Angeles, publishes a long list of video and film festivals. There are two kinds of festivals: Most charge admission to enter, and a few don't. How do you choose? Weigh your chances. Attend a festival to see if its program addresses sensibilities similar to your own. Keep in mind that many festivals show mainstream, middle-of-the-road material, while others are completely experimental. Research what each festival wants and how you can best address its needs.

Rule #11: Know What You Want. The success one achieves in creating a beautiful image has a lot to do with how much one knows conceptually about what the finished work should be.

I don't have a million dollars and I probably never will, and many of you won't, either. But knowing what we want can lead us to many avenues for producing good video work. Sure, I want digital video; sure, I want digital 3-D sound; but I'm not going to stop making videos just because I can't get these things. You shouldn't, either.

Rule #12: Know That Rules Are Made to Be Broken. Equipment keeps improving and prices keep falling. Many experts predict that by the middle of the 1990s, we'll see the emergence of digital video and digital sound technology for the video "pro-sumer." As desktop (computer-based) video becomes a more viable production alternative, some points raised here will become moot. This means that all the technological solutions described above relate mostly to the near future. But in the near future and into the distant future, keep experimenting, try some of the rules listed here, and break them to form your own.

IMAGE COMPRESSION

Data compression technologies are shaping the future of computer-based video, animation, and sound by making it possible to store vast amounts of data in small amounts of computer disk space. The use of image compression can reduce the amount of space needed to store data by more than 1,000 percent. This chapter takes a brief look at how image compression works.

BY JOHN WORTHINGTON WITH GAIL MCGREW

John Worthington is a co-founder of IFX, a company established in 1992 in Marin County, California, to specialize in new media technologies. Before launching IFX he was one of the leaders of Apple Computer's QuickTime project. He's an animator, composer, and musician who graduated from the University of California at Santa Barbara and worked at Apple for six years. Coauthor Gail McGrew is a writer and editor in San Francisco.

Image compression is a process of "squashing" the data that comprise an image in order to transmit and store it quickly and at a relatively low cost. Images take up a great deal of space in a computer's memory. On the Apple Macintosh, a typical, full-screen, full-color image (640 x 480 **pixels**) eats up 1.2 megabytes of storage space, and the kind of higher-**resolution** images used in print publishing, such as the cover of this book, require 50 megabytes or more.

The typical Macintosh computer is equipped with a hard drive that offers 40 to 200 megabytes of storage space. If you want to store several images, you can quickly use up the entire drive. You have two choices: you can spend thousands of dollars on more memory (and larger or more hard drives), or you can compress the data that make up the images and graphics—up to 1/20th of their original size, without degrading the image quality.

Image compression is typically accomplished through "compression utilities," computer programs that code the data into special space-saving formats. Restoring the image data to full-resolution form requires decompression, a process included as part of the compression utility program.

Today you can choose from two types of image compression: "lossless" and "lossy" compression. Lossless compression ensures that the original data are exactly recoverable, with no loss in image quality. The image you see after compressing and decompressing it is precisely the same as the original, down to the pixel. Unfortunately, there are limits to the amount of

pixels: Contraction of "picture element," the display dots (smallest resolvable elements) on a computer display. Picture resolution is measured in the number of pixels (usually in horizontal and vertical dimensions) used to create the image. The more pixels per inch, the higher the resolution. For example, Apple's high-resolution monitor supports 640x480 (HxV) pixels.

resolution: The measurement of image sharpness and clarity on a computer display, usually measured by the number of pixels per square inch. The more pixels, the higher the resolution and the smoother the image, with a greater amount of reproducible details. "Resolution" also applies to video and film, where it's measured by the number of horizontal lines that make up one image frame (complete picture).

compression you can achieve using lossless compression. The average upper limit is around 4:1, and actual results vary with the type of image you're compressing. This 4:1 ratio means that you might be able to squeeze a 1.2-megabyte image down to about 300 kilobytes. However, extremely complex, high-contrast images such as photographs don't compress as well.

"Lossless" compression is necessary for critical image needs. Magazine and book publishing companies, for example, might require lossless compression to save some storage space while maintaining extremely accurate, high-quality images. The standard **PICT** graphic file format used for images on the Macintosh relies on a form of lossless compression.

One field that requires lossless compression is medicine. Medical centers are exploring ways to use lossless compression to transmit X-ray images over telephone lines. A person living in a small town could go to the doctor's office for an X-ray, and the doctor could send the X-ray image data via modem to a specialist in a large city. It's vital that the data not be lost or corrupted; the transmitted image must be an exact duplicate of the original image.

In "lossy" compression, the original data is not completely recoverable. The loss of some information might decrease image quality, but compression experts say that you can lose a great deal of the data in a typical image without a noticeable loss in the apparent resolution. The trick is to discard information that is less visually important, which usually involves losing small details. Imagine a brown hill beneath a blue sky filled with white clouds. Odds are, your mental picture is fairly

complete—maybe you're envisioning some vegetation on the hill, or puffy and wispy clouds—even though I haven't supplied you with those details. The data that make up an image that detailed require many bytes of information; however, I was able to create the basic image description with 56 bits of information (56 characters, including the letters and the spaces between the words). By providing such a basic description, I do lose detail, so the image in your mind isn't exactly the same as the one in my mind. That's what "lossy" compression is all about. Almost all uses of compression techniques today are lossy, including the technique used in **HDTV**.

In general you'll always use lossy compression in your computer images, because it provides much greater compression. The gain in compression is directly related to the loss of image quality. Deciding how much to compress an image involves weighing these choices. In book and magazine publishing, you might want keep highly compressed versions of all your images as "roughs" for use in designing the publication. This would give you an idea of how the final results will appear. The final artwork, the version you send to the printer, would contain the original, high-quality images.

It's also important to maintain "minimum color depth" in your images. If your final output is going to be black and white, there's no reason you need to work with the image in **24-bit RGB** format. By working with the image in **grayscale** format, you immediately achieve a 3:1 compression savings, with no loss of image quality.

PICT: A type of Macintosh file format that can contain drawing-type graphics, charts, graphs, and so on.

HDTV: High-definition television, a new TV transmission standard that provides a way to transmit and receive about five times more video information than we can see on normal TVs. HDTV sets are larger and wider, offer better color and 4-channel digital audio, and cost many thousands of dollars. Different HDTV systems are under development in Europe, Japan, and the U.S. Experts say we'll feel HDTV's impact in the middle to late 1990s, when it slowly makes its way into our homes.

24-bit RGB: A "24-bit RGB" monitor can display over 16 million different colors at once. RGB refers to an image-encoding scheme and display output signal, based on the additive properties of transmitted light (used in video technology), that mixes red, green, and blue to create colors.

grayscale: A shade of gray assigned to a pixel in a computer image, from black to white.

Image compression doesn't only affect computer users. Anyone who uses a camera, for instance, will experience the wonders of compression when they use the Photo CD system developed by Eastman Kodak Company and Philips Interactive Media Systems Division. Photo CD lets you take your print film or 35mm slide film to a photo shop or drug store and get back a CD-ROM for about $20 for a 24-exposure roll. The Photo CD process scans any 35mm slide or negative, converts it to a digital photograph, compresses it, and stores it on compact disc. You can play the disc in the Photo CD players that connect to TV sets (these players handle audio CDs, too) or in CD-ROM drives that connect to computers. You can even have prints made from the CD.

Photo CD images are compressed for storage on the disc, then decompressed as they're accessed for display on screen. As a result, a single 680-megabyte disc can hold up to 100 digital images with the equivalent of 2,000-line resolution. (This also accelerates the process of accessing the data for screen display.) Without compression, just one of those images would require 18 megabytes of storage space. Kodak's PhotoYCC compression scheme resembles the compression scheme used for HDTV.

Photo CD also works directly with Apple Computer's **QuickTime** system, so Apple Macintosh users can click on a Photo CD icon to access and integrate Photo CD images directly into any program, from page-layout, multimedia and "slide" presentations, and even spreadsheets and word processing documents.

QuickTime: Part of the Apple Macintosh system software, it allows integration of dynamic media (sound, video, animation) within all applications.

QuickTime supports numerous compression formats, as does the Windows operating system on the IBM PC platform. Soon, most of the images displayed on any computer screen will be compressed images.

Image Compression & the Artist

Artists need to understand image compression because it will affect our creative work. When we use lossy compression to store our images, we must be prepared for the results. The polite term for those inaccuracies introduced by lossy compression is "artifacts." Artifacts can take on many forms.

One form of artifact results in a "blocky"-looking image. Blockiness usually appears because of the quantization used in most image compression methods.

"Quantization" refers to one step in the process of encoding an image's pixels, or bits, as representative numerical values for storage. Simply put, quantization involves "rounding-off" the numbers. Let's say you have an image in which the numbers from 1 to 1,000 represent a color gradient. Since we want to use fewer bits to represent each color, we quantize the 1-1,000 range to 1-10. So the "mapping" of original to new bits would start out like this:

Original	New
1-10	1
11-20	2
21-30	3

If part of the original image was represented by the set of numbers "9,10,11,12," it would be replaced in the compressed image by "1,1,2,2." When displayed on screen, this new set of numbers would appear in the image as a block, and what was originally a smooth change of color now becomes a distinct change. Additionally, because a range of colors has been mapped to a single color, the image can look flat.

This quantization also can induce "shimmering" or "sparkling," usually in video or animation. The quantization transforms an object's soft edge (such as a cloud) into a hard edge, which looks "shimmery." Sometimes the quantization creates a set of pixels that are the wrong color in only one image of the video or animation sequence. When the sequence plays back, you see a "sparkling" effect.

Some visual artists *like* these lossy compression artifacts in their work. Artifacts sometimes create unexpected effects that are aesthetically interesting. Consider the Impressionist paintings from the 19th century; they often were characterized by the artist's combining many dots of color to create the image. You don't see the image clearly until you step back 15 feet or more from the painting. Today's cyberartist might intentionally seek an effect similar to this by "overcompressing" an image.

Artists who use computers are just beginning to learn how the different types and amounts of image compression work in different images and effects. At this point, experimentation is the name of the game. Image compression technology is young—software utilities first appeared in the marketplace in 1990. The rules and standards of image compression are still in development.

The Future of Image Compression

Image compression is useful not only because it reduces the storage requirements of images, but also because it makes them easier to transmit. HDTV takes advantage of image compression to fit a higher quality image in the same **bandwidth** used by a standard television image. Cable companies use image compression to transmit more channels with the same picture quality over a single cable. In the future we'll watch interactive TV, which will merge the computer and the television, with the assistance of image compression technology.

One issue that complicates the widespread use and understanding of image compression is the lack of standards. Computer and imaging technology manufacturers, including Apple, IBM, Intel, Microsoft, Philips, and Kodak, each support their own proprietary "secret recipe" image compression system.

A few international standards for image compression have been proposed, but most are too processor-intensive to be implemented in software alone, which means they need to be supported by hardware. This makes them extremely expensive to incorporate within personal computers. Two relatively recent standards are making their way into computer systems in the form of add-on circuit boards and software packages. These standards were developed by the Joint Photographic Experts Group (JPEG) and the Joint Motion Picture Experts Group (MPEG), committees working under the auspices of the International Standards Organization. The former group has defined a proposed universal standard for the compression and decompression of still images in computer systems, while the latter defined such a standard for motion video and audio.

bandwidth: Data transmission rate.

The JPEG standard can be implemented in software on most personal computers. Most major computer manufacturers are supporting it; Apple supports JPEG in its QuickTime software, while Microsoft supports JPEG under Windows. Unfortunately, JPEG specifies a compression *method*, not a basic file format, so things get complicated if you want to transfer a JPEG-compressed image from a Macintosh to a PC. To further confuse the issue, some companies developed compression software based on earlier versions of the JPEG standard, so if you're using one JPEG-compatible software program to compress an image, you can't assume that it can be decompressed by other JPEG software.

Many of JPEG's techniques were applied to MPEG. The first stage of MPEG's activity addressed methods for encoding video on and off CD-ROM for screen display, seeking the kind of image quality associated with broadcast television. Even as the MPEG specification was being finalized for acceptance as an international standard, there were proposals for MPEG 2.0!

The bottom line with image compression is that we need to keep informed about it. As the market grows, we'll see standards emerge and cross-platform compatibility become easier.

MOVING HOLOGRAPHY

*Computer-generated, animated **holography**—what is it and how might it be applied? In this chapter Stephen Benton, inventor of the white-light transmission "rainbow" hologram seen on credit cards and magazine covers, discusses the past, present, and future of this photographic process. Much of the early work on white-light holograms (which can be viewed under normal lighting conditions) was performed in the 1970s by Steve at the imaging physics laboratory he established at Polaroid.*

BY STEPHEN A. BENTON

Stephen Benton, professor of media technology, heads the Media Arts & Sciences program and directs the Spatial Imaging Group at the MIT Media Lab. He is a Fellow of the Optical Society of America and a Trustee of New York's Museum of Holography. After working at Polaroid, he joined the Media Lab to develop a teaching and research program in 3D imaging, especially as it relates to the human-computer interface. There he and his colleagues have invented the world's first interactive holographic video system. He also is the inventor of the "alcove" hologram, which projects a computer-generated image at the viewer's fingertips and offers a 180-degree field of view.

holography: The process of making or using a hologram, which is a 3D picture made on a photographic film or plate without the use of a camera. It consists of a pattern of interference produced by a split coherent beam of light. For viewing, it is illuminated with coherent light from behind. 3D imagery dates back to ancient Greece, when Euclid demonstrated that the left and right eyes each see a slightly different image of the same object and the merging of these images creates depth perception. Based on this principle, a hologram is designed to project two different vantage points.

The Media Lab is located at the Massachusetts Institute of Technology, which is on the Charles River in Cambridge. The Media Lab is housed in a beautiful, I. M. Pei-designed building on the east end of campus, close to the heart of MIT. Did you know that MIT is the home of the new Nerd Pride movement? I co-founded the International New Media Nerd Club. We have chapters in Russia, France, and the States, but the most active chapter is in Japan. By the way, don't let other people tell you what a "nerd" is supposed to be. We're here to tell the world what nerds are! Harnessing America's nerd power is the secret to our future. If you are obsessive, compulsive, intense, and driven by some wacko vision that you can barely articulate, and perhaps are a bit socially undeveloped in the eyes of those people who themselves are the single largest threat to our future, contact me at the Media Lab and I'll send you a "Nerd Pride" pocket protector—or a button, in case you don't have a pocket on your dress.

The Media Lab consists of 12 research groups; its graduate program offers Master's and Ph.D. degrees. We have about 90 students. Many have worked in industry, learned things, and returned to school to learn even more and to contribute to the Lab's research programs. For example, one of our research groups, Electronic Publishing, is concerned with how to manage the fire hose of information that comes out of CD-ROM drives and the fiber-optic cabling that one day soon will bring information from networks to our homes. Multimedia work is concentrated in the Visible Language Workshop, where

Moving holograms
shouldn't be confused with
holographic stereograms,
which show a repetitively
moving subject.

eye tracking: Eye movement detection, referring
to a computer technology's
ability to determine precisely where the user is looking.

cognitive science: The
study of the human act
or process of acquiring
knowledge, including both
awareness and judgment.

multimedia scripting (authoring systems) is an area of research. The Interactive Cinema group is concerned with the creation of an interactive cinema-like medium. Another group is working on the School of the Future, sponsored by Lego and Nintendo among others. Most of our artificial-intelligence work is concentrated in the Music & Cognition group. The other Media Lab groups focus on important elements of the information environment of the future, such as speech research, advanced human interfaces, **eye tracking**, computer graphics, animation, and digital video. We're not talking about next year's products, of course, but about an academic research program that looks decades into the future. Our research is heavily driven by what I call "technical agendas"—hardware and software hacking, **cognitive science**, and artificial intelligence—as well as by design and aesthetics. We try to bring in people from all these backgrounds.

The group I head at the Media Lab, the Spatial Imaging Group, is interested in creating a visual interface that is dimensional, or "spatial." It's the kind of project that depends on people with many types of backgrounds—electronics, optics, computer programming, and all aspects of media—who, over the course of their education, learn to work together to make things happen that wouldn't occur in any one discipline alone.

We're not dedicated solely to holography, but over the past few years, for the first time anywhere, we've been able to produce real-time, moving, holographic images. They're small-scale, dim, and flickery— comparable to where television was around

1926—yet they represent the first toehold on this next epoch in visual technology. These **moving holograms** are actually holographic video images.

Modern holography is defined as optical wavefront reconstruction by laser interference and diffraction. It's a subfield of optics, a display technology invented by the scientist Dennis Gabor in 1948, long before the laser was invented. Nothing much happened in holography until the laser came along in the early 1960s. The U.S.-based scientists Emmett Leith and Juris Upatnieks, in 1964, were the first to use the modern laser for holography. They are the fathers of modern holography; once the importance of the concepts behind holography was made clear (in 1971), Professor Gabor received the Nobel Prize in physics.

When most people hear the word "holography," they think about the psychologically ultimate, three-dimensional imaging medium of the future. When Disneyland opened its Haunted Mansion in 1969, everybody assumed that the creatures flying around in the haunted ballroom were holograms. George Lucas' 1977 film, *Star Wars*, featured an apparition of Princess Leia projected into the middle of a room. Since then, visitors to the Media Lab have seen our large, hardcopy holograms, looked at them appreciatively, and asked, "So when are you going to show me the holograms?" Disney's Haunted Mansion actually represents a new version of an old magician's trick, a triumph of imagination over engineering, while *Star Wars'* projected apparition of Princess Leia violates at least four laws of physics. Yet it's amazing how many grown engineers think we should be able to do this already!

Suppose you want to do things like that. What would you do? You could try *lenticular* screens (cousins of 3D postcards), spinning and moving screens, or vibrating "varifocal" mirrors, all devices that produce images that are autostereoscopic—they don't require you to wear special glasses in order to see the 3D effect, and as you move around, you experience *motion parallax*, or relative motion between the front and rear of the image; you can look around the object to its right and to its left and still see the 3D image. People have long thought that intersecting laser beams ought to be capable of making a 3D display in some kind of special gas or crystal, which might come true someday. People also imagine that you can project images onto smoke with a slide projector, and that you'll see a 3D image in the smoke. If you try it, you'll find it doesn't really work. However, some connection between these methods someday may produce an image that you can generate in mid-air, but without opacity and the other important visual attributes of real objects.

Our recent work has focused on holographic video, producing moving and interactive 3D images. Holography has broken, or at least reformulated, many rules of classical optics, and the laser has made many new things possible. Indeed, we don't know what holography's ultimate limits are. We *do* know that one basic problem concerns projection, because we *don't* know how to take a beam of photons— light—and turn it around in mid-air and make it appear to your eye as something

in mid-air. Photons have no mass, charge, or magnetism, and it's hard to deflect them, except with optical elements— lenses, mirrors, or perhaps, holograms.

Therefore, the kinds of projections that are possible will take place on something analogous to a screen, which will itself be an optical device; it might be a concave mirror, lens, or a holographic screen. The optical element itself must be fairly big. If people are standing before a viewing zone that's a meter wide, the projection lens also must be about a meter wide.

Since the late 1960s, everybody believed that holographic video was simply impossible with any foreseeable technology. We conducted our first experiments in 1987, with a hologram that consisted of about 1,000 pixels. It took a few hundred seconds to compute. Since then we have developed our current system and learned more and more about programming it, so now we're down to a few seconds for each hologram.

Our breakthrough came about because we approached the concept of "information reduction" by trying to find the minimum amount of visual data that human beings need in order to perceive a high-quality, three-dimensional image. A normal hologram is capable of providing extremely precise information about its subject, with resolution down to millionths of an inch, far more than the human eye can appreciate. Also, a normal hologram provides motion parallax in an up-and-down direction as well as side-to-side, while most of our sensation of depth comes only from side-to-side variations. We reasoned that, by deliberately limiting the amount of information in the

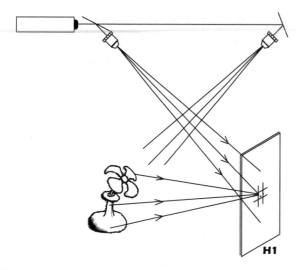

hologram, we would make it both easier to compute and easier to display. However, such insights do not usually suggest specific ways to make systems work, and it has taken us several years to come up with a really fast computing system and high-resolution display system.

We're starting to look at many applications of holographic video. For example, we're working on a holography project with Massachusetts General Hospital. We're dealing with a new kind of X-ray treatment of tumors that are located deep inside the brain. The brain is a highly complex, three-dimensional system. If you're a brain surgeon operating on a tumor, you want to know when you're missing

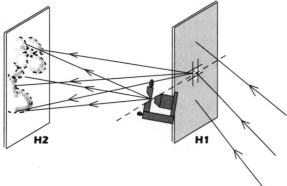

structures and when your X-ray probe is planted in the tumor and not hitting blood vessels. You also want to be able to see the same problem from different perspectives. By viewing a holographic video of the tumor and moving your head around, you will be able to understand the implications of placing the X-radiation in various ways—which vessels will be radiated, and so forth. The holographic display will let the surgeon switch between seeing a view of the anatomical landmarks and a view of the radiation doses to them.

How do we create holographic video? Our computed hologram is modelled on a type of "natural" optical hologram called the "lensless Fourier transform hologram" process, a variation on conventional holography. I'll describe how we would make such a hologram with real optics, which might make the computer model easier to understand.

We start with an object positioned in front of a photographic plate; we illuminate both the object and the plate with a laser beam. Most of the light illuminates the object and creates waves that fall on the plate. The rest of the light forms a "reference beam" that overlaps the object waves to produce a high-resolution "interference pattern." These are small areas of high and low exposure, where the reference and object waves arrive in or out of phase, so they reinforce each other or cancel out. It's all extremely microscopic and vibration-sensitive. The center of the plate records a perspective view from the center of the viewing zone. High and low parts of the plate record up-and-down perspectives, while side-to-side parts of the plate record side-to-side views.

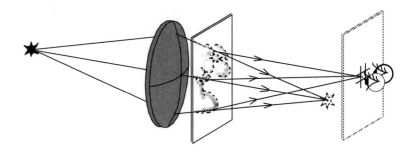

We normally illuminate the hologram and view it as though we were looking at it through a window. In modern two-step holography techniques, that first hologram is used to project an image into space by illuminating it with light traveling backwards as compared to its original reference beam (this is called phase-conjugate illumination). It travels through the back of the plate and sends an image out into space—the image literally floats out there, and if you put your eye in the right place, you can see the aerial image being formed in space. Next, we straddle that image with a second holographic plate, with its own reference beam, and record the interference pattern produced where they overlap. That's called the image plane hologram, which is the kind you see in science shops and gift stores. The trick to creating a Fourier transform hologram is that its reference beam comes from a point source that's at the same distance as the first hologram.

You view the second hologram by illuminating it through its back, focusing the light to where the reference beam point had been. Diffraction of the illumination by the microscopic interference pattern changes the direction of the light waves and creates an image of the first hologram in space. You can move from side to side and up and down within the area of the first hologram and see the 3D image of the original object.

The diagram that shows a full-aperture transfer hologram refers to "no information limiting" (the aforementioned information reduction), which means that the resulting hologram consists of an extremely fine pattern of dark and light

Viewing of a full-aperture transfer hologram, with no "information limiting."

areas. To model this hologram, we need to compute thousands of pixels per millimeter. A typical four-inch by five-inch hologram requires about ten million pixels to represent all the detail, while a typical TV image consists of about a quarter-million pixels, so you can imagine the problems we experience trying to deal with billions of pixels. The computation of this much information has stymied progress in the field for years, and the display of so many pixels still seems impossible. The solution is to reduce the amount of information so as to drastically reduce the number of pixels required.

Let's say we want to create a reduced-information hologram, one without vertical parallax. We block off the upper and lower areas of the first hologram during the transfer process by illuminating it with only a horizontal slit of light, perhaps 2mm high. This prevents the "high" and

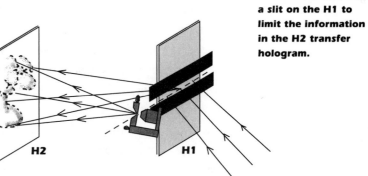

Here we transfer using a slit on the H1 to limit the information in the H2 transfer hologram.

H2   H1

"low" perspective views from being projected to the hologram so that information is never recorded. The reference beam for the second hologram is now a point source at the extreme left end of the slit. To view the hologram, we illuminate it with a vertical line of sources, or put a vertically-diffusing filter over it, to create a viewing window that is fairly tall.

Other approaches to reducing holographic information include reducing the vertical resolution and reducing the horizontal resolution to the eye's maximum capability, and sampling the horizontal parallax. We also can reduce the hologram size; today, hard-copy holograms that measure a meter square are, more or less, the state of the art. Our moving holography experiments use an image about the size of a 35-millimeter slide, roughly an inch by an inch-and-a-half. We also can reduce the angle of view; in hard copy, we can achieve almost 180 degrees of "look-around" in a single hologram. Most of the holograms that you see in shops and science museums have about 30 degrees of view angle.

For these experiments, we reduced the viewing angle to 12 degrees, just enough to let both eyes see the image and allow some motion from side to side, to enjoy the motion parallax of the image. We hate to reduce the size and angle, though, because a hologram's impact depends on large size and wide angle of view. We are already working our way back up to larger sizes and wider angles.

When we reduce the hologram to the size of a 35mm slide with a 12-degree angle of view, the number of pixels required to display it drops drastically to about 32,000 pixels wide by 192 high, or 6 million pixels (6 "megapixels") total. Displaying all those pixels still presents a challenge, because each individual pixel measures only about a micron wide, twice the wavelength of light and about an eighth of a millimeter high. We can compute this reduced number of pixels in a reasonable amount of time, but still must come up with a way to display them. Although this is not an astronomical number of pixels, they are arranged in a strange configuration. It's been difficult for us to get manufacturers involved in developing displays for this strange format, but this may change as more manufacturers come to believe that holographic video might become practical (as is happening in Japan, for example).

Most of the depth of a holographic image arises from *binocular stereopsis*. Each eye sees a slightly different perspective view, and the fusion of those differences produces a strong impression of depth. The holographic effect is enhanced by motion parallax, which I mentioned earlier: From side to side, you can move a couple of inches at arm's length and look around a bit. In developing our holographic images, the first step we take with our image-modelling software is to create **wire-frame** images. Then we introduce object opacity ("occlusion," or hidden surface removal) so the dark planes in front hide the wire frames behind them. Then we work on surface shading to create solid-shaded facets. (These days we're working on implementing something similar to **Phong shading** for more realism and to achieve highlights and blends, which are extremely important in spatial perception.) We also port in stereographic camera images—that is, images built up from several dis-

wire-frame: In computer-generated 3D graphics, wire-frame drawings appear as lines that represent the edges of an object.

Phong shading: A type of shading used in computer graphics, named after the person who formulated ideas fundamental to that shading process. Also called "normal interpolating" shading.

crete perspectives from side to side, which is how we make our hard-copy, computer-generated holograms. We also **scan** in photos of real people and bring those images up on the holographic video.

To compute, store, and distribute these computed holograms, we work with the Connection Machine II (CM2), a mini-supercomputer made by Thinking Machines, Inc., of Cambridge, Massachusetts. When we take the horizontal-parallax-only approach, the CM2 doesn't calculate the entire hologram all at once. In a normal hologram, the information of any one object point is spread over the entire hologram. In a horizontal-parallax-only hologram, that information is spread across just one horizontal line, which means we only need one line of pixels (32,000 pixels wide) in the computer's memory at a time. Otherwise, the necessary system memory would have to be huge. We literally simulate the propagation of the reference and object light waves to the hologram, where we interfere them and calculate the hologram exposure at each pixel location within a line. Our CM2 has 16,000 processors, and we can configure the system to look like there's one 8-bit processor at each of the 32,000 pixel locations. The hologram is computed a line at a time, then sent to hard disk storage or temporary storage in the frame buffer memory (the frame buffer controller was modified to allow access to two megabytes of storage on each of three memory planes, normally the **R,G, & B** memory planes). The computed pixel patterns are read out from the frame buffer memory at video rates, about 80 megapixels per second on each of three lines, so

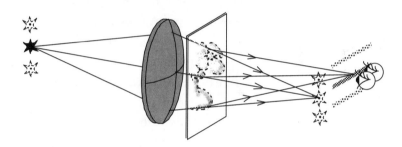

Viewing a horizontal parallax-only hologram.

the entire hologram is read out about 40 times per second.

Our breakthrough in the optical display also was related to human perception. We realized we didn't need a single liquid-crystal display screen to display all six million pixels at once. If we placed an aperture over the liquid-crystal display and moved it around, as long as we could see about 2,000 pixels—just enough to cover the pupil of the human eye—the image would look about the same, provided the image depth was no more than a few inches away from the screen. The overall image is dimmer as a result, but the important point is that the limited size of the eye's pupil (which limits its ability to see fine detail) also implies a limit to the number of pixels required at any one

scanning: The process of translating images into a form that can be displayed on a computer monitor.

R,G, & B: Red, green, blue, the primary colors of light used for displaying images in computer monitors and televisions.

instant (assuming we don't intend to view the image with a microscope).

We provide that limited number of pixels by feeding them into one end of a bar of crystalline material (tellurium dioxide) that has a particularly slow speed of sound—about 2,000 feet per second. A **transducer** that is bonded to the end turns the electrical pixel signal into a soundwave that, via the "acousto-optical effect," modulates the lightwave illuminating it. This crystal bar, then, is an acousto-optical modulator (AOM). It's long enough to hold about 2,000 pixels' worth of information between its ends. The effect is as if we had that small aperture with 2,000 pixels revealed, but now the pixels are racing across at 2,000 feet per second, so the pixels soon disappear!

We could move the AOM itself in the opposite direction at 2,000 feet per second, which would make the pixels seem to stand still, then swing it back to start a new line, but this is mechanically impractical. Instead, we move the AOM optically by viewing it through a rapidly rotating mirror (actually, one of 18 facets of a mirror wheel that is spinning at about 9,000 rpm). Seen through the mirror, the AOM's outline moves from side to side, and the temporary pixels seem to stand still behind it. That image is focused and demagnified about four times by a large-aperture camera lens to form the hologram lines at the output plane. A "nodding" mirror system moves this line up and down in order to trace out the entire hologram surface about 40 times per second. The resulting holographic video image moves fairly

smoothly, as precomputed holograms can be pulled off the computer's hard disk at a rate of about 15 images per second. The images also can be interactive—we can recompute them in real time, usually in less than a second for wire-frame images, turning a knob to rotate the hologram in any direction.

Our future work involves creating better mathematical models, or more efficient encoding, for holograms that are easier to compute. More efficient encoding means we wouldn't have to send as much information around all the time. If we can accomplish model-based encoding of the 3D image information and perform more computing on the display itself, the information becomes easy to distribute around a high-capacity network.

Over the next few years we also plan to scale up the hologram's size to a 12-inch display system. We need to devise new scanning technologies to make that work. This will involve a much more elaborate computer system with extremely high-speed frame storage and image processing. Nonetheless, in a few years holographic video will be bigger, brighter, and easier to see.

I believe that holographic video will become a practical and useful imaging technique. I hope we will reach the point where we can make it portable, something that you can look at with your own two eyes. The ability to bring holography more into our lives will depend on achieving a better match between what that technology can provide and what we human beings need to stimulate our powerful spatial thinking abilities.

transducer: A device that converts one type of energy to another. For example, the loudspeaker in your stereo system is a transducer; it converts electrical energy into soundwaves.

THE CHOREOGRAPHY MACHINE

A DESIGN TOOL FOR CHARACTER & HUMAN MOVEMENT

BY THECLA SCHIPHORST

Thecla Schiphorst is a choreographer, dancer, animator, and computer systems designer whose performance work includes integrated media dance performance. She earned her B.A. in dance and M.A. in computer compositional systems for dance from Simon Fraser University (SFU) of Vancouver, British Columbia, in Canada, and graduated with a diploma in computer programming and systems analysis from British Columbia Institute of Technology. She currently serves as artistic director at the Computer Graphics Research Lab at SFU and design consultant to Kinetic Effects, Inc. She also teaches at the Emily Carr College of Art and Design in Vancouver. For several years Thecla has worked with choreographer Merce Cunningham (based in New York City), supporting his creation of new dance using LifeForms.

"LifeForms" is a computer program that lets you create sophisticated human motion animations and access "shape" libraries of figures in sitting, standing, jumping, sports poses, dance poses, and other positions. This chapter explores the goals of Life Forms' development as a software tool that supports the design or compositional process of choreography and animation. The author, a member of the LifeForms design team, investigates how choreographers use this tool and ponders some of its cultural and social implications.

"LifeForms" is a computer tool for the creation of three-dimensional character motion. A software program for Apple Macintosh and Silicon Graphics computers, it provides an interactive, graphical interface that enables a choreographer or animator to sketch out movement ideas in space and time. Although originally envisioned as a creative tool for choreographers, LifeForms has greatly interested animators, directors, athletic coaches, and motion planners, because it enables you to create, edit, and store movement sequences for humans and other types of characters.

The world renowned choreographer Merce Cunningham, who presaged the post-modern dance movement, uses LifeForms in his creation and exploration of new dance work. In his use of LifeForms to create a dance work such as "Trackers," choreographic insight and discovery combine with technological development and exploration. In this approach, the computer technology is as much affected by the articulation of dance knowledge as dance and choreography are affected by the articulation of technological knowledge.

In the design of LifeForms, we explored the ways in which choreographers such as Merce Cunningham create movement with a tool. We then integrated what we learned from these artists into the system in a way that provides what we hope is transparent access to the creator's movement idea.

In LifeForms, you can **keyframe** movement sequences by directly manipulating a body interactively, using "inverse kinematics." You can define and use skeletons other than the human body with the same ease and flexibility that initially allowed choreographers to create dance. The system's large library of predefined movement sequences provides a source of material that can be performed by multiple human figures (or multiple user-defined figures). You can edit these figures in space or in time by using a simple, interactive, intuitive interface that supports the hierarchical nature of composition by allowing you to easily move backward and forward between alternate views and conceptual levels of abstraction. You can view various movement paths, while the computer automatically **interpolates** the animation of the movement sequence so you can view it in real time. Since dance typically is accompanied by music, you also can select audio files, cue them to various "in" and "out" points, and play them synchronously with the movement.

A Brief LifeForms History

Initially, LifeForms was designed as a computer tool for creating and planning human movement in dance and choreography. Conceived by Dr. Thomas Calvert at Simon Fraser University, LifeForms is a development that reflects his career-long interest in exploring the relationship between computer technology and research into human movement.

Dance is the most technically complex form of human movement that exists in our culture, so development of a computer tool for the creation of dance provides several research challenges. For example, dance embodies a wide range of movement possibilities and often requires great physical virtuosity that extends the limits of a human body's physical ability and training. Therefore, what is learned from a computer tool that is used to create dance can be generalized for other forms of human motion planning. Also, choreography is a compositional design task that requires a set of skills related to *creating*, *structuring*, and *forming*. Building a computer interface that interacts with a choreographer's design skill set requires an understanding of the mental model of the choreographer's design process.

As Herbert Simon noted in *Sciences of the Artificial*, "The ability to communicate across fields—the common ground—comes from the fact that all who use computers in complex ways are using computers to design or to participate in the process of design." This area of research relates to the observation and understanding of how our creative process operates when we interact with computer systems, and how computer interface designers can help provide a more intuitive, direct, and transparent relationship with the creative idea. In dance (and in animation), where the creative idea is a movement idea, the goal is to visualize and create body movement in an immediate

keyframe: Used by the computer to calculate and display intermediate frames in an animation sequence. LifeForms automatically creates smooth human motion between any two positions, or "keyframes," defined by the user. For instance, one keyframe might show a human figure with its arms held up in the air, while the other keyframe shows the figure with its arms pointing straight down. The software supplies the "in-between" frames.

interpolate: A mathematical function; to estimate a missing functional value by taking a weighted average of known functional values at neighboring points.

and responsive way, so the computer tool must become a "visual idea generator." Our initial design goals provided us with an interface that has proven valuable in other areas of computer graphics-based movement simulation.

LifeForms deals with movement in a general, direct, non-narrative way, so it interests anyone involved in planning motion. Kinetic Effects, Inc., is continuing development of LifeForms in areas targeted toward character animation (much of the software engineering has been performed by designer Chris Welman). As a result, Life-Forms now works with skeletons defined by the user, and these skeletons can represent any kind of character, not just the human body.

An adjunct development in the area of movement research has been the creation of a parameterized real-time walking interface, created by Armin Bruderlin. By parameterizing movement, you don't have to keyframe shapes based at specific points in time. Instead, you can create movement and receive real-time visual feedback as you modify parameters directly on the computer screen. The integration of this type of motion control provides for multiple methods of creating movement.

LifeForms as a Model of Design Process

The design process contains elements that are recognized as common to all creative activity. These include: the hierarchical process; alternate representations; and use of knowledge and visualization of the compositional idea.

Hierarchical process is the way in which one conceptualizes an idea in various levels and layers of abstraction. In dance there

You can define custom "skeletons" for use with LifeForms.

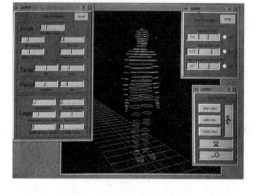

LifeForms supports the choreography of "parameterized" walking in real time.

is the high-level conceptualization of overall shape, spatial relationships, and energy flows, and the lower-level detail of how the arms, head, and fingers move in relation to one another or in relation to time. An important element in creative process is to move flexibly between these levels.

The importance of *alternate representations* lies in the juxtaposition of different frames of reference that allow the choreographer to think in various (perhaps unconventional ways) about the composition. The Latin verb *cogito*, "to think," means "to shake up." The British writer Arthur Koestler has noted that the act of discovery of creation (which he refers to as "the Eureka act") occurs when distinct representations are recognized as depicting the same object, idea, or entity.

The *knowledge* of the choreographer is context-dependent. That context is sociocultural and based on expertise and training in the physical, kinesthetic experience of dance and movement and in the cognitive forming and structuring elements of choreography. The discriminating act of selecting one's compositional material, even if done unconsciously, determines the resulting form of the artistic work. *Visualization* of the work in progress allows the choreographer to view and evaluate the movement and the dance, and represents an important step in the iterative creative loop. In most cases, it is helpful if the movement is as realistic as possible.

These elements have formed the basis for the functional design of LifeForms.

Working with LifeForms

In describing the essence of dance, Merce Cunningham once said, "Dancing is movement in time and space; its possibilities are bound only by our imagination and our two legs." LifeForms maps this viewpoint of "movement in time and space" by providing three on-screen windows in which to create dance:

• a window that allows the creation of movement sequences for a single dancer; this is called the "sequence editor window";

• a "spatial" window that allows groups of dancers to be arranged and edited in space; and

• a "timeline" window that allows the dancers' movement sequences to be moved and edited in time.

These three windows, or views, are interconnected. You can move flexibly between them by using a simple interface that supports the hierarchical nature of composition by allowing movement between conceptual levels of abstraction. Movement sequences are created automatically by smoothing the motion between the shapes created on the body. Included with LifeForms are libraries of sequences to provide a source of material that can be performed by many figures simultaneously. Movement paths can be viewed, and playback speed can be slowed down or accelerated. You also can select sounds, cue them up to your desired "in" and "out" points, and play them back in synchronization with the dance sequences.

The Sequence Editor. A movement sequence is the design "building block" in LifeForms. In dance, movement sequences are also called "phrases" or "movement motifs." The underlying rationale in selecting a sequence as the building block is that you can develop design "chunks" which enable creation to occur on a more conceptual level. A sequence can be created, manipulated, varied, and placed with other sequences at a rate that enables the visual response to provide a meaningful, creative feedback loop. This addresses our desire to move away from the constant struggle with detail that so often occurs with the computer. Without the conceptual distance provided by stepping back to a higher conceptual level, a choreographer or designer is unable to follow the iterative process that occurs naturally in all creative efforts.

In LifeForms, you use the sequence editor window to create movement for a single figure. A sequence is made up of a number of keyframes, each containing a body shape placed at user-defined time intervals. The movement is created by interpolating or smoothing the motion between keyframes. You can vary the playback speed to view or analyze the movement at different tempos.

The sequence editor window displays a three-dimensional human body (or "skeleton"), initially shown in a natural, neutral standing position. You then can create shapes for skeleton in several ways. For example, a single limb segment can be directly manipulated on the body and positioned in three-dimensional space, or existing body shapes can be copied from the library of stored sequences. Alternately, a chain of limb segments defined by the choreographer can be pulled in place through the use of inverse kinematics. (For instance, if the end of the chain was the hand and the base of the chain was the lower back, the entire chain from the base of the lower back could be moved by pulling on the hand.) An exist-

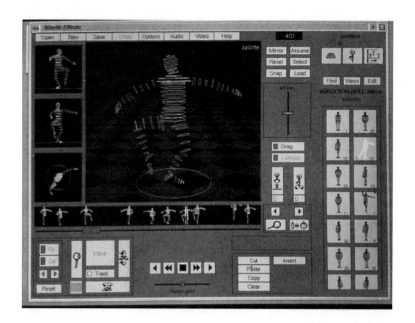

The sequence editor

ing position can be mirrored in the left or right plane.

The Spatial View Window. The spatial view, or "stage," enables the choreographer to spatially plan multiple dancers performing combinations of sequences. A character or dancer can be assigned a sequence, a starting position, and an orientation (or "facing") by directly

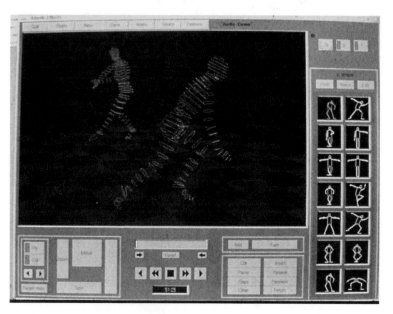

The spatial view

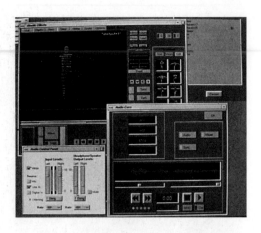

The audio window

positioning the dancer with the mouse. Movement can be viewed from any three-dimensional viewpoint, and camera keyframes can be set to enable the viewpoint to change as the composition is played back. These spatial scenes are similar to the series of storyboard sketches used in film and video production, but the interactive capability lets the choreographer zoom in or zoom out from the stage and view the composition from all angles. Movement sequences are displayed in a visual library on the right side of the spatial window. Each sequence can be viewed as a "flip animation" by selecting it with the mouse. This provides a fast, visual memory aid and enables the choreographer to quickly select movement for use in the composition. The spatial view, in conjunction with the "timeline" view, allow spatial and temporal editing to occur in relation to one another.

The Timeline View Window. The timeline view provides the choreographer with a high-level, score-like display that depicts the relationship between dancers and movement sequences. The spatial relationships of the dancers are superimposed upon the timeline display. Since changes made to temporal relationships

between figures and sequences necessarily result in changes to spatial relationships, the overlapping of views addresses this "transparency" and interrelationship between space and time and provides immediate visual feedback when changes are made.

The Audio Window. The audio window (which works only on the Silicon Graphics Iris Indigo version of LifeForms, as of this writing) enables a choreographer to play sound files with a single sequence in the sequence editor or an entire choreography in the spatial view. Cued "in" and "out" points can be edited for experimenting with combined movement and sound.

Merce Cunningham & LifeForms

In March of 1991, Merce Cunningham premiered a dance piece called *Trackers*, in which about a third of the movement was created with LifeForms on an SGI Personal Iris computer donated by Silicon Graphics, Inc. Cunningham has used Life-Forms since December of 1989. In a 1991 interview with the cable TV channel CNN, he said, "I think this technology can, in this case . . . open out a way of looking at dance and movement in a way that would be stimulating and invigorating to the whole dance field eventually." As a leading figure in contemporary dance, Cunningham is a choreographer who is world-renowned for his continuous innovation and exploration in "opening out the way one looks at," understands, and creates movement. His ability to openly embrace technological possibilities is simply an extension of how he continues the exploration of movement as a process rather than as a fixed goal.

Merce Cunningham is interested in making new dances. The words "making" and "new" offer two compelling hints that reveal how he works. The "making" is the active engagement of creative process, while the "new" reveals his attraction to discovery. This is exemplified in his description of the appeal of imagining movement with computer support: "One can *make* things with [LifeForms], one doesn't have to put things in one already knows. . . . One can make *discoveries*, and that interested me from the beginning." Cunningham did not abandon his previous choreographic methods for LifeForms; he incorporated them. For example, many of his movement sequences in LifeForms were created using chance procedures to determine how the body would move, what body parts would be used, and what shapes would be incorporated. When these movement sequences appeared "physically impossible," Cunningham would work with his dancers to discover how the sequences could be made to work. He does his work by dancing and by making dances.

LifeForms in a Cultural Context

It is important to describe not only the technology itself, but also its perceived relationship with the user—the artist—and with the work created with it and from it. In other words, it is important to place this work in some sort of cultural context.

Sometimes LifeForms, and artists' work with technology in general, is misrepresented or misunderstood by the mass media. In the same CNN segment in which Cunningham described his work with LifeForms, the CNN reporter said, "Tech-

Merce Cunningham's dance "Trackers" was choreographed, in part, with LifeForms. Photo: © Johan Elbers

nology is coming to the rescue of choreographers" and that computers will "save dancers from long, arduous, and boring rehearsals." These comments represent the kind of social attitude toward technology that often has given technology a "bad name." Also, we need to make clear the fact that dancers do *not* regularly find rehearsals "boring," although they may well be arduous or long. The kind of commitment, sacrifice, and passion that artists give to their work comes from love, not from boredom. And choreographers and dancers probably don't take kindly to the idea of being "rescued by technology," which implies some kind of victim stance and somehow misses the point of cooperative development between artist and technological design people. There is something of a gift in creating art and in designing computer interfaces that enables each way of "making" to affect the other. What can result is an education for all participating in this exploration.

Those who see technology as a "longed-for saviour to choreographers who will finally be rescued by it" must

LifeForms' Distribution:
LifeForms is distributed by Kinetic Effects, Inc. (Seattle) for the Silicon Graphics computer platform and by Macromedia (San Francisco) for the Apple Macintosh. The Silicon Graphics version runs on any SGI computer. Kinetic Effects, Inc., handles all LifeForms development work.

learn that choreographers and artists are not victims, and that an enormous amount of choreographic knowledge can enrich their ways of using and creating with technology. It is not technological constraints that hold us back from using technology in new ways (after all, technology changes at a tremendous rate), but it is the cognitive constraints, our willingness to explore beyond the constraints of our mind and our imagination, that have the greatest effect.

The Artist: Moving Toward Opening Possibilities for Discovery

As has been noted by others, the impact of technology on the artist is not limited to the expressive possibilities of equipment and techniques. It is necessary to understand the conceptual and perceptual changes that are taking place, to understand further the working of the human mind and body and the forces of the social and natural environment, and to understand the very nature of the arts themselves, their role and function in this changing world.

An interaction is taking place among the arts, dissolving the boundaries that have separated one art from the other, seeking new synthesis between the plastic arts and the performing arts and combining these, in turn, with the electronic media. Central to all our uses of technology is the artist's ability to explore possibility, discern meaning, elicit or reveal value, and elaborate vision.

Work with LifeForms was supported in part by grants from the Social Sciences and Humanities Research Council of Canada.

SECTION 4

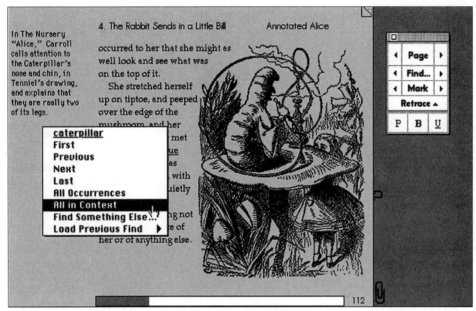

"The Complete Annotated Alice" **A Voyager Expanded Book**

INTERACTIVE MEDIA:

THEORIES

TOOLS, RESULTS

VIRTUAL WORLD WITHOUT END

THE STORY OF XANADU™

BY THEODOR HOLM NELSON

People who once considered Ted Nelson a lunatic dreamer now refer to him as a visionary. He has spent the last three decades making films and designing interactive software for personal computers, working on issues of nonsequential forms of writing (which he dubbed "hypertext") and "explorable" presentations (which he dubbed "hypermedia"), both intended for display and manipulation via the computer screen. Ted earned a B.A. in philosophy from Swarthmore and an M.A. in sociology from Harvard. He taught sociology from 1964 to 1966 at Vassar College. He's published many articles and four books, including Computer Lib, *the 1974 volume that inspired a generation of hackers. In 1979 he started Xanadu Operating Company, but didn't catch the attention of the computer industry until 1988 when Apple Computer introduced HyperCard, thus popularizing Nelson's term "hypertext." That same year Autodesk (primarily known for its computer-aided design software) purchased Xanadu and appointed Ted as Distinguished Fellow.*

Ted Nelson writes: "The gold rush is on. The hypermedia are happening. Whatever you call it, here come interactive graphics, text, video, all somehow user-chosen. But how will they tie together? If producers knew where all this was going, the rush would rival the advent of the Talkies. Meanwhile, each manufacturer says its gizmo will be the centerpiece of the hypermedia gold rush.

"Whatever it is will be very new. What will it look like? What will it run on? Where will we keep it? How will we connect it? Where do I fit in? What's in it for me? And perhaps most important, what's in me for it?

"As always, a torrent of technicalities hides simple truths. Talent, not technicality, will be the limiting commodity. Each user has at most 24 hours a day. Complicated setups will be little used. And incompatible things will fade quickly. It all has to tie together. There cannot be island universes.

"The problem lies in putting together the ideas, not the equipment. More people must learn more, faster, than ever before. This means the user must go freely through magic doors, turning corners from world to world to world, keeping track of what happens on the way. And our new media must merge production values from many technical sources, melding portions of many pre-existing productions in the hands of tomorrow's producers and artists."

This chapter explores Xanadu, a radical software concept that first occurred to Ted Nelson in 1960. The Xanadu system is intended to become the foundation for an information utility that will involve franchised information outlets located around the world.

You hear today about "Virtual Reality," meaning computer-based three-dimensional worlds. But "virtual" means something much larger: *as-if*, the way something seems to be. Virtuality means the *seeming* of what we create, and the appearance of things is the true center of software design.

Our world becomes increasingly virtual, as its appearance departs more and more from depending on the structure of physical reality. Movies and television, moving signs, recorded music and sound, the illusory continuities of broadcasting stations and political parties, all these are virtual.

Deciding the fundamental ideas of our mental and electronic universe seems to me one of the most important tasks of all, and it is the design of virtuality. I will present here that virtual universe of the mind that I and my colleagues have been working on for many years.

In 1960 I was a young academic and aspiring filmmaker, but something happened to delay these pursuits. I had a vision of new computer media and the delivery system they would need. I knew there would be **interactive** movies and interactive texts, and we would need an interactive publishing system to make them available.

But somehow this was not obvious to everybody, nor is it yet.

In my youth I had heard that computers were mathematical, engineering sorts of things. And you had to know a lot of math, and what they were really for was doing statistics, bookkeeping and astronomy, but there were some obscure interesting things about them. Well, all this sounded fishy to me; I had to know. So I took a computer course in graduate school.

And here in the textbook was a screen, you see, that could be attached to the computer. A screen! On which the computer could make patterns of dots. How about that. Now here's a picture in the newspaper. What is it close up?—patterns of dots! There's no picture you couldn't put on the screen! And you could store the picture, you could change it by the computer's responding to you. Together you and the computer could do anything.

That story about mathematical computers had been a lie, a coverup. They'd been hiding this thing. Under the rug was the most wonderful machine you ever saw. You could do anything with it. In the hands of an artist, in the hands of a filmmaker, in the hands of a writer it could become anything. This was the answer to my biggest problem—how to organize writing (something the programmers don't understand yet).

So I figured, holy smoke! I'll have to do something about this.

We are talking the future of civilization here. How we handle ideas and writings and the other media is at the center of everything. The final form that the human heritage takes is *literature*, the collection of writings and ideas and memories we save. I saw that there had to be a whole new computer-based system for the literature of the future.

And I thought I had to do it for a very simple reason—if I didn't do it, *they* would, and they'd screw it up. Unless the new literary system were clean and

interactive: Able to respond immediately to certain choices and commands made by the viewer, in such a way that the viewer's actions and decisions genuinely affect the way in which the program progresses.

unless it were simple, our human future would be crippled.

That was 32 years ago. And what I consider the most fundamental tool of human thought does not yet exist, and the work I put on hold remains unfinished. So far.

The 2020 Vision

The vision I had in the fall of 1960 was very simple and can be very simply stated. It was so simple it confused people totally. They thought, "That must not be what he means."

The idea is this. Imagine the year 2020. Billions of people, including you, are at their computer screens around the planet. And each of you is able to draw to your screen, from a common document repository of humankind, any fragment of text, graphics, audio, or video.

Demand publishing. In other words, universal electronic publishing. *Demand* publishing, meaning things come on request, right away.

Delivery is fragment by fragment, each fragment coming at a user's request. (A whole document is delivered as a series of fragments.) You pay by the **byte** for what you take.

From owned documents. Everything sent will be a portion of some stored *document*, that is, a planned contribution created and owned by some individual or publishing company. The document can be a piece of text, an illustration, a piece of recorded music, a part of a musical score, a photograph, a painting, sheet music, a segment of video, a piece of laboratory data, an architectural design. Or it can be a conglomerate including all

these types, or any other kind of information that can be stored electronically.

People often say loosely, "We'll have all the information in the world on line." Well, I don't know what that means. The word "information" is suspect; it means too much and too little. Who owns "information"? Who takes care of it and makes sure it's up-to-date?

There are these things out there called **databases**—packages of granular information, like file cards—and so much of what's in them is suspect, as is the usefulness of the more advanced database queries. You make these complicated structured queries and the answer comes back: "42." You got an answer, but you don't know what you got. Databases of this type have reached their limit.

But the real, understandable, common heritage of humankind boils down to *documents*. Notice I do not say information or data or knowledge. Because these words, "information" and "data" and "knowledge," are kind of slippery and amorphous like a zip-lock bag full of water.

But I know what a document is. A document is some kind of information package that some author created. Somebody signed it or took responsibility for the contents. And that gives you a social handle on where it's coming from, and that title tells you that this person who created it created it with some objective in mind, and the continuity of the title over different editions tells you more still. So the notion of a document is in some sense psychological and social, as well as literary.

A *document* is an information package that someone creates, and *literature* is a system of interconnected documents.

database: A large collection of data in a computer, organized so that it can be retrieved, expanded, and updated for various uses.

byte: A measure of computer data equal to eight bits; a bit is the smallest unit of data in a computer.

Each academic subject has its own "literature"—the literature in biology, the literature in economics. And then including them we have *all* literature, the much greater interconnected whole of which the others are a part, a vast interconnected system of information packages.

And what we need, as we read, is to follow connections. And that is what hypertext, and the new interactive arts, are about.

With pretty fast delivery. How fast will it come from the repository network? As "instantaneously" as a phone call gets through, which of course varies.

From a server network. Tomorrow's literary system will not be on a single gigantic mainframe, of course; it will be distributed on server machines throughout the world, coordinated by software into a single, functioning delivery system.

Digital, error-free, and playable. Because it is in digital form, the material comes without error, and your computer screen machine becomes a player with which to read, view, hear, or examine what you have summoned.

With royalty. And for each piece you automatically pay a small royalty to its publisher, as well as delivery charges to the service providers who store and ship it to you.

Come the new interactive arts. This would not be simply for yesterday's sequential paper documents, of course, but for tomorrow's new branching and interactive media—**hypertext** and *hypermedia*, as I was to name them later (in 1965). Today's novelty term, "interactive multimedia," is used so it will sound new; its popularizers avoid the synonym *hyper-*

media, which would reveal that the idea has been around for decades.

These interactive arts would not have linkages and options merely *within* individual packages (like today's closed hypertexts and hypermedia titles), but *between* the packages as well, links between documents.

A new pluralism. Because the different documents could have different authorship and points of view, the whole would be what we now call a *pluralistic docuverse*.

Of open hypermedia publishing. And that would lead to the biggest idea of all—*open hypermedia publishing*.

Now, open hypermedia publishing means the following: It means that anyone can publish a connection to another document. And a reader of the original document can say, "Who has published connections?" and go to any of the connected contributions by others—comments, disagreements, addenda, variora.

These ideas all hit me at once, a long time ago. Such a simple vision. But radical, and very confusing to people in the 1960s. Now more and more different people understand different parts of the idea, but few seem to understand it whole, even today.

What holds us back remains, as then, sluggish ideas. Then it was fear of computers. Now, we are held back by the terrible slogan that the computer enthusiasts brought out, "Wizzywig"—the most insidious piece of propaganda on behalf of stupidity that was ever contrived. Actually spelled WYSIWYG, it stands for "What you see is what you get."

What does that mean? Here I am at the screen. What I see is what I see, right? So what does "get" mean? It means *what comes out on the printer*, doesn't it? That's right, folks. WYSIWYG means we're going to use this magnificent piece of equipment, this incredible technological achievement, as a *paper simulator*; we will limit this extraordinary device, capable of enacting any set of instructions the mind of woman or man can devise—we're going to use this incredible enactor to pretend to be the surface of flattened wood pulp. (Imagine the imaginary forest that had to be cut down to make this virtual sheet of paper.) This is like using a 747 as a bus on the highway.

The alternative, of course, is to use the computer screen to show the real structure and interconnections of things—polymorphic and multidimensional. But instead Wizzywig simulates a superficial disconnected mess, the images of paper sheets and the clutter of separate papers on your desk; and gives us no general software to show you how documents and ideas are *related*.

Hypertext & the Interactive Arts

Thoughts are not two-dimensional, but until now the process of expressing ourselves on paper has been breaking the multidimensional connections of thought down into little pieces and putting them all in a sequence on two-dimensional paper.

Why should we want to do that? Because paper was what we had. Now, on the computer and its screen, we have two choices. One, we can go on breaking the thoughts into a two-dimensional structure and plastering them on simulated paper, using the computer to simulate this two-dimensional Wizzywig array of flat thought.

Or, two, we can keep the thoughts in their true, multidimensional structure and create reading and presentational arrangements that will let the reader traverse them in any direction and in any way he or she sees fit. And this, to me, is the most obvious and yet powerful thing about the computer screen world: *Ideas needn't be separated any more.*

So the term "hypertext" I define simply as *non-sequential writing*—links, possible connections to follow, reading opportunities in different directions. "Hypermedia" correspondingly means *interactive presentations.*

There are now many hypertext software products, and hypermedia, but they are amazingly incompatible. As yet there is no common data structure for these interactive arts, so what we need in order to define this arena—one of the things the world needs most—is a common system for representing and delivering them. (Not simply a low-grade player machine, as certain large companies have tried to tell us, but a grand-scale coordinate system for the documentary world of the future, and a way to navigate on it.) And that is what the Xanadu group has been creating.

The Xanadu™ Hypermedia Server

The question is, how do you go about building the world repository library? Answer: You write the software—software that will show all the connections that different people contribute, all the connections you need to keep track of.

This is what the Xanadu system is: a software package for *keeping track of interconnections of every kind*—the interconnections of ideas; the interconnections of quotations; and the interconnections of documents. Xanadu is one piece of software carrying out this one idea across a whole spectrum of needs, from the office to the vaunted system for universal electronic publishing, a single concept which has a global interpretation and a minute interpretation, both of which are really the same.

Xanadu is a literary system, in my preferred sense of "literature": it deals with *documents and their interconnections.* This works for published documents or the private documents an office will have.

The Xanadu office system (sometimes called "Little Xanadu") is just the same as the Xanadu publishing system (some-

times called "Big Xanadu")—a system for storing and delivering connected documents, multimedia, and hypermedia objects.

In both the office system and the publishing system, users at screens identically put in requests and the material flows out to supply those requests; except that in Xanadu publishing, the system transmits an automatic royalty from the user to the publisher of every fragment delivered to that user.

What the software principally provides is a generalized way to represent interconnection in documents of every kind, even though they are changing. Xanadu software handles that by two mechanisms, keeping track of two fundamental connections: *links* (of all kinds) and what we call *transclusions.*

1. The Xanadu link. The generalized link of Xanadu goes between spans, or pieces within a document or work selected by whoever made the link. A good way to visualize a Xanadu link is as a strap between a collection of bytes on the left and a collection of bytes on the right—and neither collection need be all together.

2. Transclusion. Transclusion is the other fundamental method in the Xanadu system.

Anything stored in Xanadu can be a combination of new sections and old sections stored in previous versions. The old sections are brought in whenever needed, but their origin is always noted. Transclusion can always show us the origins of what we're looking at, even in a complicated merged document. This sounds inefficient, and in some ways it is, but it

Xanadu link

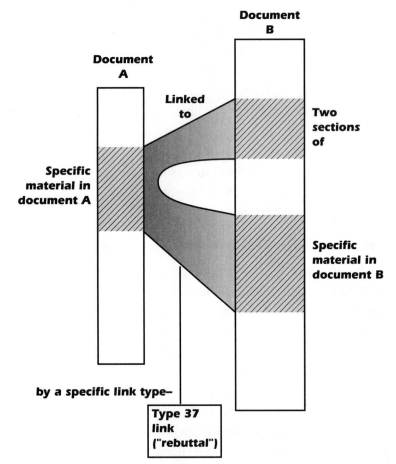

Document A

Document B

Linked to

Two sections of

Specific material in document A

Specific material in document B

by a specific link type–

Type 37 link ("rebuttal")

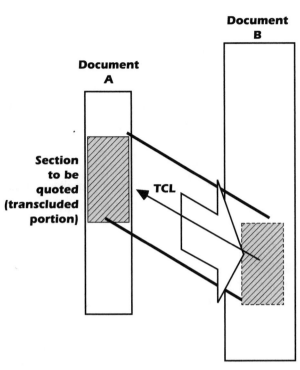

Document B

1. Transcluded section is not actually present in document B; a transclusion pointer shows where to go to get it.

◀ TCL

Document A

2. When the transcluded part of document B is sent for or read, it is automatically brought from document A, summoned by the user's screen machine.

Section to be quoted (transcluded portion)

◀ TCL

Place where transcluded portion will appear.

Transclusion

cleans up so many issues that Xanadu has been built around it.

Transclusion shows us what comes from where, because a *quoted piece is not copied*. Instead, it is brought in from its original storage when needed; but it is considered *part of* the new document, just as a family member not present at a celebration is still part of the family. We call this *transclusion* because the inclusion takes place across a document boundary.

So the idea of transclusion is that something from one document can be used in another document without copying it. It is represented in the second document as a special hidden pointer that says, "Whenever you get to this pointer, bring over the piece from that other document." This transcluded piece is intrinsically part of both documents, though its place of origin is special and called its *native home*.

Transclusion solves, to a large extent, the copyright problem, the updating prob-

lem, the versioning problem, and the boilerplate problem. I won't go into what these problems are, but if you know what they are you can see that this is a good thing.

A Data Standard

The Xanadu model also provides us with a possible basis for data standardization.

One of today's great and growing issues is how we can recapture a usable and organized world out of the jumble and morass we find now of files that are lost everywhere in different formats.

Each new program for a given purpose is typically different from most *other* programs for similar purposes, and creates stored material—files and the data structures they contain—that are likewise different from the files stored by the other programs for similar purposes.

In other words, most computer applications usually have their own incompatible data structures. Programmers

**Data structure studded
with markers**

choose a way to represent something—say, text or graphics—that is, some mixture of pure data and code markers.

Now, the code markers tend to be different for each program, and this is getting worse and worse in every area, because every programmer has the right to do it his or her way. Incompatibility grows and the data world grows daily more muddled.

But suppose we pursue a different vision: one of keeping clean data by itself, without embedded codes, and marking it by pointers off to the side. For text, the clean textual data will be the alphabetical characters, spaces, and punctuation; and we will move the data markers off to a separate package—the markers for italics, beginnings of paragraphs, and so on.

And what that means is that you can scan through the clean text and look for things in it. It also means that you can

¶
§
△
♣
∞
∏
◊

Text, text, text
Text,more text, text
More text, text,
text. and yet
more text with
special sign that
have special local
meaning. More
text, text, text...

**Same data structure
broken out as separate
collection of pointers . . .**

have *different* boxes of markers off on the side that don't interfere with each other.

So that everyone can mark up the same material without contradicting the other stuff. And that's what we have to have in a pluralistic docuverse.

The Office Foul-Up

No doubt most of you are familiar with not knowing what's in your computer files—not knowing how they're connected. What the typical office is now, in case you haven't noticed, is an accumulation of mysterious and unknown disks and files with mysterious names. We don't know where they came from or which ones quote from where. We all suffer from this problem because we don't have transclusion and we don't have linkage built into existing computer systems. What we need, I believe, is a complete revision of the way that things are stored so as to keep track of what comes from where, and what the origins, differences and connections are.

Moreover, the computer files tend to be inaccurate. We are not keeping clean computer records because users still regard paper as the final and canonical form—because the paperdigm (including WYSIWYG) is still the dominant model. A document is considered finished when some last page has been corrected with white-out. So what's in the computer is often corrupt, left behind by its paper shadow.

We cannot get these things cleanly organized until we decide the electronic version is the final and canonical copy.

So what the office really needs is a seamless and integrated pool of clean electronic documents whose interrelations are known, rather than this jumble; a seamless pool of contents which can easily be put into different combinations (documents, versions) and reused in clean and understandable ways. It means also being able to replace those stinky little file names with more sensible designations. This and more is what the Xanadu software is intended to do.

The World Repository

At the beginning I spoke of the 2020 Vision, the World Publishing Repository. This will use exactly the same connection mechanisms as the office software. And it will be on an enormous scale, potentially for trillions of linked documents. This is what our software is intended to do.

Now the notion of open hypertext publishing that I've mentioned is that anyone can add linked documents at any time which are visible at both ends of the link, even when a library gets huge. That's the hard part.

But there are many issues for such a system.

Privacy. There are fundamental issues of *privacy*.

For example, you sure don't want people keeping track of what you read. That's fundamental, but not necessarily obvious, because there are all of these good pretexts someone might have for wanting to keep track of what people read—such as research. But the overwhelming, preponderant argument is that we must not keep track of what people read because then somebody— government or employers—makes that spying the basis for how people get treated. Which then constricts what every-

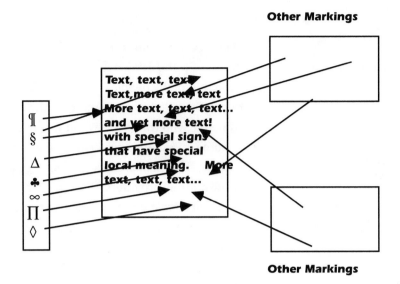

Other Markings

Other Markings

. . . permits pluralistic annotations of same materials by others

body reads, and we start reading for show, building a phony profile. Such a world would be intolerable.

(But note that we need the same seamless document environment in the world of private documents, with the additional proviso that they may link to and transclude public documents. Even for private documents, linkage and transclusion are vital facilities, and we need these features for our regular private document traffic—especially e-mail and teleconferencing.)

Then there are fundamental issues of freedom.

Freedom to read. Everyone should be free to read whatever is published. Some people want to create degrees and restricted modes of publication. This is dangerous for many reasons. I believe there should be only two degrees of availability: "published" and "private," under private control, so we do not have to outmaneuver supervisors or censors who consider particular people unqualified to read something.

publishing: *"I don't mean desktop publishing, which is a misnomer for layout."* —T.Nelson

Literary Machines: *A book published by author Ted Nelson in 1981; various revisions published by author from year to year; simultaneous mass-market edition being published, by special arrangement, by The Distributors, 702 South Michigan, South Bend, IN 46618.*

Freedom to publish. Furthermore, everyone must be free to publish. The power of **publishing** has always been in the hands of the people—we call it "Freedom of the Press"—but there is always someone who wants to restrict it.

Some information systems distinguish between "information users," or peons, and "information providers," or lords, who must put a great deal of money up front. This is intolerable. In our era more than ever, the only sensible assumption is that anyone may have something important to say, and has the right to say and publish it—and in the electronic era, the price of publishing will be going *down*.

My book *Literary Machines* just got a new chapter last week because I got around to it. That's how I like it. Sure I'd sell more copies of the book if I gave it over to a conventional publisher, but I wouldn't like it. People say, "Ted, why do you publish your own books? Why don't you go to a real publisher?" And that makes my blood boil. I am a real publisher. Anyone who publishes a book is a real publisher. The power of publication must remain in the hands of the people. Strangely, publishing is one of those terms that a lot of people don't quite understand. This is very odd. I think they don't understand it because professional publishing corporations don't want them to.

Technically, publishing means that you create documents and you hand them out or sell them— distribute them in some way, *making them public*—and the "publisher" is the person or company responsible.

And this is one of the greatest things in our country, that we have freedom of the press and you may publish anything you like at any time, without prior restraint, though of course you can be nailed later if you do something that's illegal or stomps on other people's feet. Thus a publisher, by law, is someone who makes things public and is consequently the person who can be sued for their contents or be put in jail. You're responsible for what you publish. We are free to publish without prior restraint, but not free from the consequences of publishing.

And this wonderful, wonderful thing called freedom of the press means you may publish anything you like. On Wednesday, or Tuesday, if you prefer, without asking anyone or without discussing it with any committee, or bringing it up before any editorial review board.

There's very little to it. Sell your work on the street corner—hand it out free if you like. When last seen, Walt Whitman had a baby carriage from which he was selling copies of *Leaves of Grass* in Brooklyn Heights.

In the world of print, it can cost thousands of dollars to publish something. And in the Xanadu world, what will it take to publish a document? Well, a repository fee—about $50, let's say, to publish something the size of a novel. You're paying for three years' storage of the document in three different places on the network, and the registration fee, and you've signed a little chit saying you're taking responsibility for the contents. And so now it is published.

Royalty

Then there is the issue of royalty. Since it must be legitimate to publish for money, it must be possible to manage royalty automatically in tomorrow's publishing world.

"Why can't it all be free?" people say. Because that's not how the world works. I would love to walk through the world and have people give me whatever I want and never have to give anything in return. But that's not how the world works. We have to give back; only for royalty will most publishers place things in an electronic publishing system. If true on-line publishing is to be viable, royalty must be a part of it.

Automatic royalty on each small transaction, on whatever sliver someone sends for. Why only a sliver? Because in the hyperworld, you rarely will want to buy the whole document. To look up a certain word, do you buy the whole dictionary? No, you just send for that definition.

Anyone in the world can take any fragment, paying (in their monthly Xanadu bill) an automatic royalty to some publisher for each sliver they have taken that is not in the public domain.

Free to Quote

In open hypertext publishing, you will be able to quote from any document without asking permission. How is this possible? Through the magic of transclusion.

I said before that transclusion is containing a part of one document in another without copying it. Suppose you want to quote three or four interesting documents published on the Xanadu network by authors somewhere out in the blue. Now, in the present publishing system you have to write letters, and you have to get releases and make arrangements, and so the grief and aggravation

threshold is fairly high, and authors don't quote each other very much.

But in Xanadu publishing, you'll be able to transclude any material you want into your document without asking permission, because you, the quoting author, are *not copying it*. You're simply making a transclusion pointer for each quotation, telling the reader's machine where to get that quotation. As the reader gets to the part you're quoting, the reading program in his or her machine automatically sends for the transcluded material from the other document, paying automatic royalty to the rights holder in that other document. It will also maintain automatic credit to the author of that other document, so that scholarship is perfectly sorted out. This cleans it up enormously.

You ask, "But won't you have to get permission to transclude?" No, because the original publisher has *already* given explicit permission for transclusion by signing the contract for the Xanadu publishing method.

So transclusion is a clean and simple, sweeping notion, clearing up the copyright problem enormously. It means that in this great repository, we can make many different uses of this great heritage of documents as we must in an ongoing world.

The Xanadu Group

Project Xanadu, then, was meant to be my term project in the fall of 1960 for a course called "Computers in the Social Sciences" in the Harvard Department of Social Relations. That term project will finally be finished when the Xanadu Group comes out with a major industrial piece of

LAN: Local Area Network, the most common means of connecting several personal computers into a larger system that allows users to share information and resources.

hackers: Someone who writes software or experiments with a computer's inner workings, typically with devotion and ingenuity. The term "hacker" often is applied incorrectly to mean someone who uses computers for wrong-doing or "data trespassing."

software containing this transclusive storage facility.

Of course, the project has gone through many versions. Every year or so it's been a different internal design, but always to do the same thing, more generally than before. The group I assembled on a porch in Swarthmore, Pennsylvania, in 1979 provided critical mass: Mark Miller, Stuart Greene, Roger Gregory, Eric Hill, Roland King, and me. We sat in the shade in Swarthmore and argued all summer of 1979. We agreed on one thing: "We must have the universal library and publishing system for the human race." We argued all summer as to what you did and didn't want in the World Publishing Repository, going over some of the things I've discussed—the meaning of freedom, privacy and publishing in tomorrow's electronic world. Political issues as well as technical ones.

At the end of the summer of 1979, they said, "Okay, Ted, we all agree on what has to be done"—which was quite a remarkable feat considering that these were brilliant and cantankerous people who couldn't agree on anything else—and then they said, "Now go away." And that was very depressing because I had to put down this project that I had been nurturing along for 19 years, but at least it meant they would do the work, which they understood technically better than I.

Then they labored for a decade under many circumstances; until miraculously, in February of 1988, Autodesk, Inc., a very mighty software firm, came up with money. This was because Autodesk was run by **hackers**—hackers in the good sense, not the newspaper sense—hackers meaning

people who work tirelessly on something that they believe in. Autodesk came and started fueling the Xanadu project with millions of dollars, I can't tell you how many, and we'll have a product out next year which is intended to be this server program. The World Document Repository should begin on a small scale in 1994.

Two companies. This one big idea of Xanadu has now been divided for practical reasons into two companies.

The server program, for users on a **LAN** or individually, will be from Autodesk. Xanadu Operating Company, a subsidiary of Autodesk, Inc., will be marketing this software for your generalized office applications and generalized industrial purposes.

The World Publishing Repository will be a licensing operation, vested in a company probably called Public Access Xanadu or PAX. PAX will grant licenses for publishing use of the Xanadu software, authorizing service providers to join the World Publishing Repository network. Our franchising will be rather like McDonald's, intended to assure quality and distinct, recognizable service. The service provider firms of the network will function rather like printers in the paper publishing world. (This is not an offer to sell a franchise, I must add for legal reasons.)

The Xanadu Publishing Plan

You can read all about these matters in my book, *Literary Machines*. Let me just state—to give you a sense of the timetable—that we hope to open the first Xanadu stand in Palo Alto sometime in 1994. But this in itself will not be a world-wide network, it will simply be a single stand with no more than 50 ports. You'll have perhaps two dozen Macs and PCs in the stand and the other ports free for dial-in. This arrangement should be saturated immediately, so we license more stands to qualified service providers.

See how it works? As demand increases, so will supply. It'll probably be only in Northern California at first. You'll be able to dial up from anywhere, but you'll have to come to California to belly up to the counter in a Xanadu stand—where I intend to be in a polyester uniform. Then sometime in 1995 we will open in Country 2, a place with good communication service where English is prominent and freedom of the press is not an issue. And so we will immediately be international from Northern California and Country 2, with linkage and transclusion across a unified docuverse, franchised like McDonald's. It's funny, people keep saying,

"What? Xanadu stands? I thought that was a metaphor!" You can tell them and tell them and tell them, but people won't believe you until you're there in your polyester uniform. So that, as much as the service itself, will be the proof.

Reality we have to take as given; virtuality is whatever we make it. Tomorrow's virtual world will consist of the conceptual and performing structures we design for the way we want to live. And that virtual world will be filled with information—information in idiosyncratic packages created by human beings, with their own many shapes and connections—what we have long called "documents," "works," "art pieces," "designs," "reports," and so on. Their interconnections, extending beyond paper, have in the past been lost. Designing our new virtual world to accommodate these true shapes and connections of information has been our chosen vital task.

RATTLING THE CAGES OF MULTIMEDIA MANIACS

*To cyberartists, the word "multimedia" refers to the use of personal computer technology to create, manipulate, and present information comprising multiple media: text, graphics, animation, audio, and video. "Authoring" systems and animation programs such as **HyperCard**, MacroMind Director, and Asymetrix Multimedia ToolBook make it possible for Macintosh and PC computer buffs to create eye-catching, interactive animations. MacroMind pioneered this animation software genre in 1985 when it debuted VideoWorks II for the Macintosh. Released in 1988, Director is its powerful sequel. Director allows creation of animated slide shows and full-fledged computer "movies." It provides a scripting language (also known as an "authoring" language) called Lingo, which allows creation of interactive multimedia presentations.*

Macintosh multimedia maniacs soon made Director the number-one tool for manipulating and merging files created with drawing, 3-D modeling, and animation programs. They could output the results to almost any media storage format, including videotape and videodisc.

In 1991, MacroMind merged with the software company Paracomp, which had fared well in the cyberart world with its Swivel 3-D animation program (originally developed by VPL Research, the virtual reality company). The merger begat Macromedia, which also markets multimedia presentation programs for the IBM-compatible Microsoft Windows environment, bridging the chasm between competing hardware platforms.

In this essay, Marc Canter ponders the power and potential of multimedia tools and systems.

BY MARC CANTER

Marc Canter has combined his two loves—the arts and electronics—since the early 1970s, when he majored in fine arts at Oberlin College and studied voice, opera, and electronic music. His desire to develop comprehensive tools for electronic music and video technology prompted him to form MacroMind, Inc., in 1984, to develop multimedia software. In 1992, Marc launched San Francisco-based Canter Technologies to focus on the field of interactive television.

Apple Computer developed **HyperCard** to provide computer users with a new way to organize, manipulate, and navigate through information, and to provide nonprogrammers with an interactive multimedia toolkit that has a simple, built-in authoring language, HyperTalk.

An **"interactive"** program or software responds immediately to certain choices and commands made by the viewer, in such a way that the viewer's actions and decisions genuinely affect the way in which the program progresses.

An **"authoring language"** is software that helps developers design interactive programs easily, without requiring the painstaking details and extensive skills involved in traditional computer programming.

"Windows" refers to the graphic-user interface for the DOS operating system.

The essence of multimedia is the ability to use a desktop computer to blend animation, graphics, video, sound, and text into one application, program, or "software title." The tools to do this are built into the computer; you don't have to buy and install extra circuit cards. This computer doesn't exist yet. It's almost here, but it's still the Holy Grail of multimedia. That's why a partnership must exist between the people who make hardware **platforms** and the people who make software. The manufacturers must remember that the development and distribution of multimedia requires technologists, business people, and the consumer electronics community, but the content of multimedia is driven by artists and aesthetics.

Whether it's used in training, education, sales, or entertainment, multimedia's key feature is *interactivity*. It lets you move beyond the passive, linear sequence, such as the way you watch a videotape, and actually change the order of the information presented to you.

Multimedia also can help you save money. In the world of advertising, agencies can use multimedia computer technology to create animated storyboards, or "animatics," which basically are rough drafts of TV commercials. Agencies that once spent $20,000 per animatic can now achieve similar results for $2,000.

Creative people will adapt to this new technology in many ways. The concept of real-time interaction with the media is a critical part. Just as MIDI lets us control digital musical instruments, multimedia standards will let us control computer-based graphics and video in real time.

Creative people who know how to work with the technology will exploit it to the fullest extent. People in the multimedia industry are trying to support that by creating a standard multimedia environment.

In a good interactive system, you should be able to use your mouse to interact with the environment and objects in it. We need good authoring tools to allow that. There's a difference between a true programmer, who **hacks** away in **C** or **Pascal**, versus someone using an authoring system. "Authoring system" is a generalized term that refers to any sort of program that doesn't require you to learn esoteric computer languages. It allows you to control various media devices and elements, such as graphics, sounds, and so on, using familiar English instructions.

An animator trained at an art school will get much more out of an authoring system than someone who hasn't received similar training. However, artists and other creative people don't necessarily think in programming terms. Artists do not use computer languages if they can help it.

platforms: Computer families (e.g., the Macintosh platform refers to all models of Macintosh computers).

hack: Write software or experiment with the workings of a computer.

C; Pascal: Computer programming languages developed in 1972 and 1970, respectively.

A programming screen from MacroMind Director. The Cast window lets you access and organize graphics, sounds, and text. In this example, the "character" is an animated stack of glass that grows to indicate an increase in recycled glass.

They would rather create animations in a traditional manner.

That's why one of the pressures on multimedia tool designers concerns how to provide easier-to-use products that still have the functionality of their traditional predecessors. The way I judge "ease of use" is determined by the length of each menu that appears. If it contains more than four or five items, it isn't easy to use. The ultimate "easy to use" system is called "plug and play." You just click on a command button, and maybe you highlight a file name, and the system performs the command for you.

It's this plug-and-play capability that we need for successful multimedia, and it must be something that the average person—not the technology expert—can handle easily. We need two types of tools. One type is the big, expensive, $8,000 machine, with built-in capabilities to produce real-time, 3-dimensional visuals and high-quality audio, that can spit out the master disks—the typical, advanced, professional tool that people will use to create professional-quality **3-D animation**. Once you've done those animations, you'll want to put them on a **CD-ROM** for distributing them. The second type of machine, the $300 machine, will play those CD-ROMs. The availability of these $300 machines will provide the foundation of the multimedia revolution.

Back in the time when film technology was being developed, companies created seven incompatible film projection systems, each one incorporating a different type of sprocket hole in the film. You couldn't take a film from one movie projector and play it on another. Does that sound familiar? The point is, we're trying to come up with a standard multimedia player that lets us move the same disk from one machine to the next machine.

However, the only way you can approach the multimedia world is by realizing that there never will be a standard hardware platform. Let's say you want to use the IBM Windows environment to print a word-processing document created on a Macintosh. That's what **PostScript** is all about. Want to run an animation in the latter platform that was created on the former? That's what **RenderMan** is all about. These software standards were created to allow us to move our data—it's called "data interchange"—between different platforms.

Between 1987 and 1990 we saw the Nintendo revolution, the infiltration of an **8-bit** machine into peoples' homes. We also saw the debut of the Mac II, a **32-bit** machine. In the following two years, game system machines entered the 16-bit era with the SEGA/Genesis, the NEC Turbographx and Nintendo boxes. Meanwhile, the high-end Macs improved, incorporating digital video and digital signal processing. Somewhere in the middle to late 1990s, these things will collide. There always will be a market for $8,000 personal computers. They're just going to be much more intense, and they will be able to do lots of cool stuff. But all this really won't matter until you can buy a multimedia computer for $300 at the supermarket checkout counter. And to start the multimedia revolution, we need a standard multimedia player.

People want this stuff now and they want it to be easy to use—but they also want it to be powerful. The real obstacle to overcome is in MIPS ("millions of instructions per seconds," which refers to the processing speed of the computer), and RAM ("random access memory," which refers to the storage capabilities of the computer). When we have a standard multimedia player that's fast and powerful, we'll start the *content* revolution. This content will be distributed on some sort of optical disc. That's why CD-ROM is so important; you can distribute lots of data on a CD-ROM.

If the software industry were like the fashion industry, all we'd be doing right now is selling sewing machines and scissors. That's how little we have tapped the potential of where we're headed.

If you look at the music industry and consider how much money people spend on CD players and tape decks versus how much they spend on recorded music, the "software," I estimate they spend about 10 percent on the hardware, 90 percent on software. Next, look at the computer industry. I estimate that people spend about 80 percent of their money on computer hardware, 15 percent on software, and 5 percent on service and maintenance. In general, they don't understand the concept of software. We have a long way to go, and the reason is because there are too many sprocket hole sizes. You can't just create one software title to run on one type of computer. Apple Computer doesn't sell enough computers for you to sell enough titles to send your kid to college. You have to spend thousands and thousands of dollars to convert a Macintosh title to run on IBM PC and PC-compatible computers, and on Atari computers, and on Commodore Amiga computers.

But it is possible. And the most wonderful aspect of desktop systems is that it is possible—and that we control these desktop systems ourselves. The fact that we control our information makes this a true revolution.

RenderMan: An industry-wide standard created by Pixar (Richmond, CA); enables different animation programs to represent rendered images in a standard way. (To "render" is to draw an image as it actually appears, rather than in schematic or outline form.) Issued by Pixar in 1989, RenderMan profoundly affected 3-D animation on the Macintosh. It created a standard text file format that contains a description of an image, defining the position of data, characteristics of the camera, lighting, coloring, etc. It allows graphics data to be created in one application, animated in another, and rendered in a third.

8-bit; 32-bit: Refers to ability of a computer monitor to display colors (also called "color depth"). In Macintosh parlance, an 8-bit monitor can show 256 colors at once; a 32-bit monitor can display over 16 million colors and also can perform special effects on them, useful for image processing and video production.

MULTIMEDIA WAR STORIES

Despite recent advances in digital audio and video technology, multimedia production on personal computers still presents thorny challenges. In the real world of multimedia, we face many problems caused by mass storage and computing power requirements. For example, how can we guarantee that our audio will run in perfect synchronization with our video? What happens when we show a multimedia presentation on a computer that's less powerful than the one we used to create the presentation? How do we distribute the final product? Why don't things work the way they're supposed to?

In this chapter Peter Gotcher describes some pitfalls and problems experienced by his company when they started creating multimedia presentations—and the solutions they devised. His goal, and his company's, is to help fill the ruts and defuse the bombs in the multimedia battlefield.

BY PETER GOTCHER

In 1983 Peter Gotcher co-founded Digidesign, a leading developer of computer-based, digital audio recording and editing systems. He earned a B.A. in English from the University of California at Berkeley in 1981, and worked at Dolby Laboratories in San Francisco as a technical writer before launching Digidesign in Menlo Park, California.

Multimedia caught my attention in 1988, and like many people, I bought into the idea that it would be wonderful to make interactive movies on your desktop computer, integrating audio, video, graphics, animation, all these different elements. The traditional process of making a video or animation seemed convoluted and expensive, not something I could pursue on a personal whim. Multimedia seemed like something I could pursue on my own terms.

I quickly learned that it's not as easy as some people would have you believe. You can do amazing things with this technology. It offers much promise, but it's difficult to use; it's still in the early stages of its development. In fact, there exists today something that I call "the myth of the multimedia businessperson." This myth concerns the executive who, an hour before a meeting, decides that he or she will whip up a little multimedia presentation to persuade colleagues or clients to do something. It doesn't work that way.

Multimedia is painful. It takes time and it takes talent. To "do" multimedia, you must have patience. Often, the end is worth the means, but don't let anybody tell you that it's easy. People who have created multimedia tools and titles are the pioneers in this field; there are rewards for being a pioneer, but the rewards don't come without pain and suffering. If you're committed and dedicated, you can create successful multimedia presentations or titles. But if you take a casual approach— "I'm going to come home after work and spend a couple of hours cranking out a movie"—you will be disappointed.

In 1989, Digidesign decided to investigate this thing called multimedia, focusing on the Apple Macintosh as a platform. We developed the AudioMedia circuit card, which installs inside the Macintosh II and turns it into a relatively low-cost, CD-quality digital audio recording and editing system. A month or so before our appearance at a major computer convention, where we were going to unveil AudioMedia, my marketing team came to me and said, "We want to have a great multimedia presentation to hype our new products." They wanted $10,000 to hire a multimedia production company to create a three-minute multimedia movie to show at the trade show.

I answered, "We're running around, telling people that this multimedia is a 'do-it-yourself' technology, yet we'll hire someone outside of our company to produce our multimedia demo? That's a bit hypocritical." In fact, when you go to a big computer trade show, look at the different multimedia presentations and ask the exhibitors if they did it themselves or hired

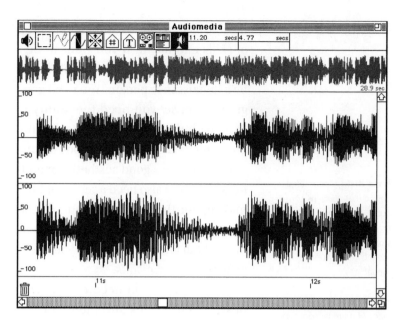

The AudioMedia system consists of a circuit board and three floppy disks. Once installed in your Apple Macintosh, AudioMedia turns the computer into a high-fidelity audio editing system. You use it to polish stereo recordings, which you can then integrate within multimedia presentations. This screen shows a graphic representation of stereo sound.

someone else to do it. I think you'll find 99 percent were created out-of-house.

At any rate, I told our marketing team that they should make their own three-minute multimedia movie. They didn't start until about ten days before the trade show. For once, it wasn't only the software programmers who were working in the office until two in the morning. It was the marketing people. Blood was coming out of their ears by the day before the show.

They worked mostly at night, because they had to handle their regular tasks during the day. Three people worked on the presentation. It took about 40 hours to write, design, and produce it, using Macro-Mind Director as the animation and authoring system. They started out with a rough script and figured they'd wing it, working out the script as they went along. They ended up scrapping their entire script, and going back to carefully and manually **storyboard** the script before actually producing it.

They also learned that producing a reasonably impressive, slick, Mac-based mul-

storyboard: A detailed, illustrated, frame-by-frame (or scene-by-scene) plan that shows all or most of a script's visual and audio elements. Sometimes it looks like a comic strip, with sketched frames above blocks of text showing dialog and narration.

timedia piece requires enormous amounts of skills and talent. If you want to be a good multimedia producer, you'd better be a Renaissance person. You need good graphic sense, you need the ability to draw with the various Macintosh paint programs, you need to know about sound or at least have a good aesthetic for editing sound. You also need a sense for filmmaking, for timing, pacing, and directing. The tools may be fairly straightforward, but without an aesthetic sense, you'll never achieve good results.

Alternatively, you need friends who possess those skills and plenty of free time, or you must have the money to hire skilled and talented people.

The bright side is that many computer software and hardware tools facilitate the transition from being an audio and video novice to being an audio and video editor, in a process that's much faster than the one you'd experience using traditional audio and video equipment.

The other problem lies in the *integration* of tools required to produce multimedia titles, or the ability to transfer stuff developed in one program for use in another program. Several companies offer good tools that help you create the different components of a presentation: animation software, sound editing tools, illustration and paint programs. But the integration of all these diverse programs still is weak. There are many obstacles to overcome when trying to move data between different applications; there's a maze of graphics and sound file formats with which to contend.

Other problems that arise when producing multimedia concern **synchronization** and timing issues. An anima-

tion created in MacroMind Director tends to run at different speeds on different Macintoshes. When you develop something on a Mac IIci and run it on the less-powerful Mac IIcx, the video runs slower and the sound goes out of sync. If you're producing multimedia on a Macintosh II, I highly recommend that you develop it using the slowest Mac you can find.

The synchronization problem makes it tough to produce a presentation for meetings on the road. I carry a ton of stuff in my briefcase—my own **hard disk**, even my own **memory chips** to install in the client's computer before I can run my demo. It's a far cry from the slide projector that you can pull out of a box, plug in, and turn on. Now you have to travel with a set of hardware alternatives and a Macintosh fix-it kit. Multimedia needs the equivalent of that slide projector, something portable and standardized. Until that happens, you'll court danger showing up at a conference or meeting, intending to do a "live" multimedia presentation.

One way to maintain synchronization is to cut all the audio into tiny chunks, small files that are triggered at various points in the presentation. (Using special commands, the presentation program can play digital audio files, or trigger CD-ROM drives to play CD audio files.) When creating audio for traditional video or film in a traditional studio, we produce long segments for the soundtrack and use **time code** to synchronize them to the picture. Using traditional equipment, we can enter commands that say, "The sound of the door slamming must occur at this precise frame number, which shows the door slamming." No similar synchro-

hard disk: A peripheral device that contains computer information and programs. Hard disks range in storage capacity from 20 megabytes to hundreds of megabytes.

memory chip: A tiny piece of material consisting of thousands of circuits and transistors; it is possible to open the computer's housing and install memory chips to increase the size of temporary computer memory.

time code: A code recorded on magnetic video and audio tape; each frame on the tape is assigned a unique address. This international standard is the basis for all professional video and audio tape editing and synchronization systems.

synchronization: The process of providing a means for an editing system to bring two or more video/audio tapes or digital audio/video data streams into exact sync, automatically. If the visual shows someone applauding, the sound of clapping should be synchronized with the action.

nization method exists for multimedia. You just trigger the sound from within the presentation program and let it "free-wheel." The sound always plays at the same speed (unless something's wrong), which can cause a problem because animations run at different speeds, depending on what type of machine you're showing them on.

There *are* systems that equip the Macintosh with time code capabilities, but they're expensive—several thousand dollars instead of a few hundred.

Less-expensive software programs that are designed to turn the Macintosh into media production and editing systems provide for synchronization. For example, Opcode Systems' Studio Vision software allows the AudioMedia system to synchronize sound to picture, and Digidesign's Pro Deck (which turns the Macintosh into a 16-track digital recording studio) can trigger a time code location. If your video or animation is running at the proper speed, you achieve good synchronization.

I don't mean to imply that multimedia is inexpensive. It's not. You need lots of hardware and software to produce multimedia presentations. Besides using Macro-Mind Director 2.0 for animations, Digidesign's Mac Proteus (a synthesizer on a circuit card) for music, and Digidesign's AudioMedia system for audio, making our own multimedia movie required the use of Adobe Illustrator and other Macintosh paint programs. Meanwhile, the Mac II required to run the movie had to contain eight megabytes of **RAM**, with a hard disk fast enough to play back digital audio.

Therefore, before you even start experimenting with these tools, familiarize yourself with the limitations of the approach and the system. That will help you chart your course. If you go into it thinking that anything's possible, you'll get frustrated. *Know the limitations of the medium before you start. Planning is vital.*

My marketing team includes two graphic designers. They're extremely talented, but they endured a hard, painstaking process to produce a large quantity of animation. We learned that a good way to produce a successful business or sales presentation with multimedia is to use many simple graphics and slides. Let the sounds provide your changing element, the part that seems "animated." A soundtrack is much easier to produce than animation, provided you have good original material.

That gets into another other issue. If you're not a musician, where do you acquire all this good material? You can't just grab bits of music off your favorite compact disc. This gets into both legal and ethical issues. For that matter, what if you're not a good graphic artist or photographer? If you aren't able to produce your own material, you may find that the administrative hassles involved in licensing music, graphics, or photos takes up a large portion of the total work involved in your project. That's why people creating multimedia productions prefer to use ready-to-go "clip art" and "clip music," a collection of pieces provided for unlimited, legal use in any form. If you're an artist, you may not want to use clip stuff, because you might ask, "Won't the use of non-original material destroy the artistic content of multimedia?" Perhaps—but for business applications, that's not generally a problem.

RAM: Acronym for Random Access Memory, the part of the computer's storage system that calls up data for reading, changing, or erasing. Data in RAM are lost when power to the computer is turned off. RAM is necessary for the computer to operate the large amounts of data in multimedia presentations, and to handle data (such as animation files) that require complex processing. When only a little RAM is available, the processor constantly swaps blocks of data into and out of RAM from the permanent storage memory; the processor can't concentrate on its main processing duties, so everything slows down. If the amount of RAM is so small that basic data cannot be shuttled into it at once, you won't be able to use very large applications or files.

Today's computer hardware and software offers better audio and video capabilities than those of products introduced just a year ago. Perhaps of greatest significance is Apple Computer's **system software**, **QuickTime**. The multimedia community needed a unifying "hub" for audio and video integration at the system software level. Apple's first-generation attempt to provide this hub, via QuickTime, represents an excellent start. It'll be exciting to see where it takes us.

● ●

THE MULTIMEDIA NETWORK

LIVING LIFE IN REAL TIME WITH "MediaLAN"

BY MARK LACAS
WITH LINDA JACOBSON

Musician, composer, visual artist, and electronics engineer Mark Lacas is president of Lone Wolf. He's put his microelectronics engineering expertise to work in several industries, including air transportation and health care. In 1983, Mark founded Fast Feedback Technologies, which developed the MicroLan Local Area Network and the "Nuclear Reactor Temperature Monitoring System" for the USS Enterprise.

LAN: A local area network is a system of software and hardware connected in a way that supports data transmission between connected devices. The most common means of connecting several personal computers into a larger system lets users share information and resources. A LAN is limited to a geographical area less than about 10 kilometers.

real time: The speed of the computer coinciding with the speed of the user; no delay in computer response time, giving the impression of instantaneous response.

patchbay: A unit with multiple inputs and outputs that let you re-route MIDI, audio, and/or video data streams to the right devices.

splitter: A device that "splits," or divides, a musical keyboard; instead of playing all types of sounds on each key, the keyboard is split into groups, each of which plays a different sound. One group might be assigned to play piano sounds, another assigned to play horn sounds.

merging: The combining of two or more MIDI data streams (from two or more controllers) to go down one MIDI cable.

When setting up a music or media production studio, you're faced with the task of orchestrating the connections and communications among your diverse digital devices. You might consider taking the local area network (LAN) approach, which provides a universal communications medium for the integration of disparate media formats. This format-independent vehicle can carry all information, transparently, between individual systems.

Problem is, traditional LANs don't operate in **real time***. They don't have to. But artistic performance and multimedia presentations usually* do *occur in real time, so the multimedia LAN must operate that way, too. If you want instantaneous results when you press a key, tap a drum pad, or click a mouse button, you can't depend on traditional LAN protocols.*

This chapter explores LAN technology that specifically addresses the stringent, real-time demands inherent in multimedia situations. It focuses on the MediaLink LAN protocol and devices developed by Lone Wolf, the multimedia LAN company. Musicians who use MediaLink include Herbie Hancock, INXS, Emerson Lake & Palmer, Tina Turner, and Motley Crue's Tommy Lee and Nikki Six.

A few years ago, my partner David Warman and I were working in our music studio, dealing with all the technology involved in modern electronic systems. We spent a lot of time setting up those systems, resetting all our **patchbays**, **splitters**, and **merging** devices, and untangling all the cables and wire. All we wanted to do was write music! We thought there had to be a better way. People develop new, more powerful devices so we can work "smarter, not harder," yet they end up causing *more* work. How can technology help

protocol: A set of rules for communicating between computers which determines the way that a network manages flow of information from "talkers" (information senders) to "listeners" (information receivers). Protocol software resides in computer memory or in the memory of a transmission device such as a network interface card. Without protocol, the computer can't make sense of incoming data streams.

fiber-optic cable: Glass or plastic fibers used to transmit information—voice, video, and computer data converted by optical transmitter to a series of light pulses. The light pulses are sent through the wire by a laser or light-emitting diode flashing on and off at extremely high speeds. At the receiving end, a light-sensitive receiver changes light back to electric pulses. Optical fibers—each one as thin as a human hair—can carry much more information than copper wires. As optical wires use light pulses, they're immune to electrical and radio interference. Currently, installing fiber-optic cable is difficult and expensive.

bidirectional: Ability for a signal to flow in either one of two directions within a single cable.

us if we spend more time butting our heads against it and less time doing creative work?

After our music sessions, we'd brainstorm on how to solve the problem. We talked about how the digital musical instrument community uses a standard called MIDI. It was created to make things easy, but it doesn't always work that way. MIDI systems are slow and hard to hook up, and you practically have to be a rocket scientist to make good use of the technology. When you work with MIDI, you keep being pulled away from the right-brain creative work by MIDI's left-brain technical requirements.

We also talked about how we use local area networks every time we tell a desktop computer to print a memo. LANs help us re-route data streams when we need to access different peripherals; they give multiple computer users access to a single device without corrupting each others' data; they let one user access a bunch of different devices, enabling their computer to cope with the idiosyncrasies of all those diverse machines. Why not take a similar approach to handle the interconnection and control of digital music, audio and even video devices?

When we researched existing network standards and LAN systems for use with real-time MIDI performance data, we found a fatal flaw in each one. Either the data transfer rate was too slow, or the system couldn't support data transmission over long distances, or it was limited in the number of devices that could function **bidirectionally** in a single system. We always ended up saying, "This approach comes close, but there's something in it that

doesn't allow for the real-time nature of what we want to do."

We assembled a pile of ideas based on the problems with existing LAN systems. Those systems suit computer networks, in which the main area of concern is *where* the data go and in what format; in real-time multimedia and music networks, however, we need to control *when* the data reach their destination. All these concepts came together into "MediaLink," our LAN **protocol** for multimedia devices.

First introduced to the electronic music community in 1989, MediaLink is a high-speed, multimedia, communications protocol that works with musical synthesizers, samplers, reverberators, equalizers, digital delays, and many different types of studio and stage multimedia equipment. MediaLink allows the real-time, simultaneous transmission of all forms of digital media information. In the MediaLink world, a single **fiber-optic** cable carries MIDI, **SMPTE**, **SCSI**, digital audio and video data simultaneously in both directions, eliminating the need for multiple cables.

MediaLink solves the problems for real-time, multimedia or artistic performance, without the connection and speed limitations inherent in other networking systems. We created this for the music community, but other areas in which people combine creativity, performance, and digital technologies will find it useful.

A Look at LANs

The devices in a LAN system interconnect in four basic configurations: ring, star, bus, and tree (*see diagram*). MIDI equipment owners use the bus configuration when they **daisy-chain** their devices using **MIDI Thru** ports. When they use a MIDI patchbay or "Thru" box, however, they form a star network.

Every LAN system is based on a certain protocol. One common LAN protocol is CSMA, or Carrier Sense Multiple Access. In this network access method, **nodes** contend for the right to send data. If two or more nodes try to transmit at once, they cancel the transmission until a random time period of microseconds passes, then try to re-send. A familiar example of the CSMA scheme is Apple Computer's AppleTalk protocol, used for simple hook-up of Macintosh computers and peripheral devices.

To understand how CSMA works, imagine entering a roomful of people. When you hear a gap in conversation, you know, "Okay, now I can talk." People tend to arbitrate among themselves who gets to talk next. If two people talk at the same time, that's a "collision." They look at each other, and either say, "Let that person talk" or "What I have to say is more important, so I'll talk." The problem with using CSMA is when *everyone* wants to talk, no one's there to prevent it. The result can be pandemonium: nothing gets through and nobody gets anything said that anyone hears.

A CSMA-based system, such as Ethernet (a common type of network), while great for connecting disk drives to computers, comes under severe limitations when you have heavy loading. "Heavy loading" happens when you have a rock band on stage playing for 50,000 people while the lights, stage effects, audio, and MIDI signals all are running through various systems. An Ethernet-type network falls apart under that kind of loading. CSMA won't work in real-time performances.

Another popular LAN protocol is the token type, exemplified by the Token Ring network which uses a ring topology and token-passing access method. This approach requires nodes to wait for their turn before transmitting data. Turns are indicated by a character sequence that passes from one node to the next.

To understand a Token Ring, imagine a room with 50 people in it. I pass a pencil around the room; whoever has the pencil gets to speak. If everybody had five

The four basic network topologies: ring, star, bus, and tree. LANs based on personal computers typically use a star topology; Ethernet LANs use the bus, while Token Ring uses the ring. A MediaLink network works equally well in a ring, star, bus, or tree configuration.

minutes to speak, you would wait hours for the pencil to come around so you could say something. Take that approach, apply it a performance network set up in Wembley Stadium or Nassau Coliseum, and you can see that a Token system suffers from the fact that the token must pass to everybody. We can forget about using the Token system in a real-time creative situation.

A third protocol for LANs is the polling approach. "Polling" is an access method in which the "hub," or the central computer, asks each node in turn if it has data to transmit. Generally implemented in a star network, the central computer directs the "conversation" on the network, telling each member when it's their turn to talk. If that main computer crashes, the entire network goes down.

MediaLink combines the best aspects of polling, CSMA, and token protocols. It lets a device with high-priority data jump into the system, say what it must say, then get back out. It doesn't give the pencil to the people who have nothing to say; instead, it lets the network know when one person wants the pencil to say something. A MediaLink network works equally well in a ring, star, bus, or tree configuration.

MediaLink goes beyond traditional LANs that use copper wire, because it uses fiber-optic cable. The electrical signals are carried as pulses of light through a cable (essentially a mirrored tube). This solves two problems inherent with copper cable: it eliminates electrical interference (which can introduce nasty hums and buzzes into the system) and allows data to move at the speed of light. When you transmit data to and from media

devices through fiber optics, the system is much easier to set up and troubleshoot.

The basis of MediaLink is the MediaLink **chip.** This chip is designed into each network device, handling communication with the network. It makes it possible for MediaLink to support real-time performance. The chip is relatively inexpensive—about $10—unlike an Ethernet system, in which the chips can cost around $50. Token Ring chips are even more expensive than Ethernet.

As the MediaLink chip is so inexpensive, we envision it being used in audio, video, and multimedia devices, including synthesizers, computers, TVs, and stereo systems. A MediaLink chip can go in every type of digital audio and digital video device. Manufacturers can design it easily and cost-effectively into equipment and systems.

When you go to the stereo store, you see stereo receivers with 20 kinds of connectors on the back panel: Tape In, Tape Out, Phono, Compact Disc, Aux, and so on. People often have a hard time setting up these systems simply because there are so many types of connectors and so many different things to connect. A LAN can solve the problem. Wouldn't you like to buy a stereo receiver that contains just one connector? Your CD player would have one connector, your speakers each would have one connector, and every other system component would have one connector. You just daisy-chain those components along a fiber-optic cable. Soon you'll even be able to use MediaLink in a wireless LAN ("Look, Ma, no cables!"). We're working with another company to achieve that through radio transmission.

When you solve the wiring problem through single-connector daisy-chaining, you achieve "logical connectivity." Let's say I want my stereo receiver to play my CD player. Instead of worrying about the six knobs on the front that connects those 12 connectors on the back, I flick a selector switch and confirm the connection on the front panel's digital readout. When I say, "I want to listen to my CD player," it's the microprocessor that figures out what connections to make, and then it makes them.

When you send a gift to a friend via overnight delivery, you don't worry about how it gets there, how many people handle it, or how many trucks carry it. Same thing with MediaLink. You put data into one end of the system and you don't worry about how it gets to the other end. You simply put an **address** on it, and away it goes.

We're not changing any standards already in existence; we're working *with* them. I own tons of MIDI equipment and I want none of it to be obsolete. MediaLink prevents MIDI obsolescence by over-coming its limitations—and it helps us gain control over the techno-spaghetti in studios and on stage.

Tapping into MIDI

MIDI, the musical instrument digital interface, is a **protocol standard** for interconnecting electronic synthesizers and other digital musical instruments and devices. When MIDI emerged in the music industry, people used it to hook together a bunch of keyboards and play them all from one keyboard.

In the past few years, however, MIDI has grown into a versatile communications technology that can be used to control all kinds of musical and performance equipment, including effects devices, mixers, and lighting controllers, and it interfaces personal computers with digital instruments. More and more manufacturers of lighting consoles, visual projection systems, laser controllers, rigging systems, and even pyrotechnics systems are adopting MIDI.

The "MidiTap" unit is the first MIDI device to exploit MediaLink. It is the

protocol standard: A set of rules for computer communication that has been widely agreed upon and implemented by vendors, users, and standards organizations. A protocol standard should allow computer-based systems to talk with each other, even those built by competing manufacturers. Examples: MIDI; SMPTE time code.

address: Data destination. To enable one keyboard to control two sound generators, for example, each sound generator must be assigned its own MIDI channel. The first one would be programmed to ignore everything on the bus except for data coded with the address "channel one." The second unit's address would be set for "channel two." To play the sound set up in the first sound generator, you'd instruct the MIDI keyboard to send to channel one.

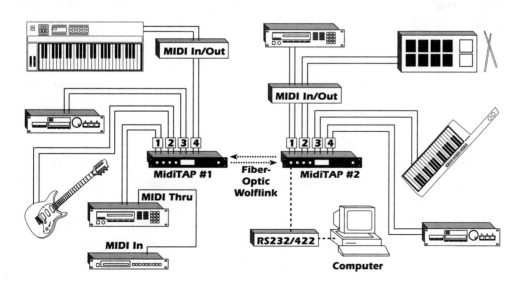

A music studio's MediaLink network; the MidiTap unit provides access to all the MIDI devices.

bridge that lets MIDI systems "tap into" the MediaLink network in real time. The MidiTap incorporates a distributed **database** operating system for setting up and managing MIDI network devices. Physically, it's a box with four independent MIDI-In connectors, four MIDI-Out connectors, an **RS-422/232** serial port for connection to a computer, and two MediaLink fiber-optic connectors. You can map the MIDI ports in any way, including full merging capabilities on all inputs. You can name, address, and access up to 64 separate MIDI devices per MidiTap with a knob on any MidiTap's front panel, and access any of those devices from any controller that's also connected to a MidiTap.

The MidiTap is considered a "node," which is a traditional computer networking term that sounds like something you get on your toe when you wear shoes that are too small. "Tap" more accurately describes that the device lets you "tap into" a data line. Even a simple MediaLink network can contain thousands of configurations of instruments, channels, nodes, and ports; each MidiTap can store 128 of these configurations, which you can recall instantly by issuing a simple MIDI command.

With each MidiTap, you can hook together many pieces of MIDI gear. A network can contain up to 253 MidiTaps. MidiTaps work over a 2.5-kilometer range. If you want your keyboard in the middle of one room, and your effects in the corner of another room, you just run the fiber-optic cable. If you're running a multimedia presentation on stage, you can control projection devices located at the back of the theater.

MIDI accommodates 16 channels of data. That's enough to connect two **multi-timbral** synthesizers, but if you're controlling a MIDI mixer, stage lights, electronic drums, keyboards, and sound effects, 16 channels can't cut it. With MediaLink and its MIDI implementation, you get enough "channels" for a *half-million* devices.

Since MIDI's bandwidth is 31,250 **bits** per second, it can't handle more than about 500 **note-on/off** events per second. Factor in performance data such as aftertouch (the instrument's ability to react to how hard you're pressing a key) or pitchbend (the instrument's ability to change the pitch of a note in a continuous, "sliding" manner), and your note limit shrinks. In large MIDI systems where lots of information travels around, the result is delayed reactions. And the data can travel in one direction only, so the system's central computer can't "know" which instruments currently are active in the system.

Even at its lowest **bandwidth**, MediaLink can accommodate 30 times as much data as MIDI. MidiTap can run at bandwidths up to two megabytes per second—with the data traveling bidirectionally.

For reliable operation, MIDI cable runs are limited to 50 feet. When you try to send MIDI data over longer cables, the data become corrupted; for example, your note-offs can get lost and you end up with droning tones. If you have to connect the mixing console in the back of a large theater to the audio systems on the stage, or you want to link the multimedia projection system in the conference room to the audio/video studio upstairs, MIDI

"Life On A Slice: The Phosphorescent Samurai & The Geisha Snail" 1991

"Life On A Slice: The Phosphorescent Samurai & The Geisha Snail" 1991

Beverly Reiser
Oakland, California.
Music by **Bill Fleming**.

Tools: Commodore Amiga 2000;
Vivid Effects' Mandala Virtual Reality
System; A-Live Video Digitizer; Tascam
PortaStudio audio mixer with Yamaha
digital sequencer, Roland keyboard
synthesizer, Yamaha electric piano.

This interactive computer/video
installation presents a fable-like narrative
in which the viewer/participant becomes
the protagonist. The participant's image
(caught by video camera) appears in
and interacts with the artwork. The participant's actions determine the ensuing
text, graphics, sounds, and story ending.

"Water Water Everywhere, Not A Drop To Drink" from the series, **"Similar But Not The Same"** 1991

Barbara Nessim

New York, New York

Tools: Macintosh IIcx; flatbed scanner;
photographs; Claris MacPaint; Adobe PhotoShop

This is a computer-generated, 3D stereo-pair
installation. Each stereo pair artwork is framed
and wall-mounted. A stereoscopic viewing
device is provided. It contains two slides
(one to view with the left eye, one for the right)
showing photos of the two images in the
artwork. Through the viewing device, each eye
sees slightly different pictures. The brain
combines the information to perceive the
picture as three-dimensional.

Michael Gosney & Jack Davis

San Diego, California

Verbum Roundtable Discussion produced by
GTE ImagiTrek; music produced by various artists

Tools: Apple Macintosh IIci; Macromedia Director 3.0;
Macintosh-based digital audio editing system

This interactive CD-ROM magazine showcases
animation and interactive multimedia works, video
clips, interactive panel discussions and feature stories
(consisting of audio recordings, text, and video),
and music and images from such cyber-savvy musicians
as Todd Rundgren, D'Cückoo, and Graham Nash.
The "reader" can interact with the magazine's
multimedia content in free-form fashion, print text files,
try software demos, follow graphic design tutorials,
and shop from a database of products and services.
The 2-disc, $49.95 VI1.0 requires a CD-ROM player,
Mac II color computer, and speakers or headphones.

*"**Verbum Interactive 1.0**" 1991*

*"**Verbum Interactive 1.0**" 1991*

Will Cloughley & Sondra Slade
San Francisco, California

Tools: 35mm photography; felt-tip marker; colored pencil; pen & ink; Kodalith lithography film; Rostrum camera (for photo-optical composites)

These images are part of a computer-controlled, multi-image presentation, in which a 9-projector slide animation system is integrated with white-light krypton argon laser beams. Projection control is provided by MultiVision system running on IBM-PC compatibles.

"Blade of Fire" 1991

CYBERARTS GALLERY

"**Body Geometry,**" 1991

"**Broadway Boogie Woogie,**" 1991

Myron Krueger

Vernon, Connecticut

Tools: Custom VIDEOPLACE computer system and software; B&W video camera; video digitization system; RGB video projection system; translucent plastic screen, with flourescent backlighting.

Both images were created with the VIDEOPLACE artificial-reality system (see chapter entitled "The 'Art' in Artificial Reality"). These real-time artworks are created by VIDOEPLACE participants. In "Body Geometry," the participant's actions create moving rectangles, triangles, and circles for inclusion in geometric compositions. In "Broadway Boogie Woogie," the participant's actions create compositions of shifting rectangles.

CYBERARTS GALLERY

Merrill Aldigheri & Joe Tripician

New York, New York

Tools: color Ikegami video camera; Sony 3/4" video recorder; Commodore Amiga 2000; Commodore Amiga 3000; Electronic Arts Deluxe Paint 4.0; Sony Type IX video editing system; musical soundtrack created by Frederick Reed on Apple Macintosh-based music production/recording system

A 25-minute video and computer animation, "Metaphoria" examines the role that metaphors play in the cognitive process, and shows how metaphors pervade thought in science, poetry, religion, and culture. The program's structure simulates metaphorical thought by creating visual metaphors, juxtaposing interviews with such leaders as Dr. John C. Lilly (pioneer in human-dolphin communication) and Professor Marvin Minsky (co-founder of MIT's Artificial Intelligence Lab) with poetry, computer animations, documentary, and dramatic movement.

"Metaphoria" 1991

Barbara Nessim

New York, New York

Tools: Macintosh IIcx; digitizing tablet; Claris MacPaint and HyperCard

By interacting with the computer, the viewer creates and keeps a unique artwork. The gallery setup consists of Macintosh computer, laser printer, paper cutter, and stapler. The Mac screen displays 200 line drawings (which Nessim input by hand into computer memory via digitized drawing tablet), each shown at two-second intervals. The screen also displays flags from 18 nations. Using a mouse, the viewer selects a flag; the computer then randomly chooses 16 drawings. The printer outputs a sheet of paper containing the flag and drawings. By following provided instructions, the viewer uses the paper cutter and stapler to assemble a miniature (2-3/4" x 2-1/4") book of Nessim's art. The chances of creating the same book twice are 48 million to one.

"Random Access Memories" 1992

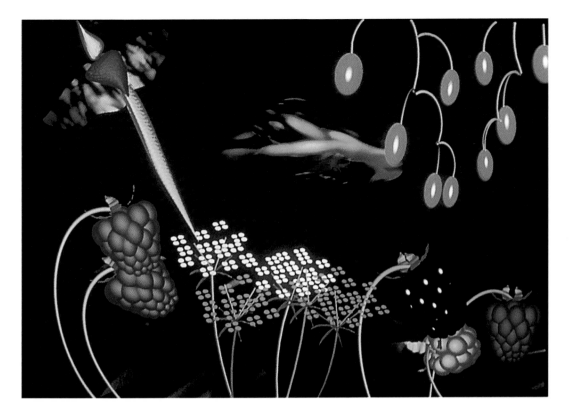

"Angels" 1990-1992

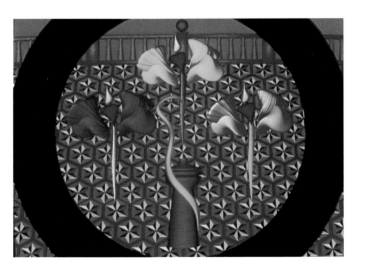

"Angels" 1990-1992

Nicole Stenger

Paris France

Tools: Silicon Graphics Iris 4D-25 workstation (for modeling of images) and VGX-320 workstation (for interactive programming); Digital Equipment Corp. DEC 5000 workstation to fine-tune models; Wavefront Advanced Visualization System; VPL Research Body Electric software for interactive programming; VPL Research AudioSphere 3D sound system with Crystal River Engineering Convolvotron digital signal processor; VPL Research DataGlove; VPL Research EyePhones Model HRX

These plates show computer-generated sketches made for "Angels," a virtual reality artpiece that the viewer/participant "enters" by donning a head-mounted stereoscopic display and virtual-reality glove. "Angels" was created by Stenger in the United States at research labs in Seattle (Human Interface Technology Lab, University of Washington) and Cambridge (Massachusetts Institute of Technology). According to Stenger, "Everything in 'Angels' is cubistic and minimalist; the idea is to visualize a paradise in which the participant can enjoy interaction with the characters."

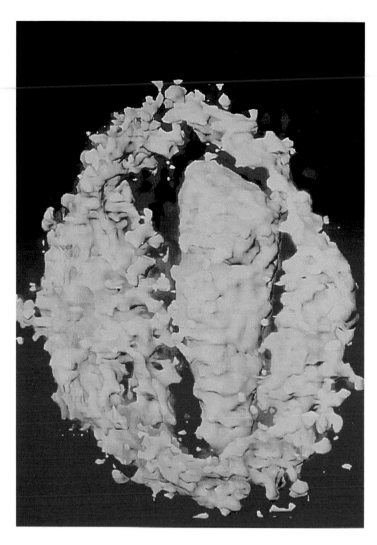

**Ellen Sandor &
Stephan Meyers of
(Art)^n Laboratory
and Arthur Olson
& David Goodsell of
Scripps Clinic & Re-
search Foundation**
Chicago, Illinois

Tools: Hewlett Packard
workstation; AT&T Pixel
Machines; Kodak Light
Valve Technology scanning
printer; cibachrome film

"HIV Reconstruction" 1991

Founded by Ellen Sandor in 1983, (Art)^n Laboratory is a team of scientists,
mathematicians, artists, and computer technicians. They use their patented
PHSCologram (skol•o•gram) technique to digitally produce autostereogram hard
copy, which does not require movement or special glasses for 3D viewing.
Invented in 1987, the Stealth Negative PHSCologram (the type shown here)
involves the creation of slightly different views of a computer-simulated object.
"Slices" of these views are interleaved into one image, printed along with a barrier
screen. The screen is composed of clear, vertical "openings" alternating with black
strips that cause the viewer's eyes to see slightly different angular views of the
backlit subject, which the brain perceives as a startling illusion of 3-dimensionality.

"HIV Reconstruction" is a computer image of the AIDS virus (HIV), which is too
small to see with an ordinary microscope. This image was created by using an
electron microscope and scientific visualization (the transformation of mathematical information, which exists only as computer data, into a picture). This image is
among the clearest yet produced of the deadly virus. It gives scientists clues to
how they can attack the virus to prevent it from spreading in the human body.

can't cut it. You need special devices to accommodate longer distances.

MediaLink lets MIDI data span distances up to 2.5 kilometers (about 1.5 miles) so you can send data across the room or across the road. I don't like to lay down music tracks in the same room that holds my computer and disk drives with all their whirring fans. Networking to the rescue! We can put the noisy boxes in in the basement, connect them into the network, and deal with them remotely.

You can use the MidiTap to merge, split, route, **map**, **filter**, and transpose MIDI data. After you set up all the connections, processing, filtering, etc., you can name, store, and recall the whole configuration as a "LanScape." A LanScape is a snapshot of the studio set-up. It helps you manage a roomful of equipment so you don't have to worry about technical details of controlling instruments and devices. A LanScape might contain the **patch** changes and volume levels for all your synthesizers and the routing, merging, and filtering for all your MIDI devices. You can set up one LanScape for composing, another for working on existing tunes, another for working on orchestration.

Let's say you spend six hours setting up your studio to work on a tune. Suddenly you get a great idea for a new song in which your keyboard would trigger a different set of instruments. You have to disconnect everything, re-set all the instruments, and finally, if you're not totally burnt out, you work on that song. Then *bang!* Inspiration hits and you have an idea for the first song. Oh, no! Now you have to reconfigure the entire system!

That's not the case when you use LanScapes. All you do is use the network management system to return to your original LanScape: you simply click the mouse on a button to reset all your synthesizers for the first tune. Rembrandt didn't have to paint a picture twice, why should you?

MediaLink supports over 32,000 "groups," or "virtual devices." A *group* carries MIDI data on multiple channels simultaneously. Each group can contain any number of devices that respond to messages intended for that group. Any MIDI message on any channel in any group can be converted into any other message and travel to any other channel(s) in any other group(s), thus eliminating MIDI's 16-channel limitation. A *virtual device* is like a custom instrument. Pick a favorite sound from one synthesizer, a second sound from another synth, and a third sound from an effects box. Combine them and name your new sound. From that point on, in different LanScapes, you can refer to that name.

MidiTap's RS232/422 port lets computers directly access the MediaLink network. The Virtual Studio software puts icons on your computer screen that represent MIDI music, audio, and lighting equipment, all in one window on a Macintosh, Atari, or IBM PC-compatible machine. You can connect any device in the system to any other device simply by drawing a line between them.

At times, I've set up and turned on my MIDI system, and no sound comes out. Then I wondered, "Why aren't the data getting through? Is there a problem at the source? Is the cable bad?" Using the

map: To send specified program numbers to connected synths when a preset sound has been changed.

filter: A device that removes unwanted MIDI messages.

patch: A sound on a synthesizer; the term is derived from the early days of modular, analog synthesizers, when patch cords were used to connect the output of one component to the input of another.

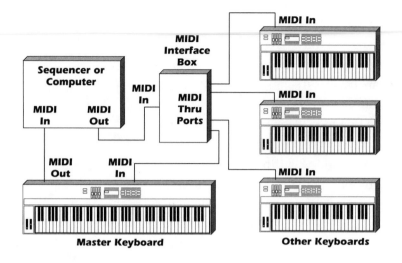

A traditional MIDI studio setup without networking capability

interrogation aspects of the Virtual Studio, I can find the problem.

Another advantage of the Virtual Studio is the ability to apply database-type searches to your equipment. In a large network, it's easy to feel deluged with information. You want to limit the scope of the on-screen display. You might say, "Today I'm going to work on orchestration, and I don't care about the effects devices." You type in the name of your desired category, and the Virtual Studio displays only the devices you want to use.

In 1992, a MidiTap system with two MidiTaps, two 12-foot fiber-optic cables, and "Virtual Studio" software retailed for about $3,000.

MediaLink At Work

I visited the folks at Peter Gabriel's studio in England a while back, and they said, "Wouldn't it be great we had a residential studio for musicians with networked computers in the bedrooms? Then, if they have an idea at 2 a.m., they don't have to go downstairs to the studio, but they can hop over to the computer and use it to hook in-

to the synthesizers down in the studio?" MediaLink makes that a reality.

It's also great for live stage use. Herbie Hancock went on European tour using MidiTaps, which solved the problem of MIDI cables running all over the stage. Herbie connected all his racks with fiber-optic cable, and used Yamaha digital audio mixers to handle the cable routing. He didn't have to deal with a rack of gear with 20 wires coming out the back, or an unreliable multi-pin connector. A single fiber-optic cable let him interconnect all his instruments to achieve logical connectivity.

If networking can solve problems by connecting electronic music devices, whether they're home stereo systems or professional studio gear, why deal with separate video feed lines, audio feed lines, and MIDI lines?

One of our goals with MediaLink is to integrate various media systems, including any data that travel through SCSI ports. A MIDI system, a digital video system, a digital audio system, and a lighting system can interconnect and send their particular types of data along a single fiber-optic cable. Any device, regardless of the system it physically connects to, can be accessed from any other system. Instant reconfiguration is possible without unplugging a single connector.

We find microprocessors in CD players, TV sets, DAT machines, cassette decks, amplifiers, and video games. Our long-term goal is to convince the manufacturers of consumer and professional equipment to put those microprocessors to work in a way that helps us better control all the machines in our lives. Our company Lone

Wolf offers a program to let manufacturers license use of the MediaLink protocol and its encoding circuitry so they can incorporate the fiber-optic connections and circuitry in their own products.

The Grand Vision

When you combine MediaLink and Midi-Taps with a **modem**, you can send a sequence from a Macintosh computer through the phone line to your friend's IBM computer. The IBM can record the sequence just as if it were happening in a live session.

Remote connectivity is important. My partner and I networked my MIDI studio in Redondo Beach, California, with his studio in Woodland Hills, California. In five minutes I can dial up his studio and link our music systems through the phone lines. Then we can have a jam session. He plays in his studio, I play in my studio, and everything we do appears at both places. It's so cool to sit at my keyboard and hear music coming out that's his music, coming from his studio!

MediaLink is designed for compatibility with the increased fiber-optic transmission speeds expected in the future. As devices that handle these high speeds become available, MediaLink will accommodate them. Then network communications will connect your local area network to a global community of people who can collaborate on creative projects. You'll be able to play a studio gig in New York from your home in Seattle.

We're also preparing to tap into other media systems, and are developing Au-dioTap, SMPTEtap, VideoTap, and SCSI-tap. In 1992 we introduced MicroTap, a communications controller that supports MediaLink in a real-time, multimedia LAN. It allows the connection of systems with anything from standard **twisted-pair** cable to plastic and glass fiber-optics. It also handles eight channels of **analog-to-digital conversion**, controls up to 30 digital input/output lines, and supports development of custom systems in Macintosh and IBM-compatible machines.

Speaking of machines, we're always seeking cost-efficient modes of transportation. How do we make cars run more efficiently? By removing weight! Imagine how much weight we could remove by using a LAN to replace the car's wiring harnesses and electronics needed to link tail lights, stoplights, brakes, and other devices. We could run a single fiber-optic cable through the car's electronics to various devices and include a low-cost chip at junctures to control the lights, gas pedal, and ignition. It's no different than a wiring system, except it's more efficient and reliable. We can extend that concept to airplanes and other mechanical modes of transportation.

The current limitations and cost of networking techniques prevent them from extending much beyond the world of computers, where networks typically connect computers, file servers, disk drives, modems and printers. If we break through the boundaries of cost and efficiency with a new networking concept, we can start applying networks to different areas with the goal of improving the quality of our daily lives.

modem: Short for **mo**dulator-**dem**odulator, a device that allows computers to send and receive information over telephone lines.

twisted-pair cable: Two pairs of copper wire inside foil, which is inside a rubber "jacket." Traditionally used to carry voice, now also used to transmit computer data. Twisted-pair is inexpensive, readily available, and easier to install than fiber-optic. Every building with a telephone has twisted-pair cable. Most important result of telephone industry's use of twisted-pair is modular cabling, which lets a company prewire a building for its phone and data services.

analog-to-digital conversion: To convert analog data into digital form for input into a computer.

MAGRITTE HATED TO PAINT

AN AESTHETIC TREK THROUGH AN IDIOSYNCRATIC
SET OF MULTIMEDIA AUTHORING SYSTEMS

In these pages Robert Edgar proposes an aesthetic goal for the development of multimedia authoring systems. He explores film art, video art, the art and business of media, and his present multimedia platform of choice: the Commodore Amiga.

Aesthetic: "I feel by means of my senses; I understand; I recognize; I comprehend."—Charles Giordano, *Synaesthetic Education*, Syracuse University, 1970.

I once read a quotation by the painter **René Magritte** in which he flatly stated that he hated to paint. At that time, in the early 1970s, I was being seduced by roomfuls of analog synthesizers, 16mm film, and brand-new ½" **video** equipment, along with the people and ideas of a still-excited New York Avant-Garde. I felt that Magritte's statement was symptomatic of a flaw; an insensitivity to the senses' intoxication. He was another artist who sold the moment for the production of an object, at the price of his own anaesthesia. As art is the production of the self, not the production of objects, it meant that his compositional strategy was fatally wrong, and his art was an index of a self-promoted poisoning.

It is now 20 years later, and my equipment is packed into my small workroom. My editing table now supports three computers; its pegboard back, which once held spools of 16mm film, now holds computer and videodisc cables. My art books share shelf space with hardware and software documentation, and my cans of film, now dusty and packed away in a closet, have been displaced by shelves of computer disks.

And what of the sticky, existential moment of creativity? The shelves of hardware and software documentation have had much to say about that, as have the reams of print-outs of computer code, and the modem flickering on the shelf above my head. While I don't deny the truth of my earlier

BY ROBERT EDGAR

Robert Edgar has created internationally exhibited multimedia productions. His interactive computer works include "Living Cinema" (for which he designed and programmed a live performance system) and "Memory Theatre One," which he describes in this chapter. He also designed an authoring system for Still Current Design, Inc. Robert used AmigaVision to produce interactive business marketing materials when he worked at Commodore. He continues to create multimedia artworks. By day he works as a media designer for Simon & Schuster Technology Group in Sunnyvale, California.

René Magritte: (1898-1967) Belgian painter.

½" video: Refers to the first low-cost, portable, black-&-white video recording gear introduced by Sony and Panasonic in the early 1970s.

perception, I've come to live with—if not accept—the cross of time required to create with computers, and even envy the free time Magritte had for his distasteful practice.

Magritte's choices were to either paint his own paintings or to look at those of others; the simple lack of color prints at that time severely reduced the quality of appropriated collages. He might have done more photography, although it was left to more recent artists to realize Magritte's strategies in that medium.

Personal computers afford us a range of choices. Their programming languages require long periods of immersion before one can master their use, but they offer the best payoff in terms of final speed and variability. Software tools, such as paint and 3-D animation programs, allow an artist to sculpt images by shape and attribute—Magritte's methods are given **algorithms** and made accessible without the necessity of learning *Trompe L'Oeil* (but *with* the necessity of learning a new set of exacting and often difficult practices).

And then there are authoring systems.

Authoring systems for personal computers have hit the store shelves. These systems, along with hardware that is acceptable if still a bit too slow in performance, give a glimpse of what we can expect when the act of authoring merges with the moment of sensual creation. Because this is the measure of our maturity: The artist can invent his or her self through multiple, simultaneous senses in real time. This inventive gesture

should be the goal of authoring system design.

From Experimental Film to Computer Programming

I like carrying a camera with me, and I shoot things that I come upon unsuspectingly, most often unrehearsed and not preconceived. I also collect video clips, and every couple of years I try to edit a selection of them into a new piece. When I was pursuing linear (traditional) filmmaking, I would edit them into a finished construct. That construct gave me a form for considering segments of the world that I might not have juxtaposed before; to smoke out new metaphors, sparked from the rubbing together of images previously unrelated in space and time.

I happily practiced this strategy for several years, until the Hunt brothers tried to corner the world's silver market. One immediate result was the skyrocketing of film costs. I no longer could afford to make my own films.

At that time, I lived in **Silicon Valley**; the Apple IIe had just been introduced. A fellow with whom I regularly played music told me about his creation of the first visual-adventure game for the Atari computer platform, and that he was creating an educational "construction set" for the Apple II. I figured that if I spent my money once on that equipment, I could program my own creative work for the price of my time. So I sold my beloved Beaulieu 16mm film camera and bought an Apple II with Paul Lutus' **GraForth**, a graphics-oriented programming language. Forth is a great programming language, and GraForth was

algorithm: A mathematical term indicating a series of instructions, decisions, and steps used to solve a problem or perform a task.

Trompe L'Oeil: French term for "trick of the eye." The purpose of Trompe L'Oeil painting is to paint 2-dimensional objects to look 3-dimensional. Used widely in theater, film, and TV, it creates such a strong illusion of reality that the viewer wonders whether the item depicted is real or a representation.

authoring system: Software that helps developers design interactive programs.

Silicon Valley: In northern California just south of the San Francisco Bay Area, this region between Palo Alto and San Jose is home to dozens of major computer and electronics companies.

GraForth: A programming language developed for the Apple II and early IBM PC, providing basic 3-D animation (object outlines) and simple musical composition.

the perfect Forth implementation for what I wanted to do.

The Memory Theatre

For years I had been aware of the **metaphysical constructions** of such Renaissance figures as Giordano **Bruno**, Robert **Flood**, and Giulio **Camillo**, all of whom were involved in creating and interpreting representations of heaven and earth. Camillo's cosmology was architectural: he created a "memory theatre," a wooden model of the metaphysical universe, just large enough for one or two people to enter. Inside, images were arranged in rows and columns and beneath each image was a drawer holding an explication of the image's symbology. One could walk into the structure of the "universe" and meditate on its meanings.

Using my Apple II, I programmed a theater comprising two rows of 12 rooms, in the shape of a **torus**, with an atrium and library in the middle. In each room I put an image with text; the top row contained my own writings, and the bottom row contained selections from found writings. Using a joystick, the viewer could move from room to room, reading the texts and viewing the images. The library contained longer passages from which the room's quotations were edited, and an additional room provided an overview of the system.

It took over a year for me to program "Memory Theatre," something I could imitate today (minus the 3-D animation) in a day's work, using an authoring system. Admittedly, I spent a good deal of that time teaching myself the basics of computers and programming, in addition to

the basics of that particular computer and that particular programming language. And, as I learned what was possible, I changed what I was doing. After all, there weren't any computer memory-theaters around for me to match. The delay between initial conception and final completion was substantial, and rather than immersing myself in the images and texts themselves, I was immersed in books on computers and operating systems. The aesthetic moment was so far removed from the practice of the programmer that the latter easily forgot the former. Not at all like the sight and smell of paint on the painter's clothes and skin, and studio walls and floor. Not like the sounds that fill the room of the practicing musician and swirl through space, creating floating volumes of texture, density, and color in the listener's mind.

No, I was just looking up a syntax to be followed once and forgotten, left behind in the back of a 3-ring binder.

From Art To Business

In 1985 I teamed up with a high-school friend and three other folks and started an Atlanta-based company, Still Current Design, to produce interactive video systems. Our first system, created for Georgia Power, used two touch-screens (monitors that act as input devices; the user touches certain points on the screen to issue commands), three videodisc players, an IBM PC/AT, a large hard drive, and a video projector. For that project we produced three videodiscs about the state of Georgia, electrical power-related concerns, and an interactive "drive-through" of an industrial park. Georgia Power built a marketing center to house the system and used it to convince businesses to move to Georgia.

We programmed the original system in BASIC, although we soon switched to **Microsoft C** for all the normal reasons (program speed, size, and range of capabilities). System maintenance required a good amount of data entry, and we continued to collect revenues for doing that. At the time our lead programmer felt little respect for authoring systems, despite the fact that an authoring system can provide tools to eliminate much of the dull, repetitive tasks of updating and revising program code. After a year of repetitious maintenance work, he saw the light. We decided to develop an authoring system.

I designed the "eMEDIA" authoring system so someone with little computer experience could quickly create a substantial interactive presentation. We integrated a fairly portable system, incorporating a real-time video **digitizer** board, a high-density **WORM** drive, and two monitors—one touch-screen and one detachable monitor for portable presentations.

With eMEDIA, you did your design work on the detachable screen. On it you created a **flowchart**; a complex flowchart would fit on a single screen. The touch-screen provided the video display. You could move from the overall interactive context to the detail-work on any single element by clicking on that element on the flowchart, then moving the mouse to the touch-screen, where you could work on single screens or video segments, or **overlay** elements directly. You could grab images and create graphics on the

touch-screen by calling up a graphics program from within the eMEDIA authoring system.

The eMEDIA system allowed someone to quickly develop a presentation, but I wanted to eliminate its two-step process and work from a mental structure, creating the presentation as I maneuvered within it. This resembles modal jazz improvisation, where one plays within and against a set of structures, as fellow musicians concurrently improvise. I wanted to extend abstract expressionist/oral poetry-influenced cinema into a single, real-time exploratory experience. And that, combined with technical knowledge and support provided by the folks at Still Current Design, led to the creation of "Living Cinema."

Back To Artwork

It struck me that everything an artist did with a paint program—create shading, blend elements, cut and paste images, and so on—involved spending hours working on an image, and then the artist would show only the finished piece. I thought that the cutting and pasting, the physical nature of the juxtapositioning of image clips, the copying of screen areas, and so on, could be used as structural elements to create their own form of poetry. I wanted to take 99 percent of the work thrown away by other artists and use it as the content of "Living Cinema." So I purchased an IBM PC/AT clone, real-time video digitizer board, speech synthesizer, industrial videodisc player, video camera, and Microsoft C, and set to work. After a year or so, I created my own narrative **paintbox**.

Here's an example of how a "Living Cinema" performance might progress: I start by playing back an image sequence that displays stills of my wife Merrilee as she slips a dress over the dress she is wearing. Using the mouse, I copy a bit of her skin and paint it over her new dress, covering it completely. I play a pre-saved quotation by the philosopher Quine, concerning someone who is replacing the wood of a raft even while floating on it. I then call up, from the videodisc, a video

segment showing a poster mounted by Australian **aborigines** on a downtown Brisbane construction site, with the headline, "We have survived."

Next, I type in a note that the aborigines have stopped **painting over earlier cliff paintings** as previous generations had done. Then I advance the videodisc to a slow-motion playback of people walking out of a pavilion. I reload Merrilee's image and grab the videodisc image through it, so where her image was, the image of the people remains frozen, but outside her outline they continue to slowly advance.

This is poetry that is exclusive to this medium. It retains a concrete nature that isn't available through a medium such as painting—although it is through digital **sampling**.

Change By Chance: Commodore & The Amiga

At Still Current Design, I started work on a dual-screen, 3-D multimedia browser that would let a user quickly dimension a multimedia database according to any three attributes, then forage through its representation, viewing the elements in an order determined both by its three axes and the moment-to-moment choice of the viewer. However, we had neither the time nor the money to develop it and although we made several attempts to acquire funding for the project, I eventually set it aside. The people at Still Current Design ended up going our individual ways. Commodore Business Machines hired me as multimedia producer, to work on a computer I had never touched: the Amiga.

As a multimedia platform, the Amiga has several advantages over other personal

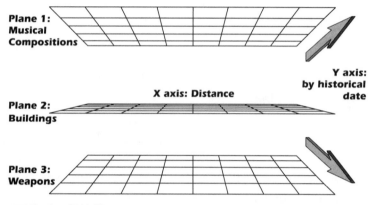

Plane 1: Musical Compositions

Plane 2: Buildings

Plane 3: Weapons

Y axis: by historical date

X axis: Distance

Multiple planes of the 3-D multimedia browser. The user can quickly dimension a multimedia database according to any three attributes, such as musical compositions, buildings, and viewpoints. The user can create additional planes, which can share attributes (above).

Once the multiple planes are constructed, the user can navigate through them (below).

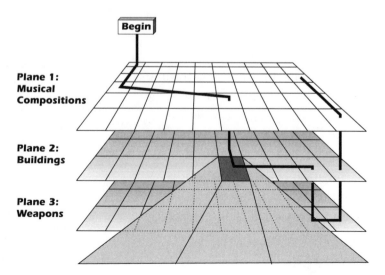

Begin

Plane 1: Musical Compositions

Plane 2: Buildings

Plane 3: Weapons

computers. It offered real-time playback of animations and digitized video. Its multi-tasking operating system allows multiple programs to run in memory simultaneously. To take advantage of simultaneously running programs, you need a way to synchronize them and handle communications among them. To do this on the Amiga, you can use an "inter-application" language called "Arexx" (built into the AmigaDos operating system, version 2.0 and later), which actually is a version of the "REXX" **mainframe** language.

Two authoring systems that employ Arexx are AmigaVision (from Commodore) and Foundation (marketed by Parallax Publishing). Both are designed for standard authoring situations, but their functionality is extended through their association with the Amiga platform.

AmigaVision is a flowchart-oriented, icon-based authoring system that lets you construct a flowchart vertically down the screen. Each icon is associated with an information window, called a "requester," in which you put information about its icon. For instance, an icon could signify an animation, and you could use the requester to indicate a particular animation and how many times it should play. Another icon could signify an **"if-then" structure**, and you could enter the **conditional statement** into the requester.

Foundation is based on a HyperCard model. Its real power comes from its extensive text language, which takes full advantage of the Amiga's video, audio, and multi-tasking capabilities. (A text language lets you write text-based programs, unlike icon-based authoring systems,

which require a programmer to move symbols across the screen to form algorithmic schematics.)

While both AmigaVision and Foundation use Arexx, only Foundation lets you call every function from an Arexx script. With AmigaVision, you can use Arexx to **pass a variable** in and out of an AmigaVision flow, thus allowing you to effect major branching decisions within the program during playback. AmigaVision, however, incorporates Arexx in a minor way, so its use in an AmigaVision program is limited. With Foundation you can call every function directly from a separate script, using it as a multimedia tool-kit in synchronization with other programs.

The benefit of this multi-tasking, multi-program approach? You can use each program for what it does best; you don't have to use a single "integrated" program that performs various diverse tasks, none of them very well.

In my current development work, I'm driving Living Cinema from my guitar through my Amiga. A **pickup** on my guitar sends MIDI data to an Amiga-based music composition program, "Bars & Pipes," by Blue Ribbon Soundworks. Bars & Pipes interprets the data so it can drive a MIDI sound module that plays back instrumental sounds, and also sends the data to an Arexx program that's multi-tasking in the same computer. This Arexx program responds by sending commands to my old PC/AT clone that is running "Living Cinema." Living Cinema controls the videodisc player, with the combined videodisc and video graphics output going into the input of my NewTek Video Toaster video production and editing sys-

painting over earlier cliff paintings: For centuries, aborigines traveled to sacred places to paint the stories of their dreams. In many of these places, subsequent generations painted over the work of previous generations. On the wall of these cliffs and caves are multiple layers of representations of a wide variety of subjects, in a wide variety of media. Today there are efforts to save some of these older walls, making them into museum pieces and effectively "freezing" the culture.

mainframe: A large, powerful computer that usually works with data "chunks" and supports scores of users simultaneously.

if-then structures: A type of conditional programming within a computer algorithm; this programming instruction can cause a program to execute a certain action if a given condition is met, as in: IF x = 4, THEN display smileyface graphic.

conditional statement: A statement specifying the condition that must be met before a result can occur, such as "If x = 4."

pass a variable: To cause a variable's value to transfer from one section of a program to another.

pickup: An electromagnet designed to "pick up" acoustic vibrations and convert them into electrical impulses.

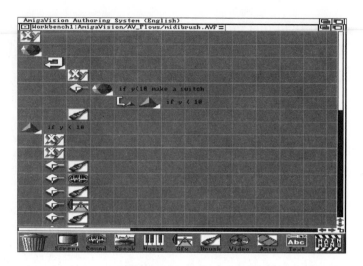

AmigaVision

customize a "traffic control" Arexx script; and I sit down with my guitar and play the system. If I could just synchronize the paint smells. . . .

VR Authoring on the Amiga

The Vivid Group's 2-D "virtual reality" system, Mandala, runs on the Amiga. [*See the chapter "The Mandala System" by Vincent John Vincent.*] Mandala combines a video camera, computer, and low-cost analog-to-digital converter with special software. A participant stands, well-lit, before a background, and can interact with programmed, on-screen elements through the software's ability to detect spatial overlap or "collisions." While seeing your image, live, on the screen, you also see other on-screen elements, such as a drum set. By moving your hand so the image of it touches the screen image of the drum, you trigger a drum sound. If so programmed, the drum bounces away from your hand, turns into a bird, and flies away.

Mandala's programming is based on a BASIC-like scripting language. The environment's power is obvious wherever the system is set up; rarely is there a computer graphics convention where Vincent John Vincent doesn't set up his system and draw large crowds. As soon as people see themselves in the monitor, they start to explore the environment—no training necessary.

A modest entry into Amiga-based "virtual reality" via interactive multimedia is Domark Software's "Virtual Reality Studio." It is designed to produce a relatively fast-moving, 3-D world that you can "populate" and edit using a combination of on-screen

Living Cinema is installed on a DOS computer and controlled by signals from the Amiga's serial port. In the Amiga, Living Cinema is controlled by a guitar's MIDI signals through the program Bars & Pipes.

tem, which combines Living Cinema's output with that of the Amiga graphics. The Arexx program also controls animations, still graphics, and audio playback through whatever authoring system (AmigaVision or Foundation) is running.

I conduct my authoring in several stages: I collect and generate source materials (digital and analog video, still images, graphics, animations, MIDI compositions, digital sounds); I write and/or

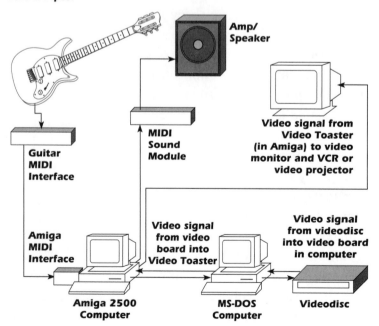

tools and a simple text programming language. Although it is designed for you to use its on-screen tools to maneuver through the virtual space, I find that the need to place the mouse cursor on a tiny button at exactly the moment when I want to interact with the space dulls the experience. It pulls you out just when you are most involved. However, I programmed my mouse and keyboard to work together, so I could use my left hand to control four or five keys to determine the effects of the mouse, which could be moved simultaneously through two dimensions using my right hand. Although I paid some penalties in program speed, it allowed me to achieve analog control over my motion through the virtual space, without the cost of "withdrawal."

A Virtual Aesthetics

When a choreographer interprets a piece of music, there is a granularity to what elements are interpreted. The rhythms of the dancer's fingers can duplicate a delicate, fast trill, whereas a torso movement can be used for musical structures of a longer duration. This exemplifies "making sense" of our environment, interpreting and cre-

"Wave Boat Rock," part of Robert Edgar's Living Cinema

ating the meaning of events in our lives.

These **synesthetic** correspondences are not just sensations; they are the roots of metaphor in the pre-language child. Whistle a wavering pitch as you draw a synchronously wavering line for a two-year-old, and be rewarded with a laugh—a laugh that comes from the child's "getting it." We come this way into the world, hard-wired to pay attention to these correspondences in order to interpret the world as we must to survive: as a poem.

The **teleological** goal of authoring systems is to provide this poem.

synesthesia: Psychological term for a process whereby one type of stimulus triggers a secondary, subjective sensation, as when a certain color evokes a specific smell sensation.

teleological: The logical development of something through time (note that the word "telescope" has the same root).

IT'S PLAY TIME

FUN & GAMES WITH INTERACTIVITY

Technology developed in the realm of big-budget, industrial and military R&D often finds its way into or onto the hands of the citizens—as was the case with the Mattel Power Glove (progeny of the VPL Research DataGlove) for Nintendo home entertainment systems. The sales of this and other computer-based and electronic toys constitute over 24 percent of the $14 billion toy and game business. Usually these toys give children (and, sometimes, their parents) their first experiences with some of the exciting technologies they'll be using in the future.

This chapter discusses the development of the Power Glove and other interactive toys and games by Mattel.

BY RICH GOLD

Rich Gold received his B.A. in electronic music from State University of New York at Albany and his M.A. in computer and performance art from Mills College (Oakland, California). In between he helped develop the first inexpensive musical synthesizer at California Institute of the Arts. A founding member of The Hub, the world's first computer network-based musical group, Rich also designed Activision's Little Computer People (the only autonomous "pet person" for home computers) and headed the Sound & Music department of SEGA-American's coin-op division. For the next five years Rich oversaw Mattel's electronic interactive toy design group. While there he served as design manager for the Mattel Power Glove, among other projects. He now works at Xerox's Palo Alto Research Center, researching ubiquitous computing and virtual reality.

The Mattel toy that you probably know best is Barbie, but I didn't work much with her. Instead I worked in a small group called "New Business Concepts" that explored unusual and weird toys, the new electronic toys and toys of the future. I worked on toys for at least two or three years before they were introduced to the market. On my first day working at Mattel, I was told, "If people ask you what you're doing, tell them, 'We're not allowed to talk about it.'"

There are toys I *can* talk about, and I can talk about how a child interacts with a toy, and how those toys interact with other appliances, electronics, and other devices found in our homes. I like to say that a toy is the child's **interface** between her hands and her fantasies, but these days a toy might have to interface with more than that. It might have to interface with the TV set in the family room, for instance.

In toy history, one of the most successful toys ever has been produced by Mattel for 20 years. I call it "Baby's First **Database Management System**," but you'll probably recognize it by its real name, "See 'n Say." When playing with See 'n Say, a child can learn about the letter "g" by moving the big plastic arrow so it points to the "g," then pulling the lever. (Until a few years

interface: (noun) The interconnection or method of communication between two objects; an interface may be hardware or software. (verb) To interconnect or communicate.

database management system: A "database" is a large collection of data (in a computer, typically), organized so that it can be retrieved, expanded, and updated for various uses; a database management system is the system used to control and/or access the information in a database.

ago she would have pulled a string, but the lever is easier, so even younger children can use the toy. Such are the realities of interface design.) When the lever is pulled, out of the speaker comes a voice that might say, "G—*girl*." Point the arrow to the letter "r," pull the lever, and you hear a voice saying "R—*rabbit*." You're probably familiar with the Macintosh computer's method of accessing information, known as "point-and-click." Well, this method is "point-and-pull." And instead of a pull-down menu, See 'n Say uses a much more efficient circular one.

I think See 'n Say is one of Mattel's best products. One interesting aspect of this database management system is that children use it to search for data before they even know what "data" is. They use this alphabet toy before they know or understand what an "alphabet" is. One reason they play with it is because the interface is so much fun. They love moving the arrow. They love pointing it at different pictures and pulling the lever over and over to hear the voice. In this toy, the interface actually drives the data. It is an interface that is so well-designed that the kid *wants* to use the toy. Compare that with your word processor.

Several years ago, a company called Landmark came to Mattel with the desire to produce a TV show called "Captain Power," a weekly half-hour program. At that time, toy companies liked to create what are known as "male action figures" to complement boys' TV shows. (Since they were for boys, we couldn't call them "dolls"!) A good example of a male action figure is "He-Man," who turns out to be the Master of the Universe. But we wanted to cre-

Mattel's See 'n Say: "Baby's First Database Management System"

ate something more than just a doll. We wanted to give the kid the capability to play and interact with the TV show itself.

This feat was accomplished with a toy called "The Striker Jet," part of the Captain Power product line. While the kid watched television, he could point his jet and shoot the bad guys, helping Captain Power. At the same time, the bad guys could shoot back at the kid. The kid got a point for each bad guy he hit and lost a point each time he was hit. When the Jet was hit five times, it "blew up" in the kid's hand. Really. This system used a wireless interface technology: You simply pointed the jet at the screen and blasted away. The show was broadcast for a year in 1987 and featured live action characters mixed with television's first computer-generated "actors."

The Striker Jet worked because patches of flashing light were "stuck to" or "keyed" onto the bodies of the bad guys. This flashing was visible; the TV show's production team hated it. However, we incorporated that flashing into the game-play itself, calling it a "guideline"; it became a "user icon" employed by the kid to determine who were the bad guys and where to shoot. With the Striker Jet, we had to worry about two interfaces: the one between the TV and the toy, and the one between the toy and the kid. In the interface between toy and kid we used the "gun" metaphor. Between the TV and the toy we used the sophisticated, albeit noticeable, "flashing chest" technology.

The Captain Power toy line was very successful, but the same could not be said for the TV show. It was cancelled after the first year. After losing half of its interface technology, the toy suffered the fate of other unsuccessful products. It was discontinued and **remaindered**.

Let's move away from cyberpunk warfare and into the exciting world of money. Most of you probably know what "Wheel of Fortune" is. In the mid-1980s it was the most-watched game show on TV; it still boasts a solid following. One interesting aspect of "Wheel of Fortune" lies in the fact that people at home tend

to play along with the contestants, trying to guess the puzzle. ("Should that blank be a 'D'?"; "I know, I know! The answer is 'Jane Fonda'!") However, there's something missing. At home you can't score points. You can't, as we say in the toy industry, "take the risks and rewards" required for good game play.

At Mattel, we thought a home game of "Wheel of Fortune" would succeed in the market. With it, the home audience could interact and score points. They could spin the wheel, risk bankruptcy, score big points, and even beat the TV contestants in solving the puzzle.

The "Wheel of Fortune Game" consisted of a small keyboard device on which you typed letters, spun the wheel, and made guesses right along with the TV contestants. It contained a tiny sensor. You aimed the keyboard at the TV, and an invisible signal encoded directly on the video told the device what the TV contestants were doing and what the answer was. As Vanna White flipped the letters on the big board, the letters also turned over on your keyboard. The scores of the TV contestants showed up on the keyboard, as did your own score. If you solved the puzzle before the contestants, and typed in the answer, you won the money that showed on your keyboard's **LCD** display. Today, all the "Wheel of Fortune" evening shows are invisibly encoded in this manner. If you can find the game at your local toy store, consider buying it, because I think you'll find it a serious challenge and a lot of fun.

The "Wheel of Fortune Game" didn't sell as well as expected. Mattel discontinued it. I'll guess why it didn't sell: because

remaindered: Mattel sold the toys to "jobbers" who in turn sell the toys to stores for very little money. This massive markdown helps move the goods out of the warehouse.

LCD: Abbreviation for "liquid crystal display," the alphanumeric display device used on such items as digital watches and calculators. An LCD uses a liquid crystal sealed between two pieces of glass and polarizers and activated by an external light source.

Mattel's Striker Jet

cockpit cover that flies off and pilot ejected when gun is hit

sensors

trigger

nobody likes to type at dinner time, which is when "Wheel of Fortune" airs. Although we solved one particular TV-to-toy-interface problem, we forgot to solve the people-to-toy one. Some interfaces just don't work when you're eating.

There's another game system that continues to sell better than anyone expected: the Nintendo Home Entertainment System. In the United States, over 20 million Nintendo units have been sold; it's said that one out of every four homes contains a Nintendo system. Essentially every kid in the United States has access to Nintendo. In fact, the average kid spends one to three hours each day playing with Nintendo. What does that mean? It means that while adults are talking about interactive television, kids are playing with interactive television. Why is Nintendo considered "interactive television"? Because the kid does something and the action on the TV screen does something unexpected as a result. Then the kid has to react to the TV action. The action/reaction continues, back and forth.

The Nintendo game differs from a "watch-me" toy, such as a wind-up toy train, or a "do-me" toy, such as Barbie or Lego, where the toy's actions are determined by the child. Despite the toy industry's current fascination with "interactivity," there are some wonderful watch-me and do-me toys . . . and some inane interactive ones.

The design of modern toys somewhat parallels the history of art. Since the Renaissance, Western artists have moved more and more toward the representation of "realism." (This is unique to the Western world.) During the Renaissance,

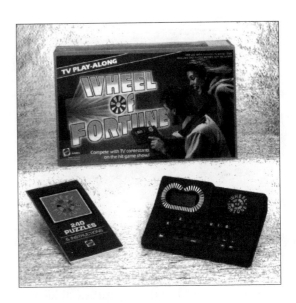

Mattel's Wheel of Fortune game

artists invented perspective painting, with the goal of recreating a scene as if you were right there seeing it. When photography was invented in the 19th century, it automated and perfected this approach, for the first time actually capturing the "skin" of reality. Then someone put a series of photographs together to make a movie, first in black and white, then in color, then on a wide screen, and now accompanied by stereo sound. Today, the technology of virtual reality aims to place you *inside* the artwork. Not wanting to buck the trend, we wanted to give kids the capability to enter their video games.

Most kids currently interact with video games using the basic Nintendo controller. This control pad contains four small buttons that control a character's or weapon's movement up, down, left, and right. It also provides two "fire" buttons and two "anything-you-want-them-to-be buttons." It is remarkable what this controller can accomplish when combined with good software and a teenager's hormones. The simplicity of the interface is dazzling—and amazing in

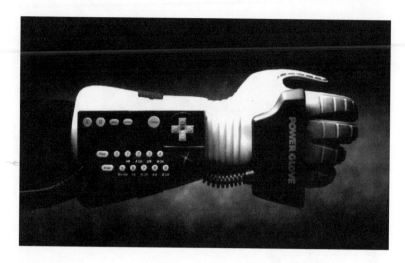

Mattel Power Glove

for about $80. Of course, it can't do everything that the DataGlove can; it's not supposed to. Nevertheless, the Power Glove—which debuted just before Christmas in 1989—was the first "virtual reality" consumer product.

At that time, Nintendo held over 80 percent of the video game market. Mattel felt that the Nintendo was the only system for which it was economically feasible to design, considering the high overhead costs of hardware and software development. We reached a licensing agreement with Nintendo, which had final approval on quality.

We knew we could develop extremely good, original software for this product. What was less clear was how the Power Glove would work with existing games. Mattel had decided early on that the Power Glove should accommodate every current game—all 150 of them! The trick was the interface problem: The games out there didn't know anything about the Power Glove. They were designed only for the Nintendo controller. We had to convert all the Power Glove motions into Nintendo controller signals so the games could understand them.

We also cooked up two new games: a street-fighting game converted for our purposes, and "SuperGlove Ball," designed by Novak of Mattel's New Business Concepts.

We spent a lot of time researching size, a classic interface problem. How big should this thing be to fit most kids' hands? We put out two sizes: large and medium, but no lefties. To you left-handed people: Sorry! Thumbs turned out to be tough, because every person moves their thumbs

the diversity of what kids and programmers can do with it.

We felt, however, that the controller didn't bring the kid *into* the video game. We wanted to give the kid a way to be even more expressive. With the help of an entertainment company, Abrams/Gentile Entertainment in New York, and a virtual reality company, VPL Research in California, we licensed the VPL Data-Glove and modified it into the Mattel Power Glove. We developed the Power Glove in six hectic months of seven-day weeks, working 14 hours a day in a small, converted warehouse. At that time, the VPL DataGlove sold for $8,000. When introduced, the Power Glove retailed

Mattel's SuperGlove Ball game for Nintendo systems

in a different way. Novak's thumb never could work the Power Glove, so he didn't use the thumb much in SuperGlove Ball. And after you wore it and played with it awhile, the glove got sweaty inside. (The biggest problem, however, was remembering to unplug the glove before getting up to answer the telephone.)

The Power Glove itself responds in four degrees of freedom: left and right, up and down, in and out, and rotation, each to about a quarter-inch resolution. Four of the five fingers are active and each has four different positions. The pinky, as we say in the toy business, was "cost-reduced-out." The glove contains two kinds of sensors. Overall hand motion is detected via **ultrasonics**, in a device located on the top of the glove, while each finger contains "bend sensors." The main difference, by the way, between the Power Glove and VPL's DataGlove—other than cost—is that the Power Glove works only when pointed in a forward direction. Luckily, that's how video games are played.

The Power Glove contains an extremely sophisticated microprocessor, programmed by Anne Graham of AfterScience. It analyzes the hand motions and performs the conversion for them. This undoubtedly is the most complex toy interface ever designed: It had to go from the kid to the glove to a different controller to the game deck to the game software and finally to the TV!

We accomplished the interface to all the different games by creating 14 "user interface metaphors" or "templates." Different metaphors were better for different games, while a few "general-purpose" templates covered the remainder. For in-

stance, we incorporated the "boxing metaphor," where you throw punches—upper left, upper right, block, even a rabbit punch. With the "driving metaphor," you place your hand as if it's holding a steering wheel which you turn left and right, with the gear-shift down below. The "flying metaphor" lets you bank left and right and drop bombs with your thumb. Again, the goal is to absorb the kids in the video game so they can feel *part* of it.

Our oddest metaphor was the "military tank." It gives you two sticks, represented by your first two fingers. Press both forward, you move forward; press both back, you go back. Pressing one forward and one back causes you to turn, more or less like in a real tank.

We used these metaphors to interface the Power Glove with the existing games, but it was not the "mode" which most interested us. Our favorite was the "raw data mode," which could provide the Nintendo system with precise information about the status of the Power Glove. Unfortunately, the raw data mode could work only with games designed specifically for the Power Glove.

"SuperGlove Ball" was the first and only game to use the raw data mode. Introduced for the 1990 Christmas season, SuperGlove Ball had two spatial metaphors. In the first one, you saw a ball bouncing around a room. This was a virtual ball that you could hit, catch, and throw. Using the ball, you tried to knock out tiles in the room. In the second spatial metaphor, after you knocked out the tiles on one of the walls, you could go through that wall into another room. The game took place inside a huge maze of rooms; in fact,

ultrasonics: Designation for frequencies of mechanical vibrations above the range audible to the human ear (i.e., above 20,000 vibrations per second; also measured as "Hz" or "cycles per second").

SuperGlove Ball put you "inside" a three-dimensional spaceship.

As SuperGlove Ball used the raw data mode, the information driving the Power Glove on the screen was extremely precise. You quickly started to consider that virtual hand as *your* real hand. At home I still play SuperGlove Ball; when I grab the virtual ball, I can almost feel it pulsing in the palm of my hand. In fact, when I hit the ball, I actually can "slice" it by rotating my hand a bit!

Both the Power Glove and SuperGlove Ball were discontinued in 1991. You can still find them sold (at a greatly reduced price!) in a few toy stores and job-lot warehouses. Mattel discontinued the Power Glove for financial reasons; we were unable to put out more raw data mode games. However, I continue to receive phone calls from scientists and artists who have adapted the Power Glove for low-cost virtual reality systems, as alternate controllers in electronic music systems, and as input devices for personal computers. Like See 'n Say, the Power Glove provides an interface that people like so much that they try to figure out things to do with it.

The biggest problem with SuperGlove Ball was that adults wanted to play it, and they *always* asked, "What are those green things bouncing all over?" I always had to explain, "They're the enemies! Go get 'em!" I've never had to explain this to a ten-year-old. Herein lies the most important lesson of toy interface design: Kids are different.

● ●

A PEEK BEHIND THE CURTAIN

By Anne Graham & Dave Ream with Peter Stone

Anne Graham launched her career at the Stanford Linear Accelerator Center in Menlo Park, California. She moved to Los Angeles in 1979 and worked with electronic musical instrument companies, then served as a designer for Oberheim Electronics, a synthesizer manufacturer. While there, in 1984 Anne co-founded the MIDI Manufacturers Association and co-wrote the first edition of the MIDI specification guidelines for companies and programmers incorporating the musical instrument digital interface into their products. Since establishing AfterScience in 1985, she and her associates have designed hardware and **firmware** for music keyboards, toys, and other interactive devices. AfterScience currently is working on projects for Fisher-Price, Hasbro, and Mattel.

firmware: A type of software that resides permanently in a chip instead of being written to an eraseable floppy or hard disk. Firmware manages communication between hardware and software.

pickup: An electromagnet designed to "pick up" acoustic vibrations and convert them into electrical impulses.

sequencer: A computer-based device that works like a tape recorder; instead of recording sounds on different audio tape tracks, it records MIDI data and selectively sends out that data for specific MIDI instruments to play back. MIDI data stored into a sequencer can play back through any MIDI instrument.

synthesizer: Electronic musical instrument that might be packaged in the form of a keyboard, guitar, drum, black box, or none of the above. Electronic (compared to "electric") instruments don't create sound on their own; they use a circuit to directly generate electrical signals, transformed into soundwaves by a loudspeaker. The first synthesizer ("Automatically Operating Musical Instrument of the Electric Oscillation Type") was shown at the Paris Exposition in 1929, while the first instrument to be called a synthesizer was the RCA Synthesizer, a 1955 invention.

Much of the final hardware and firmware design of the Mattel Power Glove was accomplished at AfterScience, Anne Graham's design studio in Venice, California. AfterScience designs systems for companies that manufacture electronic musical instruments, electronic toys, and Macintosh peripherals. Anne's design team also has worked on custom projects for film productions, computer graphics companies, and museum exhibits. This chapter briefly describes several AfterScience projects.

If you saw the 1989 film *Tap* starring Gregory Hines, then you saw—and heard—Tap-Tronics. Alfred Desio, the originator of Tap-Tronics and associate director of Los Angeles Choreographers & Dancers, came to AfterScience in 1985 with the request to help him get *more* out of his electronic tap-shoe design—which triggers music while the dancer taps away.

Al is an alumnus of the original Broadway productions of *West Side Story, Fiddler on the Roof, Man of La Mancha,* and others. The subject of many major TV and radio programs covering innovative work with tap and electronics, Al also was featured in a TV documentary about the making of *Tap,* because his Tap-Tronics dancing system was used as part of the story line.

Al's original Tap-Tronics equipment employed radio transmission to send an audio signal, from **pickups** attached to his tap shoes into various special effects and synthesizer modules. But Al wanted more. He envisioned the use of his tap transmitter system to step through, or "conduct," the notes of songs preprogrammed into a **sequencer**.

In addition to his prototype tap-controlled system, Al owned a pre-MIDI sequencer and **synthesizer** that he used to play preprogrammed songs. This meant he already had the system's front end (the radio transmitter tap pickups) and back end (the music gear), but not the necessary interface between the two ends that would enable him to realize his vision. That's when AfterScience became involved in the project.

clock: Master source of timing information. In digital circuits, a clock produces a train of high-speed pulses that are used to synchronize various functions.

sample: Brief recording of sound. A sampler is a microprocessor-based device used to record any kind of sound, store it as digital data, and play back the sound when triggered.

The Miracle Piano Teaching System shown here with the Macintosh software. The Miracle also works with the Nintendo and Super NES entertainment systems, and IBM PC and Amiga computers.

We designed a unit that takes the audio signal produced by the tap shoe pick-up and uses it to generate a series of digital **clock pulses**. These pulses are sent to a sequencer's "external clock in" input and they control the progression of a pre-programmed sequence of notes. In other words, when Al dances, each one of his taps tells the sequencer to play one or two notes, depending on the length of the particular notes. In effect, he "conducts" his musical accompaniment precisely to the rhythm of his own dancing feet.

The making of the interface box took a couple of days, but our involvement extended to subsequent improvements of the system and building the Tap-Tronics interface devices used for the film *Tap*. Al continues to use the system in "Zapped Taps," a dance show that he performs around the country.

Designing A Miracle

In 1990 AfterScience helped design the Miracle Piano Teaching System, a music-

teaching system manufactured by Software Toolworks for use with Nintendo systems and personal computers. The goal of AfterScience and the system's other developers was to create a product that would make learning basic piano skills easy and fun. The resulting $379 Miracle incorporates arcade-quality video games, historical facts, and computer-based orchestral accompaniment.

AfterScience designed the PC-board hardware and some of the instrument's firmware. The Miracle is a MIDI-compatible electronic keyboard with built-in stereo speakers. It's multi-timbral and plays over 60 voices, including piano, harpsichord, vibraphone, and many others, based on 128 digital **samples** of instruments and sound effects. Each of its eight channels can receive its own voice, and it has MIDI In and MIDI Out **ports**.

As a stand-alone instrument, the Miracle rivals other MIDI keyboards that cost far more to buy. Its 49 keys are full-sized, which is important for teaching music, and they're **velocity-sensitive** to allow piano-like expression. The Miracle comes with a foot pedal for controlling how long the notes are sustained. Also included is a software cartridge or floppy disk containing the lessons and games that teach you how to play.

Development of the Miracle System took almost nine months and involved 74 software designers, ten hardware engineers, and a ten-member structural design team. To balance out all us "techies," a graduate of New York's Juilliard School of Music came on board to design the music lessons.

The Miracle System differs from other electronic music-teaching systems because it implements **artificial intelligence** techniques in its lessons. The system recognizes 200 types of errors, which are divided into 41 categories. The system logs the player's errors and prioritizes them according to the current lesson; if you're working on playing rhythm accurately, the system will give priority to rhythm mistakes, not wrong notes. The program adapts to the player's responses, customizing individual lessons and responding differently each time a mistake is repeated. For example, if you make several unsuccessful attempts, it detects that you're having a hard time with a particular part of a song and guides you through a series of "repair frames" to help you. When you progress to the point where you can play the piece all the way through, the Miracle supplies you with a back-up band.

The Miracle's educational software contains over 100 learning levels that take into account the player's age level. Some basic lessons are fashioned after video games. For example, in one lesson you watch cartoon ducks cruise across a musical staff; when you hit the right note, the ducks quack. More advanced lessons use musical scores, ranging from "Amazing Grace" to "La Bamba," to teach musical notation, fingering, pedal techniques, music theory, and history. When you've successfully completed the Miracle lessons, you should be ready to enter an intermediate piano class.

The original Nintendo version was released a few years ago, but Software Toolworks waited until the release of IBM PC-compatible, Apple Macintosh, and Commodore Amiga versions before it started advertising. Sales took off late in 1991, reaching 40,000 units by the end of the year. People seem to like the Miracle System.

What About "Waldo"?

Another AfterScience project involved a computer graphics motion-control device used by performance-character animators Brad deGraf and Michael Wahrman to control the evil face that appears at the end of Orion Pictures' 1990 film, *Robocop 2*.

The device, called the "Waldo," uses rings and wheels mounted at various axes, somewhat resembling a set of gyroscopes, to translate hand movements into digital signals that are interpreted by a computer as motion commands. Using the Waldo is similar to sticking your hand inside a hand-puppet; with the Waldo, however, the puppet isn't on your hand, but displayed on a video screen, and you can control its movement with infinitely greater precision.

Holy CAD, Batman!

In 1991 AfterScience moved into new cyber-realms with the completion of projects that focus on the visual aspects of computer graphics and animation, rather than on sound and motion control.

That year we worked with the company General Lift on an extremely rewarding project that involved a **CAD** drawing used in the movie *Batman Returns*. Art director Rick Heinrichs, who worked on the film, asked General Lift and AfterScience for a computer-generated, "mumbo-jumbo-complicated"

artificial intelligence: Term used to describe the use of computers in such a way that they perform operations analogous to human mental abilities such as learning and decision-making; the automation of human skills that involve intelligence (understanding images, speech, and written text, problem solving, etc.).

port: Physical input provided for a connector.

velocity-sensitive: Refers to the ability of a synthesizer to measure a key's "time of travel" from top to bottom, and convert that to voltage; the faster you press down the key, the greater the note's velocity. In many synths, higher velocities cause brighter and/or louder sounds.

CAD: Acronym for Computer-Aided Design, a type of software used in many fields (architecture, manufacturing, the arts, engineering, and others) for precision drawing. CAD programs range from basic 2-D drawing tools to complex 3-D modeling systems. CAD expedites the design process by providing versatility and automation.

technical drawing of the infamous Batmobile. Rick and his colleagues—art director Tom Duffield and production designer Bo Welch—wanted to use a drawing as a set dressing for the Penguin's lair, but didn't have anyone on staff who worked with computer graphics.

They brought us Tom Duffield's drawings of vehicles used in the film *Bladerunner* to demonstrate the basic visual idea they wanted us to use as a guideline. We began by shooting photographs of the actual Batmobile. We **scanned** those images and imported them as **PICT** files to various CAD programs. Once we traced and filled out the Batmobile drawing, we surrounded it with **linear dimension lines** and elaborate, pseudo-technical imagery to make it look as complex as possible. Much of what we included has nothing to do with the Batmobile vehicle; we included things like photocopied images of jet engines and excerpts from aircraft manuals to add to the drawing's complicated appearance.

We created the drawing on a Macintosh and used Hewlett-Packard and Calcomp **pen plotters** to print it. The main technical challenge was finding the right combination of scanning, tracing, and plotting software to maintain the integrity of all the images we were combining and to properly plot the entire drawing. For different sections of the drawing and various stages of the project, we used several graphics programs: Deneba Software's Canvas, Adobe Illustrator, and ClarisCAD. We assembled and plotted the final drawing using ClarisCAD.

For four weeks we experimented with the software to create and assemble the various images. I thought our first successful drawing was only a start, a basic concept. When we submitted that version to secure approval to continue, however, the movie's art team was so pleased that they just took it as the finished piece. From there, the film's art crew photomechanically reversed the image to show white lines on a black background, and enlarged it to its final 6'x10' size for use on the *Batman Returns* set.

Envisioning Interceptor

AfterScience worked on another collaboration with General Lift. We created animation and graphics for a fighter-plane action movie, Hess Kalberg's *Interceptor*. In the film, pilots fly Stealth F117A fighters via virtual reality technology: While in the aircraft cockpit, the pilot wears a helmet that displays an entirely artificial, recreated view of the sky and cockpit, plus things that ordinarily can't be seen, such as radar fields. Using this comprehensive display of information, the pilot is better able to navigate and target planes or other "threats."

Our team created the imagery seen by the pilot inside the virtual reality helmet, imagery that is intended to help the audience understand what's going on during the flight scenes. The producers gave us much leeway to develop the "look" and the technical process we used to create the imagery.

First we analyzed the script and created our own scene-by-scene "breakdown" to determine the imagery required to convey the plotline. Then we used Electric Image on a Macintosh II (equipped with an **accelerator card** to speed up the

scan: To convert a visual image into a digital form recognizable by computer.

PICT file: A standard form of graphics file that any Macintosh graphics program can import or export.

linear dimension lines: Straight lines drawn to the length of a drawn object, which is interpreted (usually in the middle) by the length expressed numerically. Example: I-------2"-------I

plotter: A computer printer that uses computer-guided pens, rather than fixed-toner or ink-jetted dots, to output images.

accelerator card: A circuit board installed inside a computer to improve the performance of the central processing unit.

render: A computer graphics function that takes 3-D computer-generated models, removes hidden surfaces and jagged edges, and shades them by adding texture, depth, and other realistic attributes.

processing) to **render** the computer-animated landscape for the virtual reality scenes. In the fighter planes, computers assist and even perform some of the piloting by planning and recommending courses to avoid radar-detected threats. Our team represented these navigation paths to look like a "snake" sliding between and past the threats.

Our team also used the MacroMind Director multimedia authoring program to create "multi-function displays" that identified missile threats, other planes, aircraft status screens, and so on. Once all the graphics were rendered, we **compressed** the animation files. We wrote a computer- and camera-controlling

HyperCard stack that let us advance and photograph the animation files frame by frame directly from the screen of a Macintosh 13-inch display.

Some scenes comprised up to three simultaneous sequences of images that had to be superimposed. For example, we had to combine the initial virtual-reality landscape though which the plane flies, the computer-generated navigation path the pilot is supposed to follow, and various status displays showing the position and condition of the plane. We layered these sequences inside the camera, rewinding the film for each pass.

It's a crazy job, but someone has to do it. We're glad it's us.

HyperCard stack: Inexpensive, versatile HyperCard is an interactive, multimedia authoring tool and information organizer. You can use it to create stacks of information to share with other people. A "stack" is a completed file that runs under HyperCard.

compress: To translate (video, audio, digital, or combination) data into a more compact form for storage or transmission.

THE SILVER PLATTER

A LOOK AT CD MASTERING

The compact disc has revolutionized the ways we publish and distribute digital data. The evolution of audio CD technology has engendered a medley of data storage and presentation formats, including CD-ROM, CD-ROM XA, CD-ROM+Audio, CD+Graphics, CD-I, and Photo CD, along with a host of development products and services. This chapter explains the CD formats and the steps involved in CD-ROM development, production and manufacturing, emphasizing desktop development of multimedia. "With connectivity to mainstream personal computers and workstations in place, and development platform and tools rapidly maturing," author Allen Adkins says, "now is the time to learn how the CD format, like no other available media, can leverage your creative ideas into reality!"

Allen shares his insights from his perspective as president and cofounder of Optical Media International, which invented IBM PC-based, CD-ROM premastering in 1986. OMI makes CD development systems for PC and Macintosh platforms and provides CD services to Apple Computer, IBM, Sears, Digital Equipment Corp., Microsoft Corp., the federal government, and other organizations.

BY ALLEN ADKINS

*Allen Adkins is internationally recognized as an innovator in the field of CD-ROM publishing and the design of program development systems. He has extensive experience in the design of optical disc systems and multimedia interfaces. After launching OMI in 1985, Allen led the design and development of the firm's productions, including a line of CD-ROM **premastering** workstations and a digital sound library on CD-ROM (the first of its kind) for the professional audio industry. Allen also started Interactive Research Corp., which created the first interactive optical disc-based computer training system for the IBM PC.*

premastering: The part of the CD-ROM data production process that occurs prior to sending out the data to the mastering and manufacturing plant.

The CD-Audio format was introduced in 1978 and today sales of audio CDs surpass those of vinyl records and cassettes. In 1991, about 340 million CDs were sold worldwide, representing 55% of music industry revenues, while LP sales declined by 59% and cassette sales dropped 23%, according to a 1992 issue of *Billboard* magazine. One of the best things about CD is that it's a world standard: CDs made anywhere in the world can play on CD players anywhere in the world.

A CD can hold 650 megabytes of data—any kind of digital data. The runaway success of the audio CD helped decrease the cost of the technology, paving the way for the establishment of a related format: **CD-ROM**, an optical disc on which you can store all kinds of digital data. You can combine digital audio, images, text, and computer data, including data files from virtually any type of computer, in virtually any combination. Depending on the quantity ordered, multimedia CDs can be manufactured for less than $2 per disc. When we talk about "multimedia CDs," we're referring to the compact disc as a publishing medium for delivering multimedia content, or "titles," containing a combination of digital data— text, still and moving images, graphics, and audio. CD-ROM currently is the multimedia distribution method of choice, especially for PC-based applications.

The "ROM" part of CD-ROM stands for "Read Only Memory," which means that once the CD-ROM is pressed, you can't change the information on it. CDs can be highly interactive. When you use the CD with some kind of computer or microprocessor-based, home entertainment system such as a **CD-I** player, you can have tactile, multisensory, closed-loop interactivity. "Closed-loop" interactivity means that your actions and their results are part of the same system; for example, you "walk through" the 3D image of a building (the data used to construct the image is on the CD), choose a room to "enter," and that "room" is displayed on the computer screen, again using data pulled off the CD.

Hybrid products related to the original CD-Audio technology include CD-ROM XA (for eXtended Architecture), CD-I (Compact Disc-Interactive), Photo CD (developed by Eastman Kodak and Philips N.V.) and DVI (Digital Video Interactive, developed by Intel as a compressed digital-video format for use on CD-ROM). CD-ROM XA lets you have compressed digital audio interleaved with other information, be it text, graphics, compressed video, or animation. It facilitates the production of interactive multimedia titles for use with PCs and Macs. Essentially, XA is a hybrid format that uses the compressed audio format of CD-I and any graphics format. That's why it's popular for delivering entertainment and educational multimedia programs. **Photo CD** is the technology developed to electronically store, distribute, and manipulate images originating on conventional photographic film.

CD-ROM and CD-ROM XA both can play on a CD-ROM XA drive. The end user must know this in order to purchase the correct player. In the near future, all CD-ROM drives probably will be XA- and Photo CD-compatible. Today's CD-ROM players work with all manner of PCs, including Apple Macintosh, IBM PC-compatibles, Commodore Amiga, and Japan's hot **Fujitsu FM Towns** computer. Many other more powerful computer systems already support CD-ROM, and there are more to come in the future. In the meantime, the cost of CD-ROM players continues to drop; a high-quality, "name-brand" CD-ROM player that cost $1,000 in 1990 cost under $500 by mid-1992. In late 1992, Sony introduced the Bookman Portable, a hand-held CD-ROM XA computer with built-in, liquid-crystal display screen and headphone jack.

In a way, a CD-ROM player resembles a somewhat slow, read-only hard disk drive. Unlike a hard disk, however, CD-ROM is

CD-ROM: Before CD-ROM, it was not possible to have random access to huge data files on a personal computer system. The forerunner of CD-ROM in concept is the optical videodisc. Initially developed by MCA as a transport medium for Hollywood films, videodisc proved itself a much more useful tool as a storage device for the types of still photos, random-access video information, and interactive data used in training and information systems.

Photo CD: Photo CDs run in Photo CD players that connect to TV sets or in CD-ROM drives that connect to computers. See John Worthington's chapter on image compression for information about Photo CD and data compression issues.

CD-I: Developed by Philips, CD-I players hit department and stereo store shelves late in 1991. At that time the Philips "Imagination machine" CD-I player cost about $800, and about 40 titles were available, including "ABC Sports Golf" and "A Visit to Sesame Street."

FM Towns: A computer developed by Fujitsu (Japan's largest computer manufacturer) to support multimedia. Introduced in 1989, it was the first personal computer with a built-in CD-ROM drive, extensive video support, and ability to record and play digitized and synthesized sounds. It can run Microsoft Windows 3.0 with Multimedia Extensions.

a publishing medium that represents an extremely inexpensive method of delivering huge amounts of information. It's compatible with almost every mainstream personal computer and lower in cost, byte for byte, than floppy disks.

CD-ROMs are used around the world for a wide range of applications, especially by large corporate and scientific data publishers. Major software companies publish and distribute software and technical documentation on CD-ROM. CD-ROM also presents great opportunities for interactive program developers to design and create innovative, multimedia computer applications and user interfaces.

Interactive program design and user interfaces are absolutely critical to a disc's success. The choice of authoring tools used for design represents a critical decision. These are the tools that let you realize your creative ideas as hassle-free and intuitively as possible. You can choose mass-produced or custom-made development tools and authoring systems or a combination. Many off-the-shelf authoring systems work well, and they're getting better all the time. Before embarking upon a multimedia development effort, define what you want to do and learn which off-the-shelf systems can do it, including computer paint and image-editing programs and audio recording and editing hardware/software packages. Also consider the wealth of existing video and graphics material that can be converted into the digital domain. Companies exist to perform this service, and off-the-shelf products handle some of the same tasks.

When producing audio for CD, pay close attention to the way in which the sound recording is accomplished. That original (source) recording is extremely important, because CD audio playback systems tend to accentuate any noise or distortion on the original recording. Ideally, all audio is digitally recorded at a sample rate that matches the CD-audio rate of 44.1 kHz.

When producing a commercial title, as opposed to an in-house or private presentation, your first and most important consideration involves the final delivery platform. Who's going to buy your product? What kind of system will they use to play back the program? Currently, the easiest platform for developing multimedia programs is the Apple Macintosh. IBM and the MPC Marketing Council are working hard to make the PC more suitable for multimedia. It is possible to produce multimedia CD-ROMs that play on both Macs and PCs, but you must address important design and standard specification issues.

When you're developing a multimedia CD-ROM title, the ability to simulate and test it completely before it's pressed on CD is a critical time-saving and cost-saving issue. The latest generation of low-cost CD recorders provide a convenient way to produce "one-off" CDs for testing and low-volume production.

CD-ROM mastering is a straightforward process. After developing your data or multimedia application, you must convert your finished files into the CD-ROM data format: either the worldwide standard file structure, the **ISO 9660** CD-ROM volume and file structure format,

ISO 9660: The IBM-PC uses a file structure called MS-DOS when it writes data onto hard and floppy disks; the Apple Macintosh uses a file structure called HFS. A Macintosh can't directly read an MS-DOS floppy disk, nor can an IBM PC read an HFS disk. Since CD-ROM standards don't designate which file structure to use, developers initially had to create their own structures, which required extra development time and confused the computer user. To resolve this problem, a group of industry representatives met at Del Webb's High Sierra Hotel/Casino in Nevada and drafted a CD-ROM file structure proposal, commonly called the "High Sierra" file structure. They submitted the proposal to the International Standards Organization, which added a few enhancements and re-named it the "ISO 9660 standard." A computer can read an ISO 9660 disc if its operating system includes software that can handle the ISO 9660 file structure. ISO 9660 allows multiple types of computers to access the same files from one CD-ROM.

or one of the native file system formats such as Apple's HFS (Hierarchical File Structure). Various CD-ROM publishing systems automatically transfer any kind of data file from any kind of computer to this ISO 9660 format or other appropriate format (i.e., XA, CD-I, Photo CD, and so on). The finished CD-ROM theoretically can work with any computer, as long as the computer contains a **device driver** that can support the connected CD-ROM drive.

As for the CD manufacturing process, there's really nothing mysterious about it. Making a CD essentially involves printing the digital contents of a hard disk onto plastic, and putting the data into a read-only format. The process is enormously reliable; it's possible to stamp out 10,000 discs without a single error.

Optical Media International's Mac Topix CDR Pro is a CD-ROM publishing system that uses a Macintosh computer to transfer data to the Apple HFS or ISO-9660 format. It can produce a master tape and lets you use your multimedia data to simulate a CD-ROM before you actually press the CD.

OMI also developed **Unix-**, Macintosh- and IBM PC-compatible systems that include a CD recorder. All versions of the Topix system make CD recording as easy as copying files to a floppy disk; essentially they manage the outputing of any kind of data files to a compact disc. The complete system costs around $10,000 in 1992, which is a significant point, as systems with the same features cost four or five times as much in 1991. Blank discs run approximately $35 each. The resulting data discs are compatible with all existing CD-Audio and CD-ROM players.

Basically, these Topix systems do everything a multimillion-dollar CD factory does, only they create one disc at a time. Such "write-once" discs are increasingly accepted at CD manufacturing plants for volume replication. The affordable price of CD recording systems is leading to the use of CD-ROMs in many diverse applications, including data back-ups, software distribution, database publication, and custom demonstration systems.

The maximum capacity of a write-once compact disc is roughly 650 megabytes. Digital audio alone takes up about 10 megabytes per minute. At the normal video standard (video running at 30 frames per second), an entire CD could be consumed with just one second of uncompressed video! Current CD-ROM publishing is concerned with digital data compression. Video compression is of paramount importance to viable multimedia production for distribution on CD. International committees are proposing standards regarding digital video and image compression; some of these standards will allow a CD to play back full-color, full-frame motion video. **DVI** is one example of that type of technology, while the **JPEG** and **MPEG** standards and dedicated processors implementing these standards will assist the data decompression in circuit board-based compression products for Macs and PCs. These allow you to deliver all-digital, interactive multimedia with video on a CD.

The only way for compressed video to be decompressed for multimedia as it is being watched is via a special computer

device driver: Software that tells the computer how to talk to a peripheral device, such as a printer or a CD-ROM player.

Unix: One of the major operating systems for use on computer workstations. Developed by AT&T.

DVI: Digital Video Interactive, a compression/decompression technology made by Intel that plays audio and video from files on a hard disk, floppy disk, and/or CD-ROM. The computer must have DVI circuit boards installed to take the data from CD-ROM and decompress it to normal video and audio signals.

JPEG; MPEG: Refers to multimedia standards proposed by the International Standards Organization (ISO) for digital data compression and decompression. JPEG stands for Joint Photographic Experts Group. MPEG stands for Motion Picture Experts Group.

processor that is optimized for a particular compression/decompression technique. Therefore, the need for compression (provided by the CD publisher) and decompression (handled in the CD-ROM playback process) to "speak the same language" has caused a push for standards such as DVI, JPEG, and MPEG. Additionally, proprietary compression/decompression technologies are being developed by corporations such as Ultech Corp. in Japan, which seek to differentiate themselves via a more effective, faster solution to the video compression problem.

The companies that can come up with high-quality, low-cost, good authoring tool support and real-time video compression will win out as the long-term leaders in the multimedia CD arena.

● ●

CURTAIN UP! LIGHT THE LIGHTS!

DEVELOPMENTS IN COMPUTER SHOW CONTROL

BY CHARLIE RICHMOND

Charlie Richmond, who co-authored the MIDI Show Control (MSC) spec, is an audio system and theater sound designer and owner of Richmond Sound Design Ltd. and Mushroom Studios in Vancouver, B.C., Canada. His company makes an MSC-controlled audio system called Command/ Cue, which runs on the Commodore Amiga, and MSC controller software called Stage Manager, which creates and edits MSC and other types of MIDI messages, incorporating them into cues that can be triggered manually or automatically to run any kind of show.

In 1983, MIDI (musical instrument digital interface) was introduced to the music industry, but people in other fields have since discovered reasons to use this deceptively simple control protocol. One recent significant MIDI development allows computer control of the diverse equipment systems used in live performance, multimedia, and large audio-visual productions. We can expect to see this "MIDI Show Control" (MSC) standard playing a major role in theaters and performance venues everywhere.

Even before MSC Version 1.0 was officially released as part of the MIDI specification in July of 1991, MIDI was used in productions including the Broadway musical "Miss Saigon," the Las Vegas magic act of Siegfried & Roy, and theme park attractions in Orlando and Los Angeles—not in orchestra pits, but in lighting and stage managers' control booths.

The MSC protocol was championed by Charlie Richmond of Richmond Sound Design and the United States Institute for Theatre Technology, who proposed that the MIDI Manufacturers Association incorporate MSC into the MIDI spec. Today, more and more manufacturers of sound & lighting consoles, projection systems, laser control, rigging gear, and even pyrotechnics are making their equipment "MIDI-savvy."

MSC is defined as the part of MIDI called "Universal System Exclusive," which lets it run, if necessary, on the same network with music-making equipment. Each MSC message is prefaced with an individual, group, or "all-call" device number to which MSC-compatible equipment can respond individually. Pressing a "go" button on a lighting console, for example, can send a MIDI message that causes other MSC-based lighting consoles to run through a pre-programmed sequence of events. With MSC, one personal computer can handle all the control functions for lighting systems, motorized stage equipment, audio devices, videodisc players, and even pyrotechnical effects. It also can monitor safety switches; if the safety switch sends an error message, the master computer prevents improper triggering of subsequent effects. The MSC system operator can handle an enormous number of simple and complex cues, in real time, adjusting the pace and intensity of the cue sequence. The human factor still reigns supreme, with impromptu live commands taking priority over canned ones.

MIDI control can lead to tighter cues (with fewer missed), production consistency, fewer opportunities for miscommunication between stage manager and crew, and less confusion behind the scenes. The way it used to be, high-speed cue sequences turned seasoned stagehands into nervous wrecks. Board operators prayed they'd be able to identify and move multiple controls in the time it took an actor to deliver a scene-ending line and exit stage-right. MIDI can reduce these worries to manageable proportions. Now one person can control just about any non-living thing in the production, including strobes, lasers, CD players, intercoms, robots, moving platforms, slide projectors, and fog machines.

The Official Keeper of the MIDI Spec is the International MIDI Association, 5316 West 57th St., Los Angeles, CA 90056; telephone 310-649-6434.

For more information about MIDI, see Mark Lacas' chapter in this section on the Multimedia Network.

Ever since high school, when I worked as a theater sound designer for a community theater company, and later, while working at professional theater companies, I have attempted to design and build equipment that makes it easy for an operator to perform extremely complex technical functions with sound and special effects devices, live and in real time. In earlier days, these systems mostly comprised sound distribution consoles with speaker preset controls, similar to multi-scene lighting boards.

The advent of personal computers with graphical interfaces and mouse input devices provided an appropriate vehicle with which to make the move to computer control. The result was the "virtual theater sound distribution console" (or, as it is called in the theme park business, the "router/switcher"). So sweeping was the demand for this technology that our company received orders for six systems before we had fully designed the system.

People frequently ask why we chose MIDI as a basis for computerized show control. They ask that because MIDI has earned a reputation for being an inexact communication technique—not because anything is inherently wrong with it, but because it is open-ended and flexible. It is so easy for manufacturers to incorporate MIDI into their equipment that many instruments and digital devices sport unique MIDI commands, which means you face a potentially confusing, complicated situation when you combine these different pieces of equipment. But once you work out the particular idiosyncrasies of the set-up, MIDI is easy to work with. That's one reason we decided to use it for show control.

As MIDI is widely used in live presentations and concert productions, it seemed a logical format to expand upon. Just as MIDI lets us control musical elements, MSC lets us control hundreds of live production elements, including video, sound, lighting, fireworks, lasers, rigging, mechanical effects, hydraulics, and smoke and fog machines. The flexibility and simplicity of the MIDI spec allowed us the freedom to give it an extra "language" to speak, on top of the centuries-old language of music. This language—MIDI Show Control—lets us talk in the language spoken by professional production crews. If they want to use the system to run a lighting console, for example, they don't have to use such MIDI jargon as "**note-on**" and "note-off," but their own terminology, such as "go" and "stop."

MSC's users are not necessarily computer-literate. They're people who want a hardware/software package that lets them run a show, and they often don't feel comfortable with computers. They're basically moving from paper to computer.

In our MSC system software, the traditional MIDI editor contains **channel voice messages**, **system common messages**, system exclusive messages, and system real time messages. Channel voice messages include the familiar note-on, note-off messages, program change, key pressure, channel pressure and pitch-bend changes. Note-on, for example, is assigned to a particular **MIDI channel** (one of 16 available), and a note and its velocity are defined, then added to a list of MIDI messages to send to the appropriate MIDI instrument. Channel voice messages are the most common type of MIDI commands; prior to MSC, many show equipment manufacturers used channel voice messages to allow remote MIDI control of their equipment. A lighting console manufacturer, for instance, may have assigned a lighting channel to a particular note, then used the velocity data in a note-on message to determine what level the channel should go up to.

That's useful, but it doesn't make much sense to a theater lighting person who doesn't know what "note-on" means. And if your MIDI system is sending notes to musical instruments *and* lighting instruments, it's hard to keep track of what's going on. You need to remember, "The lighting is on channel two and the music is on channel four." If you forget that, you might easily edit the wrong data. This results from the fact that you're dealing with a system that hasn't been designed for anything besides musical equipment.

MIDI does make a provision for manufacturers to incorporate "System Exclusive" ("sys-ex") messages. These are open-ended commands that allow manufacturers

channel & system messages: MIDI contains two types of data: channel information and system information. Channel messages consist of note-on and note-off commands, pitch-bend changes, after-touch, and other types of music performance commands ("play a note," "play a sound," etc.). System messages are concerned with how the system is operating, not the music it's playing, and include data such as start, stop, and continue commands, timing clocks, song position pointers, etc.

Note-on tells a connected instrument to play a certain note, while note-off releases the note. Program change tells a connected device to switch to a different sound or patch. MIDI controllers such as pitch-bend and volume commands describe continuous changes in the level or position of a particular part of a MIDI device.

MIDI channels: The MIDI spec defines 16 channels through which data is transmitted along a single cable. Generally, a receiving instrument is set to respond to incoming data on one channel, and ignores everything on the other channels.

to define messages that relate to specific instrument types and models. However, sys-ex is not easy to work with because you need to consult the instrument's operation manual and figure out exactly what cryptic message you want to type into the sys-ex editor. There's an area of the MIDI spec called "Universal System Exclusive" to deal with data transmission between computers and synthesizers, but it still doesn't communicate in the same language required to run lighting and sound systems for live shows.

That's why we developed "Show Control" as a MIDI command extension. Show Control lets you communicate with a large number of different types of devices. Each

device can respond to its own particular I.D. number or to a group number.

MSC typically is used whenever two or more system controllers need to talk with each other. Often, the configuration simply comprises a live show controller telling a dedicated control device such as a lighting board or rigging system what to do and when to do it. A complex show may have several of these controller/controlled device combinations, yet each system may not necessarily communicate with the others. At the same time, a central show control system may control the other controllers which, in turn, individually control their dedicated devices.

For example, in a recent industrial convention presentation, three separate show control systems each controlled a different element—one for sound, one for rigging, and one for lights. Each system was programmed before the show in different geographic locations, so their cue sequences were not designed to coordinate with a central control system. If they were all set up in the same location, however, a central show control system could have been programmed to talk with each of the other controllers simultaneously.

It is also possible to set up two similar control consoles in a "master-slave" relationship so the operator need only run the master unit and the slave(s) will automatically follow. This allows very large systems to be easily configured for single operator operation, which means lower inventory and equipment costs and simpler shipping requirements.

When you want to use a computer with MSC software to send a command to a par-

Control screens from an MSC program

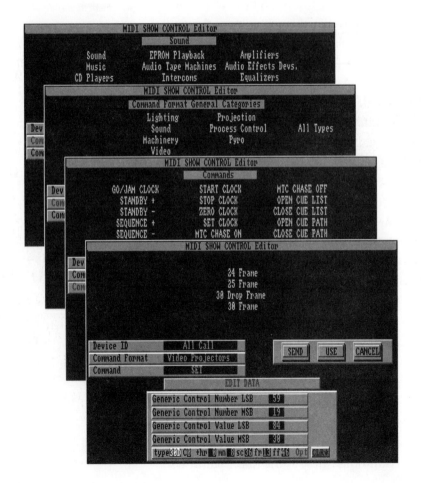

ticular device—such as telling a lighting console to bring up a purple spotlight—you treat the situation just as if you were a stage manager running a show. Conventionally, the stage manager wears an intercom headset to talk to various production and technical crew members and to call cues, such as, "Rigging, stand by cue 29." The person responsible for rigging stands by, ready to go.

When using the MSC system to make the computer call cue 29, the first thing the system operator does is select a "general command format": lighting, sound, machinery, video, projection, process control, pyro, or all-types. In the case of rigging, the general command format is "machinery."

Next, the operator chooses the specific format within the general category, which in this case is "rigging." It's possible that a large production set-up would contain more than one rigging system, so individual device numbers (I.D. numbers) can be chosen within each format. Up to 112 individual device numbers can be chosen. The system also provides 15 general group numbers to which several devices can respond. Finally, the "all-call" device I.D. provides a way to talk to all devices and groups simultaneously.

Returning to our example of "machinery" as a general category to which many different types of machinery respond, different machines also can respond to specific categories within the machinery group. For example, a record turntable can respond to the "turntable" command format but also may respond to the general "machinery" category.

In each general category, the specific categories are:

• Lighting—moving lights, color changers, strobes, lasers, and chasers;

• Sound—music, CD players, EPROM playback (solid-state sound playback devices that store digital audio in erasable, programmable, read-only memory), audio tape machines, intercoms, amplifiers, audio effects devices, and equalizers;

• Machinery—rigging, flies (systems for "flying" scenery, lights, and curtains), lifts, turntables, trusses, robots, animation, floats, breakaways, and barges;

• Video—tape machines, cassette machines, disc players, switchers, effects, character generators, still image storage, and monitors;

• Projection—film, slide, video, dissolvers, and shutter controls;

• Process control—hydraulic oil, water, carbon dioxide, compressed air, natural gas, fog, smoke, and cracked haze;

• Pyro—fireworks, explosions, flame pots, and smoke pots.

We tried to think of everything, and the MSC spec provides lots of room to add both general and specific categories in the future. No category is manufacturer-specific, which means any type of turntable (if it's MSC-compatible) can respond to the turntable message. A manufacturer that wants its turntable to work with MSC typically builds in a control unit with a MIDI port. A manufacturer of show equipment, however, typically first develops an adaptor that converts existing equipment to MSC, and eventually produces units with MSC circuitry built in. The first professional equipment to be manufactured with MSC are lighting and sound devices.

Equipment such as this generally accepts external control commands via switch-contact closures. In other words, to make a piece of show equipment do things, you connect switches to it. Commercially available MIDI control boxes that cost about $100 can be programmed to close a switch in response to a specific MIDI message. If, for example, a turntable needs a switch closure in order to start, you could connect the turntable to the MIDI box and program it to respond to an MSC command such as, "device one, turntables, go, cue 10."

The most basic command in Show Control is "go." Other basic commands include "stop," "resume," "timed go," "load," and "go off." Most basic commands let you enter a cue number that complies with many different kinds of systems. They let you program in just a simple "go" or a more complex "go cue 21.6." MSC can be made extremely simple; low-cost equipment can deal with it. If we're dealing with a simple system such as a small nightclub band's lighting set-up, we can send an "all-call, lighting, go" command and the lighting controller will simply go to the next cue standing by.

We approached MSC's development with the idea that most operating data is stored in the machines that we're controlling. For example, if we send the MSC message "lighting cue 10, go," we assume that data for cue 10 (dimmer levels, channel settings, and patching) are contained in the lighting console. If we tried to send all this information through MSC, the system would run way too slowly. So although MSC can talk to many individual controllers, we don't use it to set large numbers of controller or dimmer levels.

Some other MSC commands include:
• "All off," which lets you tell a device to turn all outputs off without forgetting where things were set. That's especially helpful with sound systems, because you can mute the sound for the moment without having it re-cue.
• "Restore," which puts things back to where they were before the "all off" command was sent.
• "Reset," which normally sets everything to a powered-up condition, to the top of the show or to the beginning of whatever it is they're currently in at the moment—the top of a cue list or the top of an act, for example.

Cue lists are a vital part of a stage manager's show orientation. My company's software, Stage Manager, allows up to 128 cue lists to run concurrently, and it sends and responds to MSC commands. Why would you want to run multiple cue lists concurrently? Two reasons: you're running a live show, and you must be able to run cues completely independently of others. One show, for example, can have separate cue lists labeled "lights," "sound," "mechanics," "effects," "rigging," "lasers," "strobes," "smoke," and "video," for example. Each list contains all the cues for each of those different elements, and each cue list can be operated independently.

Each cue list has its own clock, and each cue list can be locked to time code as well. For example, you might want to lock the sound and video systems to time code because they're controlling sound distribution and a video switcher that's receiving signals from a video tape machine supplying time code. At the same time, you might want to manually control the lighting, mechanics, and pyro so they're timed with the live action occurring on stage. Often, live action is not closely synchronized with prerecorded sound and video, so you need separately controlled cue lists.

As for the MSC spec itself, we're already working on the next version. In response to safety-related concerns, we have defined a set of fail-safe, error-detecting messages to add to MSC. Suggested uses of these messages include situations where a show is monitored and controlled from a central location, or performance conditions where safety concerns demand additional checking and redundancy in the show control mechanisms. The proposed set of safety-related commands include elaborate, stage manager-style communications along with extensive, electronic error-checking, so the MSC equipment must be somewhat more sophisticated to be able to handle it.

MSC is not a policed standard, so the people who use it must rely on the equipment manufacturers incorporating MSC into their equipment in an understandable, coherent manner. Fortunately, so far it looks like they're adopting it quickly and correctly. Many lighting control equipment manufacturers were involved in MSC's development, so they especially are incorporating it in their new equipment. MSC also will reach consumer technology, especially multimedia presentation systems. The Interactive Multimedia Association has acknowledged MSC as the prototypical language for defining interactivity between intelligent performance devices; MSC will be incorporated in future multimedia standards recommendations.

It's important to point out that MSC does not replace anybody in a stage or production crew. It will be a long time, especially in complex shows, before electronic systems eliminate human operators. The basic goal of MSC is to provide a stage manager with an electronic communication facility that is more reliable than the traditional headset system. MSC simply offers a precise way to communicate cues, so stage managers don't have to worry about the time lag between someone saying "go" and the operator's reaction time in pressing a button. Pressing buttons does not require great expertise, and most operators are glad to have MSC take over that task.

In an MSC-controlled productions, most of the time an operator is required to monitor the lighting board, run manual cues, refocus instruments, make sure the lights are operating properly, and generally keep an eye on things. Most operators are happy to pass time-critical communications to electronic systems, which gives them more time to deal with unexpected problems. As a result, the creative areas of technical expertise can benefit.

Operators and stage managers that use MSC are reporting back to us that they're extremely pleased with the results. As the developers of MSC, all we can say is merci, touché, bravo, and encore!

EXPANDING THE BOOK

TEXT & THE PERSONAL COMPUTER

When Apple Computer introduced the Macintosh Power-Book series in 1991, software designers saw it as a means to transform the notebook computer into a computer book, a reading machine that's eminently portable and easy on the eyes. Here's one designer's take on a new way to read in bed.

BY FLORIAN BRODY

Florian Brody is technical director of the Expanded Books Project at the Voyager Company in Santa Monica, California. Before moving to the U.S., he worked at the Austrian National Library in Vienna and as an international consultant in multimedia and virtual reality. He currently holds a teaching assignment at Vienna's University of Applied Art.

Books are repositories of memory but also a major part of our daily lives. Changing the look and feel of an everyday object causes many people to greet the new model as if it signalled the end of civilization as we know it. Computers have been no exception. In fact, they've been the central focus of this discussion for 30 years. When computers were big contraptions in climate-controlled rooms, their perceived Orwellian "Big Brother" threat overcast all other issues concerned with their use, but when the machines shrank—first to refrigerator size, then to the size of a box that fit on a writing desk—the issue of everyday computing became far more obvious and welcome.

When computers became "personal" in the early 1980s, it was clear to every serious typewriter user that he or she would never use a computer for writing, except perhaps as a text processor, a typewriter with a screen attached to it. This approach could prove useful, but why should one write text on a calculating machine? When I suggest today to people that they *read* books on their computers, almost all answer the same way: "Why would anyone want to read on a computer?"

Computers today are write-only devices. Everything written on a computer results in a product that comes out of the slot on a laser printer or similar device. Word processing and page-layout programs are designed to help the user produce neat, 8½-by-11 inch pages on paper. Printing on *both* sides of a page is tricky enough. What about displaying the final product on a screen for reading?

Putting Text on Screen

When I first scanned a large block of text from Paul Bowles' *Sheltering Sky* about two years ago, I wondered how it would look on a screen. I especially wondered how readable it would be. It wasn't. There is a dramatic difference between reading a database entry or a brief bit of information from an electronic dictionary and reading a *text corpus* into which the reader fully immerses himself or herself. For this task the reader needs an interface suitable for comfortable reading as well as for marking and handling the text. In most cases, the way text currently is presented on computer screens is completely unsuitable for these tasks. The text appears on the screen but you cannot get to it. You are locked out.

The Expanded Books Project

Making text readable on a screen requires a presentation that not only is agreeable to look at but also fulfills at least the basic prerequisites for reading. Text should be easy to read and not cause eyestrain. The lines of text should be short enough to limit eye movement and the topology of the text must be easily understood.

At Voyager, when we first saw the Macintosh PowerBook, we immediately understood that this would be the first machine with a screen good enough for reading. Half an hour later we had loaded the Bowles text into the PowerBook and started work on the interface, which is based on HyperCard 2.1. Six months later, Voyager introduced three Expanded

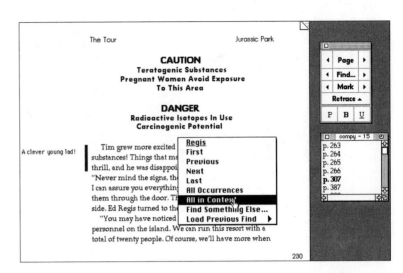

Books (*The Complete Annotated Alice*, annotated by Martin Gardner with John Tenniel's original illustrations; *The Complete Hitch Hiker's Guide to the Galaxy*, by Douglas Adams, the unabridged version containing four books; *Jurassic Park*, by Michael Crichton, with animated fractals and the pictures and sounds of dinosaurs). Each is priced at $19.95 and sold at bookstores and through software dealers. Since then we have published over a dozen more and continue to publish three books per month.

The Expanded Book's text block on the screen is sculpted after the page of a book, with a portrait orientation, with the pages structured as *pages*, not scrolling fields. Scrolling text on computer screens is a historic leftover from the time of teletype machines but, as readers learned over 1,000 years ago, fixed chunks of text on pages are much more suitable for reading. While codices and today's books offer direct access to every single page, the Expanded Books offer direct access to every single word, via a "find" feature that searches every occurrence of a word in the book on the fly and also gives you a list of the

The Expanded Book provides variable type sizes, customized word searches and indexes, and pop-up annotations and footnotes. The reader can type margin notes, underline or boldface passages, copy, paste, and print text, "paper clip" and "dog-ear" pages, and read in bed without the light on.

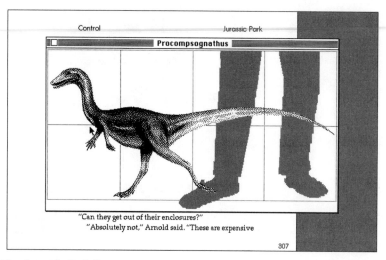

Control   Jurassic Park

Procompsognathus

"Can they get out of their enclosures?"
"Absolutely not," Arnold said. "These are expensive

307

The Jurassic Park Expanded Book allows the reader to click on the names of more than 30 dinosaurs to see the dinosaur drawn to scale and hear it roar, growl, or chitter.

backlit: Refers to a way of lighting a liquid crystal display (the kind of display used in digital watches) to brighten it and make it legible when viewed in dark places.

cyberspace: Coined by science fiction author William Gibson, in his 1984 novel **Neuromancer**, to describe a shared virtual environment whose inhabitants, objects, and spaces comprise data that is visualized, heard, and touched.

word's locations, complete with context. This makes it simple to trace the development of themes and characters.

But can you?— Yes, you can write in the margin, dog-ear corners, mark paragraphs, highlight text in bold, underline text, put "paper clips" on the pages, copy and paste text, and use the annotations wherever available to call up related text and images. You can print the text, too. You can even enlarge the text and, because the screen is **backlit**, you can read in bed under the blanket without disturbing anybody. You don't even have to hold it in your hands, because the PowerBook stays open by it-

self. Just hit the arrow button on the keyboard to turn the page.

The Experience of a Dynamic Reading Space

You can read the text that you typed into your word processor, but you can't dive into the text, as there is far too much on screen (menu bars and the like) to distract you. To be able to dive into (or, in the **cyberspace** vernacular, "jack into") the book's concepts or story, you need the text and nothing but the text. Therefore we kept the interface as clean as possible. Many hypertext novels provide exciting features that let you jump from screen to screen, interact with objects on screen, and play with buttons and amusing features, but what about the *story*, the narration? Whether writing a cyberpunk novel or a book about the law, the author wants to take you on a journey and provide a specific viewpoint. Expanded Books let you follow the author's path without interrupting it all the time, so you can get involved in the story and become a more active reader of the text.

Isn't that what the author wanted in the first place?

SECTION 5

OLD LAWS FOR NEW TECHNOLOGIES?

Rick Eberly

PROTECT YOUR WORK & YOUR RIGHTS

BY ANDY HARRIS, CAROLE BARRETT, & NICHOLAS SELBY

Many legal and ethical questions arise when we consider the possibilities of using new media technologies to store, manipulate, and distribute ideas, information, images, and sounds. These essays provide a brief look at protecting your artistic work, the legal issues involved in using new technologies to create and distribute that work, and the intricate connections between issues of ownership and freedom of speech.

BY ANDY HARRIS

Andy Harris co-owns Telemorphix, Inc., an interactive TV production company and talent agency for multimedia performance artists. Previously senior writer and new media producer for Apple Computer, Andy has produced multimedia CD-ROMs, corporate videos, and TV sitcoms, and has designed "900"-prefix telephone systems, computer-supported collaborative work environments, and low-cost, wide area network systems for computers.

copyright: Under U.S. law for works created after January 1, 1987, a copyright is effective for the life of the creator plus 50 years, or if the copyright is a work for hire or is anonymous then for 75 years from publication, or 100 years from creation, whichever expires first. It gives the copyright holder the exclusive right to produce a work, prepare derivative works, distribute copies, display the work, and perform the work. Just as a land deed defines real property, a copyright defines intellectual property. Copyright holders can transfer their copyrights by will or other legal channels to another person or entity. To secure copyright protection of your work, place a copyright notice on it (where the notice can be easily seen) as soon as the work is fixed in a medium. Proper notice on software would appear on the opening screen, instruction manual, and box, for example. As soon as possible (preferably within 3 months of creation), apply for copyright registration.

IT'S TIME TO GET INVOLVED

As a cyberartist and businessman, I'm interested in pushing the envelope of communications by merging the technologies of computers, telephones, and television. From my experience, I believe that over the next decade we'll see a mixture of for-profit and non-profit performers calling each other over telephone lines to combine visual and audio data, and distributing the results via a variety of media—satellite, telephone, cable television, broadcast television, and radio. Radically new programming will reach people's homes, crossing state and national boundaries. Some performances will take place in real time, some will be recorded.

The content of these performances will blur the boundaries between "entertainment" and "information," and in so doing will render meaningless many of our currently agreed-upon notions of community standards, **copyright** infringement, intellectual property, equal access, Fairness Doctrine, broadcast frequency allocation, local jurisdictions, and the definition of privacy. It might come as a rude surprise to cyberartists, but the world we're going to inhabit will be unpredictable, filled with litigation, lawsuits, and perhaps even censorship.

One of the first issues we need to consider concerns copyrights. Who owns what? This is all about coming to a mutually agreed-upon compromise. We're trying to protect our work, yet not be overprotective to the point that all production grinds to a halt. When the film industry first started, movies were copyrighted frame by frame! As more and longer movies were made, it became ridiculous to copyright every frame, so filmmakers now copyright the whole thing. Now, however, new technologies show that this issue is unresolved. We

must adjust to some point where we can get our work done, have it protected, make a living off of it, and yet not own every little byte of it.

It's important for artists to get involved with these issues. We must understand that such issues have a long, evolutionary background, and we must incorporate our awareness of that into how we progress from here. Consider, for example, television. The type of programming we see on television today has been shaped by decisions made in the 1920s. Becoming involved is a fundamental, integral part of being able to achieve your artistic goals and being able to protect your artistic creations.

COPYRIGHT BASICS

BY CAROLE BARRETT

Carole Barrett received her law degree from St. John's University School of Law. Licensed to practice in New York, California, and before the U.S. Patent and Trademark Office, she counsels clients on copyright, trademark, and patent issues, and has handled intellectual property portfolios, nationally and internationally. Carole founded and heads the Intellectual Property Law Center ("InPro") to provide legal counseling and dispute resolution in intellectual property and general business areas of the law.

I f we lived in an ideal world, we would enjoy a free exchange of ideas and information. If I invented or discovered something, I would let you use it freely, without charge. In this hypothetical world, if you discovered something, you would allow me the same privilege. In some actual societies— we call them "primitive" societies—this

approach works. Unfortunately, that's not how our society works.

Our society is heterogeneous. I might be willing to share my ideas with you for a while, but if I don't think you are giving enough of your ideas to me in return, I might easily say, "Okay, you can't have any more of what I have." Our society's legal system has been developed to cope with this approach to sharing, and not sharing, our creations. It's an imperfect legal system. And it's evolving. We're in a position today to help decide how it will evolve.

Our legal system allows you and me to protect our property or allow others to use it. If we wish to protect our inventions or ideas, we use the patent system, the copyright system, the trademark system, or some combination. We can protect our inventions or ideas as "trade secrets." We also can use other people's original works by acquiring permissions and licenses—for a fee, or sometimes without a fee if such is agreeable to the owner of the work or if you and the owner cross-license your individually owned property.

If I were an artist only concerned about creating art, and I didn't care about commercial applications or use of my art, I could safely avoid the system of patents, trademarks, and copyrights. On the other hand, if I intend to head into the marketplace as a commercially viable artist, I must be realistic about how I protect myself and my work.

As an artist working in the marketplace, I also must accept the fact that while I want to protect my creation, you also want to protect yours, yet we both "borrow" from each other. Borrowing is a reality. If we choose to borrow, we're taking a risk. Borrowing occurs all the time these days, as evidenced by the custom of **sampling music** with digital technology. Yet it isn't a new concept in art. In 1967, when the Beatles were in the process of recording *Sgt. Pepper's Lonely Hearts Club Band*, their producer George Martin decided he wanted to include some steam calliope music. He found a wonderful calliope recording, but he knew that using it would involve legal ramifications. So he told the recording engineer to cut the audio tape of the calliope music into one-foot sections, throw it into the air, then put it back together again. You can hear the results in the song "Being For the Benefit of Mr. Kite" on the Sgt. Pepper album.

Today we borrow in a more sophisticated fashion. We use computers to sample snippets of songs and scan parts of images, then we worry, "Am I going to get caught?" Therefore, we must understand what happens when a court looks at copyright infringement. The court examines two areas. First, it judges whether what you've taken is *substantially similar* to the original use. Second, the court determines whether you had access to what you took. The person who alleges copyright infringement must show there was a *reasonable possibility* that you could have seen or taken their material.

In judging "substantial similarity," the court determines if there are any articulated similarities between the two pieces of work. That is, would an ordinary observer, when hearing or seeing the two pieces of work, be able to articulate things in the works that are similar? If that person were able to articulate any similarities, that takes care of the first part of the court test and establishes that one work copied the other. That's not sufficient, however, to prove copyright infringement. To prove infringement, you must show that the work is sufficiently substantial to an ordinary observer. How much is "sufficiently substantial"? The courts have said that large pieces can be sufficiently substantially similar, and so too can small pieces. It's a matter of quality more than quantity.

When someone accuses you of copyright infringement, you try to prove that you did not have access to the original material, and if you did have access (which

sampling music: The United States District Court rendered its first digital sampling decision in December, 1991, preventing rapper Biz Markie and Warner Bros. from using sampled portions of Gilbert O'Sullivan's song, "Alone Again (Naturally)." (Grand Upright Music, Ltd. v. Warner Brothers Records, Inc.; WEA International, Inc.; Marcel Hall, known professionally as Biz Markie; Cold Chillin' Records, Inc.; and others.) After granting the plaintiff's motion for preliminary injunction, the court turned the case over to the U.S. Attorney's Office for criminal prosecution. The case settled before any final decision was rendered.

Using copyrighted music: The Index Departments of two major music licensing groups can help you secure the right to use licensed music in your video, film, or multimedia soundtrack. When contacting them, request the address for the specific publisher whose music you want to borrow: ASCAP, 1 Lincoln Plaza, New York, NY 10023; telephone 212-595-3050; or BMI, 320 W. 57th St., New York, NY 10019; telephone 212-586-2000.

The best way to avoid copyright infringement allegations? Get a license, or else write, perform, and record your own music. Or record music that was written at least 75 years ago. Do **not** use relatively recent recordings of music that was written a century or two ago, because the newly recorded **performance** may be copyrighted, even if the underlying composition is not. If the underlying composition is copyrighted, criminal penalties for copyright infringement do apply to unlawful copying of sound recordings.

usually is the case), you must prove that you did not injure someone by using something that was substantially similar to their work. It's a difficult thing to determine, and with all of the capabilities afforded by the new digital technologies, the courts are having a terrible time trying to deal with this.

What can we do to help? We can work to help expand or otherwise change the rules. I'd love to be able to tell you that if you use just six bars from the first 38 bars of a musical composition, you are not infringing, but I can't do that. When it comes to copyright infringement, there are no simple and easy answers. In fact, when it comes to music, the copyright law clearly provides for a license to use copyrighted material. Let's say I write and record a piece of music. Once I record it, then I *must* license it. If you request the license in compliance with the provisions of the Copyright Law, performing rights societies and mechanical rights societies exist to handle the licensing.

There are clearly defined uses provided for in the copyright law, which under certain circumstances allows one person to use the copyrighted material of another person. Such use is called "fair use." Fair use allows a non-owning party to use copyrighted material for specific purposes such as education, scholarship, and criticism. Because fair use provides a defense to a charge of copyright infringement, we see many clients who want to claim that their use falls within this provision. We always look carefully at such claims to make sure the criteria for fair use is really applicable.

One way to safely use someone else's work is by license or permission. For instance, Marilyn Monroe's estate now gives permission for people to use images of her, if they pay a fee. When someone is as famous as Miss Monroe, she can acquire the legal right, even after death, to protect herself—her estate gets compensated for others' use of her image.

We are often asked by clients to look into our crystal balls to determine whether the owner of some piece of copyrighted material will sue them. Of course, it is impossible to determine with certainty whether a copyright owner will actually file a lawsuit. But, as lawyers, it is easy to make an educated guess that the more successful the infringer becomes, the more likely the lawsuit becomes.

Because all of our clients intend to be very successful and are also very creative, we give them this advice:

1. Challenge yourself to create—that's where the real fun and satisfaction is and, incidentally, it makes looking in the mirror a whole lot easier;

2. Seek licenses on what you have convinced yourself you really need and not on what you merely want—licenses are cheaper in time, money, and energy than lawsuits, but not as rewarding as doing it yourself (see #1 above);

3. Protect the property you create so that you can be in a position of strength in your chosen field and can use your innovations to cross-license when it is to your advantage; and

4. If you don't like the law as it exists—don't just stand there, get involved!

OUR FIRST AMENDMENT: IN DANGER OF EXTINCTION

BY NICHOLAS SELBY

Nicholas Selby graduated from Harvard Law School in 1977. He has worked as a public defender and a research attorney for Chief Justice Rose Elizabeth Bird. With the California Public Utilities Commission, he represented the People of the State of California in the AT&T divestiture case. In 1985, Nick opened his own law firm in Palo Alto, California. He practices in the areas of First Amendment, telecommunications, and public utility law.

t is the year 2003. Unprecedented advances in optical-fiber transmission technologies have revolutionized the delivery of information to the office and the home. Restrictions that once prevented the Bell Operating Companies from offering information services have been removed, and what was once "Pacific Telesis" is now Pacific-Time-Warner-CNN. Fax machines at home? Passé! Cable television? A thing of the past. Now we have optical fibers delivering everything from voice mail and videos to movies and magazines over telephone lines to our voice-activated, computer-controlled, high-definition TV screens. But! Instead of having access to a wider range of information and opinion, we actually hear and see less "real" information—the kind of information that stirs controversy—than we had in 1980! Starting with the "flag-burning" amendment, the once-untouchable First Amendment has been amended 15 times in ten years. It is a shadow of a memory of the thought that aged 212 years, then died.

What distinguishes our country from the rest of the world? Our **First Amendment**. Think about all the ways our First Amendment works for us—it protects our religion, speech, press, freedom of association, even our privacy. It's an extraordinary document, but it's over 200 years old, so today there are many pressures upon it.

In a decade, the First Amendment will not be what it is today. I'd like to relate two "war stories" to give you an idea of why we should be concerned about the fate of the First Amendment.

An incident took place in 1991 that did not get much notice beyond one story in the *New York Times*. It concerned a satellite movie company. This company had a booming business disseminating R-rated and X-rated movies via satellite. People could watch movies in the privacy of their own living rooms by using a special decoder. Well, it seems there was a prosecutor—a district attorney—running for office in Montgomery, Alabama, who saw an opportunity to score political points by cracking down on this movie company, "Dial-A-Porn." This prosecutor indicted everyone he could think of, not only the distributors of the movies—the "Ecstasy Channel" and the "Tuxedo Channel"—but GTE Satellite Corporation and Hughes Aircraft, which owns Hughes Satellite Corporation. It didn't take those people much longer than a New York second to say, "This Dial-A-Porn guy is history." They disconnected Dial-A-Porn's transmission service from the satellite and the company went into bankruptcy 24 hours later. Why? Because someone in Montgomery, Alabama, decided he didn't like Dial-A-Porn.

Now, consider the fact that the dissemination of information and entertainment by telephone, over satellite, is just

Using copyrighted images: Several organizations are establishing ways for you to acquire the rights to use images and photos. In Arlington, Virginia, Electric Book is in the process of creating an electronic operation to streamline the search and retrieval of images and acquisition of licensing rights. In New York City, the American Society of Magazine Photographers is considering the establishment of a licensing entity to negotiate electronic use rights on behalf of photographers.

First Amendment: In 1791, the Bill of Rights was ratified by the States and became law. It included what is now the First Amendment: "Congress shall make no law . . . abridging the freedom of speech or of the press." The purpose of the First Amendment was, and is, to insure that the mass media will be free to report and criticize the actions of government officials and free to inform the people about public affairs.

beginning. Ten years from now it will represent an extraordinary business, so the first question I want you to consider is this: Will the community standards of Montgomery, Alabama, or some small town decide what type of entertainment is available in Los Angeles or New York, just because someone in Montgomery can pick up the telephone and access an information service in Los Angeles or New York?

Here's another story from the front lines. Right before its Thanksgiving recess in 1990, Congress passed an amendment to one of the budget acts. It was one of these "budget-buster" things where the President has no opportunity to do anything other than sign, because if he doesn't sign, the government goes broke. Jesse Helms figured, "What a great vehicle for me to add my Dial-A-Porn amendment!" He got a 96-0 vote in the Senate, and I believe, a 404-0 vote in the House, in support of his Dial-A-Porn amendment.

Note that this amendment does not deal with obscene speech, which over the past 40 years the courts have said is unprotected speech. This amendment deals with something much broader. It deals with "indecent communications" over the telephone. What are "indecent" communications? It's virtually impossible to determine the precise guidelines of what is and what is not indecent. I was in an art gallery in Los Angeles and I saw some video art that showed something terrible, something shocking: unclothed women! Maybe down in Montgomery, Alabama, this video would be considered indecent. And, as the telephone network's transmission capacity grows, we'll see

much more video content as well as audio content disseminated directly to people's televisions.

The fact of the matter is, sex is popular. One main economic engine behind VCRs when they first entered the marketplace was fueled by "adult entertainment." People finally were able to watch adult entertainment in the privacy of their own homes. The Helms amendment, however, completely threatens the dissemination of anything resembling adult entertainment over the telecommunications networks, with threats of fines as great as $50,000 a day and two-year prison sentences. In the past, when the Federal Communications Commission moved to enforce a prior version of this law—which later was thrown out by the courts—they imposed fines of $600,000 against the information providers.

When people are faced with a fine of $600,000 and the FCC offers them the chance to cop a plea to a $50,000 fine if they just go out of business and keep quiet, most people say, "Fine. See you later." This means that a very small group of people with responsibility for enforcing the law have the opportunity to limit our access to information.

The good news is that on August 13, 1990, two days before the **Helms amendment** was to have gone into effect, a federal district judge in the southern district of New York—that is, New York City—issued a nationwide injunction against enforcement of the Helms amendment.

Who influenced the FCC in writing these rules? An organization called the American Family Association. We want family values and family virtues in the

United States, right? Well, it turns out that the American Family Association is a direct mail operation based in Tupelo, Mississippi, and that the American Family Association drafted the Helms amendment for Jesse Helms. According to *Newsweek*, one of the American Family Association's primary goals is the dismemberment of the National Endowment for the Arts. This relates directly to what many artists are doing.

When you think about it, you realize there is a fine line between entertainment and political speech. In fact, the people who have defended musicians who sing controversial lyrics say that these musicians are making political statements. You may not like their political statements. These statements may be *meant* to be provocative. Likewise, Robert Mapplethorpe's controversial photographs were meant to be provocative. Do they represent "entertainment"? Or do they represent a political statement?

Artists often support progressive politicians, recognizing the importance of personal freedom. There is a connection: An assault on artistic freedom is an assault upon political freedom. An assault upon the types of graphics, music, and entertainment that can be provided over the telecommunications network is ultimately an assault upon our political rights. Jesse Helms' agenda is much larger than just cracking down on Dial-A-Porn. Dial-A-Porn is simply a convenient whipping post. It opens the door to a much larger agenda that threatens our First Amendment rights.

I've mentioned some overt threats to creative and expressive freedom, but there are more subtle and, ultimately, more dangerous threats that stem from greed, from commercial motivation. Now that the telephone companies are allowed to provide information, I think we're going to see a new commercial engine at work, funded by billions of dollars of telephone customers' money. I think we'll also see an increasing concentration of power and control over the media in the hands of a few. We see that connection today between the print media and the movies. Perhaps a giant publishing company such as Time-Warner will be bought by or will buy a telephone company for purposes of gaining control over dissemination media such as cable television and fiber-optic lines, and then, even if you have produced a great movie or video, you may not be able to distribute it to the public. This is cause for great concern. The people who run the phone companies are not the most enlightened people in the United States, nor are they the most sympathetic to the First Amendment.

Your First Amendment freedoms may not exist in ten years. Only through the vigilance of the judiciary will we have the chance to retain the First Amendment that I revere.

Helms amendment: The injunction against enforcement of the Helms amendment was subsequently overturned. In March 1991, a challenge to the FCC regulations for implementation of the Helms amendment was rejected by the U.S. Court of Appeals. The court held that both the statute and the regulations passed First Amendment muster. In May 1991, the FCC announced that it would begin to enforce its regulations, leaving telephone information providers and telephone companies facing the threat of fines as large as $50,000 per day for dissemination of "indecent" information via pay-per-call "976" or "900" services. The FCC's action left one potential means for access to such programs by telephone: where the caller pays by commercial credit card prior to listening to the message. Virtually all "adult" information providers were driven out of business by the statute and the FCC's decision, since few potential callers have credit cards and fewer still wish to divulge their credit card numbers over the phone to "adult" information providers.

FREEDOM VS. COMPENSATION

BY JOHN PERRY BARLOW & TRIP HAWKINS

"The use of new digital media—in the form of on-line information and interactive conferencing services, computer networks, and electronic bulletin boards—is becoming widespread in businesses and homes. However, the electronic society created by these new forms of digital communications does not fit neatly into existing, conventional legal and social structures. The question of how electronic communications should be accorded the same political freedoms as newspapers, books, journals, and other modes of discourse is currently the subject of discussion among this country's lawmakers and members of the computer industry." —from a 1990 press release announcing the formation of the Electronic Frontier Foundation

In this chapter, the authors discuss the social, legal, and ethical issues arising from the pervasive use of computers to communicate, to disseminate information, and to entertain.

PROTECT THE BOTTLE, NOT THE WINE

'm from the **Electronic Frontier Foundation**, which means that I represent freedom, but I represent compensation, too, in the sense that throughout most of my career I've worked with tangible objects. I was a cattle rancher. I didn't know anything about intellectual property and was forced by economics to recognize that, in the information age, there's a lot more money in bullshit than in bulls. I got out of the cattle business and now my principal commodity is what I do with my mind. So I have a direct concern with being compensated. But I don't think the systems that have been derived for seeing that I get due compensation are working.

Something about the term "intellectual property" always bothered me a bit. It sounds like an oxymoron. This was brought into real sharp focus when I saw a cartoon in the *Bulletin of Atomic*

BY JOHN PERRY BARLOW

John Perry Barlow is a writer, electronic gadfly, lyricist for the Grateful Dead, and former cattle rancher. He co-founded the Electronic Frontier Foundation.

Scientists a while back. It showed a guy on the street with his hands in the air, and a gunman pointing a gun at him. The gunman was saying, "Quick, give me all your ideas."

The background of intellectual property as a species of law is fairly old. It goes back about 200 years and traditionally was divided into two areas, patent and copyright. Patent was easily defined. Patent law described processes and ideas that could be transformed into material. That transformation into the material was a fundamental part of the process. You could not get a patent on something that couldn't make the transformation successfully and continue to work according to its design principles.

Copyright, on the other hand, was intended to protect expression of ideas—but not the ideas themselves, which is an important distinction. It's my contention that the reason copyright appeared to work so well is because, like patents, copyright involved the transformation of ideas into physical objects. Copyright worked because it was physically difficult to make a book, a CD, a film, or any of the physical objects that ideas tended to become when they were copyrighted material. As you may have noticed, this is no longer the case. Upon the invention of the copy machine, copyright ceased to work well. Go to any college campus and you can see how well copyright is working.

We now have an even trickier problem: Most information now, and all information in the future, will never undergo any kind of physical transformation. It will stay in what ought to be its natural environment, which is cyberspace, and in many respects cyberspace is very different from the physical world. Everything in cyberspace is liquid. Everything in cyberspace is mutable. Everything in cyberspace is self-reproductive. Trying to protect these rights on the basis of your ability to contain any kind of material through conversion into physicality is no longer something we can count on.

Another interesting part of treating information as a form of property is that if I steal your information, you still have it. If I steal your horse, you can't ride. I can steal your information and reproduce it a billion times and you will still have it, and what you may do with it, in terms of expressing it, will be quite different from what other people may do with it. This is called "creating."

Society has a great way of recognizing changes that the law—which has a pace second only to geological time—has a hard time keeping up with. People rapidly respond to changes in the way information is contained, and they make their own decisions about how to deal with it. Well, right now we have fairly stern laws about software protection. Do you read the fine print that comes with your software documentation? How many of you can honestly say that you have no unauthorized software on your hard disks?

What we have here is a case in which much of society has decided to diverge *en masse* from the law. Now, unless the Software Publishers Association intends to put into practice some of the great things we learned while detaining Iraqi prisoners of war, they are not going to be able to arrest all the people who copy software.

Electronic Frontier Foundation: In 1990, Mitchell D. Kapor (founder of Lotus Development Corporation and ON Technology) and John Perry Barlow established the Electronic Frontier Foundation. The Foundation: supports and engages in public education on current and future developments in computer-based and telecommunications media; supports litigation in the public interest to preserve, protect, and extend First Amendment rights within the realm of computing and telecommunications technology; helps both the public and policy-makers see and understand the opportunities as well as the challenges posed by developments in computing and telecommunications; and encourages and supports the development of new software to enable non-technical users to more easily use their computers to access the growing number of digital communications services.

For information, contact: Electronic Frontier Foundation, 1 Cambridge Center, Suite 300, Cambridge, MA 02142; telephone 617-864-0665; E-mail eff@well.sf.ca.us.

Another problem we have, because of the curious and slippery nature of information, is that large organizations, which traditionally dealt in easily definable goods—pig iron, cars, real estate, things you could easily wrap a conceptual box around—are now finding, as I did, that the money is in the other stuff, whatever that may be, and they are trying to treat it as they have traditionally treated the things they dealt with in the physical world. They're trying to assume that "intellectual property" has the same properties of containability. They don't properly recognize the difference between the idea and the expression of the idea. Increasingly we see corporations trying to hold proprietary interests, not in expressions, but in the ideas themselves. This has never been protected. Because of the confusion in the courts, it's up for grabs.

The United States Supreme Court, in the early 1980s, came down with a ruling that software algorithms were not patentable. Nevertheless, since 1982 the United States patent office has been issuing patents on algorithms like crazy. What does this mean? This means that the lawyers are going to have plenty to do. But I don't think lawyers are the answer. Any time you have this kind of social confusion, sending ten million lawyers down into the valley of death is not the answer.

The problem we're addressing here is related to freedom. The difficulties of intellectual property containment with regard to freedom have to do with this: We have entered an economic environment in which the principal item of commerce looks so much like speech that, in most cases, it's indistinguishable from speech. And if you're going to try to contain proprietary interests in that principal item of commerce by increasingly draconian rules of containment and legal methods, it is inevitable that you will restrict free speech. It is unavoidable. That's not going to be to anybody's benefit over the long haul.

Whenever government encounters a new technology of expression, the natural thing for government to do is figure out ways to control freedom. Government is not what gives you freedom. Government is what takes freedom away from you. For example, when radio came along, the government listened and heard a cacophony on the airwaves, and you couldn't get your own radio frequency because everybody was broadcasting everywhere at once. So the government said, "We must impose order here. The radio bandwidth is a limited resource, and we will allocate it. It will become a public resource." Now, that makes sense. Problem is, when they did that, they also decided that since radio was a public resource, its content had to be regulated in a way that would conform to public standards. They threw out the First Amendment. There are many things you cannot say on the radio in this country that you can say in print.

Now, instead of hearing the excuse of "limited bandwidth," we hear the excuse of "proprietary interest." The Electronic Frontier Foundation was involved in the case of a fellow named **Craig Neidorf** in the summer of 1991. He had published a purloined bureaucratic document of Bell South in his electronic newsletter. I will grant you that this document was proprietary, but then, so were the Pentagon Papers. He published the document, dis-

Craig Neidorf: In February of 1990, Craig Neidorf, then a student at the University of Missouri, was publishing an electronic newsletter (Phrack World News) when he was indicted on felony charges of wire fraud and interstate transportation of stolen property. The federal government accused him of publishing a stolen Bell South memo on the 911 emergency telephone system.

seminated it on the network, and was charged with interstate transport of stolen property. He was looking at 31 years in jail and then a wonderful thing happened. The federal government brought him into court and was so unclear on what their case consisted of that they folded after four days. They quit. They walked out of court. I've never heard of that happening before. However, Craig Neidorf is still looking at $120,000 in legal fees. This could happen to anybody. And it will happen to many more people if we continue on our present course.

The other problem, to which I alluded earlier, is that the system is broken. If we're dealing with fundamental misconceptions about "intellectual property" and how we deal with it; how do we get paid for the work we do with our minds?

It's important to consider the stuff itself and how it differs from physical property. It's an economic certainty that when there are greater quantities of a physical item, the item loses value. The more gold there is in the world, the less valuable the gold is. This is not necessarily the case with intellectual property. In fact, you could argue that the reason an antiquated spreadsheet—Lotus 1-2-3—still sells 70 percent of the software market is because it is the world's most pirated software. What happens in actual practice is that people **pirate** Lotus 1-2-3, become proficient at using it, start to feel that they want the official upgrades, service, and support, and so they buy the program. This must be occurring a lot, because the United States has a multibillion-dollar software industry that continues to be one of the most robust parts of a sick economy. Yet people aren't obeying the laws about not pirating software. Something funny is going on here.

Here's another problem that's closer to home for me. One of my gigs is as a songwriter for the Grateful Dead. Many years ago, we became tired of kicking people out of our concerts when they brought in tape decks, so we sort of formalized the fans' taping practice and gave them a place to sit so they could properly record the concerts. There are now millions and millions of copies of my songs on tapes out there for which I do not receive a dime in compensation. In no way has this hurt my economic interests. In fact, we had been playing small, 2,500-seat theaters and selling embarrassingly low numbers of records before the concert-taping and trading started to catch on, and something about the culture of this tape exchange created an enormous market for our product. The market is so large that it's frightening to me, because we don't know how to stop it now. The guys in the band are kind of old and they have to keep on dancing. I worry about them sometimes.

This is a clear-cut case in which liberality with my intellectual property was to my economic advantage—the fact that there was *more* of my intellectual property out in the world turned out to be a good thing for me.

Regarding the tape exchange in its tangible form, I take an entirely different view if somebody tries to sell a perfect replica of our *Built To Last* CD and says that it's ours. I want our attack lawyers on these people, *quick*. But that's a different premise, because you have that tangible

pirate: Make an unauthorized copy.

form that you can attach yourself to. That's not going to be the case as soon as this country gets wired—and it is getting wired fast.

Speaking of getting wired . . . I own a Next computer. Most Next software is being shipped around on the wire, because most Next owners own high-speed modems. I get programs that way all the time. That comprises an entirely different system of delivery, marketing, and copy protection, in the sense that you can acquire the software, it's disabled, you try it, then you can electronically pay for it and receive the complete version. This software delivery system resembles **shareware** but differs considerably in a few fundamental aspects, including the fact that it's much easier to pay for software when both vendor and buyer are on-line. With shareware, you have to acquire the program, enter your electronic environment, copy the program to your hard drive, then leave the electronic environment and return to the physical environment, go get a piece of paper, write on it, put it in an envelope, and go to the post office. If people don't pay for shareware, it's not because they're unethical; they don't pay for it because they're lazy. You have to make it much easier for them.

Let's return to the fundamental principle that it's not a person's ideas that count, it's what the person does with them. What counts is not thought, but execution. We must start thinking less about the wine in the bottle than the bottle itself—the containing vessel of execution. We have to think about the shrink-wrap, not the software. Again, we're going to encounter difficulties with defining the bottle or the shrink-wrap in a place that has no physicality. I think part of the answer will be technical. I hate solving social problems with technical solutions, but I think part of the solution will come in the form of software **encryption and public key** delivery to the people who pay for software services. I think part of the solution will come in the form of the service itself. As in the case of Lotus, people are willing to buy the software because they want the technical support from the software publisher. Unfortunately, that doesn't necessarily help us get software that is easier to use. It economically provides the disincentive for self-documenting software. These are tricky problems.

The ultimate protection of your economic interest in your intellectual property depends on your swiftness of delivery. If you can't get to the market with a product before your competition does, all of the intellectual property protection in the world won't make a difference. You might ask, "How can little companies with great ideas execute more swiftly than big companies?" I don't see the little companies using intellectual property protection enough, and I see the big companies using it a lot. But the big company has a hard time delivering. These huge industrial concerns are so cumbersome.

One other problem is germane to many of the concerns expressed here: How do we deal with multimedia? People won't be able to develop good multimedia as long as we have the current proprietary conditions of image ownership and as long as we try to make certain that people cannot commercially use an image they get from another source, even if it's transformed in some way, unless they pay its owner. You may not know who its owner is; in fact, you probably won't know, because the methods of tracing ownership in the environment of cyberspace are almost impossible. We'll have to come up with a new standard of fair use that includes commercialization of imagery. At the same time, we'll have to come up with some technological method that makes it easy to locate the source of an image and legally acquire the rights to use the image.

Until that happens, multimedia isn't going to get anywhere.

As long as we place the emphasis on laws rather than on ethics and as long as we're willing to use an old set of laws before we've developed a new social contract for a new environment, our freedom of expression is threatened. Freedom of expression is going to depend on responsibility in delivery, responsibility in use, and in the development of a sense of social ethics about these things.

A CALL FOR ETHICS

BY TRIP HAWKINS

W.M. "Trip" Hawkins is president of SMSG, Inc., and chairman of Electronic Arts, both based in San Mateo, California. He holds a degree in strategy and applied game theory from Harvard College and an M.B.A. from Stanford University.

When we consider the issues of freedom vs. compensation, we need to consider ethics. There is no "right" or "wrong" in ethics. Ethics isn't a religious issue; ethics concerns what's in the best interests of society. The reason ethical principles were developed in the first place—the reason we have laws—is because someone or some group of people came to the conclusion that some basic principle is in everyone's best interest. **John Locke** said that, in the formation of any society, people must give up some individual freedoms. For example, in the United States you don't have the freedom to drive on the left side of the road. It's not

smart to try to exercise freedom to drive on the left side, and we're in a much better position as a society for having agreed to which side of the road we all drive on. That's why we can't frame these "freedom vs. compensation" issues in terms of trying to maximize "freedom."

As society moves forward, it changes. On the one hand, we have the ability to create new laws; on the other hand, we have the ability to test existing laws in the courtroom. This can lead to comic results. The process of getting new laws written is incredibly time-consuming, bureaucratic, afflicted by lobbies and special interests, and beset by the need to convince Congress to create a new law. The first thing Congress asks is, "What's wrong with the law we have? Why can't the existing law cover this issue?" You need to convince them that things are different now.

Before Congress will create a new law, they say, "Let's test the situation in the court. Let the court interpret right or wrong based on the existing body of law." This

John Locke: English philosopher of the 17th century whose political ideas influenced the authors of the U.S. Declaration of Independence.

approach causes problems because of the great expense involved and because innocent people get hurt in the process.

The patent office is a good example. The patent office is a bureaucratic agency staffed by clerks who don't have much professional training. It's impossible for them to know about all the activity going on in intellectual property. Yet these clerks are granting patents and trademarks without really considering what patents have been granted previously and whether or not it makes sense to grant a patent. Therefore, it's way too easy to get a patent, and as a consequence, if the majority of patents were challenged in court, they would be defeated. Once a patent's issued, challenging it becomes a monetary issue. If you want to prove that some item is not patentable, you must prove it in court at great expense. Nevertheless, it's probably easier to get something to happen by winning in court than it is to convince Congress to make a new law about it.

We need to deal with the fact that the current laws are old. The copyright law was created at a time when most electronics didn't exist. Congress made a major revision to the copyright law in 1976, but the microprocessor was invented in 1975, so much of the technology we use today didn't exist then. Congress is kicking itself, saying, "I can't believe it. We just did this revision, and it's already obsolete again!" Congress is greatly irritated about the need to address copyright, but it must. In the meantime, over the last 15 years Congress has pushed copyright problems into the courts, when there are copyright issues—especially where computers are

concerned—that simply aren't covered by current law.

Another area of concern about copyright is that the law doesn't apply equally to different kinds of media. Organizations with special interests go into court to get a ruling that covers their particular slice of the media pie. A classic example: It's legal to rent movies and it's legal to rent Nintendo video games. (A court ruling stated that it's legal to rent movies; the Nintendo rental issue has never been tested.) Yet it is illegal to rent computer software and musical recordings. I participated in the software legislation process; it took about seven years to convince Congress that software was basically the same as records. It took that long to realize that if we have a law protecting record rental, we should have a similar one for software rental.

Congress looked at this issue by considering what was in the best interest of society. Congress didn't think, "Let's protect the rights of the inventor" or "Let's worry about the people who want to rent software." It looked at the big picture and asked, "What's best for society?"

Let's consider our ability to rent movies. The film industry went to the courts to try to prevent videotape rental, saying it would hurt the movie business. I think the reason they lost that case was because the people in the courtroom weren't sympathetic. The court said, "The film companies already released the movie theatrically. They're earning overseas revenue from it. They're making money by putting it on cable TV. They're making money by airing it on broadcast television. The movie companies are making plenty of money; why should we feel sorry for them? Meanwhile, the consumers really only want to see the thing once anyway, and if they pay a rental fee, that's like buying a movie ticket."

They looked specifically at movies and came up with an answer that fit movies. The same argument is now applied to Nintendo video games, and there's a flaw in that logic. Almost all the companies that produce video games for Nintendo systems lost money in 1991 because of video game rentals.

Software is meant to be sold. The problem with video game rental is that there is no other source of income. Software doesn't get released in theaters or shown on cable or network television. There's no way for the manufacturer to receive much of the rental income. The manufacturer sells a few cartridges to rental stores; these cartridges get used over and over, and the manufacturer doesn't receive anything for it. Juxtapose this against the existence of a music licensing group such as **ASCAP**, and consider: Have you ever noticed that when you go into a restaurant where a customer is celebrating a birthday, you rarely hear the waiters sing, "Happy Birthday to You"? That's because if they *do* sing "Happy Birthday to You," they need an ASCAP license. So they make up their own silly birthday song to get around having to license the popular one.

The same thing applies to a restaurant or store that plays the radio while customers are present. This doesn't make sense to me. The radio programming includes commercials. The record companies give their music to radio stations for publicity, the radio stations collect money from advertisers to make up for the cost of broadcasting, and if the station's playing in a store or restaurant, both advertisers and record companies receive extra exposure, which leads to a greater number of impressions and increased frequency of exposure to advertisers. Yet ASCAP says, "You cannot play the radio in your store without paying us royalties."

Likewise, you're not supposed to play a jukebox in a restaurant without paying ASCAP royalties. Much of that activity is unpoliced. ASCAP spends a great amount of money and time chasing down all the stores and restaurants with jukeboxes. All these media, in some respects, should be treated the same. Yet they're all treated differently, because some of the controlling interests spent money to pursue a court case while others are new, working in areas that aren't covered by law, and no one has the time or the money to fight a battle over it.

Another example of inconsistency in the video game business relates to the coin-operated arcade. If you sell your game for use in arcades, you just sell it once. Look at the companies that manufacture the games; their annual revenues total about $200 million. Meanwhile, the coins that kids feed into these machines, in 1990 alone, totalled $7 billion. This means that the people who designed the games—the inventors and intellectual property owners—received $200 million out of the $7 billion spent on the games. Nobody in the arcade game business thought, "Maybe we should get some royalties based on the frequency of use of the game." I'm not necessarily advocating this; I'm just pointing out some discrepancies.

ASCAP: American Society of Composers, Authors, and Publishers

Let's consider patent law as it relates to software. When the patent laws were developed, we lived in a mechanical world. Today we create problems when we try to apply patent to things that are not tangible. I would be happy if there were simply no patents for software, because of the way patentability affects a software company. A software company lives in constant terror that it might put out some product and years later someone will come along and say, "You violated my patent," although the software company had no idea about the existence of this other allegedly similar product. The patent holder basically asks the company for all the money it made through its hard labors, although the patent may represent a relatively small part of a big picture, and the patent-holder comes out on top. Many software companies protect themselves from situations such as this by saying, "We better get some patents. We can counterattack and cross-license with other companies." Instead of treating the patent as protection of intellectual property or an issue of fair compensation, they treat it as a competitive and defensive weapon. Many software companies would rather say, "You do what you want to do. We'll do what we want to do. Let's forget about patents; let's have our products covered adequately by the 'look and feel' copyright laws."

"Look and feel" copyrights (which prevent companies from selling software that significantly resembles another company's copyrighted software) do make sense, but must be applied in a strict and rigid way. Let's look at a real-world example. The idea of the spreadsheet was brought to the personal computer through a software product called Visi-Calc by a couple of guys in a company called Software Arts. They licensed the VisiCalc spreadsheet program to Visi-Corp. VisiCorp had a relationship with Mitch Kapor; he produced a couple of programs that let you create graphs with VisiCalc. At one point, Mitch had this bright idea about developing a type of program that integrated both spreadsheet and graphics, but VisiCorp thought he was out of his mind. They didn't want to pay him the money to develop it. Mitch said, "I'll sell you the rights to the programs that you're publishing for me, if you give me the freedom to do anything I want to do in this marketplace—and you can't ever accuse me of copyright infringement." They answered, "Fine," and even paid him a great sum of money for the rights to continue publishing the graphics attachments for VisiCalc.

Mitch went off and started the Lotus Development Corporation to market Lotus 1-2-3, and within a few years, buried Visi-Calc in the marketplace. The Software Arts people took their millions in royalties and complained about their 35.6 percent royalty rate, which probably was three times higher than the industry average. Software Arts and VisiCorp engaged in huge battle, which was like rearranging deck chairs on the Titanic, and both went out of business. Meanwhile, Lotus was doing well. It bought Software Arts. Not long after that, the legal department at Lotus decided that Lotus invented the spreadsheet and should sue any company that makes anything resembling their spreadsheet. Two companies could take issue with such a claim—VisiCorp and Software Arts. But VisiCorp had already promised, "We won't sue you," and Lotus had bought Software Arts. Lotus conveniently removed the potential threat of people who could truthfully say, "Hey, Lotus, you're full of baloney."

I have a problem with the copyright law being used in such a fashion. I would like to see a precise definition of "look and feel" so it doesn't apply to entire categories and market segments and thus prevent free competition. Realistically, all of us software people get our inspiration and ideas from looking at other people's work. The same thing goes for the film industry We all need sources of inspiration, but we must be able to differentiate between inspiration and true copying.

One aspect of copyright law that must be extended and clarified is "fair use." In some ways, fair use was inspired by the development of such technologies as copy machines. Again, in that case, society took a look at things like the copy machine and said, "These are great technologies. Let's give people some freedom to use them. Let's allow broadcast journalists to use bits of film clips in criticism pieces on television. Let's allow people to excerpt copyrighted material in their criticism that's published in magazines."

The people who established the fair use law clearly examined what was in the social interest, in terms of conveyance of information and the right to free speech through criticism. Fair use, however, is limited to an incredibly narrow category of items. It must be extended and it must be precisely defined to allow creative people who use the new technologies to know where the boundaries are. If I want to use a piece of music, video, or a photograph, how much of it can I use? The music industry has the concept of time duration to determine how much of a piece of music can be used and still fall within "fair use." If you use three notes from a famous song, no one will say you're violating a copyright, because it's just three notes. On the other hand, if your multimedia product flashes a famous photograph for an instant, many people will recognize the photo. This is tricky. People must now think in terms of society's interests to work out a solution that provides the right balance between having creative expression and not having obstacles that impede the invention and creation of new, interesting material.

The previously mentioned ASCAP worked out a satisfactory solution for the music industry. After spending several decades thinking about the uses of music, ASCAP established very specific prices for things, including mechanical rights to a song, rights to use the lyrics, and rights to use the performance version of an arrangement. It's all a matter of pennies; that is, ASCAP figured out the correct economic model for protecting their artists.

We don't have a similar economic model for multimedia, thus tremendous restrictions are placed on what and how we create multimedia. If your multimedia product contains 10,000 photographs, how do you determine the monetary value of one photo? If you know you have to negotiate individually with 10,000 rights holders for 10,000 photographs, you won't create a product that uses so many photographs. You'll say, "Forget it, I'll just originate all my own material." That results in higher development costs, so fewer products will be created.

The multimedia community would grow more quickly if some agency, through the legal process, could say, "We will establish parameters and a pricing structure." The economic model that works for music, however, doesn't work for multimedia. For example, it costs about a nickel to use the mechanical rights for a piece of music, based on the assumption that if you license ten songs for an album you'll pay 50 cents per album sold. No problem, you can afford 50 cents. Suppose, however, you want to produce a "Name That Tune" game on CD-ROM, and you want to use synthesized sound, which provides a compact way to store digital audio data on CD, so you literally could fit a thousand songs on the disc. If you have to pay a thousand nickels per CD sold, that adds up to $50 per disc. Nobody can afford that. Yet right now, the music industry doesn't differentiate between using music for records or compact discs and using music for CD-ROMs.

Thus, the system is discouraging creativity and the development of new products. But don't confuse this with the issues inherent in copying existing software. Software piracy is bad. You can't give away intellectual property simply because the conveyance medium is essentially free. People say, "This is an ethical issue and we should have the right to copy software because it's technically feasible to do so." Baloney. If you create something, it should be up to you to decide how to disseminate your creation. And frankly, if it weren't possible to copy software, we'd see tremendous competition; the companies that publish software products would reduce prices to maximize revenues. The reason software prices stay as high as they do is because the publishers see all these people pirating software. If you know that three out of four copies of your software are pirated versions, you make sure that you earn enough money on the fourth copy to stay in business.

Because of software pirating, many software companies have gone out of business. Yet we hear people complain, "The software companies are making a killing and they charge $50 for something that only costs them $1 to make." But few software products cost $1 to make. By the time you finish covering all the costs of development, manufacturing, advertising, and distribution, you have about $5 left over from the $50. In the future, we'll see prices come down to the point where really good software products will cost less than $20 and, in some cases, less than $10—if the market is big enough and if publishers feel that their software won't be pirated.

Companies that do attain a powerful position in the marketplace tend to look at issues—the issues of "freedom vs. compensation"—in terms of "What's in it for me?" As a society, we must get beyond this "What's in it for me?" attitude. We must look at how these issues affect our society and how they will affect the generations that follow ours.

. . . .

SECTION 6

CYBERSPACE AND VIRTUAL REALITIES

"Hanging by a Thread" **Myron Krueger's VIDEOPLACE**

THE "ART" IN ARTIFICIAL REALITY

VIDEOPLACE & OTHER NEW FORMS OF HUMAN EXPERIENCE

BY MYRON W. KRUEGER, PH.D.

Myron Krueger is an interactive computer artist who pioneered full-body participation in computer-defined aesthetic experiences. His 1970 exhibit, "Metaplay," probably represented the first combination of live video and computer images. Through his Metaplay work, Myron developed an interactive aesthetic that led to the VIDEOPLACE concept. He originated the term "artificial reality" to describe the kind of environment created through VIDEOPLACE, which could be experienced without using (or wearing) data input devices. Myron's 1974 dissertation was published in 1983 as the book Artificial Reality *(Addison-Wesley), then updated and published as* Artificial Reality II *in 1991. He has been honored with awards from both science and arts organizations, and in 1990 was selected by* Life *magazine as "a wavemaker of the decade ahead."*

The term "artificial reality" was coined by science scholar Myron Krueger in 1973 to describe his "computer-controlled responsive environments," which took an aesthetic approach to the human/computer interface. "An artificial reality perceives a participant's action in terms of the body's relationship to a graphic world," he wrote, "and generates responses that maintain the illusion that his or her actions are taking place within that world."

Myron manifested artificial reality with his creation of VIDEO-PLACE. This art installation brings video images of one or more participants into a computer-generated graphic world that the participants (and audience) view on a projection screen. Conceived in 1969, VIDEOPLACE was simulated in 1970, actualized in 1973, and has evolved continually. Myron's original goal was to discover a true computer-art form, one that would be impossible without the computer. One intellectual outcome is the concept of a reality in which laws of cause and effect are composed by an artist. VIDEOPLACE celebrates the unexpected possibilities provided by technology and simultaneously indicts the currently restricted means of interacting with computers.

VIDEOPLACE has been funded by National Endowment for the Arts and National Science Foundation. Its exhibition makes waves in museums, galleries, and conferences throughout North America, Europe, and Japan. The public is invited to experience VIDEOPLACE at its home base in the Connecticut State Museum of Natural History in Storrs, Connecticut.

This chapter explores artificial realities and Myron's belief that artificial reality ultimately will represent more than an art form . . . it will offer a new form of human experience as rich as movies, novels, and theatrical plays.

Ivan Sutherland:
Technologist who pioneered the field of interactive computer graphics and, in 1965, created the first head-mounted computer display.

CRT: Cathode Ray Tube, the popular technology (used in TV sets) that shoots electrons through a tube to a phosphorescent screen to display information.

interface: (noun) The interconnection or method of communication between two objects; an interface may be hardware or software.

The concept of "artificial reality" refers to any means by which we can create an experience that we treat as a real one, whether or not we're wearing data goggles, gloves, or other computer clothing. The essential difference between "artificial reality" and "virtual reality" is that the former is a larger class or group that includes the latter.

Virtual reality currently focuses on the use of goggles to achieve three-dimensionality and the use of gloves to manipulate objects inside the environment. The artificial reality that I implemented was two-dimensional and unencumbering. When I first developed the concept, I was aware of **Ivan Sutherland's** head-mounted display goggles containing two **CRTs** that let you look around inside a three-dimensional world. Sutherland's viewers were mechanically connected to the ceiling because of the weight of the head-mounted display. Three conditions prevented me from incorporating his invention: One, I was a grad student (at the University of Wisconsin), without money or access to such expensive graphics systems. Two, I had a personal prejudice about wearing things. Some people like to wear watches, rings, glasses, things like that. I resist them. My goal was to create unencumbering, environmental, artificial realities. Three, I wanted people to interact freely, with their entire bodies.

I started developing the concept of artificial reality in the late 1960s. As a graduate student in computer science, I had no interest in the arts. If you had told me then that one day I would work as an artist or write a book, I would not have believed you. At the same time I loved computers for the opportunities they offered, I hated the way they were and the fact that my computer science peers were unfailingly attracted to stupid issues (such as the compiler's efficiency or the task allocation on a time-sharing system, both transient issues of technology optimization) and always ignored what really needed to be done. I vowed to use my skills to humanize computers, and to use computers to provide pleasant experiences.

My ideas at that time focused on "human **interface**." Up until recently, we've applied the interface to the computer. The computer was fixed; the human adapted to it. It seemed to me the interface involved two components: the computer *and* the human. One was evolving faster than any technology in history, the other wasn't evolving at all. It seemed obvious that we should center the human interface design on the human. That meant we should study what humans can do and what they like to do. Then we should adapt the machines to them. Until recently, computer scientists resisted that approach.

In 1968, I resolved to treat the human body as the interface to the computer. Instead of *receiving input* from a *user*, I wanted the computer to *perceive* the behavior of a *participant*.

I reasoned that artists and musicians had the most satisfying relationships with their tools, so I studied them to gain insights into how people might interact with machines. I also taught a programming course for artists to see how they might want to interact with computers. At that time, using a computer was a sensory-deprivation experience. You input symbols and it output symbols. In between, it was silent and, except for some blinking lights, it was a visual blank. I implemented an **interpreter** that displayed the operation of any program—regardless of function—through sounds and visual patterns. It was more like operating a car: When you start your car, the car makes a noise; with the system I created, when you start the program, the computer made noises. When you made changes in the program, the sounds would change and you would hear audio feedback.

The idea was to let the students experience the running program through their senses rather than through symbols. The idea of experiencing a program led to the creation of an environment that you entered in order to experience the computer.

Glowflow

I participated in my first interactive computer environment in 1969, an exhibit developed with Dan Sandin (who later invented the video-image processor and, in 1976, the data-input glove), sculptor Jerry Erdman, and computer science professor Richard Venezsky. This exhibit, called "Glowflow," was controlled by traditional artistic sensibilities. Basically it was a sculpture, a computer-controlled, light-and-sound environment. On the walls of a room there were tubes filled with colored phosphorescent pigments suspended in water. The room was otherwise dark, so the glowing tubes defined the space. For instance, the bottom tube represented the floor. As people walked into the room, they saw the tube slanting slightly downward, so they would lean backwards—they thought they were going downhill. It showed the incredibly powerful role that our visual sense plays in defining reality.

Glowflow also incorporated six loudspeakers and spatial sound imaging. Sounds rotated around the room or "bounced" from wall to wall. Controlled by a Digital Equipment Corporation PDP-12 **minicomputer**, the system ran lights, loudspeakers, and a Moog sound synthesizer.

Psychic Space

In 1971, I put aside the concerns of traditional art to determine whether a medium based on interactivity was possible and what people would want to do with it. If the result was "art," great. If it wasn't, that was okay, too.

My idea was to allow a person's entire body to interact with technology. The result was the exhibit "Psychic Space," installed in the University of Wisconsin's Memorial Union Gallery. A person walked around in a room on a floor containing hundreds of pressure sensors. A DEC PDP-11 minicomputer scanned the sensors about 10 to 15 times per second, so it knew where you were standing. The information about where you stood and where you placed your feet was transmitted across campus over an audio cable and fed into a **vector-graphic** display built by Adage Corporation.

The exhibit allowed for many different types of interactions. Some involved sound alone: Your footsteps created sounds as you walked around. If you walked on a certain part of the floor, the end of the

interpreter: Part of the computer's internal software that reads and decodes instructions written in a high-level programming language.

minicomputer: A larger, more powerful computer than a microcomputer (personal computer). It can serve several users at once.

vector-graphic: Refers to the type of computer procedure used to draw outlines of objects on the screen.

room lit up—it held a rear-screen video projection screen. As you walked around, the screen displayed a graphic symbol. As you moved to the right, the symbol moved to the right; as you moved to the left, the symbol moved to the left. People were amazed. They identified with their symbol on the screen. As they moved, they were "transported" onto the two-dimensional screen, and they accepted the two-dimensional environment as their real environment.

After two or three minutes, a second symbol appeared on the screen, and every person who went into the room wondered what would happen if they moved their symbol to get acquainted with the new one. When they did that, the second symbol disappeared and a maze appeared with their symbol at the maze's starting point. Immediately they would start to walk the maze.

Now, they already learned that they had to take small steps to navigate the maze. They would mince along, taking little steps forward and sideways, and after a couple of minutes, it would dawn on them that this was ridiculous. Nobody was watching, nobody was enforcing rules about boundaries, they simply were following graphic lines on a screen. So they would lift their foot—sometimes with considerable ceremony—to cross the nearest boundary, thereby "cheating."

I knew this would happen, because I knew I would do the same in that situation. So, the first time they took a larger step to get out of the maze, the maze's boundary stretched elastically. The next time they did it, their symbol fell apart and

they couldn't continue in the maze until they returned to where they belonged. Then the symbol re-assembled. The third time they cheated, the maze would move with the symbol, so they couldn't cross the boundary. On the fourth try, the boundary disappeared and a new one would appear somewhere else. By cheating, they gained nothing.

Ultimately, there was no way to walk the maze, and by the end of the encounter the maze shrunk and disappeared. I tried letting people win, but that didn't seem to add anything to the experience. Once I assumed this perverse perspective, and didn't allow a successful navigation, people enjoyed the maze more!

The exhibit ran for ten hours each day for six weeks. We watched people and how they adapted to it, and fine-tuned the experience. Psychic Space essentially represented a composition over time. As a successful interactive composition, it pointed the way toward the kind of interactive experience in which a participant learns the rules, which later change in orderly, acceptable ways.

In general, these types of experiences don't work well when the rules change in unexpected or inappropriate ways. However, in some situations, sudden changes in the rules make for an interesting and exciting experience. It depends on how it occurs. If rules change arbitrarily, it's unpleasant. Anyone who uses a computer knows this; if you inadvertently hit the wrong key, something catastrophic can happen. The interactive art designer must work within peoples' expectations and take care not to offend them. A carefully crafted surprise is fine; arbitrary, meaningless change is not.

The Psychic Space experience influenced everything I've done since.

Metaplay

The year before I set up Psychic Space, I created Metaplay, another exhibit in the Memorial Union Gallery. Metaplay represented an aesthetic interface and simulated the type of human interface I wanted to create. I used a computer to create a **real-time** relationship between an artist in one building and a person in the gallery a mile away. We superimposed a computer graphic image over a live video image of the participant, then **rear-projected** the resulting image on an eight-foot by ten-foot screen on a wall in the gallery. Both artist and participant reacted to the screen display.

As I drew on a data-input tablet, graphics appeared over the image of people in the gallery. I often drew graffiti on them. One day, as I started drawing on the image of somebody's hand, he moved his hand, and I followed it; he moved his hand again, and I followed it again. Although I really was trying to draw something, it appeared to him as if *he* was directing the drawing. I followed his movements and, without a word passing between us, we discovered the concept of drawing together.

For the next six weeks, ten hours a day, people without any prior computer experience came into the exhibit and within a minute, learned about the possibility of drawing together. Many different interactions resulted. Sometimes when the cursor approached, a participant would

bat it away. That led me to substitute a graphic ball for the cursor. I placed the ball at the top of the screen, people would reach up and hit the ball, I'd move it across the screen, and somebody at the other end of the screen would automatically hit the ball back. Without any instruction, we had people playing volleyball with a nonexistent ball in 1970. There was no delay between understanding and participation.

The way the system worked, signals were transmitted from the computer in the Metaplay gallery to a graphics display in the computer center. One day, an epiphany occurred. On that day we were having a data transmission problem. I was in the computer center and I was talking about the problem over the phone with a colleague in the gallery. While discussing the problem, we each looked at the displays in front of us. We had trouble understanding what we were trying to describe, and suddenly I had a flash of inspiration. I told him, "Aim your video camera at your computer screen!" I already had my camera pointed at my computer screen, and as a result, we could see a superimposition of our two images. One image represented data being transmitted. The other image showed the data being received. While talking about the composite image, we naturally reached into the view-range of our cameras and pointed out things appearing on our respective screens. The result was that we both could see and point at the composite image as if we were sitting together at a table pointing to a single paper drawing.

The illusion was so strong that when the image of my hand touched the image of

real time: The speed of the computer coinciding with the speed of the user; no delay in computer response time, giving the impression of instantaneous response.

rear-projection: Allows screen sizes much larger than conventional video monitor displays. A rear-projection system throws the image onto a mirror, which reflects the picture onto the rear of a special screen.

his hand, he moved his hand out of the way. I noticed, but it didn't really register. Then it happened again and I realized he didn't want to hold hands with me. Personal distance was asserting itself in the video world! In fact, I even imagined that I felt a slight tingle, a phantom sensation, in my finger as I touched his hand.

This led to new kinds of Metaplay interactions. Sometimes we superimposed my video image over the image of the person in the gallery. I would touch or caress their image. One time my face was superimposed on the face of a young teenage girl, and with the image of my mouth superimposed over hers, I stuck out my tongue. Her reaction to this violation of her image was so strong that I realized that the image is an extension of the self: What happens to your image, happens to you. When something touches your image, you feel it. That concept became the basis for much of my subsequent work.

This also led me to redefine "telecommunication." We usually think of telecommunication as electronically mediated conversation that occurs over a distance between point A and point B. I realized that the act of communication itself creates a third place consisting of the information you share simultaneously. For example, when my son was a little boy, his friend would call him on the phone. When I answered, he'd ask, "Is Mikey here?" I started to point out his mistake, then decided he had a point. Since we were talking, in some sense we were together in the same place. Watch people while they're on the phone—some of them gesture as if they're talking to some-

one in the same room. This represents the same concept.

VIDEOTOUCH, VIDEOPLACE, & VIDEODESK

These incidents led to my 1972 proposal to the National Endowment of the Arts for a two-way installation entitled "VIDEOTOUCH." The piece was to consist of two separate environments, each containing a rear-screen video projection of a composite image of the participants in both environments. When their images touched, the composite image would generate sounds. When a participant touched an object on the screen, the computer would be able to perceive it—because the computer put the object there.

Then came "VIDEOPLACE." The concept was based on the visual information shared by two people when their images were superimposed. My goal was to create a "video place," an artificial reality in a two-dimensional world, in which the computer could perceive the people in that world. The environment would contain objects that the computer understood and these objects would "understand" the actions of the human participants, so two people in the "video place" could interact physically with graphic objects in the fantasy world.

In 1974, I wrote a proposal for the United States Bicentennial celebration, requesting federal support for a VIDEOPLACE installation that would incorporate satellites to link sites in the east coast, west coast, Europe, and Japan. Washington's reaction was interesting: the National Science Foundation said it sounded like an engineering project; DARPA (Defense Advanced Research Projects Agency) said that human/machine interaction had been done already; and NASA said, "Our satellite is over India, beaming birth-control messages down to the Indian public, but there is a satellite you can use if you can get it launched." I tried. I finally went to one place that I knew would give me a positive reception and the "go-ahead," and that was the Japanese Embassy. Indeed, they said if I could get the U.S. to do our end, they would do their end. It never did happen on a global scale, although VIDEOPLACE was an official Bicentennial project.

My proposal presented the idea that VIDEOPLACE would be a graphic fantasy world in which I would compose the laws of cause and effect. Furthermore, these laws would change from moment to moment. This brings up the question, "Can two dimensions represent a reality?" The answer is "yes." People acted like two dimensions *was* reality. In fact, today they adapt much more quickly to the two dimensions of VIDEOPLACE than they adapt to the three dimensions of the current goggle-&-glove virtual reality systems. In today's virtual reality, it takes several minutes for people to adapt to pointing a gloved finger in the direction they want to "fly." Operating in two dimensions, people adapt instantly. As soon as they enter VIDEOPLACE, they immediately start interacting successfully with the system.

I debuted the VIDEOPLACE concept in a two-way, composite space interaction exhibit at the Milwaukee Art Museum in 1975, and even then people immediately invented a way of interacting with other people in the display. They instantaneously behaved as if it were a real place,

not simply a two-dimensional view of a real place.

From 1974 to 1978, I worked with the University of Wisconsin's Space Science and Engineering Center, trading computer graphics research work for lab and office space. I built specialized VIDEOPLACE hardware that would form outlines, or silhouettes, of each participant. It would detect when and where two participants were touching each other. I didn't show this version of VIDEOPLACE publicly, because I didn't think it was fast enough—it looked about the same as today's virtual reality systems that use goggles and gloves. If I moved my hand, there was a lag before the graphics responded. This was unacceptable to me.

In the VIDEOPLACE installation, the participant faces a video projection screen (about 20 feet away) that displays her live image combined with computer graphics. Behind the participant is a large sheet of translucent plastic, backlit by fluorescent tubes to produce an extremely high-contrast image. This helps the computer distinguish the participant from the background. The projector is driven by **RGB** signals, which means that it displays much sharper colors than those seen on regular television (which uses **NTSC** signals). A black-&-white surveillance camera positioned beneath the projection screen captures the image of the participant.

The entire computer system is custom-designed. It contains 14 specialized **processors** that operate in parallel. Each participant's video image is **digitized** and fed to special processors that analyze the resulting silhouettes. They check for posture, movement (discerning even the

RGB; NTSC: RGB stands for "red, green, blue," the type of display monitor used with personal computers. The display's output signal consists of separate red, green, and blue elements. RGB monitors offer higher resolution than NTSC-type composite video monitors, because the NTSC (National Television Systems Committee) standard combines the separate RGB signals into one signal for processing, recording, and transmission. This is the current standard for TV broadcasting in the U.S. and Japan.

processor: A computer's integrated circuit that processes information.

video digitizing: The process of capturing, converting, and storing video images for use in computer applications.

slightest gesture), and so on, as well as the participant's position relative to the graphic objects on the screen. An "executive processor" tells the computer how to respond—to move an object, move the participant's image, or make a sound. A **composite** image of the participant interacting in the artificial reality is displayed on the video projection screen.

I continue to develop VIDEOPLACE. Today it accommodates the linking of two environments. Additional environments require the software to perform more complex analysis, but don't affect the system's basic operation.

Our most sophisticated VIDEOPLACE interaction dates back to 1983. It's called "Critter." Critter, a graphic creature, represents **artificial intelligence**, although "artificial personality" perhaps is a more appropriate description of what has been achieved. Critter possesses elaborate rules of behavior and the perception to drive those rules. Critter perceives your movements and engages your video image in a whimsical interplay. Critter flits

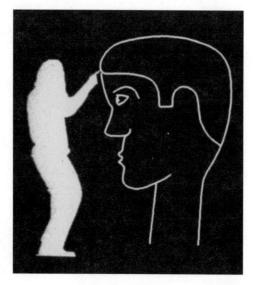

"Digital Drawing" with VIDEOPLACE

about, lands on your hand, dangles from your fingertip, and generally has a good time with you. Critter affords a playful metaphor for one of the central dramas of our time: the encounter between humans and machines.

Another VIDEOPLACE interaction is "Cat's Cradle," a variation of the classic children's game. Graphic "string" is magically attracted to the fingertips of the participants. We use **spline** curves to accomplish this. Several people can play, as the computer can identify up to 40 fingers in one-thirtieth of a second. It's something people instantaneously start playing with.

In "Digital Drawing," you can draw by moving one finger through the air. By extending all the fingers on one hand, you can erase the entire image. In one variation on Digital Drawing, you draw with "dynamic ink": If you synchronize your drawing movements with the drawing you drew previously, an animated pattern is created on the screen.

Similar in concept to VIDEOPLACE, the VIDEODESK resulted from the Metaplay experience. It consists of a light table with a video camera above it, aimed at the desk's surface, where the participant's hands rest. The camera sends information about the position and gestures of the participant's hands to the computer. A composite of the graphic images and the silhouette images of the hands appears on a monitor placed on the far side of the desk.

The image of the participant's hands can be superimposed on any application; then she can use the image of her finger to point, draw, write, or perform any operation that she normally would accomplish using a mouse, joystick, or data tablet.

Two-way interactions can occur between a participant in VIDEOPLACE and a second participant seated at the VIDEODESK. Each participant sees the same composite image on their respective screens. This image consists of the giant hands of the VIDEODESK participant and the life-sized or shrunken image of the full body of the VIDEOPLACE participant. In "Artwheels," the VIDEOPLACE participant turns cartwheels on a graphic string held by the VIDEODESK participant. In "Hanging By A Thread," the VIDEOPLACE participant can move his body to make his shrunken image swing back and forth from the end of a large graphic "string" held by the person at the VIDEODESK. Once the typical VIDEOPLACE participant understands how to behave, he starts running from side to side, while people on the sidelines encourage him. In all cases, they want to know, "Can he do a 360?" Yes, he can—and when he succeeds, the audience often cheers.

One thing we learned early on is that this type of activity is a collaborative, two-way experience. We are creating a new way for people to be together, a new way to play. When the images of two people appear on the screen, and one is doing something with the other's image, they start dealing with the issue of who has the "power." Each person becomes an instrument for the other person to play, and this plays on our common tensions about touching and personal space.

Additionally, the fact that one participant can move another's image around on the screen, and subject it to laws of physics not operating in the real world, offers unlimited compositional possibilities.

"Individual Medley," a VIDEOPLACE *interaction*

With such VIDEOPLACE interactions such as "Individual Medley" and "Body Surfacing," we provide novel artistic media for the participants to play with. Since there are no antecedents for these media, the participant has no idea what would make "good" art or what a "real" artist would do, so she lets her innate aesthetic sense guide her behavior.

We set up the VIDEOPLACE installation in such a way that each time one person

"Body Surfacing" on VIDEOPLACE

leaves the exhibit and the next person enters, they see a different interaction. One reason we do this is to combat today's standard style of art consumption, which I call "supermarket mode." Many people visit museums planning to see at least 100 works of art per hour. I wanted VIDEOPLACE to reach beyond people's desire to have "seen" art and get them to really look at it. If one of these "shoppers" glances in at VIDEOPLACE, sees one interaction in progress, and moves on, thinking they have seen it, they will be surprised when they compare notes with a friend, who saw a completely different type of interaction. This experience leads some people to return to really see the exhibit. (This is my "second strike" capability.) During every show, a few people approach me and say they returned for this reason. The 50 different interactions in VIDEOPLACE are enough to occupy some visitors for over an hour.

VIDEOPLACE's main aesthetic statement is that *response is the medium*. The composition is the relationship between what you do and what you perceive as being the computer-generated consequences of your action. The quality of the computer's perception of your actions is even more important than the responses' visual or musical quality. Realistic graphic environments are irrelevant unless you can interact realistically with them.

When a participant performs an action in a VIDEOPLACE interaction, he or she doesn't necessarily know what the system's response will be. It may be based on what happened before, or it could offer an element of surprise. We need surprises to keep people interested in responding. That's why we've always focused on fun types of interactions, and on instantaneous response.

In the term "artificial reality," "reality" refers to the causal laws that operate between your body's movements and their effect on the graphic world. As humans, our bodies evolved to move about a physical world. When the computer forces me to sit down and peck at a keyboard, it has abbreviated my world. I've always known how I wanted to interact with computers. I wanted my body back, I wanted to be physically involved, I wanted to be able to work standing up. For over 20 years, I have argued that we can instrument our environments instead of our bodies to create new worlds through which we can interact with computers—and with other people.

WELCOME TO "ELECTRONIC CAFE INTERNATIONAL"

A NICE PLACE FOR HOT COFFEE, ICED TEA, & VIRTUAL SPACE

BY KIT GALLOWAY & SHERRIE RABINOWITZ

Since 1975 Kit Galloway and Sherrie Rabinowitz have developed alternative technology systems that involve performing arts and public partici-pation. Their work has been exhibited in New York's Museum of Modern Art, Los Angeles's Museum of Contemporary Art, Italy's Venice Biennial, and the Tokyo Video Festival. During the 1984 L.A. Olympics, Kit and Sherrie modeled the Electronic Cafe concept, commissioned by L.A.'s Museum of Contempory Art. In 1987 they launched Electronic Cafe International. A year later they won the telecommunications industry's TeleSpan PACE award for ten years of leadership. Kit and Sherrie also have consulted for Xerox PARC, Walt Disney Imagineering, and the U.S. Congressional Office of Technological Manage-ment, and taught at universities. Working with Gene Youngblood, they currently are co-authoring Virtual Space: The Challenge to Create on The Same Scale as We Can Destroy.

MIDI: Musical Instrument Digital Interface. For more information, see "Hyperinstruments" by Tod Machover.

laserdisc: A laserdisc, a.k.a. videodisc, is a 12-inch plastic disc that holds thousands of video images and sound.

Over a decade before sci-fi fans first read about "cyberspace," Kit Galloway and Sherrie Rabinowitz used video as an interac-tive communications medium to pioneer virtual space. In 1977 they produced the Satellite Arts Project, in conjunction with NASA, researching the implications of using satellites to elec-tronically combine people from different locations into the same real-time virtual space. It also marked the first live, composite-image dance performance and artistic application of satellites. Dancers in locations thousands of miles from each other performed together by viewing a live composite-image satellite link-up, watching themselves with their distant partners on-screen. This chapter reviews the results of this and more recent interactive tele-com projects, particularly "Electronic Cafe International."

Established in 1987, Electronic Cafe International (ECI) is a unique venue that organizes and produces performances, dis-cussions, and a smorgasbord of tele-events in "virtual space." The worldwide ECI Network comprises over 60 affiliates and in-dividuals. Most Electronic Cafe performances incorporate the visions of several collaborating artists and occur in more than one place at the same time: videophone technology links artists who perform simultaneously in various locations around the world. A performing artist in one city might transmit video, **MIDI**, *and audio signals to another city, where the artist's image appears on a video screen while the data signals control lights, musical instruments, and video* **laserdisc** *tracks.*

Through their grassroots approach, Galloway, Rabinowitz, and associates are electronically linking cafes and public venues to create a global network of community-based, multimedia tele-conference facilities for cultural exchange.

Our original idea, back in the 1970s, was to create an electronic, multimedia composite-image space in which people separated by distance, language, values, and culture could come together to collaborate. The image itself would become a place that we named "virtual space," which differs from virtual and artificial reality because the people, places, and things are real-world items; they're not rendered by computer. Our original research was funded by Corporation for Public Broadcasting and National Endowment for the Arts, with support from NASA.

We wanted performing artists to meet in composite-image space that mixed live images from remote places and presented the mix at each location so performers could see themselves on the same screen with their partners. That became the premise for our subsequent work and experimentation.

This sort of composite image space was explored in the early 1950s by Ernie Kovacs and Steve Allen. Kovacs would superimpose his live video image onto film clips and interact with the film characters. Allen would do improvisational comedy by superimposing his live studio image with live camera shots of unsuspecting pedestrians outside the television studio.

We first explored composite-image space because we wanted to create a performance place with no geographical boundaries, in which we could collaborate with other artists. We wanted to explore the aesthetics and sense of presence in a shared performance/multimedia environment, where people don't leave their indigenous environments. That way people from varied creative and cultural backgrounds could help create a new environment in which they would collaborate on an international scale.

In designing such spaces, we look not only at their qualities and aesthetics, but how people interact when they are disembodied and their image is their "ambassador." A virtual space creates social situations without traditional rules of etiquette. The absence of the threat of physical harm makes people braver. Virtual space diminishes our fears of interaction. Still, a person is offended when the virtual-space hand "touches" body parts that wouldn't be touched normally "in the flesh." In virtual space, we learn the extent to which we "own" our image. It relates to the beliefs of some cultures; if you take a photograph of people, they believe you capture or "steal" part of their essence or soul. This is a violation of one's image. Anyone can experience this in virtual space when seeing their image violated by a person or object that occupies the same image space.

"Satellite Arts Project: A Space With No Geographical Boundaries," ©1977. The world's first interactive composite-image satellite dance performance. The dancer on the far right, Mitsuko Mitsueda, was at NASA Goddard Space Flight Center in Maryland, and dancers Keija Kimura and Soto Hoffman were in Menlo Park, California. Their electronically composited image appeared on monitors at each location. Their images responded like a mirror: When the dancers moved to the right, their images moved to the right.

If you define the aesthetic of the medium by defining the essence and integrity of the medium, then the creation of "good" art, in the case of telecommunications, means you create a situation that provides some form of communication between people and maximizes the technology's capabilities. But there must be a quality of tension that defines the "communication." If you don't create tension in the work, you're not really looking at the qualities of the medium, or the qualities of the art.

Thin Space, Thick Time: Technical Concerns

The Electronic Cafe's technical concerns include the movement of full-motion video over long distances at various speeds and the inherent satellite time-delays. The time delay represents the video signal's trip to and from a satellite. It's said that satellites are "distance-insensitive," a term referring to the cost benefits of satellite communications: Once you pay to send your signal to a satellite for transmission, no fur-

ther costs are incurred to deliver the signal anywhere within the satellite's reach. This isn't the case with transmissions delivered over the same area via terrestrial microwave or cables. Nevertheless, we believe *nothing* is distance-insensitive if it takes extra time to travel distances.

When more than one satellite "hop" is used to send get a signal from point A to point B, it can take over a half-second to arrive. This wreaks havoc on synchronized interaction between people and machines. It means you have to wait a second or two after every sentence when you're holding an overseas phone conversation. It means musicians can't enjoy real jam sessions over international satellite links. We call this condition "thin space, thick time," because you can create virtual space, but still must deal with the time component. Time takes on the added dimension of delay. We've always taken an aesthetic approach to this condition.

"Thin space, thick time" illustrates why it is so important for us to hug the surface

"Hole in Space," ©1980. Live two-way satellite connection using video screens to project life-size images. Without public announcement, we installed "Hole in Space" on the street near New York City's Lincoln Center and in a display window at a Los Angeles department store in Century City. Both screens could accommodate the images of about 15 people. People could converse with people in the other city as if they were standing on the same street corner. "Hole in Space" took place over three evenings. On the first night, people simply discovered it. They went home and told their friends, who showed up for the second evening, when it also was announced on TV in both locations. On the third night, families from miles away drove into the cities with cars full of kids to meet up with relatives on the other coast whom they hadn't seen in years.

"Aesthetic Research in Telecommunications (ART-COM)," 1982. At Loyola Marymount University, we designed and taught a multi-disciplinary lab class examining the effects, potential, and future of interactive video. These are from one of our virtual-space performances.

ISDN: Integrated Services Digital Network; proposed protocols for carrying voice, data, facsimile, and video signals across a network.

broadband: A network in which the bandwidth can be shared by multiple simultaneous signals.

bandwidth: Measurement that indicates a system's data transmission capacity. The greater the bandwidth, the greater the amount of information that can be transmitted in real time.

of the planet with terrestrial and under-sea fiber-optic cables. This would eliminate time delay because the signal wouldn't have to travel tens of thousands of miles. Less-developed nations won't see **ISDN** and fiber optics until well past the end of the 20th century. But it's vital that international human relations start *now*.

Taking full advantage of virtual space requires full-motion, **broadband** video transmission. Broadband technology promises immense possibilities, but currently isn't accessible because of its prohibitive cost. Instead, we use standard telephone lines to enter virtual space.

If we wait for the world to become wireless or re-wired before the virtual-space acculturation process begins, we delay the broad-based cultural articulation of what we want from cyberspace technology. Properly integrated with video technology, telephone lines can be used to create a sense of presence and "connectedness" with other people. Phone lines can accommodate data-transmission technology and transmit still-frame video im-

ages. In a few years, phone lines will handle as many as ten video frames per second, so while we wait for the higher **bandwidth** of fiber-optic cables, we can create an international network of informal, multimedia teleconferencing centers in which people can start developing the culture, etiquette, and skills required to live, work, play, and create in virtual spaces.

One day, virtual reality technologies will plug into this emerging network and allow full-immersion migration to virtual spaces containing people from other locations.

As wonderful as this may sound, it's important to define a technology's limits as well as its potential. Only when we understand its limitations can we use it as a medium that doesn't simply copy film or television. Western societies generally tend to abandon the responsibility of creatively applying the technology that already surrounds us. The constant high-pressure "selling of the future" drives us blindly toward the hype of emerging technologies, which we abandon in turn for the next big thing.

If we could be as conversant about the limitations of emerging technologies as we are about the utopian promises, we could sort out what we should be doing with our planet's human and material resources.

The Cafe as Cultural Community Center

We wanted to create an environment for creative people to enjoy one-to-one and group-to-group interactivities and exchanges. That's where Electronic Cafe comes in. The flagship cafe is in southern California, in Santa Monica, networked with Electronic Cafe Affiliates in San Francisco, New York City, Oakland and Santa Cruz, Calif., Santa Fe, Chicago, Pittsburgh, Vancouver, Toronto, Paris, Berlin, Japan, Seoul, Managua, Barcelona, and Budapest. We're building human networks on an international, cross-cultural, multidisciplinary scale. These networks consist of people who are getting to know each other and the technology that maintains their relationship. They're trying to creatively animate that technology by engaging in new types of conversation.

The point of Electronic Cafe is to create a community commons. The atmosphere encourages friendly conversation and serves as an amenity to the telecommunications technology. And our events typically cost $3-$5 to attend.

In 1984 we were commissioned by the L.A. Museum of Contemporary Art (MOCA) to create a seven-week project for the L.A. Olympic Arts Festival. This was the birth of the Electronic Cafe concept. We linked MOCA with five diverse L.A. communities through a telecom system, computer database, and dial-up image bank. People in the Korean community, His-

© 1989 Eric Barreau/Electronic Cafe International

© 1989 Eric Barreau & Kit Galloway/Electronic Cafe International

panic community, black community, and artsy beach community could send each other slow-scan video images, draw or write together with an electronic writing tablet, print pictures with the video printer, enter and retrieve information and ideas in the computer database, and store or retrieve images on a videodisc recorder that held 20,000 images. Electronic Cafe Artists-in-Residence helped people use

This is a Macintosh II image we created with people at a museum in Paris in 1989. We established a graphics-based dialogue as a collaborative effort with French computer-graphics artists. We sent graphics over phone lines, they modified them and sent them back. Then we changed the results and sent them, and so on.

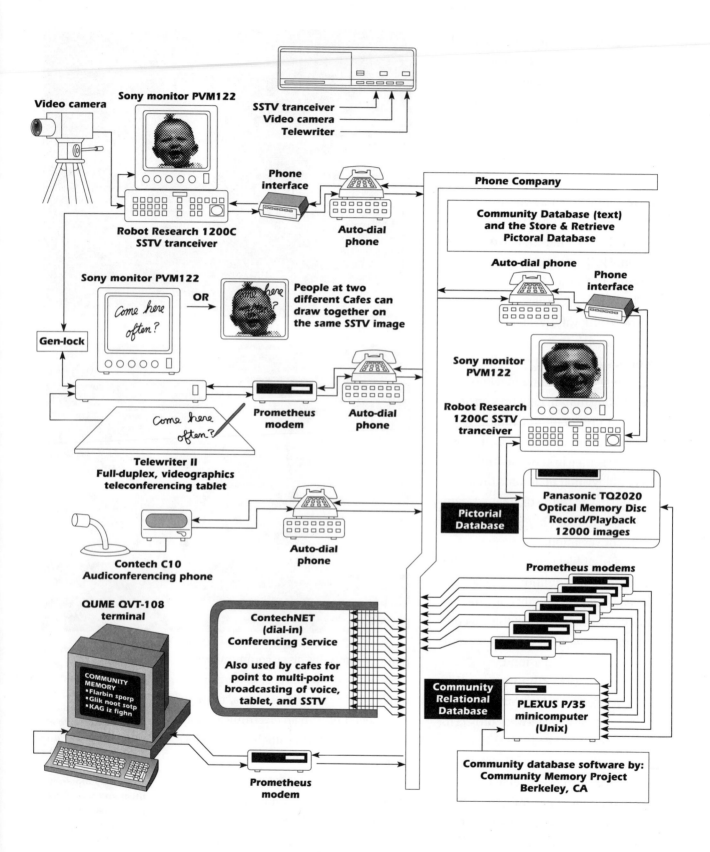

Video camera

Sony monitor PVM122

SSTV tranceiver
Video camera
Telewriter

Phone interface

Auto-dial phone

Robot Research 1200C SSTV tranceiver

Phone Company

Community Database (text) and the Store & Retrieve Pictoral Database

Sony monitor PVM122

OR

Come here often?

People at two different Cafes can draw together on the same SSTV image

Gen-lock

Auto-dial phone

Phone interface

Sony monitor PVM122

Robot Research 1200C SSTV tranceiver

Come here often?

Prometheus modem

Auto-dial phone

Come here often?

Telewriter II
Full-duplex, videographics teleconferencing tablet

Panasonic TQ2020 Optical Memory Disc Record/Playback 12000 images

Pictorial Database

Auto-dial phone

Prometheus modems

Contech C10
Audiconferencing phone

QUME QVT-108 terminal

ContechNET (dial-in) Conferencing Service

Also used by cafes for point to multi-point broadcasting of voice, tablet, and SSTV

Community Relational Database

PLEXUS P/35 minicomputer (Unix)

COMMUNITY MEMORY
• Flarbin sporp
• Glik noot sotp
• KAG iz fighn

Prometheus modem

Community database software by:
Community Memory Project
Berkeley, CA

the systems, solicit performance pieces, and transmit musical events.

These events propelled the network into a dynamic, inspirational existence. For example, Los Angeles' Korean community and black community traditionally are at odds with each other. As they met and got to know each other through the network, they wanted to visit each other! When you can make eye contact and establish a creative relationship with someone, you usually want to meet and touch them. At first people talked informally over the network, then created something together, and in many cases, ended up arranging in-person meetings.

Today, each Electronic Cafe contains the low-cost Commodore Amiga computers, which have audio and video capabilities. We also use black-&-white, still-frame **videophones** (we call them "vidphones"), color still-frame vidphones; video projectors; IBM PC-compatible and Macintosh II computers containing special circuit boards that capture video images; **modems**; computer printers; fax machines; and software for telecommunications, desktop publishing, database management, and graphics. We also have multiple telephone lines. Not all of the Electronic Cafes own video and color printers, but some locations consider them essential for documenting events.

All of this hardware and software lets EC Network affiliates exchange still-frame video images and computer graphics, enjoy video and audio teleconferencing and two-way drawing and writing in shared-screen presentations, exchange computer files, programs, electronic mail, and black-&-white images and/or text, and

conduct real-time "chats" via computer. People who own videophones or computers are welcome to dial in and join the network. We invite people to come in and encounter the technology in a nonintimidating environment.

Our Robot Research 1200C video transmission system sends color or black-&-white images over phone lines (a color image measuring 256 x 256 pixels takes 36 seconds, while a black-&-white image of the same resolution sends in 24 seconds). Images are received by another Robot 1200C or Commodore Amiga with special software. Our vidphones transmit black-&-white still images with an average 100 x 100 pixel resolution in seven or eight seconds. These vidphones (by Panasonic and Mitsubishi) no longer are manufactured, but other companies build similar systems.

One typical ECI event was "Earth Day Global Link '90," the only truly interactive global event to occur on Earth Day. It involved connections and teleperformances with Moscow, Nicaragua, Berlin, and

Electronic Cafe's Vidphone Gallery is the first public dial-up electronic bulletin board with audio & video image storage-&-retrieval. All you need is a consumer videophone and telephone to view and contribute to EC VidPhone Galleries. The current system runs on a Mac Plus with an 80-megabyte hard drive.

videophone: A device that transmits and receives audio and visual information. It transmits slow-scan stills every 5-10 seconds, while audio transmissions are continuous and two-way.

modem: A device that converts computer signals into high-frequency communication signals that can be sent over telephone lines.

These images are from a test-run telecom meeting for "The 21st Century Odyssey"; the images (captured during a single conversation) show: Barbara T. Smith in Katmandu, Nepal; Dr. Roy Walford at Bio Sphere 2 in Arizona; and, from Electronic Cafe in Santa Monica, (L-R) Sherrie Rabinowitz, CyberArts editor Linda Jacobson, space scientist Dave Ray, and Kit Galloway.

Bio Sphere 2: The Arizona-based, totally enclosed, self-sustaining environment in which eight people are living for two years. Bio Sphere 2 contains six natural climates. (Bio Sphere 1 is the earth.)

groupware: Software designed for teams of people working together on shared information.

computer musician Mark Coniglio of the Center for Experiments in Art, Information, & Technology (based at California Arts Insititute) developed a Macintosh II program, "MIDI Dancer." Using MIDI Dancer and wearing wireless motion-monitoring devices on her arms and around her waist, Dawn transmitted data about her movements to the Mac. Dawn's motions controlled the previously scored music, synchronizing it to her cadence, controlled the lighting and microphone levels, and determined when her image was captured and transmitted to the New York location.

In a current Electronic Cafe project, "The 21st Century Odyssey," performance artist Barbara T. Smith is traveling around the world with a portable vidphone system to connect with Electronic Cafe and the artists and other people she meets in her journeys. Her virtual spaces also include **Bio Sphere 2** resident, Dr. Roy Walford, communicating with us and the world through his ECI vidphone system.

Today ECI is testing limited-motion video systems and **groupware**. We are exploring ways in which digital networks allow group-to-group activities and enable a person to control objects in remote rooms.

Integration & Access

If there is one word that defines Electronic Cafe, it is *integration:* integration of technology into our social fabric; integration of distinct cultures and communities, the arts, and the general public; and integration of art forms.

When we put integration capabilities in a community center where people can

Japan. In the connection with Moscow, people discussed environmental problems and artists performed together. Children in L.A. asked the Russians, "Do you have holes in your ozone, too?"

In another Electronic Cafe presentation, a dancer named Dawn Stoppiello used technology to generate music on a Macintosh-based MIDI system and trigger vidphones that sent her image to a New York City site. Working with Dawn, witness the "creative animation" of technology, we can start to liberate people's imaginations. When artists explore this technology, we start pushing the limits of technology. We create a culture that defines how the technology can be used and encourages cross-cultural collaborations, problem-solving, and decision-making. Our hope is to create a cultural environment that helps people around the world articulate what they want in their future and determine how to get there from here.

The ability to pick up a telephone and talk to a person is the most powerful magic created by contemporary society. It is the only mechanism that lets us manage a system as large as a planet. We must recognize that this is sacred, and become a "tele-species." Through Electronic Cafes and the use of telecommunications technology, we hope to foster new kinds of artistic collaboration and experimentation that will support the tele-species.

We want to make teleconferencing systems nonintimidating and accessible to people who don't work within corporations. We want to get the technology to as many people as possible, articulate the ramifications, define the aesthetics, and topple political roadblocks. Corporate culture is not going to provide models or applications broad enough to visualize the technology's cultural application. We must acculturate it ourselves.

If the arts are to take a role in shaping and humanizing emerging technological environments, individuals and arts constituencies must start to imagine at a

At an Electronic Cafe event presented in 1992 by Center for Experiments in Art Information & Technology, renowned electronic music composer Mort Subotnick (background, right) and Kit Galloway (in baseball hat) converse with composer Conlon Nancarrow (on TV screen) in a telelink to Mexico City, where Nancarrow lives. Photo: L. Jacobson.

much larger scale of creativity. If you look at the aesthetic quality of the communication and you're true to your art form and your art logic, then you naturally put one foot in front of the other . . . and the art logic marches you right out the art institutions and into life.

Experiencing The Electronic Cafe

Electronic Cafe International is based at 1649 18th Street in Santa Monica, California. Call us at 310-828-8732, or contact us via modem at 76557.1564@compuserve.com or electronic.cafe@propalmtree.cts.com.

We're "event-driven," so the Cafe is not open on a regular daily basis. You can't walk in at any time and order a cup of java and a videophone, but you can do that during a Cafe event. Call before visiting! We also encourage arts groups to produce events at ECI. If you have access to a vidphone or computer, please join us electronically. It's easy!

THE MANDALA SYSTEM

AN ALTERNATIVE APPROACH TO VIRTUAL REALITY

Artist and dancer Vincent John Vincent was studying psychotherapy when inspiration hit, and he dreamed up the "Mandala System." He joined forces in 1984 with computer programmer Francis MacDougall at Ontario's University of Waterloo. Together they realized their vision of a machine that enables performers to dance, make music, and create art, all inside a computer world. The resulting Mandala System is an interactive technology that can take you on a journey to lands that exist only within the computer—and the mind.

Vincent's Vivid Group introduced the Mandala System in 1986. While it doesn't literally place you (your sense organs) inside a three-dimensional world, it does let you watch yourself cavorting in a computer-based, animated setting, as a video camera "places" your image within that space. In a Mandala world you can play virtual musical instruments, jog down virtual paths, and interact with an unlimited array of virtual objects in diverse, animation- and video-based environments. Today, corporations, museums, theme parks, and other institutions rent or buy custom, broadcast-quality Mandala Systems . . . while regular folks purchase Mandala software for their PCs so they can create virtual worlds at home for under $2,000.

The Mandala System attracts people because it offers a new, affordable kind of freedom of movement and creative expression. In a Mandala world, people can dance, play music, act, and paint—simultaneously. Without physically touching anything, their body movements can control such hardware as stage lights and MIDI effects devices from any distance. When used in stage performance or filmmaking, tools such as this have been used to reduce production time and costs, because effects and animation can be controlled live, and physical stage sets and hardware can be eliminated. Simply put, Mandala is an enchanting medium for artistic exploration.

BY
VINCENT JOHN VINCENT
WITH LINDA JACOBSON

Vincent John Vincent, who co-directs the Toronto-based Vivid Group, is considered the world's first virtual reality performer. ("I am not yet a master of virtual performances, but I won't stop until I am," he says.) Since his debut performance with the Mandala System in New York City's Tunnel Club in 1986, Vincent has performed with the system before audiences around the world. He and his Vivid Group colleagues sell and rent Mandala hardware and software. They also create public Mandala installations, such as museum set-ups in Washington, D.C. (including the TECH 2000 gallery of high-tech multimedia tools and toys) and at science centers, galleries, theme parks (such as Toronto's Tour of the Universe), and international exhibitions, including Tokyo's Wonderland of Science & Art.

When I started out in 1983, I wanted to integrate dance and the musical arts in a system that would let people explore themselves in a way which allowed extended creativity and interactivity. I also wanted a stage performance tool that would let a dancer create the music and work with visual images. The next year I met Francis MacDougall, a computer scientist who helped me reduce the Mandala concept from a huge morass of hardware to a smaller, PC-based system that employed a video camera as the interface between the person and the computer. Our first system simply allowed a person to control computer functions, such as calling up menus, by moving in front of the camera.

To use the **Mandala** System, you stand in front of the camera. On a nearby video monitor you see your image superimposed over computer graphics and video. You interact with the graphic objects that surround your image simply by moving your body so that your image in the monitor seems to touch objects in the environment. The computer tracks a silhouette of your body as you move, allowing your video image to fully control the computer/video worlds in real time. The video worlds in which you appear are viewed on any type or number of video displays, allowing for "hands-off" control of animation, sound, music, and various external devices through your gestures.

The first and most obvious use of this technology was in the arts and entertainment. We pursued that as the basis of the technology and created simple

screens that let you interact with on-screen images to make sound, via the computer's built-in sound chips. But we also could use the system to send signals to any digital instrument that talked **MIDI**, whether it was a synthesizer or effects device.

Back then we weren't thinking in terms of "virtual reality" or "artificial reality." We thought in terms of an interactive, visual, auditory world that people could enter. We wanted to create a multimedia tool that allowed the user to have an experience in a "computer world" that possessed some of the dynamics of the external world. The Mandala system lets you control animation, create music, and use your body as a paintbrush, so it's the ultimate performance tool.

After designing the hardware and software, we started developing animation packages. These let us bring in images, give them "paths" to travel, and let them undergo transformations. We could pick up these animated objects, throw them, and paint with them. We could create an animation of a free-floating ball and program into it the real-world physical characteristics of weight, gravity, and friction; if you threw the virtual ball

MIDI: Musical Instrument Digital Interface, the technology that lets electronic instruments communicate with each other and with computers. With a personal computer, some software, and a few MIDI-controlled instruments, one musician can write, perform, and record an entire orchestral composition.

mandala: From the Sanskrit word for "magic circle," a mandala is a circular design (although it may take other shapes) containing concentric geometric forms, images of deities, and other symbols. It is an archetypal symbol of totality or whole experience, representing a state in which all aspects of self have been fully integrated, where the "psychic center of the personality" reigns, as Carl Jung wrote. Practitioners of Eastern religions meditate upon mandalas to create certain states of awareness and foster spiritual growth. Mandala images intended for contemplation or as expressions of feeling or awareness also flourish in mythology and the arts.

against a virtual surface, it would react like a real ball would.

In the system's initial stages of development, many people asked, "What can you do with it besides dance and play music?" We spent the next two years developing the system in terms of its animation capacity. With the addition of Susan Wyshynski to our creative team, we focused on creating different applications to show the broad range of potential uses. Much of that was driven by the jobs we took to support the company. For instance, we worked on corporate presentation projects and sales promotion videos.

Even at that level, people were excited about the real-time nature of the Mandala System: You could enter a computer world and control objects in real time. At that time we worked with animation; people wanted to see real images, video. So we developed our high-end Mandala System, which incorporates video stored on laserdisc. We **chroma-keyed** together the images from the camera and the images from laserdisc and **genlocked** both sets of images underneath the computer animation. These three levels of video and computer animation are married and controlled by the user's interaction with the animation.

As a medium for storing graphics, the laserdisc player goes way beyond the computer system in terms of its image storage space and **resolution.** We wanted to create worlds similar to those in the film *Who Framed Roger Rabbit?* We want to let people step into an animated world and feel as if they're a part of it. This is facilitated by the

quality of the video images we can press onto laserdisc.

Mandala's Components

The basic Mandala System, which we sell for about $8,000, provides two layers of video, allowing the user's live silhouette or real image to be incorporated with computer animation. The components are:

• Commodore Amiga 2500HD computer with monitor, 40-megabyte hard drive, and three megabytes of RAM;

• color video camera and cables;

• video genlock with **RGB/NTSC** video output;

• **video digitizing** board from A-Squared Live!;

• multi-connector serial circuit board for interfacing everything;

• MIDI adaptor and sound synthesizer;

• **authoring software**, video digitizing software, and operation manual with tutorial video;

• 12 Mandala environments (three video games, six musical instruments, three bodypaint screens).

We also offer a high-end system for about $16,000, which provides three layers of video allowing the user's real image to be incorporated with computer animation and pre-recorded or live video. It consists of the hardware and software equipment listed above but replaces the standard NTSC video camera with an RGB video camera and adds an industrial laserdisc player (for television-quality video) with a laserdisc containing many pre-made Mandala computer/video worlds, plus a chroma-key video switcher and four-channel audio mixer.

video digitizing: The process of capturing, converting, and storing video images for use in computer applications.

authoring software: Software that helps developers design interactive programs relatively easily, without requiring the painstaking details and extensive skills involved in traditional computer programming.

chroma-key: An electronic matte that lets one image be matted on top of another without image bleed-through. Resembles an electronic blindfold. (A "matte" is an effect or device that blocks out an adjacent element, signal, or light.)

genlock: In computer graphics, a device that aligns the data rate of a video image with the data rate of a digital device, to digitize the image and enter it into computer memory.

resolution: The measurement of image sharpness and clarity on a video display terminal, usually measured by the number of pixels per square inch.

How does it work? Basically, your image passes through the camera into the computer and appears within the computer/video world on the video display. The computer always knows where your image is, and when your image comes in contact with the animation, it immediately produces video and sound effects. Most of our installations employ a set of icons, consisting of graphic triggers that you can turn on and off. The system is not based on gestures, but on interaction with the triggers. You essentially become the "mouse in the computer" (the input device kind of mouse, not the furry one!) and can control these computer functions; meanwhile, the camera is your joystick.

As current laserdiscs support analog video only, we're experiencing the limitations of the system. This means the user progresses in a linear fashion through the various 3D worlds, instead of having the ability to move freely between all the different worlds. Digital video would allow such random-access navigation.

The system runs the video at a rate of 30 frames per second (by way of comparison, standard movie film runs at 24 frames per second). If you add a large amount of animation, this frame rate drops. The solution is to add faster **processors**, which brings the speed back to real-time.

In 1991 we released a $595 Mandala VR Authoring Software package that works with any Commodore Amiga computer. This software lets you create interactive environments that can be entered and controlled through any type of video camera. You create scenes using standard Amiga paint programs and create graphics from digitized video or from scratch.

It controls laserdisc players, too, so you can incorporate TV-quality video.

The software has single-pixel accuracy of interaction, which means each dot on the screen has the potential to be an interactive controller. You have interactive control over animations, graphics, and video elements, including "body-painting" (your video image can paint the screen in different ways). It supports **sprite** and **cel** animation, picture-flipping sequences, moving picture backgrounds, and includes various forms of instantaneous scene transitions. It even features 3D simulation (animation appears in front and behind your image, which can appear as a silhouette or gen-locked video image).

Setting up a scene in which your video image juggles virtual bowling balls, or other interactions where your virtual hand moves animated characters, is not difficult. The software lets you program the juggling balls with gravity, friction, and bounce. If you make the balls the weight of boulders, juggling would be difficult. A "magnetism" effect allows objects to attract or repel others based upon their proximity.

The system also supports "inter-object communication," or interaction between two or more virtual objects. For instance, your video image might pick up a virtual can and pull out a virtual worm, which then is chased by a virtual bird. There are simple ways for any object to trigger another. Contact-oriented communication is also possible. An object's intersection with another can be used to trigger new "states" or events in either or both of the involved objects.

RGB: Abbreviation for Red, Green, Blue, the type of display monitor used with computers. RGB monitors typically offer higher resolution than NTSC-format video monitors. (The NTSC method eliminates color detail and limits color intensity to prevent distortion during signal transmission.)

NTSC: Abbreviation of National Television Systems Committee, the part of the Electronics Industries Association that prepared the color TV-broadcast standard approved by the FCC in 1953. NTSC is the current standard for TV broadcasting in the U.S. and Japan. NTSC-format video is a color television format with 525 scan lines and a frame rate of 30 frames per second.

processor: The heart of a computer, the integrated circuit that processes information and performs calculations.

sprite: Screen image, moveable under program or manual control through an input device. Sprites may be characters (such as those in video games), cursor shapes, or specific patterns. Defined by a 2-dimensional array of pixels, they normally are smaller than full-screen size, unlike **cels**, which are complete animation frames.

The software is heading toward emulation of more real-world physical properties, while at the same time adding speed-oriented features such as object-oriented, 3D-rendered images.

The system also works as an electronic musical instrument and sound effects generator, because it allows MIDI control of external devices, Amiga sound files, and popular music sequencer programs.

Mandala at Work & Play

While we use Mandala in performance to take the audience on audio/visual journeys into computer worlds that they view on large screens, Mandala also enables new communication, entertainment, and educational activities. For instance, we created an installation for the NHL's Hockey Hall of Fame that features a simulation goalie-training game, "You Be the Goalie." The idea is to knock virtual pucks away from the net. You stand before a monitor and watch the screen, on which your image is combined with those of a real net and

real players. When the puck is shot at the goal, you block it by moving your arms and legs.

In 1991 we installed a Mandala System in the Smithsonian Institution's Information Age gallery, using two cameras and two interconnected 40-inch TVs to display panoramic scenes. The same set-up is in another place in the museum. People on two different floors can talk to each other and interact with the graphics, which include animated drum kits and synthesizers and images about the history of information processing.

We've also customized Mandala Systems for business applications, including trade show presentations and video-wall installations. One trade-show client was B. F. Goodrich; we created a Mandala world that lets you "walk through" its history, from the workings of a tire factory to the manufacturing of space-age plastics for the home.

The next step involves using Mandala in telecommunications, as an interactive teleconferencing tool. Bell Canada used Mandala for real-time, transcontinental communication between locations in Toronto, New York, Atlanta, and Paris. The system itself was in Toronto, with camera and screen installations in each of the other locations. People in each city could control the computer functions and graphics; from the main system in Toronto, a video loop is sent to each site.

In this kind of teleconferencing, we do experience a time delay, but not a great one. If you're in Toronto and another person is in New York City, there is about a ¼-second delay. In 1988 we set up a real-

time, musical performance interaction between Paris and Toronto. The resulting delay between locations was about 2½ seconds. I was playing music in Paris to accompany a band in Toronto, but I couldn't play strict leads over a tight rhythm section. We had to keep it loose because of the time delay. Teleconferencing technology has advanced since then, so the delay is minimized.

Video game producers and TV show producers also like the Mandala concept. The Nickelodeon cable channel uses it for the "Nick Arcade" children's game show, in which contestants race through virtual worlds such as a giant pinball machine. "Cyberia," a television program produced by college students on U*Net (a U.S. network of college TV stations), also incorporates Mandala. "Cyberia" presents computer animations and electronic music videos; the host enters a Mandala world containing digitized images and simple animations to introduce the clips. In one segment, the host was located in the center of the screen, while animated circles moved outward from the center. A virtual chicken bounced about in the background, while a virtual egg floated around. The egg cracked and turned into a fried egg. Each time the egg transformed, it triggered the sound of a drum.

Mandala is a great educational tool. In fact, the Toronto school system incorporates Mandala into classroom activities. Our first efforts in that area involved producing an educational video in which Mandala taught children how to spell. The child stood in front of the camera and saw herself placed inside a bowl of al-

phabet soup. By grabbing the colored letters, the child assembled words. When she touched the right letters, they flew up to form the word, the word was pronounced, and a picture corresponding to the word appeared on the screen.

In current school uses of Mandala, the teacher steps into a live "Sesame Street" type of scenario in spelling class. She pulls letters out of an animated hat; they then animate and pronounce themselves. The students watch it on video monitors. After the lesson, the students step into the world and do what the teacher did. They also create their own presentations.

If you can see information, hear it, and play with it, you absorb more of it. This kinetic approach to involving the whole body in learning adds to the educational process. Teachers and students can step inside an unlimited number of Mandala worlds of their own design. It's the blackboard of the future.

Today, the Vivid Group functions primarily as a production company, creating custom Mandala installations. We also sell the Mandala Virtual World Authoring System, which includes all the hardware and software for people to create their worlds. They can import their own graphics and develop their own applications. We rent systems, too. Besides selling the low-cost Mandala software for the Amiga, we're developing similarly priced software packages for the Apple Macintosh and the IBM PC (the latter with graphics **rendered** in 3D).

We're extremely interested in Mandala's use in health care and physiotherapy, particularly for disabled people who can use it to control devices such as lights and telephones. Funded by the Canadian government, we're developing a circuit board that lets people use the system to control electronic equipment such as the TV, VCR, and stereo system, access modems and telephones, and turn on and off lights. The same system also might serve as an office machine controller.

We continue to upgrade our processing chips, moving from 68030 to faster 68040s, which gives us much more processing room for gestural analysis. We are moving beyond just recognizing the person's location in the Mandala world to being able to distinguish body parts and how they're functioning in the interaction with and manipulation of graphic elements.

We'd like to make Mandala available to more of the public by providing it on many different computer platforms. And one day, we'd like to project images not just on video screens, but as holograms. In recent Mandala systems that use

stereoscopic glasses and 3D imagery, we take a step toward realizing that dream.

Fighting Technology with Technology

We've tried to use the Mandala System to encourage creativity, while attempting to avoid violent applications.

In one application, we wanted to promote a future of clean energy sources to fuel the onslaught of technology. In 1991 we created a virtual reality simulation of a world 20 years in the future, entitled the "Transpersonal Energy Conversion Matrix." Designed for the St. Louis Science Center, it was based on the concept of machines that absorb the kinetic energy generated by our daily activities and turn it into the energy needed to run the world. The goal is to optimize energy production so we no longer need fossil fuels or have to live in fear of nuclear madness.

Our premise was based on the concept that in the future, our environments will contain millions of tiny sensors and gadgets designed to help optimize our daily activities so we have more time for simply living and being. Microlevel energy collectors and generators will be everywhere, absorbing the kinetic energy from our actions. Energy will be collected from doors, machines—anything that moves. Even our sports events will be oriented toward energy creation; they'll take place in huge arenas where energy will be collected from players' movements and audience response.

On April 22, 1992, Earth Day, we moved this concept one small step closer to reality. On that day the Transpersonal Energy Conversion Matrix installation ran off alternative energy generated by human activity and solar power. It also featured the world's first solar-powered virtual reality performance.

At the Vivid Group we see virtual reality as a window opening up at the end of the 20th century that offers people empowering opportunities to physically and cognitively experience altered and alternative perspectives of realities that we dream about.

• •

VIRTUAL REALITY: A STATUS REPORT

BY JARON LANIER

Jaron Lanier is chief scientist and co-founder of VPL Research, Inc., the virtual reality technology company. Recognized as one of the most brilliant thinkers in software and human-computer inter-face issues, Jaron was the first to use the term "virtual reality" to describe what happens when you combine VPL's DataGlove, EyePhones, Body Electric software, and other "Reality-Built-For-Two" tools. Before forming VPL, Jaron enjoyed widespread acclaim for his creation of "Moon-dust," one of the best-selling software games of 1983. Jaron also is a critically acclaimed musician and recording artist (Point Music, a Polygram label) who plays contemporary stringed and reed instruments as well as rare and ancient instruments from around the world.

"Virtual reality" essentially is a technique for creating "simulated experience"; that is, an experience of a simulated external world. It does this with the help of computerized clothing that covers your sense organs. Your sense organs—eyes, ears, and skin—connect you with the outside world, letting you know that the world is there. By covering these senses with computerized clothing that can provide the stimulation which the senses would receive in an alternate reality, we can simulate, to some degree, the experience of being in that alternate reality.

A **virtual reality** system is a general-purpose simulator, something that simulates what your sense organs would perceive in various environments. The limitation is the computer. Computers can only generate so much, because their speed is limited, so the graphics at this point tend to look cartoon-like and grainy, and the world moves somewhat sluggishly. You easily can tell you're in a virtual world. All these elements, however, will improve over time, as the technology improves.

The most celebrated item of clothing in a virtual reality system is the head-mounted display, or "virtual reality goggles." The head-mounted display was first proposed and built in the 1960s by Ivan Sutherland. VPL Research now designs and builds a line of head-mounted displays called "EyePhones." Essentially, this helmet places a video screen in front of each eye that fills your field of view with moving images. Each eye is presented with a slightly different image, to create a three-dimensional illusion. When you move your head, the scene around you changes, just like in the the physical world. You have to create that basic relationship between your head and the outside world in order for virtual reality to simulate presence in a virtual space.

The images you see in the EyePhones are not pre-taped. They're generated by real-time computer graphics, which

virtual: Being such practically or in effect, although not in actual fact or name. IBM started using the word in the late 1960s to refer to any nonphysical link between processes or machines, such as "virtual memory" for random-access memory being simulated using disk drives.

reality: (1) The quality or fact of being real; (2) a person or thing that is real; fact; (3) the quality of being true to life; fidelity to nature; (4) Philosophy: that which is real.

virtual reality: A computer-generated, multi-sensory representation of data. Virtual reality occurs in cyberspace, but cyberspace does not necessarily involve virtual reality (it's been said that "cyberspace" is where you can find your ATM money and where your phone conversations take place).

position-tracker: A system that tracks the movements of parts of the body and sends information about position and orientation to the computer for processing. Typically attached to the head-mounted display, but other hardware sensors such as VR gloves, joysticks, and "yokes" also provide digital signals generated by the physical actions of the participant in the virtual world.

requires a powerful, expensive computer. It completely recreates the scene in front of you 30 times a second, using **position-trackers** to adjust to your head position. You move your head to the left and the scene rotates right. By constantly cancelling out your head movement this way, it creates the illusion that you're moving around inside a stationary, external world. This is the fundamental illusion that leads to the sense of presence. The principle of head-tracking suggests that when we think about perception—in this case, sight—we shouldn't consider eyes as "cameras" that passively take in a scene. We should think of the eye as a kind of spy submarine moving around in space, gathering information. This creates a picture of perception as an active activity, not a passive one.

The EyePhones also include built-in earphones, through which you hear sounds that seem three-dimensional, coming from all different directions, depending on what's happening in the virtual space.

VPL Research developed the other celebrated piece of clothing, the **DataGlove.** When you wear the glove, it puts your hand inside the virtual space. It measures exactly your hand movements and how your fingers bend, tracking your hand's location in the space, and creates a picture of your hand in three dimensions that matches where your hand is in the virtual space. You can see this hand when you put on the EyePhones and DataGlove to enter a virtual reality. Having your hand in there allows natural interaction with the virtual world. You can touch and pick up objects like you do in the physical world. It helps create a vivid illusion that you're

there, although instead of a normal body you have a cartoon body, represented by a hand created by the computer.

One element in simulation that's seeing a lot of development work is tactile feedback in the gloves. "Tactile feedback" means that when you touch a virtual object, you actually feel something on your fingertips. Since 1985 we've built experimental gloves with various kinds of tactile feedback, using things that push against your skin. In 1991 we started shipping gloves with two forms of feedback, which we worked on with collaborators. One form was originally developed at Rutgers University. It involves a metal arm that ends in a ball under your palm; the arm reaches out to press its small metal fingers against the underside of your fingers. It can force, or restrict, motion. Another type of feedback was developed at Advanced Robotics Research Labs in England and also by an inventor named Jim Henigan. It's an air-pressure glove that relies on a bizarre illusion. We start with a glove covered with sensors on the inside of the hand. The glove contains air pockets, like small capillaries, that you fill. While wearing the glove you pick up an everyday object, such as a telephone. As you reach for the phone, the computer records the bends of your fingers, and while you're lifting the handset, the computer records the amount of pressure felt by different points on the inside of your hand. Then it comes up with a "map" based on the bend amount vs. the amount of pressure at a given point. You scale the proportions of the various measured pressures and play them back through the cap-

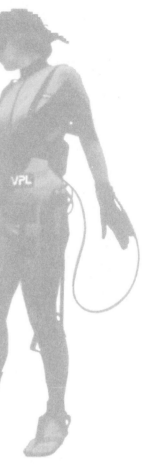

VPL DataSuit

DataGlove; VR glove:
Gesture recognition device that enables navigation through a virtual environment and interaction with 3D objects within it. A lightweight glove lined with sensors that detect motion and send signals to the computer, the VR glove is packed with fiber-optic cables along fingers and wrist, and an orientation sensor for navigation and virtual object manipulation. "DataGlove" is a VPL Research trademark.

illaries in the air-pressure glove. Then you can recognize a virtual object by feeling it. The amount of pressure that can be applied to your hand is much less than that provided by the real object, but it's a great effect. It has great entertainment value, and also can be used to identify tools you might need to grab from behind your head.

These two main forms of feedback differ greatly. One is *tactile feedback*, which affects your skin's natural sensors. The second is *force feedback*, which affects the natural sensors in your muscles and tendons. Tactile feedback acts on your skin locally with texture or pressure sensations, while force feedback actually affects the movement, or resistance to movement, undertaken by your limbs.

Right now we're not working on implementing aroma and taste. It is possible to simulate smell, and research has been done in presenting aromas to the nose, but a problem lies in the fact that there is no spectrum for smells; we can't invent new smells synthetically. We only have a catalog of smells from which to work. From an entertainment point of view it would be worthwhile to associate a smell with an environment, but it's outside the usefulness of the types of applications we develop at VPL Research. As for taste, well, it's too disgusting to think about! We would need to design and build some type of weird effector that you would stick in your mouth. We don't want to deal with that.

Various other human sense organs, such as the inner ear, aren't accessible to the clothing approach, so we're not dealing with them currently.

Recording The World

How do you "scoop up," or record, your physical environment? The subject of using cameras to develop virtual worlds represents an important frontier of development in the next decade.

Several approaches are possible. One involves a depth-scanning camera that knows where it is in space and can measure depths for each pixel it sees. You would move the camera around an environment and it would record both the environment's geometrical shapes as well as the surface appearance of objects in the environment. If you could send the camera's output to a database and just move it around to grab the environment and turn it into a virtual world, that would be splendid.

It is feasible to build this camera today, but it will take a while to design, build, and otherwise acquire all the necessary components. I don't know of anybody who's close to having a prototype of this camera, but parts of some components are almost ready to be demonstrated. In a few years we'll see research results.

Current VPL Systems at Work

VPL Research started as an education company, focusing on products for kindergarten through high school. One of VPL's founders, in fact, came from the Learning Company. We spent three or four years of wasted effort, because there's no money in the educational world. Now we contribute our resources to education by teaching a class for fifth and sixth graders at a school in the San Francisco Bay Area. They learn to build their own worlds on an Apple Macintosh at the school, then come to VPL Research to experience going inside these worlds.

In the mid-1980s we started selling virtual reality equipment, concentrating on industrial applications. One application helps architects. They use virtual reality as a communication tool that lets them put their clients "inside" a computer model of a building and helps verify the correctness of these models. They also use virtual reality to design buildings; the architect and client can go inside the model and change it while they're inside.

My favorite examples of virtual reality helping architects are in Berlin and Tokyo. There's been much rebuilding in east Berlin; the city government of Berlin asked Art+Com, a research and art institute in Germany, to use our virtual reality systems to plan it. We've been working with the city government and Art+Com to model Berlin piece by piece. We started in 1991 by modeling a subway that had been buried underneath the Berlin Wall. Now we're creating virtual versions of buildings that are being remodeled or built in east Berlin. We have the beginning of a complete Berlin, with all the city blocks filled in, with at least a box of the right size for each building. Several buildings are fully modeled, including a national gallery and office buildings. We're gradually creating a complete planning model of the city.

In Tokyo a VPL system is being used in a kitchen showroom at a department store. You walk in there and tell them the measurements of your actual kitchen, which the salesman records into the computer.

Architect's model of a Berlin subway project. Using a VPL system, the architects and clients are able to "walk through" the model to test the design.

Then you put on the goggles and glove and suddenly you're in a room the size of your kitchen. You say, "Let's put a refrigerator here," and you build a kitchen by designing it. You can try different appliance models, open cabinet doors, turn on water faucets. If you like the kitchen, you sign a form and a few days later the store delivers the appliances and fixtures and installs them at your house. This system has met with great success. It paid for itself in a couple of months and we're expanding it now to more stores in Japan. Our long-term goal in working with Matsushita, the Japanese company that runs the department store, is to give people the ability to build a complete simulated house and go inside to design it. The vision is to have people designing their own products, which is the direction Matsushita wants to take. It may not be a world-shaking application, but it gives people a way to design their own environment. It's empowering. Imagine that approach applied in other areas of life, and you can see its implications.

The concept of placing someone inside a simulated space so they can design it has been applied in other industries. We've helped manufacturers design cars, for example. A VPL system currently is being used to model a new sports car in Germany. Meanwhile, a simulation of a space station running at NASA, based on the VPL system, helps them plan maneuverability.

Another area using virtual reality involves maintenance training and documentation of large assemblies. A typical user is a company that makes complex mechanical assemblies, such as engines or transmissions, and sells them around the world. When repairs are needed, they send out field technicians to repair an engine that they sometimes have never seen before. So the company simulates the engine in virtual reality and uses the simulation as a documentation system and as a training tool to teach people about it. Even more importantly, virtual reality can be used to design an engine that's easier to take apart and put back together and be built in sequence with other parts that it connects to.

A good example in this area is Boeing, with whom we work in conjunction with the HIT Lab at the University of Washington. When Boeing puts together a plane, the big question is how long will it take to assemble and how vulnerable are

we to mistakes? By designing a new airplane in software first, then letting workers assemble it that way, we can see what it takes to solve problems before building the actual plane.

Another way to use VR is for displaying abstract information efficiently. Moving around inside a space provides a much more natural mode of understanding that space than having to use our minds to construct abstractions of information about that space. For many people, learning how to drive around L.A., for example, is easier than learning how to do complex mathematical equations. But there's actually much more data involved in figuring out how to drive around L.A. than there is in understanding math. When you transfer complex information into a more natural mode of understanding, you increase a person's ability to understand that information. It can be confusing to plot a bunch of numbers as a complicated graph to see on a screen. But if you turn that graph into a giant simulated sculpture that you can crawl around inside, the data often is easier to understand and analyze. We've done some of this type of work with geological and financial data. We also did a project with Lawrence Livermore Labs to visualize quantum wave equations. This application area is part of the larger field of scientific visualization.

Another VR application area involves ergonomics and training. Virtual reality is the most physical computer interface, because it puts your body inside the simulation. If NASA wants to design a space contraption and figure out how the astronaut would handle it, NASA can use vir-

Using the VPL virtual reality system, you can test-drive a Model T or a late-model Ferrari —or even a future vehicle of your own design.

tual reality to model it and understand how the human body fits into it and works with it. VPL makes full-body data suits, which typically are used in applications in this area.

Until now, we've tended to sell expensive virtual reality systems, costing hundreds of thousands of dollars. In 1992 we entered the lower-priced market, with systems that sell for under $75,000, which opens the door for a new set of applications. Our newest low-end system is almost as powerful as our original high-end systems!

Experimental Applications

Other VPL Research VR applications are in the experimental phase. In a joint venture with MCA/Universal Studios, for example, we're inventing a new kind of theater. The theater is large enough to be located in shopping centers, but not as small as a video game arcade. It's modeled after a movie theater, a general-purpose facility that presents different shows, instead of the kind of fixed-show approach of rides and attractions in theme parks. We call these productions "virtual movies," or "voomies." Voomies are especially exciting because they incorporate live performers. The performer is inside the space along with you but appears to you as a virtual being. This virtual being can transform into all kinds of different shapes but also runs the show and keeps things moving. We call the performer a "changling"; we even plan to open a school to train changlings. The way they'll interact with audiences resembles the work of stand-up comics more than any other type of performer; because they don't

know what kind of people they're going to entertain, they must be ready to deal with anything, make the show end on time and, overall, provide for better entertainment. The first voomies are science fiction. Once the theaters are in place, we'll see many different types of voomies and voomie producers.

Our other primary development area involves "medical media systems," VR applications for surgeons. This is headed by Dr. Joe Rosen, a surgeon on Dartmouth University's faculty. The project involves two types of virtual reality applications. One uses virtual reality to create medical simulations. We've already simulated a surgical procedure from start to finish. It involved an instrument company that designed a widget which helped fix part of the abdomen after an operation. The company had difficulty training people how to use the widget outside of an actual operation. First they tried using plastic models of abdomens, video, and interactive multimedia, and then they came to us. We were able to teach people how to use the widget in a virtual reality simulation.

Another way to use virtual reality is to give surgeons a better user interface for working with new surgical instruments. Many of these are miniaturized instruments at the ends of tubes inserted into the body, generally called "endoscopes." Surgeons use endoscopes to perform procedures without opening the body with an incision, thus reducing the required amount of anesthesia and increasing general safety. One limiting factor in their use, however, is their user interface. The device uses a fiber-optic cable to transmit images, in some cases stereo images, which the doctors view to help them control extremely small instruments. During an endoscopy procedure, the operating room can look like a TV studio with multiple monitors and people turning knobs and yelling at each other. Our goal is to replace this interface with a head-mounted user interface so the surgeon can intuitively control the devices.

We can draw an analogy here to the fighter pilot who operates millions of dollars worth of gear and must must make split-second, life-or-death decisions. For years people have known that fighter pilots require the most sophisticated user interface, providing the best ways to control the gear. Unfortunately, such a user interface-intensive approach has never been attempted for surgeons. We hope that VR will make a difference.

Reality Conversations

One important developing area involves the ability to program a virtual world while you're inside it. The virtual world contains a "liquid" type of environment; it's flexible and malleable in ways unlike the physical world. It's slow, grainy, cartoon-like, and awkward, but it's flexible—you can do things you can't do in the physical world. The trade-off for visual quality is flexibility. You take advantage of that trade-off if you can become fluent in making virtual worlds and compose the contents of the virtual world on the fly. You even can design a three-dimensional computer body to look however you want to look, like a gazelle, perhaps, or an octopus.

Another critical development involves connecting VR systems so two or more people can share an experience at the same time in the same virtual world. If two people enter the same simulated place, they can look at each other and view a virtual representation of the other person. The key is that you have the same general mode of interaction as in the physical world—you can make eye contact, play ball, do projects together. You have a sense of the physical space between you and them, and a sense of the "body music"; the individual's style of movement is preserved. That's essential, and as important as vocal inflection and style.

Given that people can connect in the same virtual world, and given that these people can develop the skills to program that world so they can change themselves into something else, you have a situation that supports extreme creativity in a philosophically unprecedented manner.

What might virtual reality be like in the fairly near future? My vision is that it will turn into a next-generation telephone: You go into your living room and put on glasses and a glove. You can still see your living room through the glasses, but suddenly you also see new furniture in the room, furniture that you can touch and feel with the glove. It's a set of shelves lined with fish tanks. Instead of fish, the tanks contain little people running around in various scenes. In one tank the little people are playing a new form of football on a 3D field. Another tank contains a shopping mall; people are walking around in there, trying on clothes and buying things. In another one there's a city council meeting with a developer proposing a building; people are arguing about it and flying around the building to see it from different perspectives. Another tank holds a real estate office where you can visit different homes. Another one has a bunch of kids walking around a swamp and looking at dinosaurs. They're in school. Each one takes turns being a tyrannosaurus rex.

These little people are all real. Like you, they're networked together, having group experiences from their homes. When you put your gloved hand into a tank, the tank gets very large and surrounds you, and you fly down into the scene and join the group.

Through virtual reality, I see great possibilities for communication. We must look further into the future to picture these possibilities, because we need not only the technology, but a culture of users who have grown up using the technology—people who can program the contents and actions of a virtual world in an improvisational manner.

One striking thing about the physical world is that we're essentially powerless in it. A child has an incredible imagination that isn't limited by the physical world, and it takes a long time and a series of shocks to realize, as an adult, that you really can't change things in the physical world. As people mature, they realize there's one small tool in the physical world that they can control quickly and use to refer to other parts of the world that they cannot control quickly. This tool is your tongue. Virtual reality gives us another tool: We can directly create experiences for each other to share our imagination. I use the terms "post-symbolic communication" and "reality conversations" to talk about this new possibility of communicating by building a world together instead of talking about the world. This form of communication essentially involves shared, lucid dreaming. For me, this is what will make all our work worthwhile and what will turn virtual reality into an incredible cultural adventure.

THE ART OF BUILDING VIRTUAL REALITIES

Virtual world designers don't have an easy job. How do they even begin to tackle the issues involved in building successful applications for virtual reality (VR) technologies? This chapter explores their goals and challenges. Steve Tice describes his company's ground-breaking work in product design and visualization, performance animation, and entertainment. After years of viewing people's behavior in virtual environments, noted author, philosopher, and interface expert Brenda Laurel presents a few dramatic rules for "experience design."

BY STEVE TICE & LINDA JACOBSON

*Steve Tice is the president and CEO of SimGraphics Engineering Corporation, in South Pasadena, California. Previously he supervised advanced computer graphics design and simulation at Rockwell's Space Station & Systems Division, which developed one of the first VR-based design and operations simulators. SimGraphics designs and integrates systems and tools for virtual reality and simulation applications. In 1989, SimGraphics released the "VR_Workbench" development platform, incorporating a Hewlett-Packard minicomputer, StereoGraphics **stereoscopic glasses**, and VPL Research's DataGlove. It was the first commercially available "toolkit" for systems and software development of VR applications on Unix-based PC workstations.*

VR IN VISUALIZATION, ANIMATION, & ENTERTAINMENT

You exert undivided mental effort to figure out the mathematical equations used in a financial report or science problem. That's a conscious process. The preconscious process of visualizing information involves color, light, form, and depth perception. If you give information to your brain in a form that takes advantage of your preconscious visual processes—instead of requiring your brain to interpret abstract lines and columns of numbers—you'll gain a faster, greater understanding of the data.

Scientists have used visualization techniques for years. Now, since virtual reality technologies help give the sensation of inclusion in a 3D model, they're figuring out ways to use VR to represent abstract data in three-dimensional form, so they can view data in space as a whole or in detail, see elements in association with each other or individually, and link those elements. That way they can make judgments faster than if they were to

stereoscopic glasses: Used for data visualization and simulation systems. SimGraphics uses StereoGraphics CrystalEyes stereo-viewing glasses. These glasses provide a lower-cost, higher-resolution alternative to the immersive VR goggles. Wireless, battery-operated LCD glasses operate with computer workstations and are infrared-controlled from an emitter on a stereo-ready display monitor or large-screen projection system.

view the data in numeric form. (That's because we humans possess extensive spatial knowledge—the same knowledge that lets us slam the snooze button on the alarm clock without looking at the nightstand.)

The fertile combination of visualization techniques and VR systems is sprouting up in the fields of architecture and product engineering, facilitating the design of objects ranging from houses to snowmobiles to helicopters. Designers can experience a "reality" that's not physically real. That's the same reason medical doctors use VR to treat tumors, aircraft pilots use it to learn to fly, and film animators use it to create cartoon characters. And because VR lets people experience alternate realities, companies are building VR systems for home entertainment, theme parks, stage, and screen. One day, participating in virtual reality experiences will be a common occurrence.

Definitions of Virtual Reality

Contrary to popular notion, however, you don't always need goggles and gloves to experience virtual reality. In our view, "virtual reality" refers to technologies or environments that provide realistic cues to some or all of the senses, sufficient to engender in the participant a willing suspension of disbelief. A successful VR application delivers both quality content and an experience; thus, virtual reality essentially represents an evolution of user interface studies and human factors-based application design.

The use of goggles, gloves, and/or full-body datasuits represents one of the three major VR implementations, or delivery environments. This implementation is called "immersive" or "inclusive" VR, because the participant feels as if he or she is inside the graphic, or virtual, world.

The second type of VR implementation is called "desktop VR." It involves viewing the 3D world through a "window" on a stereo viewing monitor or on a screen inside a simulator cab. The participant "steers" through the virtual world using physical controls provided by special 3D data input devices.

The third type of implementation is "third-person VR," in which you view and steer an image of yourself interacting in the virtual world (this is the type of implementation used in Myron Krueger's VIDEOPLACE and Vivid Effects' Mandala System—also the approach used by a TV news weatherman when he looks off-screen to see his image superimposed on an image of the weather map). In VR applications, this implementation often involves a theatrical sort of set-up that incorporates a viewing stage, video monitors and projectors, performance animation, and video imaging.

Components of VR Applications

The tools and techniques involved in creating virtual worlds—and allowing people to experience and manipulate those worlds—include:

• input devices and user interfaces—head/body position trackers; **2-6DOF** joysticks with or without force feedback; 6DOF "force balls" (also called **"torqueballs"**); 6DOF mouse; voice recognition; keyboard controls; input gloves; video imaging;

• input device **modeling** and mapping;

• databases containing information for generating computer-based environ-

2-6DOF: two to six degrees of freedom; refers to an interface device's ability to track and represent spatial position (x, y, and z axes) and orientation (roll, pitch, and yaw).

torqueball: A 6DOF trackball that allows movement of perspective. Its name refers to the type of force you apply to it in order to navigate within a virtual space. You control this graphic input device by rolling, twisting, and squeezing a stationary ball mounted in box (to move a cursor on screen, you roll the ball in the direction you want the cursor to move).

modeling: Used in computer-aided design and the creation of virtual worlds, "surface" modeling helps conceptualize 3D objects with complex, irregular surfaces, such as a cuckoo clock. "Solid" modeling helps create the object and show its inner workings (a cuckoo clock cut in half to reveal its gears).

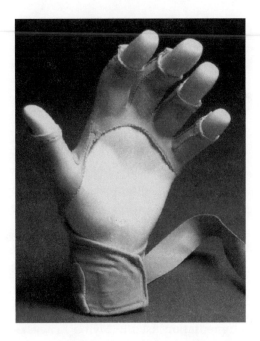

The CyberGlove, an 18-sensor instrumented glove designed by Virtual Technologies

ments, "agents" (characters), objects and behavioral rules for simulation and cues;

• 3D modeling and simulation of the environment, agents, events, object characteristics and "personalities";

• cue (or "stimulus")-generation subsystem(s), providing visual, audio, tactile, motion, and olfactory sensations;

• output device mapping; and

• output devices—head-mounted or boom-mounted visual displays; video monitor/projection; motion base platform; **tactile/force feedback**; olfactory cue generators.

Desktop VR for Performance Animation

One of the first desktop VR systems that SimGraphics developed is the Assembly Modeler program designed for Northrop Aircraft. This system lets Northrop's engineers design and test airframe assembly parts in a 3D virtual world. They manipulate objects in the same way they'd handle real parts on the shop floor—and they save millions of dollars in develop-

ment costs by eliminating the need to build full-scale mock-ups. The Assembly Modeler uses an interactive input device, the "Flying Mouse," to let two people work collaboratively on an item's assembly. These people can talk with each other (by telephone) from separate locations as they watch themselves simultaneously working with the same part on their computer display screens.

The Flying Mouse is an unusual data-input device that SimGraphics developed in 1990. It looks, feels, and acts like a standard mouse, except it has "wings" jutting out from its sides. When you place your thumb and fingers under these wings and lift the mouse, the on-screen cursor enters 3D mode, letting you move the mouse around in the air to control a computer scene or object with six degrees of freedom and movement (X, Y, Z, pitch, roll, and yaw axes). This allows complex manipulation of objects in 3D space for computer-aided design, visualization, and other applications—even film and video production.

SimGraphics is working on VR applications in product engineering, marketing, and entertainment, using the Flying Mouse and our VR application development system, VR_Workbench. The Workbench is a library of tools for building diverse, highly interactive, engineering, communication, and entertainment applications of visual simulations and virtual realities. One major area of interest (and fun) involves using these technologies to create and operate synthetic characters in "performance animation environments"—animation technology for real-time performance.

In 1991 we used the VR_Workbench to develop the Performance Animation

tactile feedback/ force feedback devices: Output devices that transmit pressure, force, or vibration to provide the VR participant with the sense of touch. Tactile feedback simulates sensation applied to the skin. Force feedback simulates weight or resistance to motion.

System (PAS). PAS facilitates the creation of computer-generated 3D characters for live performance. It's essentially a tool-kit that lets animators control cartoon characters in real time, and instantaneously morph (change) into other characters and objects. In other words, the movements of characters and objects are directly controlled by the movements of a human operator. PAS incorporates various VR system components (graphics databases and 3D imaging for output, the Flying Mouse and special facial and body armature for input). The quality of the animations is high, better than broadcast-quality. We optimize the graphics simulation using tricks learned from flight simulation technology, including **texture mapping** and **reflection** mapping. Many artistic skills are required to build real-time animated models for VR systems.

The first "Performance Cartoons" were created with PAS in 1991 by Mr. Film, a Southern California animation company. They starred the life-size "Suzy Surfer." Her movements on top of a gleaming surfboard (projected on a large screen) and the perspective of the "virtual camera" are controlled in real time by professional puppeteers—or even by audience members manipulating the Flying Mouse. A couple of stored procedural routines determine where her arms should be and how she balances over the surfboard. This is calculated in real time on a "Skywriter" (a Silicon Graphics computer). As her position is changed, the character is morphed, which means that multiple databases are interpolated to create smooth transitions between Suzy's movements.

SimGraphics worked on a PAS project for Nintendo of America in 1992, when we simulated the face of the Mario character for the introduction of the Super Nintendo System at the Consumer Electronics Show. The animation was entitled "MIRT": Mario In Real Time. On a large screen, we projected a colorful, 3D image of Mario's head; he announced the new game system and fielded questions from the audience. Backstage, an actor wore the PAS armature over his face. This contraption positions digital sensors on the actor's forehead, chin, lips, and jaw, and detects the movement of his facial muscles, translating that into Mario's facial expressions. He controlled the position of Mario's head with the Flying Mouse, making him nod and shake his head, spin it around, tilt forward and backward. It was all very smoothly animated. The actor lip-synced Mario to talk to the audience. A video camera aimed at the audience fed the signal to a video monitor backstage, so the actor could see who he was talking

texture/reflection mapping: *Refers to the processes of imbuing a computer graphics image with the appearance of lifelike texture (smooth, rough, rippled, etc.) and light reflections and characteristics.*

SimGraphics and Mr. Film created "Suzy Surfer," a real-time performance animation using VR technology.

to. The audience members used microphones to talk to Mario, so the actor could hear everything going on. He was behind the scenes, interacting with them in a way reminiscent of the Wizard of Oz in Emerald City interacting with Dorothy and her buddies. ("Pay no attention to that man behind the curtain!")

(For those of you interested in the specifics, the actor's input data went to a Silicon Graphics 420 VGX workstation, which handled all the animation.)

Not too long after the fun and games with MIRT, we developed a PAS application with even greater potential to improve the quality of human life. Working with neuroscientist Dave Warner at the Loma Linda Medical Center Children's Hospital (Loma Linda, California), and the computer animators at Mark Sorell & Associates in Los Angeles, SimGraphics created "Eggwardo." This good-natured creature was designed to help medical scientists determine whether real-time performance animations can help educate and habilitate children and educationally challenged adults. We brought Eggwardo into the hospital where he interacted with children who were terminally ill. Some kids couldn't even leave their beds, so Eggwardo's image was sent to the TV monitors above their beds, while they talked to the actor over the phone and watched and listened as Eggwardo joked with them and asked how they were feeling and if they'd taken their medicine. The idea is to use Eggwardo, and others like him, to help communicate with therapy patients and mitigate the fears of children who face surgery and other daunting medical procedures.

How do we use PAS to create a character such as Eggwardo, Suzy, or MIRT? First we develop the storyboard, in which we define the characters, their typical actions, facial expressions and body poses, and determine the desire for morphs, special effects (zooming in, shrinking the character, warping its face, etc.), character interactions, and props.

Next, in the offline pre-production stage, we compile and build visual databases and create special effects functions. These databases contain the information about the characters' or objects' characteristics for motion and special effects.

In phase three, online pre-production, we handle user calibration—matching the actor's or puppeteer's movements to the system—mix the characters' poses and expressions, map the input devices, and set up real-time modeling and geometry parameters.

Then we head into production. We actually record the real-time performance of actors, puppeteers, and camera operators, handling morphing, kinematics, and dynamic modeling of objects and characters, which will allow operator-induced "super-motion," such as the exaggerated jaw dropping and eye bulging you see on cartoons. This way we achieve quality and coordinated choreography of character movement. Each contributor to the overall process has a complete, independent PAS setup: actor, camera, camera director, special effects producer, and production director. We record all the data digitally, because we reuse it in the next phase of the process, post-production.

Post-production involves traditional animation and rendering, **compositing**,

compositing: Combining of signals.

and optical techniques, with frame-by-frame output to the display system.

We see performance animation contributing to different areas in the arts and entertainment. People will use it to produce content for film and video broadcasting; they'll use it in live performance (not only in the performing arts for stage production, but for creative content development and direction), and theme park and other entertainment attractions.

Amusement & Entertainment Applications

Virtual reality is exciting the people and organizations involved in the amusement and entertainment-attraction business. They're working on VR applications for mass public consumption, including theme-related, multi-sensory attractions, exhibits, and products for the home and public places. This means we'll see VR in theme parks, theaters, and "location-based entertainment spaces"—amusement/entertainment attractions located in a public place other than a theme park, such as a shopping mall or a stand-alone, family amusement center. These applications will feature realistic visual and sound capabilities and such technologies as wide-angle and/or 3D visual displays, motion simulation, tactile feedback, olfactory generation, 3D sound imaging, and user networking.

What kind of VR experiences can we expect to entertain and amuse us? Everything ranging from "passive rides" (brief rides that combine film/video with motion) to interactive games (brief gaming experiences with limited interactivity and branching; VR video games),

interactive exhibits (multimedia educational exhibits that include VR components), and interactive movies (long-form, complex experiences that include synthetic characters, such as those developed with performance animation technologies).

VR technology might also be found behind the scenes in film and television production. VR systems can help movie production teams pre-design sets, scenes, and special effects, simulate camera shots, and use **telepresence** systems to run motion-controlled props. Using this type of simulation technology can offer realistic scene simulation from many simultaneous vantage points. Just as Northrop Aircraft saves money by testing parts assembly in a virtual world, a movie production company can save money by testing the effectiveness of virtual sets and staging.

VR Implementation Philosophy: Creating Experiences

The primary goal of developing a VR application is to create "believable illusions" that encourage or enhance creativity and productivity. Toward that end, VR application designers must first analyze the multi-disciplinary tasks and requirements needed to assemble accurate, complete "experiences." They must determine what tasks will be performed by the participant in the VR environment, determine requirements for enabling the performance of those tasks, and choose the overall implementation type (desktop VR, third-person VR, or immersive VR). In subsequent development phases, the designers must opti-

telepresence: The experience of immersion in a remote (and/or simulated) environment; also refers to the remote operation systems that translate human movements into the control of machinery such as robotics.

mize user interface features and develop consistent user interface and virtual object behavior.

The quality of the simulated experience or entertainment depends on a variety of factors. These include:
- Level of activity;
- Emotional, cognitive, and sensory engagement and participation; and
- High-fidelity sensory cues
Sensory cues include:
- visual (color, stereo, should have great field of view and high resolution)
- audio (3D, multichannel, should have wide frequency range and high **signal-to-noise ratio**)
- motion (should provide participant with multiple degrees of freedom, and acceleration/displacement capabilities)
- tactile/force feedback (of proper magnitude)
- other cues (wind, temperature, smell).

VR can be effectively employed today in many applications. To create VR applications today that can evolve to satisfy our needs tomorrow, we need to accomplish extremely methodical system design. A well thought-out application development process allows implementation of systems that aren't technology-specific.

There's a great future for VR technology in the production of performance and promotions. There's also a great future for this technology in the development of home entertainment systems. The type of material that will attract new users—parents, women and men, and older couples—will include adventure and role-playing games. We don't need "bang, bang, shoot-'em-up" games to create an exciting experience, even in a limited environment.

Meanwhile, as the price/performance ratio improves for key system components, robust and generic systems will find more suitable, diverse applications.

signal-to-noise ratio:
Measure of noise in an audio recording or reproduction system. The noise typically sounds like hiss, hum, or a combination of both. It's expressed as a measure of how much louder an average signal is than the noise which is there when no signal is present. The higher the "S/N" reading (expressed in decibels), the better the equipment performs.

ON FINGER-FLYING & OTHER FAULTY NOTIONS

BY BRENDA LAUREL

Brenda Laurel is a veteran of the computer software industry; since 1976 she's worked as a programmer, software designer, marketeer, and researcher. Her academic background is in theater. She holds an M.F.A. and a Ph.D. in theater from Ohio State University. Since 1987 she has worked as a consultant in interactive entertainment and human-computer interface design for such clients as Apple Computer, LucasArts Entertainment, and the School of Computer Science at Carnegie Mellon University. She co-founded Telepresence Research with Scott Fisher in 1991. In 1992 she joined Interval Research Corporation as a research scientist. A widely published author, Brenda's blend of computer science and drama can be sampled in her book, Computers as Theatre *(Addison-Wesley, 1991).*

enabling technology:
Technology that makes another technology possible. The enabling technologies of virtual reality include stereoscopic viewing devices, computer graphics, and 3D sound.

When asked to discuss how we balance the technical limitations against the creative concerns of creating **enabling technologies** for virtual reality applications, I realized that we actually deal with two classes of technical issues. One involves the technical capabilities that we know are necessary, which present problems for which we can see possible solutions, and which can benefit from progress made in increments over the past few years. That's the case in the areas of image generation and three-dimensional audio. The other issue involves technical problems where we don't know what the solution might be or what direction to take to discover the solution.

For example, consider the problem of how we give people the sense that they're moving through large virtual spaces. Solving the navigation problem is not simple. **Pointing and flying** is an emblematic way to accomplish that, but it doesn't give you the kinesthetic satisfaction of being able to move all over the place. Some great developments, such as Fake Space Labs' BOOM visual display, work toward providing partial solutions to this problem. Using the BOOM display to view and move around in a virtual space (through buttons mounted on either side of the display holder), people aren't limited to pointing their fingers; they can grab their hair or flap their arms like they're airplanes. It's fun to watch people in suits do this. We also considered putting a huge trackball in the floor, but you'd need an eight-story building to accommodate it. People at the University of North Carolina are building treadmills to allow you to walk through virtual space. Nobody has come up with the winning answer to the question of virtual locomotion.

The same thing can be said about the sense of touch in virtual space, whether you talk about force or mass. Researchers such as Margaret Minsky are working on many promising projects, but no one has come out with the "silver bullet."

In the areas of smell and taste, we've barely scratched and sniffed the surface.

Another area that needs much more progress, in which we don't know what the

The **Virtuality VR game system**, created by W. Industries Ltd, is an example of a complete virtual reality system, incorporating a stereoscopic display helmet and a hand-held control stick.

silver bullet might be, is that of speech processing. In a virtual world you want to be able to talk to and be understood by synthetic characters, and those characters must be able to generate speech back. If we constrain things into cartoon-quality stuff, we can start to use speech today, but doing serious discourse and understanding is beyond our reach right now.

In addressing these important creative concerns, however, we've learned that our creative work is constrained not so much by technical limitations as it is by pragmatic concerns. At least that's how it seems from my part of the world. On every level of development we're faced with the fundamental issue of equipment cost and

Pointing and flying:
Refers to the method of navigating in virtual space when wearing a VR glove, which requires pointing your finger and "flying" in the direction you want to go.

availability. An enormous amount of interesting work could be taking place in such places as the San Francisco Art Institute and various university departments, but can't right now because the technology is too expensive. It's a question of waiting until this equipment is sold in large enough volume that it's to somebody's benefit to push down the costs.

The only way we can address the creative issues is through meeting the key challenge of identifying system configurations and applications that can be sold. Telepresence Research only works on products, installations, and prototype projects that possess at least one research problem that we can identify and solve—small, tractable problems that developers can be confident about solving in a way that results in marketable products and services.

In pursuing VR research, the major challenge involves the configuration and funding of labs that support people who have the right skill sets. These skill sets are diverse and eclectic; I call the people who possess these skill sets "fusion craftsmen." They're coming along now, through colleges and graduate programs, with backgrounds in both computer science and the arts, such as narrative art, literary criticism, and graphic design. Creating spaces in which these people can work as interactive designers is another current pragmatic problem.

This problem brings up the issue of creating tools for these people to use. There is a huge difference between the kinds of tools required today by the first-generation artist in the VR business and the tools that will be required by second-generation artists. Today we have to build tools that optimize skill transfer from other domains, such as choreography, sculpture, screenwriting, etc. Tomorrow we'll see artists who got tossed in the VR pool and learned to swim when they were six weeks old, so we won't have this concern about helping people from other domains master skills across domains—rather, we'll optimize the skills of people who are familiar with the VR medium. Making that point to people who commission and fund tools today is sometimes difficult, but the strategy for accomplishing it is simple. Right now, the best thing to do is strap an artist to an engineer. They look cute that way, too.

Another limitation that involves both technical and pragmatic issues concerns the *conceptual* limitations. Exactly what is it that we think we're doing with VR, and what do we think will be the ideal outcome? What is the Holy Grail?

One such conceptual issue involves what I call "sensory combinatorics." We're working in a multisensory medium; we're trying to cram as many senses as we can into telepresence and virtual environments. How do these senses interact with each other? How do you design for this medium?

The first time I visited Scott Fisher's lab at NASA, I came in all aflutter and kicked around with the helmet thing and got it on and got all wired up and was instructed in finger-flying. Then I was in this virtual space. I saw a Space Shuttle—rather a wire-frame model of the Space Shuttle. Low-resolution—this was 1986—running at four to eight frames per second. No audio. Simple, open, geometric shapes. Scott said, "Fly forward." I was in a cargo bay, flying forward. The bulkhead was in front of me and it consisted of an open geometric form, a little wire-frame thing *ka-chunking* along. Yet, as my virtual body was about to pass through the bulkhead, every nerve ending fired. My brain screamed, "You are approaching a solid object!" I got through the thing, and I tried to figure out how to get back, and I couldn't figure out whether I should turn around or point, and I tried both ways, and I got all wound up in the cable, and Scott threw me out of the lab.

The point is, the illusion *worked*, even if it took place in what we consider today to be an impoverished technological and sensory environment. It fooled my brain. The automatic responses of my body behaved as if I were passing through a solid object. This stuff does work, and it works in environments that are low-performance, low-resolution, and low bandwidth, compared to what we strive for today. What helps make it work is a tight coupling of kinesthetic and visual information. As I moved my head and my body, the world responded—even at four to eight frames per second, with a lag between my actions and the system's reactions. It was that kinesthetic/visual connection that created my brain's reaction. Adding audio amplifies the brain's reaction. Improving the visual frame rate amplifies it even more. This notion of sensory combinatorics, then, concerns not so much the resolution and bandwidth as it does with putting senses together properly in multi-sensory environment.

"Electronic media alters the ratio between the senses," wrote Marshall McLuhan. An obvious example is the way audio affects the perception of video. In the computer game business, we learned that high-resolution audio caused people to report that the game's graphics were higher resolution. It doesn't work the other way, though; really high-res video does not cause people to report that the little beeps on their PC are suddenly rich, full-bodied sounds. Something interesting is going on here. In one case, audio pulls video along, and in the other, a disparity shatters the illusion. This also exemplifies what I mean by "sensory combinatorics." Investigating this stuff and using it can make a huge difference in the quality of the virtual reality product.

Audio also pulls us along in a dimension that we might call "involvement," or the dimension of "constructive involvement": pulling stuff out of the imagination of your user to achieve a very deep level of participation. It turns out that audio is a whole lot better at that, in general, than video. When you create an audio-intensive environment, the effect tends to work better. (That's not *always* true, but it's true enough often enough that it's worth looking at.) Horror movies, for example, are generally shot at darker, lower resolution and the audience sees only partial imagery, but in a very vivid auditory environment. Haunted houses also are frightening. Remember being scared by peeled grapes and spaghetti and all the eerie sounds? The peeled-grapes-and-spaghetti principle supports constructive involvement.

Audio is much better than video at creating a sense of real space. Multisensory photo-realism is a false Grail. The computer graphics world is obsessed with resolution, and specifically, with photo-realism. In virtual reality it translates into an obsession with turning up all the knobs—video, audio, smell, touch, taste. There are a couple of things wrong with that attitude. McLuhan suggested that media that saturates your senses also cauterizes your imagination. I think that principle has been amply demonstrated by what's happened since he formulated it. As a community, we need to balance the hunger for the hype and real rush that this technology can deliver against the need to elicit engagement and imaginative participation from people in these environments.

Yes, indeed, you can design VR experiences that fry people's brains and make their eyes turn into little spirals until they stagger off and barf in your lap, but that may not be the outcome you want. I could be wrong; a guy from Las Vegas visited Telepresence Research a while back, and he was susceptible to motion sickness. He tried our VR demo, and after about a minute, he turned green, ran up to the front office, ate a Dramamine, came back and said, "I'm sick as a dog. This is fantastic!" So who knows?

Finally, we need to broaden our view of applications, audiences, and "feel" in terms of what we produce and the models we use to design applications in a virtual environment. I'm talking specifically about growing out of the war-games approach to VR applications, whose audience is the adrenalin crowd. A wonderful thing happened to me the other day. I was talking to some guys—very, very straight guys who run alternative movie theaters. They were talking about using some VR stuff in the lobbies of their movie theaters and said, "We don't want any of that war games stuff, because that's a really narrow demographic." And I said, "Praise the Goddess!" After 15 years of righteous indignation, finally we get some dweeb in a tie telling me that providing war games doesn't make economic sense. I love it.

We need to start asking, "What will be fun to do with VR besides create Flight Simulator Fu?" There's the ancient art of war and there's the ancient art of play, right? I've spent hours and hours in kindergarten watching kids, and there is stuff that goes on when kids play that we could easily map into this VR business, such as the way kids assert things to each other. They'll say, "OK, pretend this is Rome. And pretend it was on the street. And pretend I did this. And pretend I did that. Okay? Let's go get pizza!" They're in and out of role-playing and world-asserting seamlessly. There's no mode shift for them. When you give them little doodads like rocks they can put dresses on or potatoes they can stab stuff into, they go nuts. There's a level of ambiguity that's necessary about these toys, these little props. There's an appropriate level of fuzziness about them that optimizes them for children.

The point is, our notion of activity often seems bounded by what we thought we wanted from "computer games." The rest of the time, atavistic folks like me run around and rant about dramatic plot and narrative, but there are, in fact, many wonderful alternatives for collaborative, imaginative play that are right in front of us every day, if we just notice them, start working with them, and try figuring out how to recreate them with the technology we already have.

● ●

ENTER THE EXPERIENTIAL REVOLUTION

A VR PIONEER LOOKS BACK TO THE FUTURE

"There are increasing demands today for ways and means to teach and train individuals without actually subjecting the individuals to the hazards of particular simulations. . . . Accordingly, it is an object of the invention to provide an apparatus to simulate a desired experience by developing sensations in a plurality of the senses. . . . Another object of the invention is to provide a new and improved apparatus to develop realism in a simulated situation." —from U.S. Patent #3,050,870, "Sensorama Simulator," 1962

Over three decades ago, Mort Heilig combined 3D film technology, electric motors, music, sounds, and aromas to create Sensorama, an "immersive" art experience disguised as an arcade-style attraction. It was really a demo he developed in search of support for his invention of a multi-sensory, ultra-wide angle, 3D movie theater with controlled localized sound, aromas, and rotating seats on a motion platform. Mort also patented his own head-mounted display (a 3D TV viewing helmet) in 1960. Few people paid attention—until the birth of the "cyber" generation.

In this chapter Mort relates his experiences and views, and explores the potential (good and bad) of the new media technologies.

've been working in this field they call "virtual reality" for 40 years; I am a filmmaker. I've been making films for 40 years, and have produced over 100 documentaries in the United States, Central America, South America, and Europe. I've also managed to produce a feature film, *Once*, that was invited to the Cannes Film Festival where it received a wonderful reception.

BY MORTON L. HEILIG

Mort Heilig is a cinematographer, director, and inventor who studied filmmaking in Rome before launching his career in the 1950s as a documentary filmmaker. He lives in Southern California and runs Supercruiser, Inc., purveyors of fun-loving sports vehicles.

Selections from "The Cinema of the Future" by Mort Heilig, first published in 1955:

"When a primitive man desired to convey to another man the emotional texture of an experience, he tried to reproduce, as closely as possible, the elements that generated his own emotions. His Art was very simple, being limited to the means provided by his own body. . . . With time, a specific word-sound became associated with the impressions, objects, and feelings in man's experience. Words were useful in conveying the general structure of an event. . . [but] even then not a thousand of his choicest words could convey the sensation of yellow better than one glance at yellow, or the sound of high-C better than listening for one second to high-C. And so side by side with verbal language they evolved more direct forms of communication—painting, sculpture, song, and dance. . . . For all the apparent variety of the art forms, there is one thread uniting all of them. And that is man, with his particular organs of perception and action. Art is like a bridge connecting what man can do to what he can perceive."

Back in 1952, when I returned to Manhattan from Europe, I went down to Broadway to see a presentation, "This is Cinerama!" It was a pivotal experience in my life. The film began in the conventional 16mm format, then went to 35mm format. Then they announced, "Ladies and gentlemen, *this* is Cinerama!" The curtain opened, and suddenly I was riding on a roller coaster! No longer was I vicariously experiencing the thrill of the ride through the actor. I felt like I was on that roller coaster. I felt the vertigo and the excitement. I realized this was a highly pivotal transition in the form of audio-visual communication.

I became very excited. I thought, "Why stop at a picture that fills only 18 percent of the spectator's visual field, and a two-dimensional picture at that? Why not make it a three-dimensional image that fills 100 percent of the spectator's visual field, accompanied by stereophonic sound? If we're going to step through the window into another world, why not go the whole way?" I wrote an article about this concept, and about the need for art to appeal to all our senses. Titled "The Cinema of the Future," it was published in the Mexican architectural review, *Espacios*, in 1955. I sat back and waited to see if anything would happen. Nothing did.

In that article, I wrote that hundreds of sense impressions stimulate the sensory nerves every second of the day, but only one or a few at a time are permitted to enter the *realm of higher consciousness*. The human brain shifts rapidly from element to element within each sense and from sense to sense, in the approximate proportion of sight, 70 percent; hearing,

20 percent; smell, 5 percent; touch, 4 percent; and taste, 1 percent, selecting one impression at a time according to needs. These unite into the dynamic stream of sensations we call "consciousness." The Cinema of the Future, I postulated, would represent the first direct, complete, and conscious duplication of this ratio. Since the conventional movie screen fills only 5 percent of the spectator's field of vision, it automatically represents his or her point of visual attention; the director needs only point the camera to control this point of attention. But with the invention of a means to fill 100 percent of the spectator's field of vision with sharp imagery, the director must solve the problem of visual attention another way or lose his main aesthetic power.

I decided to invent that means myself, so I designed and patented "The Experience Theater." My design provided a way to use all the technology then available to create a theater that provides audiences with the total illusion of reality. I determined that the way to do that involved breaking full sensory information into various components—sight, smell, motion, sound—and dealing with them individually. The audience would enjoy multi-dimensional experiences, with full color and motion on film, and complete peripheral vision: The screen accommodated visual imagery extending 180 degrees horizontally and 155 degrees vertically. The vertical range is extremely important; most peripheral vision systems have concentrated primarily on the horizontal viewing range. These types of films were shown in a theater shaped like a dome, in which people look up at the inside of the

"Desiring to convey the full richness of experience in more life-like form, men combined the 'pure' Arts into the 'secondary arts' of opera, ballet, and theater. . . [but] the essential factor of control was missing. Not only did the artist have to master visual, musical, choreographic, and verbal materials, not only did he have to limit the scope of his imagination to the practical limitations of a theater and depend on the collaborations of dozens of singers, painters, dancers, musicians, and actors, but even after he had masterminded every detail and rehearsed the cast into perfect form he had absolutely no way of fixing his creation so it could remain exactly the same whenever and wherever played. This was an impasse until the arrival of a strange newcomer on the scene—the machine. The machine with its genius for tireless repetition and infinite exactitude was an extension of the limbs and will of man. It could be trusted to perform all his purely mechanical operations, freeing his energies for more creative tasks."

dome. But we don't deal with life that way; we don't lie on our backs, looking up at reality. We look *forward* at reality. Back then it seemed obvious to me that we had to put the dome in front of the audience, not above it.

The screen I designed would fill not 5 percent of your visual field, as did the local movie theater screen, or the 18 percent of Cinemascope, or the 25 percent of Cinerama. It would fill 100 percent of your visual field. The human eye has a vertical span of 150 degrees and a horizontal span of 180 degrees. (The nude eye actually has a vertical range of 180 degrees, but this is reduced to approximately 150 degrees by the brow and cheeks.) That vertical field is difficult but not impossible to provide. Even the planetarium 30 years ago provided a wide vertical peripheral field. The Cinema of the Future would provide it along similar lines, using a screen that curved past the spectator's ears on both sides and beyond his sphere of vision above and below.

This approach, when integrated into the Experience Theater, led to a host of problems, such as light bounce. When you project images onto large, domed screens, the projection lights bounce all over the place, which washes out the image. I solved that problem by controlling the light energy, thus maintaining the image contrast and color values. Another problem concerned audience seating. In conventional theaters, people in the front row enjoy a clear visual field, vertically and horizontally. But for the people *behind* them, they block about 40 percent of the information from below the horizon. By placing the seats on a very steep incline, I

eliminated one problem, but created a new problem with moving audiences in and out of the theater. I solved this by designing the seat to rotate. The spectators could leave or enter the theater at any time without disturbing other spectators.

My design also included stereophonic sound. Actually, it provided for a multiplicity of speakers—about 30 speakers on the walls, the sides, top, and bottom, so the sound could come from any direction. This provided tremendous aesthetic possibilities for handling directional sound. A sound could move through space and its precise location could be controlled.

After designing that part, I thought, "We have imagery, we have sound, but what about the other senses?" Then I added smell, which could be controlled. At that time, a few mechanical aroma-projection systems existed, but they had serious problems. You need to control the amount of smell close to the nose, which is the only way you can instantly change the smell. Unfortunately, the aroma systems back then worked by pumping the aroma into the air-conditioning system. Once they got the aroma into the environment, they had no way of getting it out. When you changed the film scene from a flower market to a city scene, you were stuck with the flower smell, and a tremendous amount of smell contamination. My design, however, solved that problem.

The Experience Theater also provided temperature variations, motion and vibration, and wind (forced air) against the audience's bodies. A critical component of the design was the seat, which vibrated and tilted. In regular theaters, the seat is just a place to park your body, and the presentation comes from the wall in front of you. In the Experience Theater, the seat is an integral part of the presentation, and a costly one at that.

I wrote in my 1955 article, "The Cinema of the Future, as presented in the Experience Theater, will far surpass the 'Feelies' of Aldous Huxley's *Brave New World*. It will be a great new power, surpassing conventional art forms like a Rocket Ship outspeeds the horse, whose ability to destroy or build men's souls will depend purely on the people behind it."

In 1960 and 1961, I tried to market this theater design. In every situation I found myself working my way up a bureaucratic ladder to the key decision-maker who had the power to provide the funds to build this theater. I was rebuffed over and over again. To influence the key decision-maker, I presented my concepts using slides on a peripheral screen, but I always ran up against the problem when the decision-maker would ask, "How would this look in motion?" I thought that question was almost ludicrous, and used to say, "Stick your head out of a window of a moving car. That's how it'll look." They didn't understand. I finally faced the reality that I had to design a little one-person theater, so to speak, to persuade the decision-maker. The model theater would sacrifice some of the full-blown theater's architectural grandeur, but when the lights are low in a full-blown theater, it's just you and the screen anyway. At least the model theater would give the *illusion* of the excitement I thought a theater of this kind could generate. That's what motivated the construction of something I

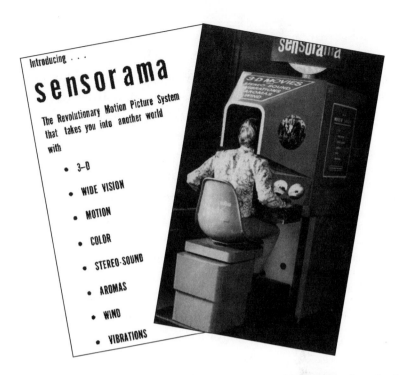

called the "Sensorama Simulator." It initially was a way to present a full range of sensory information in a dynamic fashion. Sensorama had three-dimensional images, peripheral vision, binaural sound, and it gave you smells on cue, blew air against your body, and vibrated your entire body. All of this sensory information was synchronized with the film imagery in a way that provided what I hoped was an exciting experience.

Halfway through building this thing, I realized it was a valid invention in its own right, with the potential to serve as an arcade attraction, or a sales demonstration system, or even an educational tool. And that's what it turned out to be.

I finished building Sensorama in 1961. I had to devise every component. At that time there was no film for that type of system, and no camera that could shoot that type of film. I designed a three-dimensional, side-by-side 35mm cam-

"Sensorama is a simulator that gives one person at a time an illusion of reality. It is a semi-portable automatic machine that can be plugged in anywhere electricity is available. The illusion of reality is achieved by providing the viewer with a wide range of sensory information. All of this information is perfectly synchronized with the picture (aromas, wind, and vibrations change instantly). All the control information is on one piece of film. Sensorama is completely automatic. The viewer activates it by depositing a coin or pushing a button (depending on application)."

era. To create the types of films I had in mind, the camera had to be highly portable; this was unusual back then, because 3D cameras were monstrosities that weighed over 200 pounds and were awkward to use. People in the industry still consider my camera advanced, because few 3D cameras can shoot straight out with wide-angle lenses. Most 3D cameras can't shoot anything wider than 45 degrees.

I used my camera to shoot five short films for the Sensorama Simulator. One film starred a belly dancer who enticed the viewer; you could smell her perfume. Another film featured a dune buggy ride in Pismo Beach and a helicopter ride over Los Angeles. Another took you on a high-speed motorcycle ride through New York; you felt the wind against your body, smelled the car exhaust fumes, and felt the seat handles and foot platform vibrate in synchronization with the speed of the vehicle and sounds of the motor. Another film put you on a date with a girl, playing on the beach and walking through flower markets. The fifth film was especially interesting because I shot it from the point of view of a bottle going through a Coca-Cola bottling plant. I went through all the machines in the building. My idea was to use this film to interest the Coca-Cola people or some industrial company in the Sensorama as a sales tool.

When I realized that Sensorama had potential as a coin-operated machine, I added the appropriate components. In 1962 it debuted on 52nd St. and Broadway in Manhattan. First I installed it in New York, and later, when I moved to California, I installed it at the Santa Monica pier. Another Sensorama was placed at Universal Studios. Overall, Sensorama was quite the success and received a fair amount of press. It was written up in *Popular Photography*, *Saturday Evening Post*, and various film industry newspapers, such as the *Hollywood Reporter*. *L.A. Weekly* compared it to the "feeling machine" in Aldous Huxley's *Brave New World*.

I also realized the possibilities for using Sensorama to watch television. Television wasn't very advanced, there weren't computers to speak of, and video was in its infancy, but I thought you could use a head-mounted television set (the 1960s version of virtual reality goggles and gloves!) to present 3D color imagery and binaural sound. I designed a system like this, creating a small display to work out some of the optics issues. I didn't put a television in there, but I did include 3D slides with extremely wide peripheral effects, and stereophonic sound. I also designed the interocular (focusing) controls, and the capability to include smells in this mask. The device was patented in 1960.

I remember bringing my little viewer model to the David Sarnoff Research Center, the research arm of RCA in New Jersey. I had the honor of meeting with Vladimir Zworkin, the inventor of electronic television. I said to him, "I think there's a future for this kind of device in television. I would love to come out here and build it. I don't have the financial resources or the electronic knowledge to build it, but with your technicians, I could put something together quickly that would be very, very interesting. It has enormous potential in the areas of entertainment and education." They just patted me on the head and said, "You're a bright young man, keep it up, and try it on your own."

Well, I'm still here, but RCA is not, and this tale of RCA's reaction to my invention was the story of my life. You might ask, "These are neat inventions, how come you never got them off the ground?" The only one that succeeded in any way was the Sensorama Simulator, but that was only after it had been turned away by everybody in the industry. Only two individuals helped me: John Miller in New York helped start a company, and then Don Werby, a real estate developer in San Francisco, saw the machine in an arcade and after pursuing me like crazy, expanded the company and helped build more Sensorama machines.

I tried hard to realize the dreams behind Cinema of the Future, the Experience Theater, and the television viewing mask. I approached every major film studio. I went to NBC Television. I banged on doors and asked, "Where's your research and development department?" They didn't know what I was talking about and always directed me to the camera department. I even approached the government. You name it, I went there, desperately trying to secure funding to build the theater or the television mask or more Sensorama machines. I was turned down at every corner.

At that time, I was cutting a feature film on the lot at MGM. All the production was taking place overseas then, and the lot was virtually empty. I said to MGM's management, "You have this huge studio, and it's empty. You have these great camera technicians sitting around, playing pinochle. You have a lot of money.

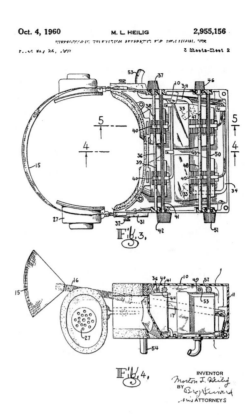

Drawings from Mort Heilig's patent documenting "stereoscopic television apparatus for individual use."

You have the best 70mm laboratory in Hollywood. Why don't you give me some of your resources. I don't want it all for myself. We'll share in whatever comes out of this. Just let me build a prototype of my theater!" Again, I was turned down, I was not a "practical" guy. They were the beancounters and executives and important businessmen. They were the practical guys, not me. Well, I'm still here, but MGM is not. The lab is gone, which is sad, because it was Hollywood's best 70mm lab. The Japanese now are on the lot, and MGM is struggling for its life.

MGM's attitude was and is characteristic of the film industry. From an industry standpoint, it's hard to explain why there is such blindness about new technology. In science fiction films taking place two or three centuries in the fu-

"The cinema of the future will no longer be a 'visual art,' but an 'art of consciousness.' When a great many sense materials are presented in sharp focus simultaneously, the spectator must do his or her own selecting. This situation is so life-like that it gives the spectator the sensation of being physically in the scene. [Scenes such as] Cinerama's famous roller coaster sequence will, I am sure, be used to great effect in the cinema of the future, but it must be used with great discretion. For aside from being very tiring, after one too many loops, the spectator may be so thoroughly convinced that he is shooting the chutes as to throw up on the lady in front of him. . . ."

ture, people fly around on rocket ships, saying things like, "Scotty, beam me up" and "Scotty, beam me down," but when they need to communicate with the master admiral at headquarters or another civilization on another planet, they look at big, flat, two-dimensional television screens. Yet that type of screen won't exist in 200 years!

That blindness exists not only at the highest corporate levels of the film and television industries, but with people on the street. If you were to stop a man on the street and ask, "What will transportation be like in 100 years?" he will come up with interesting ideas: "Rocket ships and rocket belts and maybe anti-gravity suits!" If you ask him, "What will our communication media be in 100 years?" you'll receive a blank stare, or maybe some comment about wristwatch television. People assume we'll always have two-dimensional, rectangular movies and TV.

When I spoke to the head men at the studios, or the head of a theater chain, they would say, "I would love to build this theater, but where am I going to get the films for it?" Conversely, when I went to the filmmakers, they would say, "I'd love to make a film like this, but where am I going to show it?" The only way to solve this problem was by having one company handle both ends, which is what all innovative companies have always done: Cinerama built its own theater, made its own cameras, and made its own film; Showscan built its own theaters, makes its own films, and so on, even today.

I figured the Walt Disney organization was the only place with enough money, technology, and imagination to create

the future cinema. I pitched my theater concept to Disney on several occasions. They kept inviting me back. Finally they offered me a job as a design consultant with Walt Disney Imagineering, the design arm of the Disney organization, and the division that creates all the theme park rides. It was a dream come true for me to be there, because I met many brilliant designers and artists who had the money to do marvelous things.

Disney had everything necessary to create the Experience Theater. Unfortunately they didn't see it that way. They put me to work on projects that didn't interest me. I was able to accomplish one positive thing: I dragged them kicking and screaming into 3D. They originally didn't appreciate 3D film. I guess it's a natural for a company that's running a theme park not to be a 3D film booster: When you go to a movie theater, you see a two-dimensional image and have a certain limited experience. When you take a ride on "Pirates of the Caribbean," you experience a total environment, a three-dimensional place. If you installed a 3D film theater with complete peripheral and sensorial imaging, you might lessen people's motivation to go on all the rides in the theme park.

Nevertheless, I wanted to work with 3D film, and I managed to pull Disney into it. I designed "Magic Vision," a life-size, rear-projected, three-dimensional image against which live actors would work in the foreground. It was inspired by a system designed in Czechoslovakia that debuted at the Montreal World's Fair in 1967. That system displayed a front-projected, two-dimensional image with actors working in front of it, interacting with objects and characters on the film. It used a slotted, elastic screen; so, for example, if a character on screen ran down the stairs, at the appropriate moment a live actor who looked exactly like the on-screen one would dive out through the screen and perform in front of it. I thought, "I'm going to do something like this, only better." I converted the two-dimensional image to 3D, which enhanced the illusion of a real actor interacting with projected characters. I also rear-projected the image, which was a first; no one had ever rear-projected 3D film. Rear-projected, three-dimensional images worked with live characters, handing objects back and forth to each other, kicking and chasing each other, popping each other's balloons. It was really something, but none of the top executives at Disney ever came to see it.

Eventually I left Disney. As you probably know, they finally came up with their own 3D system, first presented at Epcot Center in Orlando, Florida. They were surprised at its phenomenal success. Today, you find some of the longest lines at Disneyland at the 3D film attraction, "Caption EO," starring Michael Jackson. Disney took a similar approach with "Star Tours," which is not three-dimensional, but features 70mm film with motion simulation. It's an amazingly successful attraction.

In any event, frustrated by my inability to acquire funding, I set aside all my inventions. I went on to do other things to pay the rent, such as making films. I put the Sensorama machine in my backyard and forgot about the whole thing.

Years later, a sequence of events occurred like a piece of thread rolling out from a spool. Suddenly people wanted to know about Sensorama. It started when Scott Fisher of NASA mentioned Sensorama at a conference. I received phone calls from television producers in Holland, Germany, and England. They all wanted to see the Sensorama machine, which was buried under a big tarp in my backyard, being claimed by the vines. It caused me to imagine how a nuclear disaster might destroy everything in the world, and a few centuries from now, aliens would walk in my backyard, see a mountain of vines, hack away at it, pull back the moldy tarp, and suddenly see this strange thing emerge. Then they'd accidentally hit a switch and, like the Volkswagen in Woody Allen's film, *Sleeper*, the machine would jump to life, all its lights working. The aliens would assume it was some kind of a God from our civilization, and they would sit on the motorcycle seat and punch the buttons.

I mentioned this thought to the TV producers: "What a curious view they're going to have of our life when they look at the Sensorama belly dancer and experience this motorcycle ride!" The British producers decided to dramatize that. They dramatically pulled the tarp aside, and I think they really wanted to see Mort Heilig under there with a long, grey beard, sort of like Rip Van Winkle coming out from under the tarp, winking and blinking at the lights, saying, "I've been asleep for a couple of hundred centuries. Interview me!" I *have* been winking and blinking, you might say, at all the wonderful new TV and computer screen displays, but I have

"Art draws upon science for its cold and abstract findings into warm, sensual imagery that can be apprehended by any man, emotionally orienting him to the world and organizing his physical energy for constructive action."

not been dead for 30 years. People seem to see me today as if I'm surfacing like Rip Van Winkle, going through culture shock, but I'm not. I like to think I'm going to *give* some culture shock.

The advantage of not being involved directly in the more recent virtual reality technology affords me a different perspective. I'd like to share some of my perspective with you, by taking a good look at the forest, rather than the trees.

There exists a process in animals and humans that is so automatic, so rapid, as to seem one indivisible act. This process consists of three basic phases. When primitive people walked the earth, their lives were based on the continual cycle of these three phases, all working in harmony and balance. One example is a primitive man walking through the jungle who suddenly hears the growl of a lion. The first phase, *perception* (the noise and mental image of the lion), involves the reception of isolated impressions or facts. The second, *feeling*, involves the result of the integration of these isolated facts with the human's inner needs into an emotional unity that prompts and controls action (the man's sensation of danger and terror). The third, *action* (turning to run, or lifting a club to fight), represents a change in one's physical relationship to the world.

With the forming of society, different people concentrated on each of these three phases, and by casting the results of their labor into concrete forms (that could be passed from person to person, generation to generation), they created Science, Art, and Industry. The goals of each are clear. Science wants to bestow the maximum of knowledge on humanity. Art wants to digest this knowledge into the deeper realms of feeling, generating emotions of beauty and love that will guide the energies of humanity to constructive actions. Industry wants to act upon the material world so as to procure more living energy for humanity.

Each field has experienced differing amounts of success in reaching its goal. Science has come the closest because it has uncovered the individual's scientific thought processes and codified them into a clear, systematic method of experimentation. Science makes more discoveries in one year than previously were made in entire millenia. Science also has efficient ways of distributing its findings to humanity.

Industry also made great strides toward its goal, because production geniuses such as Ford have rationalized it to the "nth" degree. They have instigated assembly-line, mass-production techniques that pour out more food, machines, and fuels in one year than were produced in centuries.

Art today is the furthest from reaching its goal. The world is woefully barren of peaceful, tolerant, humanitarian feelings and the Art that should create them. And this is because, as yet, Art has evolved no clear-cut methodology to make it as efficient as Science and Industry in creating its product. Art is now struggling to achieve this.

The field of Industry, and more recently, the field of Science, are going through revolutions. Obviously, the industrial revolution tremendously amplified a person's power to act. We can do things now in great volume, on a massive scale, with tremendous power and a huge range that were unimaginable just a century ago. In the realm of information, through the application of scientific knowledge and through the use of telescopes, microscopes, computers, and satellites, we're launching the information revolution.

These revolutions share certain basic characteristics:

• They're based on scientific foundations. The industrial revolution would not exist without physics and chemistry. The information revolution would not exist without electronics, mathematics, and logic.

• They require technology. In the industrial revolution, the basic technologies were the steam engine, electric motor, and steel. The basic engine of the information revolution is the computer.

• They require education. You need schools to teach the skills required to support the revolution. The Industrial Revolution launched engineering schools, and, later, business schools. The information revolution launched computer science, electrical engineering, and artificial intelligence.

• They require groups of people working together. A modern factory organizes tens of thousands of people who each contribute to a final manufactured product. The same thing goes for the information revolution. Groups of scientists work in large laboratories, pursuing more and more information.

• They require large amounts of capital. You cannot manufacture cars or build computers unless you apply large funds. No longer can the lone, unfunded craftsman work in a small shop if his goal is to reach the mass market.

• They require mass distribution and consumption of the product. This is obvious with respect to the Industrial Revolution, and fairly obvious in the realm of information distribution, in terms of telephone, computers, and satellites. A tremendous amount of information is enjoying mass distribution. The result is that the poor person of today possesses more physical power and more information than the most exalted emperor in medieval times. Just by climbing into a car, a poor man today can propel his body through space at 70 miles an hour. An emperor in the past could only dream of that velocity. A poor man today can eat food from the far corners of the earth, and with the flip of his finger, switch on lights and heat. The emperor couldn't.

As Buckminster Fuller said, in modern industrial societies we each have perhaps a hundred slaves working for us all the time, but they're not human slaves, they're mechanical slaves, electrical generators, and so forth. We don't even see them, but they're there.

So we have an enormous extension of our physical powers, and information coming to us through television and radio. Thanks to computers and fax machines, we can communicate information from one end of the globe to the other, instantaneously. This concept of power is dramatically illustrated in wartime situations, when somebody in Washington has the power to push a button and kill a million people, ten thousand miles away. This person's ancestor was a caveman who wielded a club to kill animals or one

". . . The Cinema of the Future will become the first art form to reveal the new scientific world . . . in the full sensual vividness and dynamic vitality of our consciousness."

person at a time. Now this person can kill many more people (and animals) with much less effort.

With all his enormous physical power and his tremendous stores of information, does modern man *feel* more? What's in his heart? That's where I think we're coming up short. In many ways, modern people feel much less than primitive people felt. In our rush to achieve physical security and access to information, we have circumscribed our emotional and sensorial lives.

We can't even compare the act of a primitive man going to work to hunt bison with the act of a yuppie going to work in an office. Walking through a jungle was an experience filled with sensorial richness, danger, excitement, colors, sounds, smells, and temperature variations. We have *sterilized* our environments. We've built concrete walls. We've eliminated smells, hidden the moving of the clouds, and blotted out the sensorial richness of our natural environment. We've even stabilized the temperature—in the summertime we keep cool, in the wintertime we keep warm. We wanted to make ourselves comfortable by eliminating the extremes of temperature and the dangers of the real world, and we've succeeded to the point that we're sensorially deprived. Perhaps it is because we live in a puritanical Anglo-Saxon culture that we've never assigned much importance to these things; this society has equated emotion, sensory experiences, and sex with "the work of the devil," something that must be dominated, controlled, and eliminated so we can get on with the business of living.

Consequently, our culture hasn't assigned great weight to the arts or to sensorial richness. It's different in Latin and Far Eastern cultures. These cultures always considered the arts vital, and always respected their artists as prestigious leaders of the community, even "national treasures." In America, art is basically something that supports other things. If your living room wall has a crack in it, you cover it with a painting. The painting has no validity in itself. Instead of honoring artists, we honor industrialists—the Carnegies, Fords, Iacoccas—by giving them great prestige because they wield the kind of power that we believe in.

More recently our society started honoring the "crazy scientists." Before 1945, American society viewed the scientist as a loony. He was some guy shut up in an academic ivory tower. The popular image of scientist was Einstein with his wild hair: someone who couldn't tie his own shoes, someone impractical and forgetful. Lo and behold, those crazy scientists came up with the atom bomb and they ended the war. Suddenly, everybody—including the government—realized, "These crazy scientists have knowledge that can be translated into tremendous military power, so we should respect these guys and give them some money!" Science thus became respectable. Scientists became important.

Our society, then, highly respects the industrialists and businesspeople who give us physical power, primarily because they help us make lots of money. The scientists earned our respect when their work led to power and, also ultimately, to money. The artist, and the type I call the "experiential people"—the people responsible for putting all this information together and giving us an appropriate direction for our physical power—still earn little prestige.

Science put us into trains, cars, submarines, and airplanes—whizzed us above and beneath the earth, filling our senses with a million new and dynamic impressions. Science attached microscopes, telescopes, microphones, thermometers, and computers to our senses, stretching their range a thousandfold. Then, on conveyor belts of theory, Science brought facts from the buried eons of history, from the center of the electron, and from the corners of the Universe. The mind of the modern human has been flooded with a million new facts, not the stable, static facts of the ancient world, but dynamic concepts in which everything—atoms, continents, empires, and galaxies—are in a constant flux of change.

Similarly, the body of Industry has driven its feet of coal and oil deep into the earth and bound the globe with arms of steel track. Food stuffs and machinery flow through the arteries of commerce from one corner of the earth to the other. But most of its action is eyeless. It grows in spurts and dashes and then, like a crazed epileptic, grinds itself to bits. The miners, farmers, truckers, sailors, and office workers from one end of the earth to the other are making this great giant move without in any way seeing the results of their actions; consequently, they are incapable of controlling them. And so like some powerful giant whose mad brain is filled with brilliant, disconnected bits of information, society is heading down a path of phenomenal

destruction and suicide. Science has given us an atomic mind and Industry an atomic body, but we have no atomic hearts. Without an atomic heart, we can't put everything together in a way that helps us control our actions, preventing us from destroying ourselves.

What are the consequences? On a local level, you see crime in the streets; a perfect example is drive-by shootings. A kid with a gun in his hand holds enormous power and knows exactly what he's doing. Yet he feels nothing. On a global level, you see situations like the Persian Gulf war, also known as the "Nintendo War." Here, enormous firepower was applied while we watched a sanitized version of it on television. We were acting (as opposed to perceiving or feeling)—we were blowing up a country—and watching it on television. Did we feel anything? We felt the need to protect the American soldiers. But when those bombs exploded, and we watched the neat, little blips of dust on the TV screen, did we feel the fear, the terror, the horror, experienced by the people on the ground? No.

One of the consequences, I believe, is the drug problem. People who lead sensorially deprived lives—*experientially* deprived lives—try desperately to fill this void, and one way to do it is with drugs. They're trying to experience, in a very concentrated fashion, and to feel. Perhaps if they led lives richer in sensorial experience and emotional fulfillment, they wouldn't need drugs, and there would be much less crime.

Emotional content is vital to life. We know that infants who are not fondled and handled will die. We know that one of the cruelest things we can do to a person is isolate him in prison and deprive him of companionship. We're starting to wake up to the fact that our lives are sensorially deprived. We're beginning to see that we need more than the industrial revolution and the information revolution. We're beginning to undergo what I call the "*Experiential Revolution.*" Large groups of people are starting to work together, basing their projects on the science of psychology, perception, and emotions, with large application of financial and technological resources, all to produce and mass-distribute *experiences*. We're at the beginning of a sensorial experiential revolution.

Ultimately we will enjoy the all-encompassing, 21st-century versions of Cinema of the Future and the Sensorama Simulator. We won't necessarily encumber someone in head-mounted displays and wired gloves; we'll get beyond that. It's a given. We will produce total environmental situations which people can enter and react to. The ability to react intensifies the experience. In the future we'll witness the development of emotional media of communications and experiences so powerful that it's hard to imagine them now, just as it was impossible 40 years ago to imagine the power of computers. These new sensorial media will be so powerful that in many ways, as with any kind of powerful instrument, they will have enormous capacity for harm—and enormous capacity for good.

Each time we developed a means of having more extensive power, we found that we must regulate it. We don't let an unlicensed individual fly a 747. There's

too much power, too much at risk. We don't let an unlicensed individual run a nuclear power plant. I hate to say this, because it sounds fascist, but these new media will be so enormously powerful and overwhelming that you could put somebody through an experience of terror and fear that could literally kill him in his seat. Therefore, I visualize a time when we'll have to train and license people to use these media in a responsible way.

The power for good will be equally enormous. These media will have a revolutionary impact on our schools, which now are falling by the wayside because they're so boring. The new media will have a revolutionary impact on hospitals and on therapy. Today when a someone is ill, we slam the body down on a bed and do nothing for the mind. Indeed, we completely sterilize the environment and frustrate the patient's mentality.

The new media also will alter the way we design cities. They will change the balance of international power. In the past, the country with the most industrial and military power enjoyed the most prestige. Today that prestige is reserved for countries with the most economic power. Ultimately, the country that comes up with what I call "experiential power," sensorial power, emotional power, will emerge as the dominant culture. If I were to put my bets on particular countries, I would put them on Italy and China. Both countries have a long tradition of valuing sensorial experience.

Finally, an area of enormous impact will be religion. Today many people have fallen away from religion. When they want to have a religious experience, they might go to a cathedral or a temple. A cathedral is a machine designed to give you an emotional experience of a religious nature. It has temperature control, large volume of space, carefully controlled acoustics, stained glass windows—all elements intuitively or consciously designed to blot out the everyday world, remove you from your "normal" life, and place you into a contemplative frame of mind so you can communicate with the eternal verities. The new media will lead to the creation of the electronic temple. They will pour new wine from a new bottle.

When humanity finally travels into space, we'll come up against certain limits. Today we're extremely proud that we can move cities, divert rivers, flatten mountains. When we get out into space, we'll find that our physical powers are extremely limited. We won't be able to move stars or shift galaxies. Likewise, our intellectual powers will be limited. There's no limit to what we can learn and understand, but the complexity of the universe is so enormous that one day we'll have to realize that we're never going to understand it all.

That leaves us with the area of the emotions, the experiential sphere. That's the one area in which our powers are unlimited. In it we can experience the stars and the galaxies *ad infinitum*, and evoke the feelings of compassion, adoration, and love that have been characteristic of religion from the beginning of time. In fact, the great religious leaders have always understood that it is our capacity to feel and respond that provides the final goal of human existence. We cannot define the need to feel in terms of human power, because now we know that our power is limited. We cannot define the need to feel in terms of reason, because ultimately, even our reasoning powers are limited. We may have to define it as our ability to feel, to have compassion, to love, and to offer adoration to a God, if you will. That, in turn, may provide us with a kind of power we little understand, but which is extremely important, in the balance of the universe.

The experiential revolution is extremely important, and I think it holds our greatest hope for the salvation of humanity.

• •

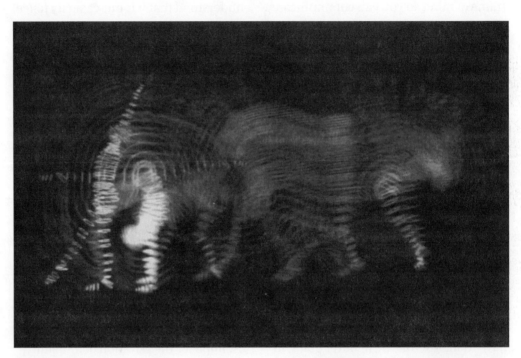

"LifeForms" choreography software

APPENDIX: SOURCES & RESOURCES

MAKE BACK-UPS EARLY & OFTEN!

Now that so many wondrous techno-tools-for-creativity are available, let's hope a good deal of their development is driven by artistic concerns rather than by (or at least as much as) the industrialist's lust for more/bigger/better/faster.

Technology evolves ever so rapidly. By the time you read this, a few—and eventually many more—of the tools and techniques mentioned in *CyberArts* will be surpassed by more powerful systems. We've discussed technology (brands, models, capabilities, performance, price) that will change, but the concepts, objectives, and philosophies remain the same.

At this stage of the game, artists continue to need (and should demand):

• reduction in the cost of product and application development;

• establishment of standards and cross-platform compatibility;

• tools that work well together;

• widespread distribution, because creating art with the new technologies requires talent, time, and money, but just having these ingredients doesn't mean the results will be experienced by many (although we sure can have a blast during the process of creation. And isn't that the idea?).

In the meantime, while you're absorbed in your work, remember to keep an arm's distance from that computer screen. Don't forget to stretch those shoulder and back muscles, breathe deeply, and blink often.

Oh, yes . . . always stay informed. After all, *techknowledgy is empowerment.*

—*Linda Jacobson*

SUGGESTED READING

Overviews & balancing perspectives

The Media Lab: Inventing the Future at MIT by Stewart Brand (New York: Viking Penguin, 1987)

Computer Ethics by Tom Forester & Perry Morrison (Cambridge, MA: MIT Press, 1990)

Digital Visions: Computers and Art by Cynthia Goodman (New York: Harry N. Abrams, 1987)

The Graphics Artists Guild Handbook, Pricing & Ethical Guidelines (New York: Graphic Artists Guild, 1992)

Computers as Theatre, by Brenda Laurel (Reading, MA: Addison-Wesley, 1991)

The Art of Human-Computer Interface Design, edited by Brenda Laurel (Reading, MA: Addison-Wesley, 1991)

Four Arguments for the Elimination of Television by Jerry Mander (New York: Quill, 1977)

Understanding Media by Marshall McLuhan (New York: Signet Paperback, 1964)

Computer Lib by Theodor Holm Nelson (Redmond, WA: Microsoft Press, 1987)

Technopoly: The Surrender of Culture to Technology by Neil Postman (New York: Alfred Knopf, 1992)

Understanding Computers by Nathan Shedroff, Sterling Hutto, & Ken Fromm (Alameda, California: Sybex, 1992)

Art & Physics by Leonard Shlain (New York: William Morrow & Co., 1991)

• Music & sound technologies

MIDI for Musicians by Craig Anderton (New York: AMSCO/Music Sales Corp., 1986)

Musical Applications of Microprocessors, Second Edition by Hal Chamberlin (Indianapolis, IN: Hayden Books, 1987)

The Musician's Home Recording Handbook by Ted Greenwald (San Francisco: Miller Freeman/GPI Books, 1992)

Synthesizer Basics, edited by Brent Hurtig (Milwaukee: Hal Leonard Publishing, 1988)

• Imagery, video, & computer graphics

Video Lighting & Special Effects by J. Caruso & M. Arthur (New Jersey: Prentice Hall, 1990)

The Art of David Em: 100 Computer Paintings by David Em (New York: Harry N. Abrams, 1988)

Making Art on the Macintosh II by Michael Gosney & Linnea Dayton (Glenview, IL: Scott, Foresman & Company, 1989)

Computers & the Imagination: Visual Adventures Beyond the Edge by Clifford A. Pickover (New York: St. Martin's Press, 1991)

On Photography by Susan Sontag (New York: Farrar, Straus & Giroux, 1977)

• Cyberspace & virtual reality

Cyberspace: First Steps, edited by Michael Benedikt (Cambridge, MA: MIT Press, 1991)

Artificial Reality II by Myron W. Krueger (Reading, MA: Addison-Wesley, 1991)

Virtual Reality by Howard Rheingold (Old Tappan, NY: Simon & Schuster, 1991)

ORGANIZATIONS

A select listing of membership organizations and foundations of interest to those who use computer technology for artistic/creative reasons.

Association of Computing Machinery
SigCHI (Special Interest Group on Computer-Human Interaction)
SigGRAPH (Special Interest Group on Computer Graphics)
1515 Broadway, 17th Floor
New York, NY 10036
212-869-7440

Art & Science Collaborations, Inc.
PO Box 040496
Staten Island, NY 10304

Audio Engineering Society
60 East 42nd Street
New York, NY 10165
212-661-8528

Electronic Frontier Foundation
1 Cambridge Center, Suite 300
Cambridge, MA 02142
617/577-1385

Interactive Multimedia Association
9 Randall Court
Annapolis, MD 21401
410-626-1380

IMA Intellectual Property Task Force
1 Fifth Street
Cambridge, MA 02141
617-864-6606

International Interactive Communications Society
PO Box 1862
Lake Oswego, OR 97035
503-649-2065

International MIDI Association
5316 West 57th Street
Los Angeles, CA 90056
213-649-MIDI

Multimedia PC (MPC) Marketing Council
1730 M Street NW, Suite 700
Washington, D.C. 20036
202-452-1600

National Center of Supercomputing Applications
    152 Computing Applications Building
    605 East Springfield Ave.
    Champagne, IL 61820
    217-244-2005
National Computer Graphics Association
    2722 Merilee Drive
    Fairfax, VA 22031
    703-698-9600
Small Computers in the Arts Network, Inc.
    Box 1954
    Philadelphia, PA 19105
    215-667-9390
Software Publishers Association
    1730 M Street NW, Suite 700
    Washington, D.C. 20036
    202-452-1600
YLEM: Artists Using Science & Technology
    PO Box 749
    Orinda, CA 94563
    415-856-9593

TECHNOLOGY SOURCES

A select listing of manufacturers, developers, & consultants whose wares are described or mentioned in CyberArts.

Ad Lib
    220 Grande-Allee East, Ste. 850
    Quebec, QC, Canada G1R 2J1
    418-529-9676
Alesis Corp.
    3630 Holdrege Avenue
    Los Angeles, CA 90016
    213-467-8000
Artificial Reality
    Box 786
    Vernon, CT 06066
    203-871-1375
Asymetrix
    2110-110th Ave. NE, Suite 717
    Bellevue, WA 98006
    206-637-1500
Autodesk
    2320 Marinship Way
    Sausalito, CA 94965
    800-525-2763

Blue Ribbon Soundworks
    1293 Briardale Lane NE
    Atlanta, GE 30306
Broderbund Software
    PO Box 6125
    Novato, CA 94948-6125
    800-521-6263
Brown Wagh Publishing
    130-D Knowles Drive
    Los Gatos, CA
    408-378-3838
Crystal River Engineering
    12350 Wards Ferry Road
    Groveland, CA 95321
    209-962-6382
Digidesign
    1360 Willow Road
    Menlo Park, CA 94025
    415-688-0600
Domark Software
    550 S. Winchester Blvd., #200
    San Jose, CA 95128
    408-246-6607
Electronic Cafe International
    1649 18th Street
    Santa Monica, CA 90404
    213-399-1051
Exos
    8 Blanchard Road
    Burlington, MA 01803
    617-229-2075
Fake Space Labs
    935 Hamilton Ave.
    Menlo Park, CA 94025
    415-688-1940
Focal Point 3D Audio
    1402 Pine Ave., Ste 127
    Niagara Falls, NY 14301
    416-963-9188
FM Towns Center
    101 California Street, Ste. 1775
    San Francisco, CA 94111
    415-616-9700
Horizon Entertainment
    PO Box 14020
    St. Louis, MO 63178

Lone Wolf
1509 Aviation Blvd.
Redondo Beach, CA 90278
310-379-2036

Macromedia
600 Townsend Street
San Francisco, CA 94103
415-442-0200

NewTek
215 E. 8th Street
Topeka, KS 66603
1-800-765-3406

Opcode Systems
3641 Haven, Suite A
Menlo Park, CA 94025
415-369-8131

Optical Media International
180 Knowles Dr.
Los Gatos, CA 95030
408-376-3511

Parallax Publishing
471 Lighthouse Ave.
Pacific Grove, CA 93950
408-646-1032

Philips Interactive Media of America
11111 Santa Monica Blvd, Suite 700
Los Angeles, CA 90025
213-444-6600

Richmond Sound Design
1234 W. Sixth Avenue
Vancouver, BC V6H 1AS
Canada
604-732-1234

SimGraphics
1137 Huntington Drive
South Pasadena, CA 91030
213-255-0900

Software Toolworks
60 Leveroni Court
Novato, CA 94949
415-883-3000

StereoGraphics
2171 E. Francisco Blvd.
San Rafael, CA 94901
415-459-4500

Telepresence Research
320 Gabarda Way
Portola Valley, CA 94028
415-854-4420

Verbum Interactive
670 Seventh Ave., 2nd Fl.
San Diego, CA 92101
619-233-9977

Virtual Technologies
PO Box 5984
Stanford, CA 94309
415-599-2331

Vivid Group
317 Adelaide St. W.
Toronto, Ontario M5V 1P9
Canada
416-340-9290

VPL Research
Metro Center Building
950 Tower Lane, 14th Flr.
Foster City, CA 94404
415-312-0200

W Industries
3 Oswin Road
Brailsford Industrial Park
Leicester, LE3 1HR
England
44-533 524 127

Wavefront Technologies
530 E. Montecito St.
Santa Barbara, CA 93103
805-962-8117

INDEX

7971